Scheler's Critique of Kant's Ethics

SERIES IN CONTINENTAL THOUGHT

EDITORIAL BOARD
CLAUDE EVANS, Chairman, Washington University
ALGIS MICKUNAS, Secretary, Ohio University
DAVID CARR, Emory University
JOSE HUERTAS-JOURDA, Wilfred-Laurier University
JOSEPH K. KOCKELMANS, Pennsylvania State University
WILLIAM MCKENNA, Miami University
LESTER EMBREE, Dusquesne University
J. N. MOHANTY, Temple University
THOMAS M. SEEBOHM, Johannes Gutenberg-Universität Mainz
RICHARD ZANER, Vanderbilt University

INTERNATIONAL ADVISORY BOARD
SUZANNE BACHELARD, Université de Paris
RUDOLF BOEHM, Rijksuniversiteit-Gent
ALBERT BORGMANN, University of Montana
AMEDEO P. GIORGIA, Duquesne University
RICHARD GRATHOFF, Universität Bielefeld
SAMUEL IJSSELING, Husserl-Archief te Leuven
ALPHONOSO LINGIS, Pennsylvania State University
WERNER MARX, Albert-Ludwigs-Universität
DAVID RASMUSSEN, Boston College
JOHN SALLIS, Loyola University, Chicago
JOHN SCANLON, Duquesne University
HUGH J. SILVERMAN, State University of New York, Stony Brook
CARLO SINI, Università di Milano
ELISABETH STRÖKER, Universität Köln
JACQUES TAMINIAUX, Louvain-la-Neuve
D. LAWRENCE WIELDER, University of Oklahoma
DALLAS WILLARD, University of Southern California

Sponsored by the Center for Advanced Research in Phenomenology, Inc.

Scheler's Critique of Kant's Ethics

Philip Blosser

OHIO UNIVERSITY PRESS

Athens

Ohio University Press, Athens, Ohio 45701

© 1995 by Philip Blosser
Printed in the United States of America
All rights reserved

99 98 97 96 95   5 4 3 2 1

Ohio University Press books are printed on acid-free paper ∞

Library of Congress Cataloging-in-Publication Data

Blosser, Philip.
    Scheler's critique of Kant's ethics / Philip Blosser.
        p.   cm. — (Series in Continental thought ; 22)
    Includes bibliographical references (p.   ) and index.
    ISBN 0-8214-1108-X
    1. Scheler, Max, 1874–1928. Formalismus in der Ethik und die materiale
Wertethik. 2. Kant, Immanuel, 1724–1804 — Ethics. 3. Ethics. 4. Values.
I. Title   II. Series.
B3329.S483F623   1995   94-45367
170′.92 — dc20   CIP

Contents

Acknowledgments *vii*
Abbreviations *ix*
Introduction *xi*

Chapter One. Historical Introduction 1
   Kant and Scheler: A Study in Contrasts 1
   Historical Background 3
   Scheler's View of the "Kantian Problem" 7
   The Importance of Scheler's Critique 10
   Notes 19

Chapter Two. The A Priori: Form and Phenomenon 27
   The Problem 27
   The Kantian Legacy and Phenomenological Background 29
   Scheler's Critique of the Kantian A Priori 33
   Scheler's Critique in Perspective 42
   Notes 50

Chapter Three. Moral Good and the Nature of Values 59
   Formalism in Kant's Ethics 59
   Scheler's Critique of Kantian Formalism 62
   The Question of "Empty Formalism" and the Concept
      of Material Ends in Kantian Ethics 69
   Scheler, Heidegger, and the Being of Values 75
   Notes 88

Chapter Four. Moral Feeling and the
   Perception of Values   99
      Kant's Theory of Moral Feeling   100
      Scheler's Critique and Alternative   105
      Comparative Assessment   112
      Notes   119

Chapter Five. Duty and Its Phenomenological Basis   125
      Kant's Theory of Moral Obligation   125
      Scheler's Critique of Kantian Deontologism   128
      The Phenomenological Basis of Scheler's Critique   132
      Critical Appraisal   137
      Notes   151

Chapter Six. Conclusion: Some Final Thoughts
   on Scheler's Critique   159
      Moral Action and Moral Disposition   159
      Human Nature   162
      Scheler's Interpretation of Kant   168
      Philosophical Implications of Scheler's Critique   170
      Notes   176

Appendix I: Is Scheler's Ethic an Ethic of Virtue?   179

Appendix II: North American Dissertations on Scheler   189

      Bibliography   195
      Index   211

Acknowledgments

The material in Appendix I: "Is Scheler's Ethic an Ethic of Virtue?" was previously published in *Japanese and Western Phenomenology*, ed. P. Blosser, et al. (Dordrecht: Kluwer Academic Publishers, 1993), pp. 147–59. It is reprinted here by permission of Kluwer Academic Publishers. A large part of my discussion of Kant's theory of moral feeling at the beginning of Chapter Four was published in substantially the same form in my article "A Problem in Kant's theory of Moral Feeling," *Lyceum* Vol. 3, No. 2 (Fall 1991), 27–39. I am grateful to the editor, David Banach, for permission to draw on this material.

Abbreviations

Kant

BG	*Der einzig mögliche Beweisgrund zu einer Demonstration des Daseins Gottes (The One Possible Basis for a Demonstration of the Existence of God)*
GMS	*Grundlegung zur Metaphysik der Sitten (Foundations of the Metaphysics of Morals)*
KGS	*Kants Gesammelte Schriften (Kant's Collected Writings)*
KpV	*Kritik der praktishcen Vernunft (Critique of Practical Reason)*
KrV	*Kritik der reinen Vernunft (Critique of Pure Reason)*
KU	*Kritik der Urteilskraft (Critique of Judgment)*
MS	*Die Metaphysik der Sitten (The Metaphysic of Morals)*
Prol.	*Prolegomena zu einer jeden künftigen Metaphysik (Prolegomena to Any Future Metaphysics)*
R	*Die Religion innerhalb der Grenzen der bloßen Vernunft (Religion within the Limits of Reason Alone)*
TP	*Theorie und Praxis: Über den Gemeinspruch: Das mag in der Theorie richtig sein, taugt aber night für die Praxis (On the Proverb: That May Be True in Theory, But Is of No Practical Use)*

Scheler

E	*Vom Ewignen im Menschen (On the Eternal in Man)*
F	*Der Formalismus in der Ethik und die Material Wertethik (Formalism in Ethics and Non-Formal Ethics of Values)*
GW	*Gesammelte Werke (Collected Works)*
IR	"Idealismus-Realismus" ("Idealism and Realism")
IS	"Die Idole der Selbsterkenntnis ("The Idols of Self-Knowledge")
LdT	"Lehre von den drei Tatsachen" ("The Theory of the Three Facts")
OA	*Ordo Amoris (Ordo Amoris)*
PE	"Phänomenologie und Erkennnistheorie: (Phenomenology and the Theory of Cognition)")
Res.	*Das Ressentiment im Aufbau der Moralen (Ressentiment)*
S	*Wesen und Formen der Sympathie (The Nature of Sympathy)*
Stel.	"Die Stellung des Menschen im Kosmos" (Man's Place in Nature)

HUSSERL

CM   *Cartesianische Meditationen (Cartesian Meditations)*
EU   *Erfahrung und Urteil (Experience and Judgment)*
FTL *Formale und transzendentale Logik (Formal and Transcendental Logic)*
Ideen *Ideen zu einer reinen Phänomenologie und phänomenologischen Philosophie, I (Ideas Pertaining to a Pure Phenomenology and to a Phenomenological Philosophy, Book I)*
K   *Die Krisis der europänischen Wissenschaften und die transzendentale Phänomenologie (The Crisis of European Sciences and Transcendental Phenomenology)*
LU   *Logische Untersuchungen (Logical Investigations)*
Z   *Die Vorlesungen zur Phänomenologie des inneren Zeitbewußtseins (The Phenomenology of Internal Time-Consciousness)*

HANS REINER

DI   *Duty and Inclination: The Fundamentals of Morality Discussed and Redefined with Special Regard to Kant and Schiller*

Introduction

IN 1928 HEIDEGGER CALLED HIM the strongest philosophical force in all of contemporary philosophy. I. M. Bochénski, in a popular survey of contemporary European philosophy published in 1947, called him the most brilliant thinker of his day. Manfred Frings, in an introductory work published in 1965, compared his work in ethics to Aristotle's and Kant's and called it one of the most profound, erudite, and ingenious works in the history of philosophy. Gadamer, Sartre, Merleau-Ponty, Hartmann, Cassirer, Buber, Maritain, Marcel, Ingarden, and other philosophers of international reputation have acknowledged their debt to him. Even Pope John Paul II wrote a doctoral dissertation on him.[1]

But, for all of that, Max Scheler remains a comparative unknown in the English-speaking world. There are reasons for this, as we shall see. Among others, these have to do with changing trends and styles of philosophy, the dwindling support for almost any kind of intuitionism, the ascent of Heideggerian existentialism and its repudiation of all philosophies of value. Still, even after all of these factors have been examined, the neglect of Scheler's work among contemporary students of phenomenology, the lacuna of studies in English devoted to him, and the widely overlooked wealth of material in his early ethical work remain something of a mystery. Even a greater familiarity with the parallels that exist between Scheler and contemporary currents of philosophy, such as critical theory and its view that moral norms are arrived at through communal discourse, would undoubtedly spark a renewed interest in Scheler's remarkable insights.

My interest in Scheler's critique of Kant runs back nearly a decade. I have always had a profound respect and admiration for the philosophy of Kant, and an appreciation of his indispensable importance for understanding contemporary philosophy generally. But as I began to study the works of Husserl and other phenomenologists, I also began to see increasingly the importance of Kant for understanding phenomenology specifically. In one way or another, like the other seminal thinkers of the phenomenological movement, Husserl appeared to find his philosophical point of departure within the legacy of Kantian ideas and assumptions. While critical of Kant and differing sharply with him on fundamental issues, Husserl also took over certain features and assumptions of his philosophy, such as its transcendental subjectivism and apriorism, adapting them to the phenomenological project. In view of this, the fact that Scheler's *magnum opus* contains an extensive appraisal and critique of some of the most fundamental presuppositions of Kantian philosophy seems especially significant. The more I read of Scheler, the more I began to see the value of a project dealing with his critique of Kant in *Der Formalismus in der Ethik und die Materiale Wertethik*, which would possess the virtue of focusing in a single project three important strands of philosophical interest: phenomenology, Kantianism, and ethics. Furthermore, with the exception of a handful of German articles and dissertations from the 1920s through the 1940s, the issue had remained untouched, and, in the English-speaking world, the project envisioned was virtually unprecedented. At the same time, however, the project presented a number of daunting challenges. For one thing, it involved rehabilitating the work of a philosopher who has been largely ignored over the past few decades or dismissed as passé. This meant that the reasons underlying the erosion of Scheler's tremendous earlier appeal, such as Heidegger's repudiation of value theory, would need to be addressed at some point, in order to make possible an even-handed reassessment of Scheler's phenomenology of value and ethics. Another difficulty was the unavoidable structural complexity of such a project. It involved, in effect, *three critiques* — my own "critique" of Scheler's "critique" of Kant's ethics, which, after all, is itself a "critique"[2] of the metaphysical foundations of morals. None of these difficulties made the project an easy one, but its intrinsic virtues, in the final analysis, rendered it eminently worthy of the challenges it entailed.

The present study cannot, of course, lay claim to comprehensiveness in its treatment of Scheler's philosophy or, most certainly, of Kant's. Its goal must be the comparatively modest one of endeavoring to unravel and examine the main strands of contention involved in the Schelerian critique. To this end, our primary source material can be fairly conveniently restricted, for the most part, to Scheler's aforementioned *magnum opus* (itself a tome of impressive size) and, for purposes of critical comparison, a number of key passages from Kant's ethical works; and the secondary literature can be restricted, on the whole, to the relatively few works and articles that most directly engage the Scheler-Kant question.

The study is divided into six chapters and two appendices. Each of the chapters constituting the body of the work contains a brief analysis of the Kantian position or discussion of the basic questions at issue in it, an exposition of Scheler's critique of the Kantian position and its presuppositions, and a detailed appraisal of Scheler's critique.

Chapter One, the historical introduction, not only introduces the reader to the basic anatomy and significance of Scheler's critique as a challenge to the fundamental assumptions of Kantian ethics, but offers an extensive historical discussion of the philosophical background of Scheler's critique and its overall place and significance within modern philosophy. In its opening paragraphs, a few remarks are made comparing and contrasting Scheler and Kant as philosophers and persons. I have always thought it important to know something about the personal lives and backgrounds of the philosophers whose theories I am considering.

The theories may stand or fall on their own merits, it is true, but they are not disembodied Platonic abstractions. They are human productions of a given personal, historical, and geographical ethos or horizon. And although the productions may be eidetically independent, strictly speaking, from the horizons which give them birth, the latter are not unrelated to the former, utterly, but connected somehow. In fact, there is sometimes the possibility, as some say, that an examination of the horizon may even help to illumine the philosophy. Whether or not this is the case in the present instance, others will have to judge for themselves. In any case, before outlining the theories at issue in this study, I begin with a few remarks and observations about Kant and Scheler personally, as well as about their intellectual milieu.

Chapter Two, "The A Priori: Form and Phenomenon," is devoted to an examination of Scheler's critique of the basic assumptions underlying Kantian apriorism. The importance of this issue for ethics, of course, lies in the insistence of both Kant and Scheler upon a rigorous grounding of ethics in some set of principles that can be grasped a priori. The discussion, at this point, requires an elaboration of the basic differences between phenomenology and the Kantian critical philosophy on questions of epistemology and metaphysics. It also requires, among other things, distinguishing Scheler's conception of the a priori from Husserl's.

Chapter Three, "Moral Good and the Nature of Values," centers on Scheler's criticism of the "empty formalism" of Kant's conceptions of duty, moral law, reason, and the categorical imperative as canons of moral worth, and Scheler's contention that such notions cannot be expected to provide the material content needed to serve as the grounding principles of ethical theory without being grounded themselves in a theory of material value. Any proper assessment of these claims, of course, requires an examination of the often-neglected "material" or "teleological" concepts within Kant's ethics, as well as the Heideggerian repudiation of Value Theory, which has probably done more to undermine the philosophical reputation of Scheler's ethics than any other single factor.

Chapter Four, "Moral Feeling and the Perception of Values," offers an extended analysis of Kant's theory of moral feeling and the problematic dualizations of reason/sensibility, will/inclination, spontaneity/receptivity, and noumena/phenomena underlying his analysis of affectivity in moral experience. Scheler's concept of an *ordo amoris*, an order of affectivity with its own ordering principles independent of reason, leads him to argue that the perception of values is not primordially a matter of intellectual choice or will, but of passive intentionalities belonging to one's pre-reflective experience. This, in turn, allows him to recast the traditional problems of hedonism, eudaemonism, and the relation of virtue to happiness, in untraditional new forms.

Chapter Five, "Duty and Its Phenomenological Basis," deals with the fundamental problem of moral obligation and its basis. Scheler's critique here hinges on the contention that Kant's formalistic conceptions of moral law, as expressed in the formula of the categorical imperative, prevent his ethics from being, in any material sense, an ethics of "insight." Rather, by trying to derive the conception of moral worth from a formula of obligation, Kant's ethics becomes instead a "blind" ethics of duty. No matter what pains Kant takes to show that the moral worth of an action resides in its being performed for duty's sake alone, Scheler's claim is essentially that there is something still more basic than duty—namely, the good—which can be defined only by reference to material values. At this point, Scheler's ethics itself is confronted by perhaps its greatest challenge: showing how a normative ethical theory can be founded upon a descriptive phenomenological theory of value.

Chapter Six, "Conclusion: Some Final Thoughts on Scheler's Critique," falls into several parts. The first two sections present some concluding thoughts on a few ancillary aspects of Scheler's critique, including his analyses of moral action, moral disposition, and human nature. These are followed by a brief discussion of the overall accuracy of Scheler's interpretation of Kant, and a detailed conclusion dealing with the general philosophical implications of Scheler's critique.

Appendix I, "Is Scheler's Ethic an Ethic of Virtue?" presents an extensive discussion of Scheler's concept of virtue, comparing it with those of Kant and Aristotle, and asking whether it escapes the basic difficulties of "post-aretaic" ethics scrutinized in Alasdair MacIntyre's masterful study, *After Virtue*. Appendix II contains a list of dissertations written on Scheler in English in North America since the mid-1930s.

In the present study, references to the key works of Kant and Scheler, as well as of Husserl and Reiner, will use the abbreviations provided in the list following the table of contents. Most references will include a cross-reference to an English translation, where such exists. Thus *F*, 125/104 indicates a citation to page 125 of the German edition of Scheler's *Formalismus*, and to page 104 of the English translation. By consulting these translations the reader will see for himself or herself where we have adopted this or that translation entirely, adapted it to our own translation, merely consulted it, or even translated the text quite differently—as in the case of the term *Gesinnung*, which Frings and Funk render as "basic moral tenor," but which we prefer to translate as "moral disposition" for reasons of style.[3] The only exception to this pattern of cross-references will be in the case of those works by Kant whose translations contain the conventional pagination of the German critical edition (*KGS*, Akademie edition). In such cases, for the sake of brevity, only the German pagination will be given.

For his accommodating support and helpful advice through various stages of this project, I am grateful to Professor Lester Embree of Florida Atlantic University. For their comments on earlier drafts of portions of this work, I owe special thanks to Professor Thomas Seebohm of Johannes

Guttenberg Universität in Mainz and Professor John Scanlon of Duquesne University. For a number of helpful insights on Scheler's relation to Husserl, shared at various conferences as well as through his books and articles, I am grateful to Professor Manfred Frings of DePaul University. I am indebted also to Professor Jack Caputo of Villanova University for his personal counsel, encouragement, and inspiration at stages along the way, as well as for some of his publications, which were helpful to me. For help in procuring various books and articles, I am thankful to Dick Rojcewicz of the Simon Silverman Phenomenology Center at Duquesne University; to my friend, Dr. Jim Bratt, who acquired for me the important study by Ingeborg Heidemann from Harvard University; and to Burl McCuiston of the Rudisill Library at Lenoir-Rhyne College. Support for the completion of the project was made possible through a generous leave of absence from Lenoir-Rhyne College in the autumn semester of 1990, as well as by a number of generous in-house grants through the offices of Dr. Robert Spuller, the Vice President for Academic Affairs of that institution, and by the invaluable secretarial assistance of Sonnie Cooke. I would be remiss not to mention my debt of gratitude also to Ms. Holly Panich, Associate Director at Ohio University Press, and her fine staff of professionals, for their part in bringing this book into print—especially to Helen Gawthrop for her oversight of the project as Production Manager, and to Mary Gillis for her meticulous work as copy editor.

Finally, I owe incalculable gratitude to my wife, Lori, and our four sons, Christopher, Jonathan, Benjamin, and Nathaniel, for their steadfast personal support and inspiration.

NOTES

1. The dissertation, which the Pope wrote in his native Polish under his personal name of Karol Wojtyła, is entitled "Ocena możliwości zbudowania etyki chrześcijańskiej przy założeniach systemu Maksa Schelera" (Catholic University of Lublin, 1959), and addresses the question of how far it is possible to establish a Christian ethic on the foundation of Schelerian principles. Cf. also his work, *Das Problem der Trennung von Erlebnis und Akt im Lichte der Anschauung Kants und Schelers, Primat Des Geistes* (Stuttgart: Seewald Verlag, 1979), and *The Acting Person*, trans. Audrzej Potocki (Dordrecht: D. Reidel, 1979), a book written in English and based on his earlier work in phenomenology.

For Martin Heidegger's remark see his "In Memory of Max Scheler (1928)," trans. T. Sheehan, in *Heidegger: The Man and the Thinker,*, ed. T. Sheehan (Chicago: Precedent, 1981), 159; for I. M. Bochénski, *Europäische Philosophie der Gegenwart* (Berne: Francke A. G. Verlag, 1947), translated into English by D. Nicholl and K. Aschenbrenner under the title *Contemporary European Philosophy* (Berkeley: University of California, 1961), 140; for Manfred S. Frings, *Max Scheler: A Concise Introduction Into the World of a Great Thinker* (Pittsburgh; Duquesne University, 1965), 103; for Scheler's influence generally, see Paul Good, ed., *Max Scheler im Gegenwartsgeschehen der Philosophie* (Bern: Francke, 1975), passim.

2. The word "critique" here is being used, of course, in different senses. Kant's "critique" refers to establishing the limits of reason and should not be equated with "criticism" in the usual sense.

3. In contrast to Manfred Frings' and Roger Funk's expression "basic moral tenor" (*F*, 131ff./111ff.), "disposition" is not only less awkward but also as suitably imprecise in English as *Gesinnung* is in German. It is also the conventionally more accepted translation. See, for example, *Kant's "Critique of Practical Reason" and Other Works on the Theory of Ethics*, Thomas Kingmill Abbott, trans., 6th ed. (London: Longmans, Green and Co., 1909), 331; *Religion within the Limits of Reason Alone*, by Immanuel Kant, Theodore M. Greene and Hoyt H. Hudson, trans. (1934; rpt. New York: Harper & Brothers, 1960), 20, 64.

There is only one possible obstacle to this conventional translation in Scheler's case, and that is a passage (*F*, 137/117) in which he explicitly states that the *Gesinnung* "is not a disposition" ("*keine Disposition ist*"). But since his purpose there is to distinguish the *Gesinnung* from an unintuitable hypothesis assumed to underlie empirically given deeds—what he calls "character" ("*Charakter*")—the problem is merely semantic and does not warrant the creation of an entirely new (and unwieldy) expression. Cf. "*Gesinnung*" in Rudolf Eisler, *Kant-Lexikon* (1930; rpt. Hildesheim: Georg Olms Verlagsbuchhandlung, 1964).

Historical Introduction 1

Kant and Scheler: A Study in Contrasts

It is hard to imagine two more different men than Immanuel Kant (1724–1804) and Max Scheler (1874–1928). Temperamentally, Kant was every bit the classic university professor, the devoted lecturer, and desk scholar. Although he enjoyed the company of friends and was an entertaining conversationalist, he always remained a study in self-discipline, a bachelor of such regular habits that the fabled housewives of Königsberg are said to have set their clocks by his daily walks. Scheler, by contrast, found the quiet of a library or study intolerable, preferring the constant bustle of people and clink of glasses, scribbling his thoughts on the back of train tickets, menus, or letters. With him, as Nicolai Hartmann noted, philosophy streamed forth as an overflowing expression of that which filled his life, so that living and philosophizing became indistinguishable.[1]

Kant made a conspicuous show of disassociating himself from the "ecclesiastical faith" during university processions, as Karl Barth once noted.[2] But he retained entirely the pathos of his childhood Pietism in the emphasis on personal faith, moral earnestness, and the strength and purity of an indomitable good will, which pervaded his life and work. By contrast, Scheler was a convert to Roman Catholicism and, for a significant period of his life, was even regarded as a leading philosopher of the Church.[3] But even the would-be Catholic seemed to lack almost entirely Kant's exemplary qualities of self-discipline. The "rigorous" Kant never allowed himself the amenity of marriage. Scheler was not only married, but married three times, and the succession of broken relationships that marred his career and alienated him from the Church became a deep and personal tragedy of his life.[4]

Kant followed with interest the French Revolution and other political and social events of his day but always retained the detached posture of an academic observer. He was well versed in the geography and culture of distant places but never set foot outside of his native province. His interest ranged across an amazing breadth, taking in everything from "lunar volcanoes" to theology, but he always remained concerned preeminently with the critical, metaphysical questions of foundation underlying these other areas of interest. By contrast, Scheler was actively involved in the immediate politics of his time, keenly aware of living in and for his age, always confronting and addressing the social, economic, political, and spiritual crises of his times. From 1917 to 1918 he served in the German Foreign Office, accepting missions to Geneva and to The Hague; and after the war he applied himself with a sense of mission to the spiritual reconstruction and reunification of Europe and the creation of a new sense of European solidarity.

These differences of temperament, concerns and orientation are reflected also in differences of prose style. The reading of Kant's critical works, even for many Kant enthusiasts, is often a tedious ordeal, while reading Scheler, for anyone, is usually not. Kant's critical writing is disciplined and organized but dry and deficient in examples, as he himself admits (*KrV*, A xviii). But the impression given by Scheler's works could hardly be more different. His paragraphs are sprawling and unwieldy but rich in suggestive examples. As Alfred Schutz observed: "Overwhelmed by the wealth of his discoveries, he lived in a continuous haste of mind. He had to proclaim so many lucid insights that he staggered, bewildered by cognition and inebriated by truth. This explains the frequent inconsistencies of his thought and the lack of structure of his writings."[5]

But nowhere is the contrast between Kant and Scheler more pronounced or more important than where their interests converge in the issues of philosophy and ethics. For it is at this point that a fundamental component of Kant's philosophy—the notion of "form"—stands in sharpest relief from what is most basic in Scheler's philosophy—the notion of "material content," or, better still, "phenomena."[6] It is here that Kant's much discussed "formalism" comes into conflict with Scheler's "phenomenology," and the questions about the transcendental grounding of philosophy, the nature of moral value and obligation—indeed, questions about human nature itself—are all reopened for renewed debate.

The present study is devoted to this contrast, this confrontation, this engagement between the Kantian and Schelerian alternatives. It is devoted to the problem of formalism in Kantian ethics and, by the same token, to the question of Scheler's non-formal alternative. Most generally, it is devoted to Scheler's "critique" of Kantian ethics—a term used advisedly in view of Scheler's reflective-phenomenological, as opposed to argumentative-critical, method.

A word of caution is in order here. While every effort has been made to represent Kant's ethics fairly and accurately in this study, the focus throughout is on Scheler's critique and alternative, not necessarily on the details of Kant's ethics. The reasons for this are two-fold. First, the study of Kant's ethics and its manifold problems of textual interpretation and conceptual systematization is a major industry in its own right. A thoroughgoing treatment of these matters clearly lies beyond the scope of this book. Thus, for the most part, we shall simply assume a basic and conventional familiarity with Kant's ethics, even while pressing this conventional view, at times, beyond what some interpreters would find acceptable in order to try to expose possible points of strain and weakness. Second, Scheler's own interest was in the general import of Kantian ethics rather than in the details and problems of Kant's texts. Accordingly, this generality is reflected to some degree in our own study and must be borne in mind against any inordinate expectation of exegetical thoroughness in our treatment of Kant. This should not be thought to betoken either a predilection towards a cavalier treatment of Kant or a predisposition to accept in advance the interpretation of Kant that emerges in the Schelerian critique. It is a matter, rather, of what is possible within the limitations of a study such as this.

In the remainder of this chapter we shall examine briefly the historical background of Scheler's position, summarize Scheler's own view of the problem of "formalism" in Kant's ethics, and briefly assess the importance of his critique in light of current discussions in philosophy and ethics. The sharply critical Heideggerian repudiation of all philosophy of "values"—a pointed complement to the more recent deconstructionist developments and the widespread criticism of all forms of foundationalism—must figure to some degree in the latter assessment.

Historical Background

THE EARLIEST SIGNIFICANT CHARGES of "empty formalism" to be leveled against Kant's ethics were made by Schleiermacher and Hegel. These followed hard on the heels of well-known jibes about Kant's "rigorism" and "gloomy and monkish asceticism" made popular by the satiric verses and essays of his contemporary, Schiller, and were followed, in turn, by similar charges by Schopenhauer, J. S. Mill, and others.[7] But the major, immediate formative influences on Scheler's own understanding of the "Kantian problem" were different from these, due primarily to intervening historical and intellectual movements. Most basically, these influences consisted of four interrelated developments in the recent history of philosophy—the movements of Lebensphilosophie, Neo-Kantianism, Value Theory, and Phenomenology.

Lebensphilosophie, or "vitalism" (or even "life philosophy," as it is sometimes called after its German name), is a movement that is notoriously amorphous and hard to define. It is identified with the emergence, in the last century, of the "social" or "human sciences" (*Geisteswissenschaften*) and is sometimes discussed under the heading of "philosophy of culture" or even "philosophical anthropology." Its emergence is identified chiefly with the name of Wilhelm Dilthey, but, as a movement, it is sometimes seen as embracing such diverse figures as Goethe, Schopenhauer, Nietzsche, Henri Bergson, Rudolf Eucken, Georg Simmel, Wilhelm Wundt, Ernst Troeltsch, Max Weber, Eduard Spranger, Karl Mannheim, Nicolai Hartmann, and even Scheler. At least in part, Lebensphilosophie was a reaction to the emergence of positivism, which was itself a reaction, led by Auguste Comte and others (such as J. S. Mill), against the perceived excesses of metaphysical speculation in later German Idealism. The positivists, in response to this alleged overextension of the "noumenal" in Idealism, enshrined the "phenomenal" realm of "positive facts" as the only true reality, but in such a way that the positing subject was excluded from consideration as irrelevant. In reaction to this exclusion, Lebensphilosophie devoted increasing attention to the historical relativity and psychology of the experiencing human subject.[8]

This current of thought was first introduced to Scheler formally when he studied philosophy at Berlin in 1894 under Wilhelm Dilthey and Georg Simmel, and the following year at Jena under Rudolf Eucken. But already from his early years, Scheler was familiar with the broad current of "vitalism" through his acquaintance with Nietzsche's writings, of which he was an avid reader. Later he also became a devoted reader of Henri Bergson. Through these philosophers Scheler was exposed to various claims regarding the historically and culturally conditioned nature of philosophy, the relativity of values, and the irreducibly spiritual dimension of human life represented in the *Geisteswissenschaften*. Whatever influence such ideas may have had on Scheler, they could hardly have disposed him favorably toward the largely unhistorical, abstract, transcendental formalism of Kantian ethics.

Neo-Kantianism was a vastly diverse movement, comprised of complex, and sometimes contradictory, rival interpretations of Kant, stemming from rival schools with somewhat differing areas of interest. In part, at least, it may be viewed as a neo-idealistic reaction against the irrationalistic implications perceived in the outright relativism and historicism associated with the Lebensphilosophie movement—a reaction paralleled in England by the Neo-Hegelianism of F. H. Bradley and J. McTaggart. A not insignificant fact of Scheler's own development is that he had as one of his own teachers at Jena the Neo-Kantian philosopher, Otto Liebmann, whose *Kant und die Epigonen* (1865) and famous motto ("Back to Kant") eventually earned him the title, "Father of Neo-Kantianism." Both Scheler's dissertation and *Habilitationsschrift* reveal his early immersion in problems central to the Neo-Kantian agenda: the problems of distinguishing and delineating the realms of logical and ethical principles, and transcendental and psychological methods. Friedrich Lange had already subjected the materialism of the philosopher of science, Ludwig Büchner, to well-founded criticism from the Neo-Kantian perspective in his famous *History of Materialism* (1866), and, while rejecting Kant's view of the rational necessity of an intelligible but unknowable world, defended the legitimacy of a postulated ideal world as the product of poetic fancy (*Dichtung*). Likewise, while rejecting the notion of the thing-in-itself as a mistake, Liebmann left open a field for value decisions that do not depend on claims to valid knowledge, but only on human will as determined by culture.

Both the Marburg and Baden schools of Neo-Kantianism, with which Scheler seems to have been familiar, continued to expand the notion of cognition to include broader formal laws and categories of the understanding. Hermann Cohen stressed the historical development of ideas in cultural consciousness and set forth a view of logic in which logic was regarded as generating its own content as well as forms.[9] In this sense, Cohen's philosophy was less narrowly "formalistic" than Kant's, although it was perhaps no less "constructivistic." Wilhelm Windelband, meanwhile, considered the "epistemological problem" to be reducible to an axiological one, since the truth of a judgment, in his view, is not determined by its conformity to a thing-in-itself, but to an experienced obligation to believe it—that is, to an experienced logical, ethical, or aesthetic value or norm, in the light of which the judgment is made. Heinrich Rickert explicitly drew on the hylemorphic schema of the Kantian legacy in his view that the material content of a system of values cannot be derived from general axiological forms, but must be drawn from the material (content) of concrete culture and history. Furthermore, he expressed the view that the whole realm of values may be conceived simultaneously as "real" and yet as "nonexistent," anticipating questions about the ontological status of values in Scheler.[10]

The thrust of this Neo-Kantian influence, then, was to present Scheler with an expanded, non-formal, material view of cognition—a view that complemented, at least in this respect, the influence of Lebensphilosophie from Dilthey, Simmel, and Eucken. Yet the influence of Neo-Kantianism itself was not unmixed. For if Scheler welcomed certain features of Neo-Kantianism, he also rejected others. For example, he ultimately rejected what he called the "constructivism" of the Kantian philosophy—the view that the objective order of the world is imposed upon it by the order-conferring subject—an idea as much a legacy of the Neo-Kantians as of Kant. Furthermore, Scheler's attack on Kantian "formalism" may have been evoked, in part, by the "formalistic" and "panlogistic" conception of transcendentalism governing the multiple forms of cognition in Neo-Kantian interpretation.

Value Theory (*Werttheorie*), or "axiology," as it is often called by English-speaking writers, is a movement loosely associated with Neo-

Kantianism, which arose under the influence of Rudolph Hermann Lotze (1817–1881). Lotze sought to secure a realm of independent significance for human "values" against the encroaching advances of the natural sciences, whose pervasive positivism threatened to reduce the totality of human experience to a dimension of quantifiable "facts." On the Continent, the later development of the value theory movement was carried out chiefly on two fronts. In Germany, as we have seen already, it was developed within the Baden school of Neo-Kantians established by Windelband, and later elaborated by Rickert and others. In Austria, it was developed by Franz Brentano and his two disciples at the University of Vienna, Christian von Ehrenfels and Alexius Meinong, within the so-called Second Austrian School of Values.[11] Brentano's lecture before the Vienna Law Society, later published under the title of *The Origin of Our Knowledge of Right and Wrong* (1889), had already forged a way between what was regarded as the abstract formalism of Kant and the somewhat arbitrary consequentialism of the British utilitarians, proposing the existence of an order of a priori ethical intuitions of comparable rigor to that of formal logic. In their respective works, Ehrenfels and Meinong took over and expanded upon Brentano's ideals, seeking to lay a foundation for a general theory of values as a systematic and a priori science.

Scheler was acquainted with these developments, which, along with the expanded notion of "value" current in the writings of philosophers as diverse as Nietzsche and Edmund Husserl, offered a generic conception of value and an acquaintance with various attempts to classify intuitive laws of valuation and "regional ontologies" of values. These "material" notions of value—encompassing what were called the "value phenomena" of such fields as ethics, economics, aesthetics, jurisprudence, education, and perhaps logic and epistemology—provided some of the basic constituents in Scheler's critique of Kantian "formalism" in ethics.[12]

Phenomenology, whose roots may also be traced to the Austrian, Franz Brentano, emerged as a movement under the leadership of Edmund Husserl, who exploited and developed the notion of "intentionality" pioneered by Brentano. Like Brentano and the value theorists, Husserl rejected the naturalistic and positivistic assumptions underlying prevailing theories of science; but unlike them, he rejected Lotze's view that a realm of significance for human concerns could be secured against the encroachments of natural science and positivism by setting up a dualism of two realms—a realm of real facts and a realm of ideal values. Far from providing a resolution of the actual problem, such a bifurcation of experience only led to the major dilemma of the age—the infelicitous choice between the incompatible philosophies of naturalism or positivism, on the one hand, and of idealism on the other. The dilemma, as noted by J. H. Olthuis, posed hopelessly unacceptable alternatives: "Naturalism is scientific, but value-less; that is, it is incompetent to answer the important questions of life. Idealism is value-sate, but unscientific; that is, its answers are will-o'-the-wisps which help no one."[13]

Scheler had already been exposed to a kind of phenomenology, prior to meeting Husserl, in the descriptive psychology taught and practiced by certain of his contemporaries, such as Carl Stumpf, with whom he studied while in Berlin. But it was only in 1901, when he was introduced to Husserl at a party in Halle hosted by Hans Vaihinger for collaborators on the journal *Kant-Studien*, that Scheler met what he considered to be the decisive influence on his philosophical career. The phenomenology of Husserl at that time was not yet the transcendental phenomenology worked out a decade later in his milestone publication, *Ideas* (1913). But whatever may be said about the nature of Husserl's influence on Scheler, or about the differences between their ultimate conceptions of phenomenology, it was Husserl's conception of "categorical intuition," in the final analysis, that served as the key to Scheler's critique of Kantian philosophy and opened the way for his own theory of value, which was based on the phenomenological notions of "essential intuition" (*Wesensschau*) and the "material a priori."[14]

Scheler's critique of Kantian ethics must be seen against this background. It was this background of these four contemporaneous philosophical developments that formed the intellectual culture within which his conception of the problem of "formalism" in Kantian ethics took shape.

Scheler's View of the "Kantian Problem"

WHAT SCHELER WANTED WAS AN ETHICS that addressed the material content of moral experience with the same rigor that Kantian ethics appeared to have achieved in its treatment of the formal elements. Scheler essentially agreed with the Kantian insistence that the foundations of ethics must be unconditional and a priori, that morals cannot rest on anything as unpredictable as the anticipated realization of contingent goods or ends. A consequentialist ethic would not do. But he rejected the Kantian inference that the "material contents" of moral experience therefore could have no place in determining the morality of an action. He could not accept the Kantian assumption that the determining ground of morality can be found in nothing other than the form of an agent's will.

On the Kantian view, according to Scheler, the only principle of lawfulness conceivable in morality was that contributed by the rational subject; in other words, the form of universality expressed in the categorical imperative. But the material elements given in the inclinations, desires, and feelings of moral experience could never be known to have their own moral lawfulness independently of the rational subject. Hence, the morality of an action was supposed to be decided in a purely formal way, excluding from consideration such phenomena as the actual material contents (or objects) of willing and desiring.

In order to make sense of Kant's formalism at this point, it must be remembered that Kant was involved in a struggle to make room for morality in the face of the prevailing mechanistic views of the science of his time. Spectacular advances in the physical sciences seemed to be leading rapidly towards a completely mechanical understanding of nature, including human nature. The ideal of science, with its mounting record of technical conquests over nature, was rapidly encroaching upon what seemed to be the last vestiges of the ideal of free human personality. The ultimate philosophical implications of this shift were embodied preeminently in Humean empiricism, which seemed to undermine the very idea of free human personality essential to morality and, furthermore, the ideas of God, the soul, the external world, substance, and causality (and thereby, ironically, the foundations of science itself). Only against this background can we begin to make sense of Kant's psychology, his distinction between phenomenal and noumenal realms, and his attempt to secure the determining ground of morality in a (formal) maxim of the will, and not, in the final analysis, by a consideration of the will's (material) objects.

But at this very point, claims Scheler, Kant uncritically took over elements of the empiricist theory of the will. According to this theory, the *contents* of willing originate by being kinesthetically posited in "representations" of anticipated pleasurable effects or reactions. Only by assuming such a theory of will, says Scheler, could Kant reasonably have concluded that all attempts to determine the morality of willing by reference to its material contents (or objects) must result necessarily in a consequentialist ethics, a contingent ethics of realized ends, an "ethics of success." By contrast, Scheler insists, the phenomenon of willing itself contains nothing more than a conation in which a content to be realized is given, and given originally independently of any "representation."[15]

In Scheler's view, the Kantian orientation prevents one from arriving at a clear, coherent account of moral experience. Indeed, Scheler insists that Kant himself remained forever blind to the fact that, at the center of his ethics, the "moral ought" of the categorical imperative implicitly presupposed precisely what he intended its formalism to exclude: material insight into the actual values implicit in an "ideal ought," or in what Kant called the "moral law."[16] Hence, the greatest error of Kantian ethics, according to Scheler, lies in its neglect of those elements of experience that are given a priori as the basic phenomena of moral experience—namely, values. Values, according to Scheler, can be shown to exhibit themselves in an objective a priori order of ranks and, thereby, to furnish an index of reference (correlative to an a priori "logic of preference") necessary for rigorously grounding a phenomenological ethics.

Accordingly, Scheler set for himself a two-fold task: first, to establish a new foundation for ethics in a phenomenology of material values; and, second, to carry out this project by simultaneously offering a fundamental critique of Kantian ethics. His evident strategy was to offer a decisive exposé of the Kantian formalist ethic, which to his mind represented the most compelling and rigorous moral theory of all modern philosophy, with the intention of thereby reinforcing the cogency of his own material, phenomenological approach as a viable alternative. With this strategy in view, Scheler distilled from Kantian ethics eight basic presuppositions, which he set forth as a foil for the development of his own critique. These he inscribed in the opening pages of his major work, *Der Formalismus in der Ethik und die Materiale Wertethik* (1913–1916).[17] In the English translation by Frings and Funk, they read as follows:

1. Every non-formal ethics must of necessity be an ethics of goods and purposes.
2. Every non-formal ethics is necessarily of only empirical-inductive and a posteriori validity.
3. Every non-formal ethics is of necessity an ethics of success [or consequences]. Only formal ethics can treat the basic moral disposition [*Gesinnung*][18] or willing based upon it as the original bearer of the values of good and evil.
4. Every non-formal ethics is of necessity a hedonism and so falls back on the existence of sensible states of pleasure, that is, pleasure taken in objects. Only formal ethics is in a position to avoid all reference to sensible pleasure-states through the exhibition of moral values and the proof of moral norms resting on such values.
5. Every non-formal ethics is of necessity heteronomous. Only formal ethics can found and establish the autonomy of the person.
6. Every non-formal ethics leads to a mere legalism with respect to actions. Only formal ethics can found the morality of willing.
7. Every non-formal ethics makes the person a servant to his own states or to alien goods. Only formal ethics is in a position to demonstrate and found the dignity of the person.
8. Every non-formal ethics must of necessity place the ground of all ethical value-estimations in the instinctive egoism of man's natural organization. Only formal ethics can lay the foundation for a moral law, valid in general for all rational beings, which is independent of all egoism and every special natural organization of man.

Scheler saw it as his task to expose the lack of warrant for these presuppositions phenomenologically and, by the same approach, to establish the warrant for his own alternative ethical theory based on a phenomenology of material values. Our task will be, in turn, to examine Scheler's critique of Kantian ethics and to assess the viability of his alternative.

The Importance of Scheler's Critique

THE PHILOSOPHICAL RELEVANCE and significance of the Schelerian critique must be assessed in terms of three issues that converge in it—first, its challenge to Kantian ethics; second, its phenomenological approach; and third, its implications for moral theory generally.

THE CHALLENGE TO KANTIAN ETHICS

As for its challenge to Kantian ethics, the significance of Scheler's critique has been all but buried beneath the history of confused and confusing arguments surrounding the issue of "formalism" in Kant. This has been true especially in the English-speaking world. One reason for this is the fact that, until the comparatively recent translation of Kant's later works, such as his *Doctrine of Virtue* (1964), the principal works from which students derived their knowledge of Kantian ethics were those that often lent themselves to facile caricatures of Kant's "formalism." Abetting this tendency has been the all too frequent transposition and reconstruction of Kant's "formalism" within an Hegelian-idealist framework or utilitarian-consequentialist orbit of considerations; in neither case could justice be done to the integrity of Kant's own views.

Another reason is that the role and nature of teleology in Kant's ethics has never been widely understood. Not only is this a matter of logically relating the formal motives and determining ground of practical reason to its material ends and purposes, as Kant does in his *Doctrine of Virtue* and *Critique of Judgment*; it is also a matter of understanding how a "deontological" system of ethics can be related to, and perhaps be lodged within, a larger "teleological" framework such as he envisions in his political and historical writings.[19] But ever since the modern rejection of ancient and medieval views of natural teleology during the Scientific Revolution and Enlightenment, this has become no easy matter. For after the teleological assumptions of Aristotelian physics were rejected, "reason" was no longer regarded as capable of supplying a genuine comprehension of humanity's "essential nature" or "true end" in any scientific or speculative sense. This is at least arguably as true of Kant as it was of most any of his philosophical contemporaries or successors.[20] This problem has contributed to the difficulty of understanding the issue of "formalism" in Kant's ethics.

Thus, in one way or another, either the old charge of "formalism" has been taken up in largely superficial attacks on Kant or else, among partisans of Kant, the more substantive issues underlying the charges have not been perceived clearly or faced squarely. Examples of such failings may be found, respectively, in the treatments of Kant offered by Richard Taylor and H. J. Paton. On the one hand, in his study of *Good and Evil* (1970), Taylor relentlessly attacks and ridicules Kant's ethical formalism as "empty" or "barren," despite many cogent arguments that exist against the view that Kant's categorical imperative is devoid of content, and without addressing substantively the "material ends" of ethics specified by Kant himself (Taylor, xii, 108–14). On the other hand, in his study of *The Categorical Imperative* (1947, 1948) a couple decades earlier, Paton utterly failed to address any of the real difficulties with Kant's formalism of the kind raised by Continental writers such as Scheler, Nicolai Hartmann, and others (74–77, 116, 249f.). And even where Scheler's views themselves are mentioned, all too often they are perfunctorily dismissed, as they are, for example, by Lewis White Beck in his commentary on Kant's *Critique of Practical Reason* (118). This is no less of a problem than if Scheler's phenomenological approach was simply taken over with a few revisions and left fundamentally unquestioned among some of his followers.[21]

Some of those who come to Kant's defense against the charges of "formalism" emphasize the necessity of a formal principle in ethics. But they point out that, far from neglecting the material contents of willing in moral experience, Kant in his later works regarded the material ends of willing as playing a decisive if not fundamental role, contrary to what some of his critics have supposed. The question is also raised as to what, exactly, "formalism" refers to when used in criticism of Kant. Must we distinguish, perhaps, several kinds of formalism—for example, "logical," "substantial," and "procedural" formalism—as John Silber does? ("Procedural Formalism," 233). Should not the formalism of Kant's ethics be carefully distinguished from that of his theoretical philosophy, as Paul Schilpp insists?[22]

Interpretations among English-speaking philosophers run the spectrum. This can be seen particularly in the differing explanations that are offered regarding the categorical imperative as the formal principle of Kant's ethics. For example, C. D. Broad and L. W. Beck have argued that Kant's categorical imperative is more accurately understood as a rule of syllogism than as a premise from which to deduce specific conclusions. A. R. C. Duncan and T. C. Williams see it as a description of the nature of the moral action executed by practical reason, not as a criterion determining the rightness or wrongness of conduct as such. M. G. Singer, as well as Paton and Beck, on the other hand, stress that specific procedures for applying Kant's formal rules allow one to address the material content of moral experience. And Alan Donagan, like H. H. Schroeder much earlier, accents the importance of the second formulation of the categorical imperative in showing how concretely Kantian ethics addresses specific performances of moral experience.[23]

German scholarship of the last half-century, on the whole, has maintained increasingly that Kant's ethics not only allows, but demands, a non-formal (material) development.[24] And in the 1920s Heidegger lent the considerable weight of his opinion to the view that Kant, in his conception of the *personalitas moralis*, held a rich *phenomenological* notion of *nonsensible* moral feeling that utterly disarms Scheler's critique of Kant's alleged formalism.[25] But such views, even if prevalent, have not gone uncontested; and questions remain, as we shall see, about how Kant's relationships to later German philosophy, to Neo-Kantianism, and, in particular, to the phenomenological movement, are to be understood.

All of these considerations signal the importance of assessing Scheler's critique on its own merits, of seeing how far it genuinely penetrates and illuminates the issue of "formalism" underlying Kantian ethics, and of assessing in what way it may constitute a real challenge and perhaps in some ways a viable alternative. Any such assessment requires a consideration of Scheler's phenomenological perspective and its relation to the critical philosophy of Kant.

Since a substantial treatment of Scheler's phenomenological approach can be found in our next chapter, and a detailed discussion of the philosophical implications of his critique is offered in the concluding part of chapter six, we shall limit our remarks in the following sections to some observations of a general historical nature.

Scheler the Phenomenologist, and His Influence

The phenomenological approach of Scheler's critique is important for several reasons. For one thing, his critique of Kantian ethics appears in his major work of moral philosophy, *Formalismus*, which represents one of the first clear, sustained and programmatic applications of the phenomenological method to a material field of investigation—the field of ethics and value theory. Whatever the differences between Scheler and Husserl—and certainly there are important differences, not the least of which was Scheler's rejection, in the manner of the Munich-Göttingen school, of Husserl's "transcendental" turn around 1913—there is no question that, in an important sense, Scheler's *Formalismus* represents a kind of "test case" of applied phenomenology. Husserl never published a work on ethics, but only works concerned with foundational questions or "beginnings."[26] Further, although there are other, perhaps more systematically developed, phenomenological treatments of ethics than Scheler's—notably Hartmann's massive *Ethics* (1926)—Scheler's work is the earliest and the more genuinely seminal in an historical sense; and only Scheler's work contains a thoroughgoing critique of Kantian formalism[27] and presses the contention that a genuinely normative ethics must be capable of offering moral guidance.[28]

Scheler's phenomenology of moral experience is not without its own genuine brilliance. In many respects it is a piece of genius. Care must be taken, in fact, to protect a proper appreciation of Scheler's genius from being undermined by the perception of excessive enthusiasm on the part of some Scheler scholars. This is a possible perception, for example, when a leading authority on Scheler says that the latter's work "unquestionably represents the chief contribution to ethics in this century, and is along with Aristotelian Ethics and Kant's *Critique of Practical Reason* the most profound, erudite, and ingenious work on ethics to be found in the history of philosophy" (Frings, *Max Scheler*, 103). Indeed, the litany of expressions of awe and admiration for the genius of Scheler are hard to overlook. His influence was considerable. The impact of his work was felt not only in Europe but in many other parts of the world. One finds it, for example, among scholars in the former Soviet Union; even more decisively in Japan; and through the work of Ortega y Gasset, in Latin America and the Spanish speaking world as well.[29]

In light of this, the comparative ignorance about Scheler in the English-speaking world is surprising at first. This has been attributed to a number of probable causes. The most general and obvious of these is the growing rift, since Bertrand Russell's defection from the camp of British Idealists around the turn of the century, between the approaches of "analytic" philosophy in the English-speaking world and of the so-called speculative tradition of Continental philosophy and phenomenology. On the "analytic" side, the rise of logical empiricism and of a new antipathy toward intuitionism, led to the development of emotivist and other noncognitivist metaethical theories (such as those of Charles L. Stevenson, Richard B. Brandt, and J. L. Mackie), which have been deeply inimical to the sort of approach taken by Scheler, as we shall see in the following section.[30] More specific causes may include Scheler's pro-German writings at the outset of World War I; the view—unwarranted in light of his later writings—that he was a proto-Nazi; the bad press he therefore received in his first exposure to American and British audiences; the suppression of his writings by the Nazis, ironically, because of his Jewish ancestry on his mother's side; his allusive, unconventional style of writing; his apparent inattention to foundational questions of epistemology and metaphysics; the slow completion of his published collected works; the impression of disorder given by the present state of the Schelerian *corpus*; and the lack of English translations of many of his works.[31]

But much of what could be corrected in all of this has been remedied. Manfred Frings has done a considerable share of the work needed to remove many of these obstacles. His editing of Scheler's posthumous manuscripts, a task he took over from Maria Scheler, the author's widow, and his translation into English of works of key importance, along with David Lachterman and others, have helped to make available material to dispel some of the negative prejudices against Scheler and pave the way for a constructive assessment of his significance and the assimilation of his work into the world of English-language scholarship. The translation of *Formalismus* by Frings and R. L. Funk, which appeared in 1973, has been especially important in view of the comparative lacuna in ethical studies among English-speaking phenomenologists. The results of this work over the past three decades may be assessed by tracking the progress of American dissertations written on Scheler (see Appendix II).

Despite this, Scheler remains a surprisingly little-known philosopher, especially for one so universally acclaimed such a short time ago. There remain two related and perhaps overriding factors behind this. One is the sharp decline in the popularity of Value Theory since World War II in Germany as well as in the English-speaking world; the other is the eclipse of Scheler, along with Husserl and other phenomenologists, by the advent of Heidegger on the philosophical scene, first in Germany and then in the United States. And it is in this connection that the implications of Scheler's critique must be developed.

THE PLACE OF SCHELER'S CRITIQUE IN MODERN PHILOSOPHY

The implications for ethics generated by Scheler's critique are especially significant for a tradition of ethics that reaches from F. Brentano to N. Hartmann on the Continent and from G. E. Moore to J. N. Findlay in the English-speaking world.[32] The idea of a general theory of value, as it was first developed in a grand way on the Continent (as described above), had some influence in Britain on the work of Bernard Bosanquet, W. R. Sorely, and others. But it would be wrong to assume, because of its current decline in the English-speaking world, either that the development of Value Theory was chiefly a Continental affair, or—to the extent that it did hold sway in Anglo-American circles—that it was a Continental import. In fact, Findlay claims that a closer study of the neglected later chapters of Moore's *Principia Ethica* (1903) would show him to be, at least within the English-speaking world, "one of the prime founders of axiology," no less than the earlier chapters make him the "father of modern meta-ethics." In any case, the idea as well as the term "axiology" was first introduced in the United States by W. M. Urban, in his highly respected *Valuation: Its Nature and Laws* (1906), and by Hugo Münsterberg, who taught at Harvard at the turn of the century. Subsequently, the concepts and vocabulary of value theory were taken up by R. B. Perry, John Dewey, D. W. Prall, E. W. Hall and others, and found perhaps its most notable exponent in J. N. Findlay during his years at Yale.

Although this tradition has had some recent exponents, the decline of widespread interest in Value Theory as a philosophical movement is now evident. As recently as 1970, Risieri Frondizi could point to the publication of *The Journal of Value Inquiry* as one of many evidences of "a growing interest in value theory" in his preface to the second edition of his *What is Value?* And in his 1972 anthology, *Contemporary European Ethics*, Joseph Kockelmans included a major section on "axiological ethics," with selections by René Le Senne, Hans Reiner, Raymond

Polin, and Georges Gusdorf. But today these philosophers are widely dismissed as passé in Europe and remain virtually unknown in the English-speaking world.

Why is this? In 1976 Hans Reiner addressed this question in an essay entitled "Is Value Ethics Out of Date?"[33] He attributed this decline of interest to the ascendancy of existential philosophy and waning interest in ethics in post-World War II Germany and to the general rejection of intuitionism among English-speaking philosophers.[34] On the reasons for dissatisfaction with intuitionism, he referred to what William Frankena had written in his *Ethics*:

> There are a number of reasons why intuitionism, for almost two centuries the standard view among moral philosophers, now finds few supporters. First of all, it raises several ontological and epistemological questions. An intuitionist must believe in simple indefinable properties, properties that are of a peculiar non-natural or normative sort, a priori or non-empirical concepts, intuition, and self-evident or synthetic necessary propositions. All of these beliefs are hard to defend. (103)

While "hard" to defend may not mean "impossible," as Reiner goes on to try to demonstrate in the case of his own intuitionist axiological ethics, Frankena clearly offers some indication why intuitionist theories have fallen on hard times.

The first reason for the decline of interest in Value Theory, then, was the development of a reaction against the view that moral disputes could be settled by appealing to a supposedly universal ethical intuition. This position, popularized in Britain by the Bloomsbury Circle, had been developed by G. E. Moore. (Regan, *Bloomsbury's Prophet*, xi–xiv, 3–10, 20–28). But it seemed too precariously parochial a view, far too likely to endorse culturally biased values, and in any case the intuitionists constantly disagreed among themselves. This led to the development of various noncognitivist theories such as those of the emotivists, who concluded that "ethical intuitions" really express subjective feelings rather than evidencing any kind of direct knowledge of moral properties or ethical truths.

A second reason for the decline (one not discussed by Reiner), was the rise of logical empiricism with its insistence that only two kinds of cognitive language are possible—analytic statements (such as definitions or tautologies) and factual statements that can be empirically tested. On these grounds, conventional definitions of ethical terms were considered permissible, as well as psychological and sociological accounts. But moral judgments were viewed as problematic. On the one hand, they are not definitions and therefore not analytic. On the other hand, they do not refer to empirically observable properties and therefore are not empirically verifiable. Hence, logical positivists such as A. J. Ayer concluded that moral judgments cannot be cognitive at all. And this also reinforced the emotivist thesis, worked out in different ways by Charles Stevenson and others, that moral judgments must be noncognitive utterances, used to express and arouse emotion.[35]

A third reason (and one mentioned by Reiner), is the ascendancy of existential philosophy and waning interest in ethics in post-World War II Germany. This development is no less important than the two philosophical developments just mentioned or the rise (to which they contributed) of noncognitivist metaethical theories deeply inimical to the sort of approach taken by Scheler. Just as important for the decline of interest in Value Theory among Continental philosophers, and also for the decline of interest in Scheler, has been the emergence of Heidegger as a major philosophical force to be reckoned with. This was not simply a matter of Heidegger capturing the limelight from Scheler; it was a matter of his raising serious new questions concerning the very being of the values upon which philosophers such as Scheler sought to erect systems of ethics. In this light, the chief defect of Scheler's phenomenology, like all philosophies of value, was the weakness of its treatment of the *ontology* of values. The insufficient development of this fundamental aspect of Value Theory has left it especially vulnerable in a philosophical climate that has been distinguished, since the 1930s, by the major "growth industry" of Heideggerian ontology, making this appear to be probably the most critical defect of Scheler's *Formalismus*. While it is true that Scheler developed this dimension in some of his later works and even took issue with some of the views of Heidegger's *Being and Time*, these reflections occurred relatively late in his career and found their way into print only much later, after his death and after his career was eclipsed by the swift ascent of Heidegger's; and, consequently, these facts are scarcely noted even now.[36]

The question of whether Scheler's value theory possesses a sufficient philosophical foundation is also raised from another direction by transcendental phenomenology. Like Husserl after his transcendental turn, some of his disciples—especially, perhaps, those of the Mainz school, such as Gerhard Funke and Thomas Seebohm, although others such as J. N. Mohanty also come to mind—have suggested that phenomenology ultimately requires a critical grounding in transcendental subjectivity in a sense at least analogous to Kant's.[37] From this perspective too, then, Scheler's critique of Kant is regarded as suffering a critical defect: the lack of a sufficient transcendental ground.

The Schelerian critique does suggest at points that the problems of ethics and epistemology ultimately intersect in the ontology of values. This is true especially of the way Scheler founds moral obligation in a priori intuitions of value essences. Other thinkers, as different as Chisholm and Windelband, have picked up on this issue and proposed that the problem of knowledge is ultimately reducible to a problem of ethics—that "truth" in epistemology boils down in some sense to the issue of "obligation" in judgments or propositions.[38] Scheler himself would not have welcomed exactly such a view. But his own view of the "ideal ought" (examined in chapter five, below) is freighted with implications about how the "ought" of ethics is ultimately grounded in the "is" of certain interrelations among values, which, he claims, can be "known" *a priori*.[39]

Whether or not something like a "transcendental deduction" can be provided for a general theory of values, as Findlay once suggested, perhaps remains a moot question (*Axiological Ethics*, 81f.). But the issue as to how specific moral actions and dispositions may be evaluated, and how such evaluations are to be grounded, and what ontological status such evaluations may have, remains a vital one within the interchange between Kantian "critical" philosophy and phenomenology—from Scheler and Husserl to Heidegger and beyond.

If the weakness of its ontological analysis and phenomenological grounding is its chief apparent *defect*, the most serious *obstacle* before the Schelerian critique may lie in the recent ascendancy of a type of philosophical thought—both on the Continent and in the English-speaking world—that regards the very project of endeavoring to secure a *ground* or *foundation* of any kind as philosophically pointless and passé. In analytic philosophy, this trend came to expression in the criticisms of "foundationalism" that have emerged over the last decades. In Continental philosophy, it came to expression in examples of the post-structuralist deconstruction of philosophical theories founded upon "metaphysics of presence."

Against this background, Scheler's effort to ground his ethics in a phenomenology of objective values may appear naively "foundationalist" or hopelessly "metaphysical." This is the view, for example, that pervades Parvis Emad's particular "Heideggerian" exposé of the notion of "constant presence," which he regards as implicit in Scheler's theory of intentionality (*Heidegger*). The defect and the obstacle coincide, interestingly, in Heidegger's oblique criticisms of Scheler and of Value Theory. Heidegger categorically dismisses philosophizing in terms of "values" in Scheler's manner because all thinking in terms of "values," in his view, lacks an *adequate* ontological reflection on the Being-in-the-world of *Dasein*, and because an adequate reflection would reveal the *impossibility*, presumably, of the kind of metaphysical foundation that is being sought for ethics in a Platonic realm of immutable essences or "values" (see chapter three, sec. 4, below).

As I have already suggested, this sort of account is by no means accepted universally as signalling the end of a phenomenological approach to moral experience, let alone of moral philosophy in general. Not only have serious questions been raised by Emmanuel Levinas, Hans Reiner, J. N. Mohanty, Gerhard Funke, Werner Marx and others about Heidegger's philosophy and about the deconstructionist paradigm, but, despite widespread skepticism about metaphysics, the discussion of ethical issues continues to unfold in various new directions among contemporary philosophers. Some of the more interesting studies that come to mind are those of Alan Donagan, Alasdair MacIntyre, Robert Nozick (who continues to employ the language of "values" and "foundations," though in a new way), and, from the phenomenological side, Hans Reiner (who does the same) and Robert Sokolowski.[40] And by no means have either the Heideggerian or Derridian accounts succeeded in overriding the issue of the irrepressible data of value—phenomena as given in pre-theoretical experience, of which perhaps one of the most stalwart champions in this century was Herman Dooyeweerd (*A New Critique of Theoretical Thought*). The claim made by Emad and others that no viable "metaphysic of presence," or metaphysical grounding, exists to serve as a conclusive theoretical foundation of philosophy or ethics as traditionally conceived does not entail the complete absence of *some* kind of "presence" or grounding in pre-theoretical experience; if philosophy must abandon its Hegelian pretensions to omniscience, this does not mean that it must necessarily give up its aspirations to genuine, if limited, knowledge.[41]

Among the most interesting implications of the Schelerian critique for ethics generally are those that are concerned, not with traditional analytic problems of consequentialism, deontologism, decisionism, moral judgments, and the like, but with the issues of human nature and human virtue. For example, a basic and fascinating question, for Scheler, concerns what sort of person is virtuous. It is not hard to guess why people often believe that virtuous actions will lead to happiness. But why is it, Scheler seems interested to know, that virtuous actions often seem to flow from people with a profound sense of spiritual well-being? Could it be that the moral value of human actions is fundamentally linked to the kinds of dispositions possessed by their human agents? The attention devoted to questions of virtue and character gives the Schelerian critique special currency amidst the lately resurgent interest in "ethics of virtue." These issues are dealt with in the appendix entitled "Is Scheler's Ethic an Ethic of Virtue?"

Even so, some of the most important implications of the Schelerian critique concern very traditional sorts of ethical questions about the nature of moral action, the basis of moral obligation, the source of moral values, and the like. It is in connection with such issues that Scheler comes into open conflict with the fundamental assumptions of the Kantian moral philosophy. Most notable here are the implications of the Schelerian critique for (1) Kant's metaphysical bifurcations of reason/sensibility, will/inclination, and noumenon/phenomenon; (2) his presupposition that whatever order we discover in our moral experience can be nothing other than an order imposed upon it by the law-giving rational subject; and (3) his formalistic conception of reason, moral law, and duty. Scheler's concepts of the "essential intuition," "*ordo amoris*," and "material a priori," as we shall see, strike at the heart of the Kantian system. If Kant's bifurcations of experience can be shown to be phenomenologically unwarranted, if his assumption that reason is the only source of order in moral experience can be cast into doubt by the discovery of examples of nonrational ordering principles in human experience, and if his grounding principles of "reason," "moral law," and "duty" can be shown to lack determinate content, then the Schelerian critique and alternative may pose a challenge, not only to Kantian ethics, but to contemporary ethics as well.

Notes

1. The best biographical material available on Kant and Scheler in English includes Ernst Cassirer's *Kant's Life and Thought*, trans. James Haden (New Haven: Yale University Press, 1981) and John R. Staude's *Max Scheler, 1874–1928: An Intellectual Portrait* (New York: Free Press, 1967). A standard French treatment is Maurice Dupuy, *La philosophie de Max Scheler, son évolution et son unité*, 2 vols. (Paris: Presses Universitaires, 1959). For N. Hartmann's assessment, see "Max Scheler," *Kant-Studien* 33, Nos. 1–2 (1928), ix–xvi.

2. "Kant did not, like Rousseau, go to Holy Communion, did not, like Lessing, call Luther to witness. Instead, when the university of Königsberg was proceeding in solemn procession from the Great Hall to the church for the university service on the *dies academicus* Kant used ostentatiously to step away from the procession just as it was entering the church, make his way round the church instead, and go home." Karl Barth, *Protestant Theology in the Nineteenth Century: Its Background and History* (Valley Forge: Judson Press, 1973), 267.

3. In his "third period," Scheler renounced "theism" altogether, in any conventional sense of the word, as he indicates in his preface to the third edition of *Formalismus*. Biographical sources indicate some influence of his mother's Judaism in Scheler's childhood, as well as a tempestuous relationship to the Church throughout his life, involving a series of reconversions and renunciations of faith.

4. However, at least some of the notorious rumors that circulated about Scheler's womanizing were doubtless malicious (Staude, *Max Scheler*, 7).

5. Alfred Schutz, "Max Scheler's Epistemology and Ethics, I," *Review of Metaphysics* 11 (1957), 305.

6. What is meant by the "material" in Scheler, whenever it is contrasted, as here, with the "formal" in Kant, must be understood in terms of phenomenological essence. The German adjective *material* is a technical term and refers to "content," not, as the German *materiell* does, to "matter." Since there is no similar distinction conveniently available in English, some authors substitute the negative adjective "non-formal."

7. Schleiermacher, in his *Outline of a Critique of Previous Ethical Theories* (1803), and Hegel, first in his essay on *The Scientific Ways of Treating Natural Law* (1802–1803), and then in his *Phenomenology of Spirit* (1807), and later in his *Philosophy of Right* (1821), attacked the "barren contentlessness" of Kant's categorical imperative, the "abstractness" of his insistence on "duty for duty's sake."

The relevant essays of Schiller include *On Grace and Dignity* (1793) and *On the Aesthetic Education of Man* (1795). The best current discussion of the Schiller-Kant controversy is that of Hans Reiner, *Duty and Inclination: The Fundamentals of Morality Discussed and Redefined with Special Regard to Kant and Schiller*, trans. Mark Santos (The Hague: Nijhoff, 1983), esp. 26 n. 8, and 29–51.

The relevant works of Schopenhauer and J. S. Mill include the former's treatise, *On the Basis of Morality* (1840), and the latter's *Utilitarianism* (1861). The attack on Kantian "formalism" was later extended in other directions by philosophers such as John Dewey, in his *Outlines of a Critical Theory of Ethics* (1891) and *Theory of Valuation* (1939).

8. One of the most reliable introductions to the developments in this period can be found in Michael Ermarth's *Wilhelm Dilthey: The Critique of Historical Reason* (Chicago: University of Chicago, 1978).

9. Scheler's early view of logic was not dissimilar, as can be seen from the published manuscripts intended for a projected, but never completed, two-volume work on logic, where he opposes Lotze's and Husserl's view of "correspondence" to an "objective truth in itself," insisting that, rather, thought generates its own truth. See Max Scheler, *Logik*, I, ed. R. Berlinger and W. Schrader, Elementa, 3 (Atlantic Highlands: Humanities Press, 1975), 1:140–65. For Cohen and other Neo-Kantians discussed below, see n. 10 below.

10. Brief but helpful introductions to Neo-Kantianism include the classic accounts by the Neo-Kantian, Ernst Cassirer, "Neo-Kantianism," *Encyclopaedia Britannica*, 14th ed. (1930); W. Tudor Jones, *Contemporary Thought of Germany*, 2 vols. (London: Williams & Northgate, 1930); as well as Joachim von Rintelen, *Contemporary German Philosophy and Its Background* (Bonn: Bouvier, 1970); and Lewis White Beck, "Neo-Kantianism," *Encyclopedia of Philosophy*, ed. Paul Edwards (New York: Macmillan, 1967).

11. The "First Austrian School of Values" was a school of theorists about *economic* value, which included such figures as Karl Menger, Friedrich von Wieser, and Eugen Böhm-Bawerk. In fact, as J. N. Findlay notes, the word "axiology" was introduced into philosophy by Wilbur M. Urban in 1906, in his book *Valuation: Its Nature and Laws*, in order to translate the German *Werttheorie*, which the Austrian economist von Neumann had introduced into economics. See J. N. Findlay, *Axiological Ethics* (London: Macmillan, 1970), 1; cf. Nicholas Rescher, *Introduction to Value Theory* (Englewood Cliffs, NJ: Prentice-Hall, 1969; rpt., Washington, DC: University of America Press, 1982), 30; and Risieri Frondizi, *What Is Value?: An Introduction to Axiology*, 2nd ed. (La Salle, IL: Open Court, 1971), 41.

12. For brief but helpful introductions to Value Theory, see, in addition to the works by N. Rescher and J. N. Findlay already cited (in n. 11 above), William K. Frankena, "Value and Valuation," *Encyclopedia of Philosophy*, ed. Paul Edwards (New York: Macmillan, 1967). A frequently cited German classic is Oskar Kraus, *Die Werttheorien: Geschichte und Kritik* (Brünn, 1937). See also Jean Héring, "De Max Scheler à Hans Reiner: Remarques sur la Théorie des valeurs Morales dans la Mouvement Phénoménologique," *Revue d'Histoire des Sciences et de leurs Applications* (Paris) 40 (1960), 152–64; and John N. Findlay, *Values and Intentions: A Study in Value Theory and Philosophy of Mind* (London: George Allen & Unwin, 1961).

13. James H. Olthuis, *Facts, Values and Ethics* (Assen, The Netherlands: Van Gorcum, 1969), 5.

14. For Scheler's relationship to Husserl, see H. Spiegelberg, *The Phenomenological Movement*, 2d ed. (The Hague: Nijhoff, 1976), 1: 228f. Spiegelberg's discussion is based on Scheler's own account of the relationship, which can be found in his essay, "Deutsche Philosophie der Gegenwart," in *Deutsches Leben der Gegenwart*, ed. P. Witkop (Berlin: Wegweiser, 1922), 197f. While it is clear that Scheler owed his basic phenomenological orientation to the influence of Husserl, there is some difference of opinion over who influenced whom in the case of Value Theory. Alois Roth claims, in *Edmund Husserls ethische Untersuchungen* (The Hague: Nijhoff, 1960), 166, that the manuscript of Husserl's lectures on ethics in the summer of 1920 (F I 28 in the Husserl Archives) reveals clear evidence of the "immediate influence" of Scheler's notion of "love" as the fundamental disposition in the apprehension of values. Yet any familiarity with the work of Brentano would suggest that this notion was available to Husserl through Brentano's writings prior to 1900. See, for example, Franz Brentano, *Psychology from an Empirical Standpoint*, trans. A. C. Rancurello, et al. (1874, London: Routledge & Kegan Paul, 1973), 198f., 222–24, 235ff. A more detailed discussion of the philosophical relation between Scheler and Husserl follows in chapter 2.

15. *F*, 143/123 (see n. 17 below). More will be said about Scheler's theory of the will in the discussion of values in chapter 3.

16. This is a claim more recently elaborated upon by Hans Reiner, *Duty and Inclination* (henceforth cited as "*DI*") 15f., 156. Reiner, like Scheler, argues that Kant's moral philosophy presupposes a concept of value.

17. This work, which is published in Scheler's *Gesammelte Werke*, Vol. 2, ed. Maria Scheler (Bern: Francke, 1954), and appears in English under the title of *Formalism in Ethics and Non-Formal Ethics of Values*, trans. M. S. Frings and R. L. Funk (Evanston, IL: Northwestern, 1973), will be cited hereafter as "*Formalismus*" in the text, or simply abbreviated as "*F*," followed by the pagination of the German and English editions, respectively. Thus, the citation for the present reference is *F*, 30f./6f.

18. Frings and Funk translate *Gesinnung* by "moral tenor" or "basic moral tenor" throughout *Formalismus*. For historical as well as stylistic reasons, however, I prefer to use "moral disposition" or "basic moral disposition."

19. See, for example, the relevant essays available in convenient English anthologies of *Kant's Political Writings*, ed. Hans Reiss, trans. H. B. Nisbet (Cambridge: Cambridge University Press, 1971), and Kant's *On History*, ed. L. W. Beck, trans. L. W. Beck, et al. (Indianapolis: Bobbs-Merrill, 1963).

20. For a good discussion of this point, see Alasdair MacIntyre, *After Virtue* (Notre Dame: University of Notre Dame Press, 1981), 53ff.

21. While Scheler may have had such followers, only an undiscerning and unsympathetic critic would attribute such an uncritical borrowing of Scheler's views to a philosopher of the stature of Nicolai Hartmann, in his *Ethics*, trans. S. Coit, 3 vols. (1932; rpt. Atlantic Highlands: Humanities, 1975).

22. Paul A. Schilpp, "Ethical Formalism," in *Dictionary of Philosophy*, ed. D. D. Runes (Totowa, NJ: Littlefield, 1962), observes that "Kant very early conceived and developed the more critical concept of 'form'—not in the sense of a 'mould' into which content is to be poured (a notion which has falsely been taken over by Kant-students from his theoretical philosophy into his ethics), but—as a method of rational (*not* ratiocinative, but inductive) reflection" (98, col. 1).

23. For C. D. Broad, see his *Five Types of Ethical Theory* (Totowa, NJ: Littlefield, 1965), 122f.; for L. W. Beck, his Introduction to *"Critique of Practical Reason" and Other Writings in Moral Philosophy*, by Immanuel Kant, trans. and ed. L. W. Beck (Chicago: University of Chicago, 1949), 21–23. For A. R. C. Duncan, see his *Practical Reason and Morality: A Study of Immanuel Kant's "Foundations for the Metaphysics of Morals"* (Edinburgh: Thomas Nelson & Sons, 1957), chs. 1, 7, 10, 11; and for T. C. Williams, *The Concept of the Categorical Imperative* (Oxford: Clarendon, 1968), chs. 4, 7–10. For M. G. Singer, see his *Generalization in Ethics* (London: Eyre & Spottiswoode, 1963), 217–20, cf. 251f. For Alan Donagan, see his *Theory of Morality* (Chicago: University of Chicago Press, 1977); and for H. H. Schroeder, "Some Common Misinterpretations of the Kantian Ethics," *Philosophical Review* 49 (July 1940), 424–46.

A brief survey and summary of these interpretations, as well as a cogent development of Donagan's basic line of argument, can be found in the excellent article by Ping-cheung Lo, "A Critical Reevaluation of the Alleged 'Empty Formalism' of Kantian Ethics," *Ethics* 91, No. 2 (Jan. 1981), 181–201.

24. On recent German scholarship, see Gerd Wolandt's "Nachwort," in *Kant und Scheler*, by Karl Alphéus, ed. B. Wolandt (Bonn: Bouvier, 1981), 402f; also cf. the discussion of "The Question of 'Empty Formalism' and the Concept of Material Ends in Kantian Ethics" in ch. 3, sec. 3, of this book for a more detailed treatment of this issue.

25. Martin Heidegger, *The Basic Problems of Phenomenology*, trans. A. Hofstadter (Bloomington: Indiana University Press, 1982), 133, 136. Cf. the discussion of Heidegger's criticism of Value Theory in chapter 3 below.

26. Husserl's lectures on ethics were only published posthumously in the form of manuscripts collated and edited by A. Roth in *Husserls ethische Untersuchungen* (see above, n. 14). See also Ullrich Melle's edition of Husserl's *Vorlesungen über Ethik und Wertlehre: 1908–1914*, Husserliana 28 (Dordrecht: Kluwer Academic Publishers, 1988).

27. But see Lewis White Beck, "Nicolai Hartmann's Criticism of Kant's Theory of Knowledge," *Philosophy and Phenomenological Research* 2 (June 1942), 472–500; cf. n. 28, below.

28. Reiner's phenomenological ethics does not rest on a significant critique of Kant or a claim to be normative in any practical sense. It consists primarily of refinements on an already historically established phenomenological project, particularly as developed by Dietrich von Hildebrand, and lacks the seminal importance and scale of Scheler's work.

Hartmann denied that moral philosophy could offer more than general criteria for a universal ethics. He did not think that ethics should try to teach what one ought to do in particular situations, dismissing this view as mere casuistry. On a certain level, however, this could be construed as a denial that ethics can offer actual normative directives (*Ethics*, 1: 30ff.), a position vigorously opposed by Scheler (*F*, 23/xxxi). But even Scheler himself never produced the sequel to *Formalismus*, which he said would go beyond the latter's foundational character—a sequel he promised, both in the concluding paragraph of *Formalismus*, and in his preface to its second edition.

Not only does the reason for this remain in question, but also the reason for what sometimes seems to be a pattern of hesitation on the issue of ethics among major phenomenologists and existentialists generally. Husserl never published a work on ethics during his lifetime. Sartre never published the work on ethics that he promised in the concluding sentence of *Being and Nothingness*. The ethical ambiguity of Heidegger's philosophy has been much discussed, and his abhorrence of any reference to "values" is notorious in such of his writings as his "Letter on Humanism," translated by F. A. Capuzzi, et al. in *Basic Writings*, by M. Heidegger, ed. D. F. Krell (New York: Harper & Row, 1977), 189–242. Cf. also Bernard J. Boelen, "The Question of Ethics in the Thought of Martin Heidegger," in *Heidegger and the Quest for Truth*, ed. Manfred S. Frings, 76–105 (Chicago: Quadrangle Books, 1968); and Werner Marx's *Is There a Measure on Earth? Foundations for a Nonmetaphysical Ethics*, trans. Thomas J. Nenon and Reginald Lilly (Chicago: University of Chicago Press, 1987), chs. 1, 2.

29. Cf. Introduction, above, for Scheler's influence in Europe. For a sampling of his influence in the Soviet Union, see Edward M. Swiderski, "Phenomenology in the *Filosofskaja Enciklopedija*," *Studies in Soviet Thought* 18, No. 1 (Feb. 1978), 57–66, and Joseph L. Navickas, "N. Lossky's Moral Philosophy and M. Scheler's Phenomenology," *Studies in Soviet Thought* 18, No. 2 (May 1978), 121–30.

For Japan, see Hirotaka Tatematsu, "Selected Bibliography of Major Phenomenological Works Translated into Japanese and of Major Phenomenological Writings by Japanese Authors," in *Japanese Phenomenology*, ed. Y. Nitta and H. Tatematsu, Analecta Husserliana, 8 (Dordrecht: D. Reidel, 1979), 279f., which indicates the number of Scheler's works in Japanese translation as six, in a projected fifteen volume set. That was written in 1977; when I checked on the progress of the series (*Scheler Chosakushu*) in 1982, the entire set was already complete. See also Minoru Uchiyama, *Das Wertwidrige in der Ethik Max Schelers*, ed. Gerhard Funke, Mainzer Philosophische Forschungen 4 (Bonn: H. Bouvier Verlag, 1966); and especially Eiichi Shimomissé, *Die Phänomenologie und das Problem der Grundlegung der Ethik: An Hand des Versuches von Max Scheler* (The Hague: Nijhoff, 1971).

For Latin America and the Spanish-speaking world, see José Ortega y Gasset, *The Modern Theme*, trans. J. Cleugh (New York: Harper, 1961), 60ff.; "Max Scheler: un ubriaco di essenze," *Ethica* 7 (1968), 161–67; as well as his earlier work, "Max Scheler," *Neue Schweizer Rundschau* 34 (Oct. 1928), 725–29.

In the mid-1970s, A. Lichtigfeld could still speak of "A Scheler-Renaissance," *Tijdschrift voor Filosofie* 37, No. 4 (Dec. 1975), 711–15, though this would hardly be an accurate description of the last few decades of Scheler scholarship throughout the world.

30. Cf., for example, the emotivist theory of Charles L. Stevenson, "The Emotive Meaning of Ethical Terms," *Mind* 46 (1937), rpt. in *Readings in Ethical Theory*, 2d ed., ed. Wilfrid Sellars and John Hospers (New York: Appleton-Century-Crofts, 1970), 254–66; *Ethics and Language* (1944; rpt. New Haven: Yale University Press, 1976); and the "definist" approach of Richard B. Brandt, who redefines moral judgments in terms of factually testable psychological categories, in *A Theory of the Good and the Right* (Oxford: Clarendon Press, 1979), 2–12, 208f., and his "The Future of Ethics," *Nous* 15 (1981), 38; and the antirealist theory of J. L. Mackie, *Ethics: Inventing Right and Wrong* (Harmondsworth: Penguin Books, 1981), 25–27, 35–37, 40–43, who argues that the objectivity ascribed to moral concepts is due to a process of "objectification" whereby people project their attitudes and conventions upon an external reality.

31. The best recent survey of these issues is David R. Lachterman's Translator's Introduction to *Selected Philosophical Essays*, by Max Scheler (Evanston, IL: Northwestern University, 1973), xivff. The selection of essays translated for this volume is especially helpful in dispelling the myth that Scheler was disinterested in questions about "foundations," either epistemological or metaphysical.

See also Wilfrid Hartmann, "Max Scheler and the English Speaking World," *Philosophy Today* 12, No. 1 (spring 1968), 31–41. Scheler's bad press in the United States is exemplified by George N. Shuster's Introductory Statement for the "Symposium on the Significance of Max Scheler for Philosophy and Social Science," to which the March, 1942 issue of *Philosophy and Phenomenological Research* (Vol. 2, No. 3) is dedicated. For Scheler's later writings on peace and pacifism, see his "The Idea of Peace and Pacifism," parts 1 and 2, *Journal of the British Society for Phenomenology* 7 (Oct. 1976), 154–66; 8 (Jan. 1977), 36–50. See also Manfred S. Frings, ed., *Max Scheler (1874–1928): Centennial Essays* (The Hague: Nijhoff, 1974), and his "Max Scheler: Focusing on Rarely Seen Complexities of Phenomenology," in *Phenomenology in Perspective*, ed. F. J. Smith (The Hague: Nijhoff, 1970), 32–53.

32. For G. E. Moore's affinity to the Schelerian perspective, see Scheler's remark in his preface to the second edition of *Formalismus* about Moore's "similar views on many points concerning the problem of values" (*F*, 13/xxi). Similar affinities might be traced through Moore's illuminating and favorable review of Franz Brentano's *The Origin of the Knowledge of Right and Wrong* in the *International Journal of Ethics* 14 (1903), 115–23, or J. N. Findlay's comparison of Moore and Meinong in his work, *Meinong's Theory of Objects and Values*, 2d ed. (Oxford: Clarendon, 1963), see esp. ix f.

33. Reiner's essay first appeared in *Zeitschrift fr Philosophische Forschung* 30 (1976), 93–98, and was later translated and included in the English edition of his *Duty and Inclination*, 263–69.

34. Although the rejection of intuitionism in analytic philosophy is associated with the linguistic analysis of Ludwig Wittgenstein, John Austin, A. J. Ayer, and Charles L. Stevenson, it finds perhaps its clearest expression in the critique of intuitionism offered by P. H. Nowell-Smith in his widely esteemed *Ethics* (1954).

35. See, for example, A. J. Ayer, *Language, Truth and Logic*, 2d ed. (New York: Dover Books, 1946), ch. 6. For Charles Stevenson and others such as Richard Brandt, see n. 30, above; and J. O. Urmson, *The Emotive Theory of Ethics* (London: Hutchinson University Library, 1968), which is primarily a study of Stevenson's *Ethics and Language*.

36. See Max Scheler, "Reality and Resistance: On *Being and Time*, Section 43," trans. Thomas J. Sheehan, *Listening* 12, No. 3 (fall 1977), 61–73; rpt. in Thomas Sheehan, ed., *Heidegger: The Man and the Thinker* (Chicago: Precedent, 1981), 133–44. This is a translation of a portion (pp. 259–69) of part 5, "Das emotionale Realitätsproblem," of "Idealismus-Realismus," *GW*, 9. In his prefatory remarks to the article in *Listening*, Sheehan writes: "Immediately after *Being and Time* was published in February of 1927, Heidegger sent a copy to Max Scheler, who in September of that year composed a forty-page fragment on the book.... In a letter of August 6, 1964, Heidegger wrote to Manfred Frings: '... During the winter semester of 1927–28 Max Scheler invited me to Cologne for a lecture at the Kant Society, of which he was the head.... During that visit—I stayed at Scheler's house for three days—we spoke together for

the last time and discussed in detail how the formulation of the question in *Being and Time* was related to metaphysics and to his conception of phenomenology'" (61). Part 5 of "Idealismus-Realismus" represents the fruit of this encounter, and Scheler's own marginal notes in his copy of *Being and Time* appear in *GW*, 9: 305–40. See also M. S. Frings, "The Background of Max Scheler's 1927 Reading of *Being and Time*: A Critique of a Critique through Ethics," *Philosophy Today* 36, No. 2 (Summer 1992), 99–114.

For Heidegger's criticism of Scheler and the philosophy of values, see Parvis Emad's chapter, "Heidegger on Transcendence and Intentionality: His Critique of Scheler," in Sheehan, *Heidegger: The Man and the Thinker*, 145–58; and especially the book-length treatment by Emad, *Heidegger and the Phenomenology of Values: His Critique of Intentionality* (Glen Ellyn, IL: Torey Press, 1981). Heidegger's own criticisms, which offer only a tenuous basis for some of Emad's claims, are nowhere developed systematically but can be found in scattered comments throughout his works. Most often cited, perhaps, are his comments in his "Letter on Humanism," a translation of which is provided by F. Capuzzi and J. Glenn Gray in Heidegger's *Basic Writings*, 193–242. These criticisms are discussed in some detail in ch. 3, sec. 4, below.

37. Gerhard Funke, *Phenomenology: Metaphysics or Method?*, trans. David J. Parent (Athens: Ohio University Press, 1987). See also Thomas M. Seebohm's Foreword to that work, as well as his Preface to *Kant and Phenomenology*, ed. T. M. Seebohm and J. J. Kockelmans (Washington, DC: Center for Advanced Research in Phenomenology and University Press of America, 1984). But compare the views of Aron Gurwitsch, who contested the need for grounding in a transcendental "ego," for which he could see no conclusive evidence. "Phänomenologie der Thematik und des reinen Ich," *Psychologische Forschungen* 12 (1929), 279–381.

38. See Roderick M. Chisholm, "Evidence as Justification," *Journal of Philosophy* 68 (1961), 730–48, and Richard B. Brandt, "Epistemology and Ethics, Parallel Between," *Encyclopedia of Philosophy*, ed. Paul Edwards (New York: Macmillan, 1967), 3: 7; on Windelband, see Lewis White Beck, "Neo-Kantianism," *Encyclopedia of Philosophy*, 5: 472.

39. On Scheler's view of the relationship between truth and obligation, see his *Logik*, 1 (see above, n. 9), where he rejects the notion that logic is in some sense the "ethics" of thinking, and states that normative laws are, rather, grounded *within* thought and therefore cannot themselves ground thinking. Cf. the similar points he makes in criticism of Windelband and "assessment" theories of value in *F*, ch. 4, part 1.

40. Alan Donagan, *The Theory of Morality* (see n. 23, above); Alasdair MacIntyre, *After Virtue* (1981), *Whose Justice? Which Rationality?* (1988); Robert Nozick, *Philosophical Explanations* (Cambridge: Harvard University Press, 1981); Hans Reiner, *Duty and Inclination* (1983); and Robert Sokolowski, *Moral Action: A Phenomenological Study* (Bloomington: Indiana University Press, 1985).

41. For a brief, but wide-ranging, thoughtful, and very stimulating response to deconstructionist developments, see George Steiner, *Real Presences* (Chicago: University of Chicago Press, 1991); and cf. ch. 5, n. 16, below.

The A Priori: Form and Phenomenon 2

The Problem

THE CONCEPTS OF THE "A PRIORI" and "a posteriori" have a history fraught with notorious ambiguities. Already in the antecedent Greek distinction between the *proteron* and *hysteron* there is a kindred indefiniteness: something may be "earlier" or "later," Aristotle noted, in one of two ways—either *te physei* (in nature) or *pros hemas* (in regard to us).[1] In the evolution of later European thought about the a priori, from the scholastic distinction between *ex prioribus* and *ex posterioribus* down to modern analogues, new and complicating accretions attached to these views, compounding the original complexities. The a priori came to be identified with the "formal" and "rational," while the a posteriori came to be related to the "material" and "empirical"; and, as Paul Moser points out, the epistemological distinction between "a priori" and "a posteriori" knowledge came to be identified with the metaphysical distinction between "necessity" and "contingency" and the semantic distinction between "analytic" and "synthetic" truth.[2]

These developments form the background and point of departure for the transcendental-critical concept of the a priori that emerged in the Kantian tradition, as well as for the phenomenological concept that appeared in Scheler's critique of Kant. It is not by accident that Scheler's critique of Kantian ethics turns on the concept of the a priori. For this concept in many ways constitutes the keystone, not only of Kantian ethics or of the Kantian system as a whole, but of a basic current of the Western metaphysical tradition, whose identification of the a priori with the "formal," the "rational," the "necessary," and the like, Scheler rejects. Moreover, Scheler's main purpose, so far as the concept of the a priori goes, is to dismantle the traditional interpretation in order to reconsider the concept from an innovative, phenomenological point of view. The subsequent divergence between the understandings of the logical empiricists (both in the Vienna Circle and the Anglo-American tradition) and of the continental phenomenologists, as well as their mutual isolation from each another, has complicated the question as to what philosophers mean by the "a priori" and how they understand its relation to such affiliated notions as analyticity, necessity, the nature of propositions, essences, and the like—at least until recently.[3]

In this chapter we shall proceed, first, by discussing briefly the nature of Scheler's opposition to the Kantian perspective and, second, by examining the Kantian concept of the a priori and the background of Scheler's position in the phenomenology of Husserl. Third, we will analyze in detail Scheler's critique of the Kantian a priori and then, finally, conclude with a critical appraisal of his own position.

The concept of the a priori is fundamental to the philosophies of both Kant and Scheler. It was understood by them, however, in quite different ways. This fact confronts one in an immediate linguistic difference: Kant uses "a priori" in the more conventional way as an adverb or adjective ("to know something a priori" or "a priori knowledge"), while Scheler uses it not only as an adjective ("a priori essence") but, less conventionally, as a noun ("the a priori") or as part of a nominal phrase ("the material a priori"). Kant's view is related intimately to his critical idealism, transcendentalism, subjectivism and formalism, and is ineluctably embedded in the presuppositions of his methodology, faculty theory, metaphysics, epistemology and logic. Scheler's view is related to his understanding of the phenomenological method he adapted from Husserl, and is embedded deeply in his notions of phenomena, essence, intuition, and value. The two views differ radically.

Scheler's critique of "formalism" in Kantian ethics, as well as his development of his own "material" alternative, turns on the issue of the a priori. In Kantian ethics the categorical imperative expresses the a priori proper to moral judgment. Ethics must have an unconditional foundation, and this foundation lies in the formal a priori relation established between the will and the moral law. The determining ground of moral willing, therefore, is (and must be) something that can be discovered by reason independently of the sensible faculties, without consulting the contingent relations between the will and the specific material ends toward which it is directed in empirical experience. The basis of moral action cannot be anything so capricious and fleshy as experience, but must reside in the a priori judgments of pure practical reason.

In Scheler's view this Kantian proposal is untenable. It is not merely that it seeks a level of abstraction that is impossible to attain, but that it succumbs to the metaphysics of purity and sublimation, which regards reason as a sanctuary to be protected from the contamination of experience; and so, revisited by all the devils of that metaphysics and its tangled dualisms and dilemmas, Kantian ethics cannot give proper account of this preeminent fact about ourselves—that our primordial comportment toward the world is *affective*, involving the pre-theoretical apprehension of values (*Wertnehmung*). Every mode of intellectual reasoning, conceiving or judging always *already* presupposes an affective experience of the value of that about which one reasons, conceives or judges. Hence, the very project of determining the will in a purely formal manner apart from the "material" value-contents of willing, after the Kantian a priori manner, is self-defeating.

Yet Scheler was not prepared to dismiss the Kantian demand that ethics be grounded in unconditional a priori principles. He agreed implicitly with this demand in rejecting any contingent ethics grounded in the anticipated realization of particular, empirical goods or ends. For Scheler, as for Kant, the metaphysics of morals must not be empirical. Ethics must not be arbitrary. Accordingly, the issue for him became: How can ethics be grounded in the data of the material value-contents of moral experience and still be based on a priori principles? And his answer to this question—a wrenching question from almost any conventional point of view—rests on a rejection of the alternatives posed by Kantian ethics: *either* a "formal a priori" ethics *or* a "material a posteriori" ethics. These alternatives, in Scheler's view, rest on a false dilemma and mistaken correlation. His own answer sets forth an alternative between these terms, the possibility of a new correlation: a *material a priori* ethics—a proposal no less radical than Kant's *synthetic a priori*. Accordingly, Scheler's critique of Kantian ethics turns upon an altogether un-Kantian, phenomenological understanding of the a priori—on the notion of a *material a priori*, or, more explicitly, on an *a priori of material content*.

The Kantian Legacy and Phenomenological Background

ALTHOUGH THE NOTION OF THE A PRIORI, as such, is nowhere developed thematically by Kant in a substantial way, it functions throughout his transcendental system as one of its most fundamental operative concepts. It lies at the very heart of his "Copernican Revolution" and constitutes the basic problem underlying the critical outlook. The basic agendum of Kant's three *Critiques* consists in the essentially conservative task of mapping out the legitimate spheres of competence of theoretical and practical reason, in order to safeguard the possibility of scientific knowledge and moral conviction against the skeptical inroads of Humean empiricism. Since the possibility of science and morality rests on the possibility of genuine a priori knowledge, the task of critical philosophy is to demonstrate the validity of such knowledge without appealing to experience or to anything outside of the cognitive operation itself, yet without falling back upon the divine warranties claimed by Cartesian innatism.

The Kantian notion of the a priori involves a cluster of mutually supportive and interrelated elements, all of which collectively form the basic structural features of the Kantian philosophy. Some of these elements are revolutionary and new, such as the subjectivist turn implicit in the Kantian "Copernican Revolution" and the critical methodological concept of "transcendentalism." A priori knowledge is possible, in the Kantian view, because the formal conditions that render experience intelligible are furnished by the rational subject. The most basic principles of order and lawfulness, in morality as well as in science, are imposed by the rational subject upon experience. Yet other elements are hardly new, for the Kantian view of the a priori was developed within a context of a number of common historical conventions and assumptions. Probably the most prominent of these include epistemological assumptions about the relation of intelligible "form" to sensible "content," and about the logical criteria of "necessity" (as opposed to "contingency") and "universality" (as opposed to "individuality"), as well as psychological assumptions, such as those inherited from Wolff and Tetens about "higher" faculties of cognition, feeling, and desire (reason, taste, will) governing "lower" ones (sensibility, pleasure, inclination), and those about the higher faculties being purely "active" and "spontaneous" while the lower ones are "passive" and "receptive." But one can also place the Kantian concept of the a priori within the context of traditional metaphysical themes, where it can be seen as identified implicitly with "being" and "constancy" (as opposed to "becoming" or "change"), "unity" (as opposed to "diversity"), and "intelligibility" and "supersensibility" (as opposed to the "irrational" and "material").

Scheler takes issue with virtually every facet of this schema. His critique of the Kantian a priori is decidedly phenomenological; indeed, it cannot be understood apart from a proper appreciation of this fact. Whatever the differences between Scheler and others within the phenomenological movement, his conception of the a priori is inseparable from what he calls his "methodological consciousness of the unity and sense of the phenomenological attitude," which he credits to the works of Husserl (F, 11/xix). In the early part of *Formalismus*, where he defines his own view of the a priori, Scheler refers to Husserl's concept of "categorial intuition" in the *Logical Investigations*, a concept whose significance for him we know from his reflections nearly a decade later concerning his first meeting with Husserl in Halle in 1901.[4] The outline of Scheler's views can best be discerned against this background of Husserl's influence, particularly as it pertains to the Kantian position.

The web of relationships that connect Husserl to Kant and Neo-Kantianism is complex. There are evident lines of dependence as well as important differences between them. What is clear, on the one hand, is Husserl's assimilation of the transcendental motives of Kantian philosophy (at least by the time of the publication of *Ideen* in 1913), and, on the other hand, his rejection of its implicit psychologism, its neglect of clear noetic analysis, and its bifurcations of form and matter, understanding and sensibility, noumena and phenomena, appearances and things-in-themselves.[5] Husserl could very well agree, in principle, with the Kantian project of attempting to secure a priori knowledge from the encroachments of Humean skepticism. He could very well agree, in principle, with the Kantian attempt to ground such knowledge transcendentally in the subject. Recourse to causal explanations appealing to relations between the subject and the "external world" was no more possible for Husserl, as a basis for a priori knowledge, than it was for Kant. The problem for Husserl was that the Kantian position tended, in the words of Dufrenne, "to psychologize the transcendental" (12). It committed one to the metaphysical presuppositions of Kantian anthropology and faculty psychology. By contrast, the phenomenological demand for presuppositionless attention "to the things themselves" required the suspension of all judgments pertaining to the worldly existence of the empirical subject of consciousness. The subject matter of phenomenology was thereby limited to the "pure" content of consciousness itself. In this way all acts of consciousness and, correlatively, all *objects* of consciousness became proper subjects for phenomenological investigation; they were considered capable of being clarified and grasped "eidetically," that is to say, in their "essential" structures.

Husserl could accept, in principle, the Kantian claim that nothing is "given" in experience but "phenomena." But what is primordially *given*, in his view, is not a seeming chaos of irrational sensations (as in Hume), which is rendered intelligible only by having a priori forms imposed upon it by an order-conferring mind (as in Kant). Rather, the categorial forms articulated in thought are the articulations of the presentational forms or eidetic structures of phenomena themselves.[6] The a priori forms that render experience intelligible, in Husserl's view, belong to the *material content* of experience. They are *given* in the identificational forms and meanings that eidetically structure experience. Within the Kantian system, of course, the notion that a priori forms, categories, and ideas—which are the *conditions* of the possibility of experience—could be experienced or intuited *themselves* is an impossibility.[7] The notion was dismissed by Kant under the title of "intellectual intuition"—something possible, if at all, only for a purely rational being such as God. But something very close to this idea became a methodological cornerstone in the development of Husserl's philosophy under the name of "essential intuition" (*Wesensschau*).[8]

Husserl developed and refined this concept throughout his career. Already in the *Logical Investigations* (1900, 1913) his views of intuition and thought were developed in a distinctively non-Kantian direction. Of particular interest is his sixth investigation, where he distinguishes between "sensible" and "categorial" intuition—the capacity for bringing ideal objects or meanings (such as the universal essences of negation, conjunction, unity, number, and the like) to full intuitive understanding. It is in this context that he offers his verdict on the Kantian view of the a priori: "All the main obscurities of the Kantian critique of reason depend ultimately on the fact that Kant never made clear to himself the peculiar character of pure Ideation, the adequate survey of conceptual essences, and of the laws of universal validity rooted in those essences. He accordingly lacked the phenomenologically correct concept of the *a priori*" (*LU*, 2:203/833).

The problem with the Kantian concept, says Husserl, is its deficient conception of "pure Ideation"—by which he means "essential intuition." What Kant grasped in his exceptional admission that the forms of intuition (space and time) are themselves "pure intuitions," his system prevented him from allowing in the case of other categorial essences. This failure was due, at least in part, to the traditional metaphysical dualism at the center of the Kantian system, which set the faculties of sensibility and understanding over against each other. Lack of clarity about the nature of thought and intuition prevented the Kantian analysis from realizing its transcendental aspirations for the a priori conditions of knowledge. The formal analytical a priori was defined by reference to principles of logic that were taken to be self-evident; but these principles themselves could not be said to be a priori in the same sense as propositions whose analytic character is determined by these principles. The possibility of synthetic a priori judgments was traced back to the general psychic constitution of human subjectivity; but the factual laws of empirical psychology could not be said to be a priori in the same sense as the categorial forms of thought and their ideal laws. Hence, in each case there is a lack of "transcendental rigor," which Husserl, in the overall charge he brings repeatedly against the Kantian conception of the a priori, attributes to "anthropologism" or "psychologism."[9]

For Husserl, then, the a priori is a property of essential intuition and of intuited essences, not principally of logical propositions or of the relations between the terms of such propositions. The a priori defines the invariant essential structures of the contents of intuition, and, as such, is something phenomenologically given. At times, in fact, it may be taken to be synonymous with "essence."[10] It must be remembered, however, that the concept of essential intuition always remained itself a problem for continued investigation for Husserl. As a result, particularly in his later career, the notion underwent complicating transformations in the course of its development, notably in conjunction with the concepts of "constitution" and "passive synthesis." This meant that the role of prior position-takings and of a passive synthetic "agency" had to be given due consideration in the analysis of various strata of essential intuition, and even the founding stratum of essential intuition as "passive" could not be regarded as sheerly "receptive."[11]

Scheler's Critique of the Kantian A Priori

SCHELER ASSIMILATES MOST, IF NOT ALL, of the Husserlian analysis and supplements Husserl's criticisms of the Kantian position with a penetrating critique of his own. In his attack on Kantian "formalism," particularly, and in his subsequent attempt to substitute a theory of the "material" a priori, Scheler is even more radical and direct than Husserl himself—a fact which may explain why Scheler's statements, more than those of Husserl, drew the fire of Moritz Schlick in his famous article, "Is There a Factual A Priori?" (1930–31).[12] Before we proceed to Scheler's critique of the Kantian view, however, it may be helpful to examine briefly his own positive statements about the a priori.

In a frequently quoted passage from *Formalismus*, Scheler offers the following definition: "We designate as *'a priori'* all those ideal units of meaning and those propositions that are self-given by way of an *immediate intuitive* content in the absence of any kind of positing (*Setzung*) of subjects that think them and of the real nature of those subjects, and in the absence of any kind of positing of objects to which such units of meaning are applicable" (*F*, 68f./48). Like Husserl, Scheler identifies the a priori with the *content* of essential intuition (*Wesensschau*), or what he calls "ideal units of meaning." These are "self-given," according to Scheler, not produced by a faculty of cognition; they are given by way of *material* presentation, not imposed on experience by subjective form; they are given immediately, apart from questions about the existence of the subject of consciousness to which they are given or of the objects of consciousness that may exemplify them in the natural world.

If we call the content of such an intuition a "phenomenon," or call such intuiting "phenomenological experience," says Scheler, we must not think of this "phenomenon" as having anything to do with the Kantian distinctions between "appearance" and "reality," or "phenomena" and "noumena." For what we mean is nothing more than what is *essentially given* in experience. If we call the contents of such intuition "a priori," we must not think that this is ultimately because of logical principles we may formulate concerning them. For these principles cannot be a priori in the same sense as the original contents of intuition about which they are formulated. Rather, these principles and their formulations are themselves grounded in the essentially given contents of phenomenological intuition. Phenomenological experience therefore precedes the articulation of logical forms and principles. As such, Scheler's concept of the phenomenological a priori belongs neither to the Kantian realm of "sensibility" nor to the Kantian realm of logical "form," but to what he calls the sphere of phenomenological "facts."

In an early unpublished essay called "The Theory of the Three Facts" (1911–1912), Scheler distinguishes between the facts of natural, everyday experience (*natürliche Weltanschauung*), scientific experience (*wissenschaftliche Erfahrung*), and phenomenological experience. He lists four characteristics of the last, which he calls "pure facts": (1) they must be identifiable essences independent of any variable sensuous elements in intuition; (2) they must have the character of an ultimate *foundation* of the merely sensory components of natural facts, which are "founded"; (3) they must be completely independent of symbols in their given identity; and (4) they pertain (a) in the "broadest sense" to the essence of objects in general and serve as the basis of pure logic or theory of objects (*Gegenstandtheorie*), and (b) in the "narrower sense" to particular ontological realms of objects where they serve to distinguish particular essential relationships, such as the foundedness of color upon extension. (LdT, 449f./219ff.).

In *Formalismus* Scheler offers two criteria by which to distinguish *how* such "facts" are given—criteria which serve simultaneously to distinguish the phenomenological perspective from all others. Phenomenological experience, he says, yields such "facts" (1) *immediately*, without any mediating signs or symbols—a point already made in his earlier essay—and (2) *immanently*, or purely, within "lived" (*erlebt*) experience. To this he adds a somewhat confusing criterion by which to discern the *essentialness* of a given datum of intuition: "it must already be *intuited* in the attempt to 'observe' it" in empirical experience (F, 70/50). What this means is that the essentialness of a phenomenological fact is evident when it must already have been *intuited* in order to observe empirical instantiations of it. For example, in order to recognize the Japanese maple outside my window, I must already have a concept of what a Japanese maple is. Essences, or phenomenological "facts," are given "a priori" in the sense that they are given "prior" to, and as conditions of the possibility of, empirical experience. They constitute the presentational forms or eidetic structures that make possible the experience of empirical phenomena. Essentialness therefore consists in the a priori "self-givenness" of a content of intuition independently of, and as a condition for the possibility of, sense experience.

What is clear from this analysis is that Scheler uses a number of terms interchangeably and not always consistently. In their adjectival forms, these include "intuitive," "essential," "phenomenological," and sometimes "a priori"; in their nominal forms—in various contexts and with various qualifications—these include "a priori," "essence," "content," "fact," "phenomenon," and the like. Furthermore, it is clear that by these he does *not* mean to refer to the contingent facts or phenomena that can be known only *a posteriori* from empirical experience. He is referring to the essential presentational forms of phenomena that are articulated in thought and given as the intentional correlates of identificational consciousness, the objective content of essential intuition. No criterion of verification may be found by referring beyond or outside of this content; rather, this content is self-authenticating, just as "seeing is believing." This is the heart of the a priori for Scheler.[13]

Scheler's critique of the Kantian "a priori" takes the form of a detailed criticism of several epistemological and metaphysical theses implicit in the Kantian analysis.[14] These involve the tacit identification of the a priori with the first term in each of the following six sets of classic distinctions: (1) *"form"* versus "content," (2) *"thought"* versus "sensation," (3) *"spontaneity"* versus "receptivity," (4) *"necessity"* versus "contingency," (5) *"universality"* versus "individuality," and (6) *"subjectivity"* versus "objectivity." In addition, there is Kant's "transcendental" interpretation of the a priori, which is related to the thesis of "subjectivism" and falls under the more general phenomenological criticism of the "anthropologism" of the Kantian philosophy. Let us consider these in detail.

FORM AND CONTENT

In his attack on the *"formalism"* of the Kantian conception, Scheler puts the issue more sharply than Husserl: "The identification of the 'a priori' with the 'formal,'" he declares, "is a *fundamental error* of Kant's doctrine" (F, 74/54). The problem is that the opposition between the formal and material is not equivalent to that between the a priori and the a posteriori, as the Kantian view assumes. Rather, the former is a "relative" distinction having to do with the universality of concepts and propositions, whereas the latter is an "absolute" distinction founded on the acute difference in the kinds of contents fulfilling the concepts and propositions concerned. Scheler illustrates his point with examples from logic and arithmetic. The a priori character of the logical proposition "'A is B' and 'A is not B' cannot be simultaneously true" is *formal* in respect of its universality, on account of which *any* object can stand for A and B; however, it is *material* in that it is based on phenomenological insight into the fact that the being and non-being of something at the same time and in the same respect are irreconcilable in intuition (F, 74/53). Likewise, he notes, $2 \times 2 = 4$ is "formal" for plums and pears alike but is itself fulfilled only by the "material" content of a mathematical intuition. Similarly, in respect of propositions that hold good a posteriori, it is just as possible to distinguish the logical form from the material content, since the contingent facts by which they are verified are also the facts by which their logical form is materially fulfilled. Hence, Scheler introduces the distinction of formal and material as a *secondary* distinction *within* both the sphere of the a priori and of the a posteriori.[15] Thereby he endeavors to show that, while the distinctions may intersect, they are in no sense equivalent.

THOUGHT AND SENSATION

A second basic error of the Kantian view, according to Scheler, comes from identifying the a priori with what is "thought" or what has been added to "sensible content" by "reason." This view, which rests on a dualism running back to the Greeks, results in both theoretical and practical distortions in the Kantian philosophy.

But the concept of the "sensible" (or "sensible content") as such, tells us nothing about what actually determines a specific content as *content*. This concept of "sensibility," according to Scheler, indicates not *what* a given content is, such as a sound or a color, but merely *how* it is given to us. In no case is it anything *in* the color or *in* the sound. Why, then, did Kant identify the "given" element in cognition with "sensible content"? He did so, Scheler suggests, because he assimilated uncritically the atomistic empiricism of Hume regarding "sense impressions." The fatal result of this identification is that one asks what *can be* given instead of simply asking what *is* given. One assumes that nothing "can" be *given* at all when sensory stimuli, sensory functions, and sense organs are lacking (*F,* 75/55). In Kant's case, this assumption led to the conclusion that all contents of experience that *exceed* the elements of "sensible" contents (such as relations, forms, values, space, time, motion, being, unity, truth, causality, and the like) must be something *added* to it by the formative activity of the knowing subject. But this supposition, Scheler argues, is not supported by the phenomenological evidence.

An unprejudiced examination of what *is* given in experience, says Scheler, shows how arbitrary it is to restrict the "given" to the "sensible." For example, what is given originally in the perceptual experience of a cube is not anything like the "sense data" or "sense impressions" of the bare perspectival profile of the cube; rather, what is given is "the cube." In fact, to perceive the "sensible contents" of the profile requires a complex series of acts *subsequent* to the act of perceiving "the cube" *as such*. One must (1) reflectively grasp the relation between the individual consciousness and what is given to it; and (2) understand the *perceptual* character of the act of seeing in which not everything appears that was given originally. Furthermore, to apprehend the profile, one must (3) determine the perspectival relation between one's body, its physiological functions of perception, and the perceptual contents experienced in perceiving. But even this does not yet yield "sensible contents"; for in addition to this one must (4) distinguish the variable correlation between certain contents of experience and the experienced changes of the state of the lived body.[16] Hence, when one asks phenomenologically what in experience fulfills the concept of "sensation," one discovers that it is *not* a specific content of intuition. "Sensation," as such, is never strictly "given" at all; it is only a name for a specific relation between states of the lived body and appearances in the outer (or inner) world. What is given in experience therefore cannot be restricted to so-called sensible contents.

This holds in the practical sphere of volition no less than in the theoretical sphere of cognition. Just as Kantian theory limited what can be given in the knowing of objects to "sensible contents," so it limited what can be given in the willing of ends to "sensible feeling-states" of pleasure or pain. These were seen as affecting the will as reactions to contingent ends to be realized in willing. Hence, according to Kantian ethics, anything in the sphere of willing that *exceeds* the affective content of such feeling-states (and could determine the will a priori) must be contributed by the rational subject. According to Scheler, however, this view is mistaken. It may be true that in acts of mere *wishing* one attends to desired sensible feeling-states, even without intending their actual realization; but in acts of *willing* there is a marked absence of attention to such feeling-states; instead, there is a pronounced focus on the value of those ends whose actual realization is intended. What is given primordially in willing, then, is a valued *good* (e.g., sugar); only subsequently and secondarily does one encounter feelings of value (agreeableness of sugar) or sensible feeling-states (pleasant feeling of sugar on the tongue). The Kantian view is mistaken, therefore, says Scheler, in suggesting that what is given in the sphere of willing is only (a posteriori) sensible feeling-states of pleasure and pain.

In conformity with the ancient dualism that exhausts human life in the contraposition of "thought" and "sensibility," Kantian philosophy identified the a priori with the logical and therefore subjective pole of "thought," and the a posteriori with the non-logical and therefore objective pole of "sensibility." The basic error of this view, says Scheler, is its assumption that the only principle of lawfulness in experience is that conferred upon it by the rational subject's "thought." But the *whole* of human act-life, and not only our acts of analytical thinking, exhibits a lawfulness *independent* of human organization; and this lawfulness, including the lawfulness of logical thought, is not simply conferred by the rational subject upon experience, but belongs originally to the given content of experience. Accordingly, besides acts of analytical thinking, Scheler insists that there are numerous non-logical acts of feeling, preferring, loving, hating, willing, and the like, which possess a priori structures not borrowed from "thinking." These structures, he says, must be shown to be independent of logic. Just as there are a priori contents of logical thought, so there are a priori contents of our emotional act-life. With this in mind, Scheler borrows the expressions of Blaise Pascal's *Pensées* and speaks of an a priori *"ordre du coeur"* or *"logique du coeur."*[17]

Spontaneity and Receptivity

In keeping with his phenomenological method and his exclusive commitment to the evident "facts" concerning the a priori, Scheler rejects all attempts to reach behind these facts in an effort to "explain" them. Such attempts always go beyond the given facts and are therefore unjustifiable. Hence, he rejects the Kantian distinction between the "spontaneity" of thought and "receptivity" of sensibility as an unwarranted means of trying to explain the a priori. According to this distinction, every appearance is necessarily a "product" of the "formative" or "synthetic" activity of the understanding. This hypothesis leads to the "mythology" of productive rational activity, says Scheler, which results in a *"purely constructivistic explanation* of the a priori contents of objects of experience, an explanation based on the very *presupposition* that only a 'disordered chaos' is 'given' " — either in the form of "sensations" or in the form of "inclinations" (F, 86/66). But there is nothing in the content of experience that calls for this complex, constructivistic explanation; it is demanded only by the atomistic sensualism that Kant borrowed from Hume on "blind faith." Of course if the world is pulverized into a medley of "sensations" and man is dispersed into a chaos of "drives," there is no alternative: *"Hume's notion of nature required a Kantian understanding, and Hobbes's notion of man required a Kantian practical reason"* (F, 87/66, emphasis in the original). But there is not a shred more of phenomenological evidence to support the Kantian remedy of formalism than there is for the English malady of sensualism.

Scheler discerns in this Kantian "constructivism" a metaphysical attitude of hostility towards the world, a distrust of the given, an anxiety about the "world outside me" and "nature within me." Nature is viewed with fear, as a "chaos" of inclinations and sensations that must be formed, organized and controlled (F, 88/67). This attitude is reflected in the *locus* assigned to the a priori in the Kantian scheme of faculties and their functions: the a priori is derived from the functions of judgment and willing instead of from the content of intuition as the basis of judging or willing. At the *bottom* of this attitude, says Scheler, is a "Puritan" spirit of distrust of human nature and its impulses, so far as these are not subject to systematic, rational self-control. In this sense, the Kantian view lacks essential *insight* and is *blind* to the objective world of essences that are given a priori in the presentational forms of experience.

NECESSITY AND CONTINGENCY

Necessity, in Scheler's view, (1) pertains only to *propositions* (e.g., the relation between premise and conclusion), not to facts of intuition, except derivatively, and (2) is a *negative* concept insofar as "only that whose opposite is impossible can be necessary."[18] As such, the concept of "necessity" cannot help to elucidate the nature of the a priori, since necessity itself is grounded in the positive evidence of an essential a priori facticity: "Whenever we speak of 'necessity,' we must presuppose as *true* those propositions *according* to which propositional relations are necessary.... But it is clear that *these* propositions and their *truth* cannot be reduced to any 'necessity' that would differ from mere 'mental constraint.' They are *true because they are a priori evident"* (F, 95/74). The necessity of logically necessary propositions is based on *insight* into essential logical relationships, which itself cannot be reduced to the "necessity" that obtains among logically necessary propositions.

At points, Scheler's analysis becomes muddled and confusing, as Karl Alphéus, among others, has shown.[19] What is clear is that Scheler holds what Quine and others have called an "intuitionist" conception of the foundation of logic. Logical necessity, on this view, is founded on intuitive evidence. For Scheler this means that the a priori is not based on necessity, but necessity on the a priori of evidence in essential intuition. This relationship between necessity and the a priori is extended by Scheler beyond logic to morality, although the relationship between the "necessity" involved in each is not entirely clear.[20] The necessity of moral obligation, he says, has its foundation in the intuition of a priori connections among values. What is *good* is not based on "necessary obligation"; rather, "necessary obligation" is based on insight into what is good.

Universality and Individuality

Universality fares no better as a criterion of the a priori than necessity. In no sense, says Scheler, does it belong to the nature of essence. Essence, as such, is neither universal nor particular. The essence "red," for example, is neither universal nor particular as such, except as it is considered in relation to objects of which it may be predicated ("All Soviet flags are red"). This does not mean that a priori knowledge is never marked by universality, as it clearly is in logical propositions. But it means that even the a priori universality of such propositions is never grounded in the formal, logical conditions of a subjective faculty of concepts, but rather in essential evident "facts": "Hence the a priori is *not* dependent on *propositions* (or *even* on acts of judgment corresponding to them). It is not dependent, for example, on the *form* of such propositions and acts (i.e., on the 'forms of judgments,' from which Kant developed his 'categories' as 'functional laws' of 'thinking'). On the contrary, the a priori belongs wholly to the *'given'* and the sphere of *facts*" (F, 70/49).

This means, first, that individual essences are no less possible than universal essences; and, second, that essences only become universal or particular by virtue of a relation to subjects capable of intuiting them. A proposition based on an a priori essence is intuitively universal ("All Soviet flags are red") only for those subjects capable of the same insight (e.g., who are not blind or communicatively impaired). Hence, there can very well be a priori insights that lie within the capacity of some individuals and not others.[21]

This means, according to Scheler, that the Kantian attempt to ground the a priori in subjective rational functions is misleading and self-defeating. For it confuses the *nature* of the a priori with the subjective *capacities* or *activities* by which we apprehend it. Scheler therefore stresses that the a priori and the a posteriori have nothing to do with the distinction between "innate" and "acquired" qualities. The latter two concepts are causal-genetic concepts, and, as such, cannot define the character of the former relation, which concerns *types* of insight and *natures* of "essence" and "reality." On the one hand, the a priori cannot be "innate," since its nature as essence is something absolutely objective, in the sense that it is not relative to (or dependent upon) anything like "inherited dispositions." On the other hand, a priori insight cannot be regarded strictly as "acquired"—even if "a priori insights become *factically* [sic] realized" in persons through heredity, tradition, and acquisition (F, 99/78f.). The reason for this is that the *capacity* for realizing the a priori must be considered relative to certain native dispositions, much as the capacity for perceiving colors may vary according to such factors without affecting the a priori essences of colors themselves (F, 99/79). Hence, the *nature* of the a priori must be distinguished carefully from the *capacity* by which it is apprehended.

SUBJECTIVITY AND OBJECTIVITY

Scheler's most general criticism of the Kantian view concerns its "subjectivism." Most of the discussion of "subjectivism" in *Formalismus* is devoted to the Kantian attempt to link the a priori to the criteria of "necessity" and "universality," which Scheler regards as concealing an unjustified metaphysical hypothesis about the being of the rational subject underlying the logical form of judgments. But Scheler also sees the subjectivist thesis as related, first, to the more general problem that Husserl called its "anthropologism" or "psychologism," and, second, to the "transcendentalism" of the Kantian philosophy, which he (Scheler) rejects.

In the first instance, he says the a priori is misunderstood as "a law of the acts of an 'ego' or a 'subject,' e.g., as the form of the activity of a 'transcendental ego,' a so-called consciousness as such" (F, 96/76). But for Scheler, the ego is neither the point of departure for intuition nor the producer of essences but itself a *positive content* of intuition.[22] Hence, what Kant endeavored to "explain" by means of the hypothesis of transcendental apperception can be "described" phenomenologically without recourse to any such hypothesis through a more careful analysis of the relations between (1) the *nature* of the "act" and "object," and between (2) the *act* and "person" and the *object* and "world" (F, 98, n. 1/78, n. 45).

In the second instance, according to the Kantian "transcendental" thesis, the "laws of the objects of experience" are assumed to conform to the "laws of the experience of objects" (F, 92/71). What does this mean? Scheler sees Kant as conflating a number of important distinctions by focusing on (a) the essential interconnection between the essences of acts and of objects without giving due consideration to (b) the essences of "qualities" and "contents" given in acts, or to (c) the essences of acts themselves. Kant then goes a step farther and treats the essential relation between experience and objects as a *unilateral* one, arguing that a priori laws of objects must conform to the laws of experience. But why should we think that? Why should we assume that our "understanding" prescribes laws to "nature" or that our "practical reason" impresses its "form" on a manifold of chaotic "inclinations"? The only things we have any clear evidence of "prescribing" to nature are "conventions" (such as scientific signs or symbols). But these are certainly not "a priori" in the Kantian sense; and there is no clear evidence that even Kantian forms or concepts or ideas are "a priori" in the sense prescribed by their transcendental pretensions.

But if this is the case, the a priori does not pertain simply to the *conditions* of the possibility of experience, as in Kantian philosophy; for in a broader sense, it becomes a matter of *experience itself*. It is not something that can be "deduced" from the forms of judgment, as in Kant, for it is itself a matter of intuition to which even the judgments of the understanding must conform. In a broadly expanded and carefully qualified sense of the word, then, Scheler can speak even of the "empiricism" of the a priori (F, 72/51), much as Dufrenne speaks of the "empiricism of the transcendental" (7), though not in the sense of Kantian "sense empiricism." Scheler writes: "It is therefore not experience and non-experience, or so-called presuppositions of *all* experience (which would be un-experienceable in *every* respect), with which we are concerned in the contrast between the a priori and a posteriori; rather, we are concerned with two *kinds* of experience: pure and immediate experience *and* the experience conditioned and mediated by positing the natural organization of a real bearer of acts" (F, 72/52). In other words, the difference between the a priori and the a posteriori corresponds to the difference between phenomenological and mundane (non-phenomenological) experience, such that a priori essences function as "structures" and "formal laws" in mundane experience, becoming the "content" and "objects" of intuition only in phenomenological experience. In this sense they are "phenomena."

This means that, in spite of himself, Scheler does not entirely abandon the transcendental theme of a priori conditionality.[23] For, even though he declares himself unequivocally opposed to "transcendentalism," he admits that "there does exist a lawfulness of the 'conforming' in a sense quite different from Kant's" (F, 94/73f.). What does this mean? "Real things, goods, and acts," he explains, "are what 'conform' to the a priori content of experience." That is to say, the *real* stuff of *mundane* experience "conforms" to the *essential* stuff of *phenomenological* experience, in the sense that phenomenology discovers the structures already contained within mundane experience—structures by virtue of which mundane experience receives or possesses its categorial and recognitional forms.[24] The a priori conditions of mundane experience are found in the identificational structures of phenomenological experience. These "phenomena" do not *conceal* a transcendentally antecedent world of conditioning "noumena" as in the Kantian philosophy. Rather, they *disclose* the "things themselves" in their identificational structure. This, of course, is neither the transcendentalism of Kantian philosophy nor quite even that of Husserlian phenomenology, for Scheler rejects in both the recourse to *subjectivity* as a way of adducing the a priori conditions of experience. But the transcendental theme of a priori conditionality remains in Scheler, notwithstanding his denials, in the form of a kind of "transcendental essentialism."

Scheler's Critique in Perspective

AT LEAST SUPERFICIALLY, Scheler's basic difference with the Kantian perspective takes the form of a reversal of the latter's "Copernican Revolution." In baldest terms, Scheler's a priori is (1) not "subjective" but *"objective,"* (2) not "formal" but *"material,"* (3) not generated by the "spontaneity" of thought but *given in the "receptivity" of intuition*, (4) not "independent of all experience" but *phenomenologically "experienced."* Beyond these apparent reversals, Scheler dispenses with at least two features of the Kantian account, namely (5) its anthropological hypothesis about psychical "faculties" and (6) its logical criteria of "necessity" and "universality."

In several other respects, Scheler's differences are somewhat subtler. While (7) explicitly rejecting Kantian "transcendentalism," Scheler does not thereby reject the conditional structure of transcendentalism[25] as such. Rather, he shifts the conditionality from subjective laws of acts to objective relations of essences. Furthermore, within the context of traditional metaphysical themes, we have seen that the Kantian concept of the a priori is identified with "being" and "constancy" (as opposed to "becoming" or "change"), "unity" (as opposed to "diversity"), and "intelligibility" and "supersensibility" (as opposed to the "irrational" or "material"). But (8) whereas the Kantian a priori concepts and ideas represented the *constant formal features* of cognition over against empirical processes, Scheler's a priori essences represent the *constancy of the material content* of cognition over against the fluid pre-conscious experience of the meaningless "resistance" of reality.[26] Again, (9) where Kantian forms and concepts served to unify a given manifold of sensations, Scheler's essences serve that purpose only in relation to objects for which they can serve as common predicates ("All Soviet flags are red"), or in relation to subjects by which they can be inter-subjectively intuited (e.g., by all those who are not blind and can see or visualize the color "red"), as we saw in Scheler's discussion of "universality." Finally, (10) while the Kantian a priori was identified with the "intelligible" or "suprasensible" and set in opposition to the "sensible," as if the former were not given in experience, such is not the case with Scheler's concept of "essence." Rather, essence is discerned within reality as that which structures it and renders it meaningful.[27]

The cumulative effect of Scheler's critique is to call into question the transcendental-rational "constructivism" of the Kantian account. The Kantian dualities (a priori/a posteriori, formal/material, spontaneity/receptivity, rationality/sensibility, noumena/phenomena, and the like) suggest that whatever *order* we discover in moral experience is an order imposed upon it by the activity of a *rational subject*. By virtue of his "Copernican Revolution," experience becomes, for Kant, a construct of the mind. The most basic laws that govern experience reside within, and are contributed by, the rational subject. What is *given to* the subject in empirical experience, whether in the experience impressions of external or of internal sense could never disclose lawfulness or orderedness in and of itself *apart from* the lawfulness and orderedness contributed by the subject. For Scheler, however, *there is no phenomenological evidence for this supposition*. There is no adequate reason for supposing that the nature of the a priori is formal and not material, that it is produced by thought and not "given" in intuition, that it is rooted in the transcendental conditionality of subjective laws of acts and not in objectively given essential relations among phenomenal "facts." The effect of Scheler's critique is to call into question the fundamental dualistic metaphysical framework presupposed by the Kantian "Copernican Revolution."

It would be misleading, however, to suggest that Scheler's position represents a simple *reversal* of Kant's—as it were, a Ptolemaic counter-revolution. For Scheler's alternative is neither a simple reversion to pre-Kantian, pre-critical options, nor simply the affirmation of the "material," "objective," "a posteriori" side of Kant's distinctions over against the "formal," "subjective," "a priori" side. For, as we have seen, Scheler makes use of some of these traditional, metaphysical categories in quite non-traditional ways. For example, he no longer contrasts the "a priori" with the "a posteriori" or the "material." Kant's distinction between "a priori" and "a posteriori"—typically identified in his work with the classical distinctions between "form" and "matter," "intelligibility" and "sensibility"—are displaced in Scheler's thinking by the distinction between "essence" (identified with "phenomenological fact") and "reality" (identified with "resistance").[28]

Accordingly, Scheler's effort to develop an alternative to the Kantian a priori is unavoidably linked to two issues which, according to Thomas Seebohm, governed the early controversy between phenomenology and Neo-Kantianism from its beginning: (1) the question whether the a priori is subjective or objective, merely formal or also material, and (2) the question whether phenomenology itself needs an ultimate grounding in a transcendental subject (Preface, vi).

On the first of these questions, we have seen Scheler's answer: the a priori is "material" and "objective," not "subjective" and merely "formal"; but it is "material" and "objective" in the sense of *phenomenon* in phenomenology, not in the sense of *empirical object* in Kantianism (let alone in pre-critical realism). Scheler's most notable insight at this point lies in his exposé of the Critical Philosophy's uncritical presuppositions stemming from 18th-century Enlightenment dogmas about the autonomy and self-sufficiency of reason. Where is the evidence that the ultimate source of the ordering principle which governs our moral experience lies in the experiencing *subject*? Where is the evidence for the presumption that the only form of such order or lawfulness is ultimately *rational*, whether the lawfulness experienced lies in the orderedness of desires, or inclinations, or moral perceptions? True, Scheler does not take into consideration what Husserl called "passive synthesis" or "passive constitution." But even if he had, this would not have altered the force of his argument; for the question finally turns, not on whether subjects play an active role in constituting the ordered world of their moral experiences, but on whether that order *originates in themselves*. Scheler's "material a priori" re-opens the question as to the ultimate source of the lawfulness that orders moral experience while acknowledging that, in fact, we do *experience* such lawfulness as a phenomenological fact.

On the second question, as we have seen, Scheler's position is more complex. On the one hand, he seems largely satisfied that there is neither any evidence that phenomenology, with its concept of the a priori, is grounded in any sort of transcendental subject, nor any evidence that it ultimately requires such grounding. On the other hand, his claim that the mundane experience of reality finds its identificational structure in the phenomenological experience of ideal essences seems to concede the existence of some sort of transcendental grounding structure, even if it is not that of a transcendental "subject." But in neither case is Scheler's position articulated with sufficient clarity and substance to bring resolution to the issue. While he does become more explicit about what the phenomenological reduction is in his later writings, his phenomenological method is never conclusively defined. Perhaps it may be said that he is engaged in a pre-transcendental phenomenology of the life-world, as was Alfred Schutz. In any case, Scheler's position leaves him vulnerable to criticism on two sides. On the one hand, it leaves him open to the criticism of *existential* phenomenologists, such as Heidegger, who argue that his position lacks an adequate analysis of fundamental ontology.[29] On the other hand, it leaves him open to criticism by *transcendental* phenomenologists, such as Funke, who insist on the necessity of rigorous grounding in a transcendental subject.[30]

Granted, in his later philosophy Scheler does offer a variation on the ancient microcosm-macrocosm theme in which he reasons from the act-object correlation between individual "persons" and their individual "worlds" to a structurally analogical correlation between a "person of persons" and corresponding "world of worlds." In this light one might venture to argue that he does try to ground his phenomenology in the "transcendental subjectivity" of God. But Scheler's speculations at this point take him far beyond what may be called phenomenologically evident and plunge him into a bog of metaphysical hypotheses on the origin of evil and the problem of theodicy from which he seemed incapable of extricating himself in his later years.[31] If there is any evidence that phenomenology and its conception of the a priori are grounded, or require grounding, in a transcendental subject (which the early Scheler denies) it is unlikely to be found in this direction, at least as Scheler develops it.

The position taken by the early Scheler and other early phenomenologists against any kind of quasi-Kantian grounding of phenomenology in a transcendental subject was eventually rejected by Husserl, who moved increasingly in the Kantian direction, making a "transcendental turn" and seeking to ground phenomenology in the "transcendental ego." But the issue remained a subject of dispute among subsequent phenomenologists. Not even every transcendental phenomenologist followed Husserl at this point. Aron Gurwitsch, for example, while recognizing the necessity of some sort of transcendental conditionality, contested Husserl's insistence on locating this conditionality in a transcendental "ego," for which he could see no conclusive evidence, in his essay "Phänomenologie der Thematik und des reinen Ich." While the correlativity of "subjectivity" and "objectivity" in the intentional act-structure was never in doubt, disagreement centered on whether or not this correlative act-structure itself evidences or requires a particular grounding in a transcendental subject.

In the context of Scheler's concerns, for instance, some might be tempted to ask why we may not speak of "transcendental objectivity"—why we may not regard the essential act-structures of phenomenology as grounded transcendentally in the "objective" conditions of the possibility of experience. Construing the matter in this way may not only seem consonant with the intent of Scheler, but also may attract especially those of a metaphysical realist or epistemological intuitionist stripe.[32] Without considerably more justification than this, however, it would fail to satisfy Husserlian phenomenologists that the real conditions of transcendental grounding have been met.[33] It would also fail to persuade most contemporary philosophers that the issues involved in the current controversy over antirealism (Feyerabend, et al.) and deconstruction (Derrida, et al.) with its attendant cluster of ontological, epistemological, and semantic issues, have been adequately dealt with. Moreover, it would fail to address an apparently ineluctable dilemma at the heart of the phenomenological analysis of the a priori—the dilemma of how to understand the *origin* of the a priori after "splitting" it, as Paul Ricoeur observes, into subjective and objective "sides."[34]

Now, it is true that "object" is, in Husserlian phenomenology at least, a term whose denotation includes everything "subjective." But when the matter is put, as Ricoeur states it, in terms of a subject-object schema, only two possibilities seem to be finally available—either the a priori must be understood in terms of the free creative *subject* or described in terms of the static, structured *object*. From this vantage point, even if one tries to do justice to both sides of the polarity,[35] one may still question, with Ricoeur, whether it is legitimate to split the a priori into two parts, whether it can ultimately be accounted for in this way. The case is not appreciably altered by recognizing, as Husserl did, the phenomenon of "passive synthesis," which shows that the founding stratum of perception is never sheerly "receptive" but is always the result of a passive synthetic "agency."[36] This only pushes back the problem, for one must still ask about the relation between this passive synthetic "agency" and the world constituted by it. Nor is the problem overcome by the notion of a "universal *a priori* of correlation"—a notion Husserl developed of a correlation between an "ontic Apriori" and a "constitutional Apriori" that is concretely inseparable from it in order to account for both sides of the polarity (*K*, §46, *FTL*, §97). But although the subject and object of consciousness are "bracketed" so as to leave only the "content" of consciousness itself, this "content" nevertheless remains an *object* of consciousness; and, as such, it is accepted ultimately either as an objectively structured datum received by consciousness or as a constituted product of a structure-conferring transcendental subject. There seems to be no satisfactory middle ground within the dualistic schema. The ordering principle cannot come from both object and subject, world and mind.[37]

The dilemma that arises from this perspective concerns the *origin* of the a priori as such. One might reasonably ask why we should trouble ourselves about such a question at all, even if others have done so (see Virgil C. Aldrich, "The Origin of the Apriori"). Why should we think an ordering principle "comes from" anything at all? This in turn, of course, raises the question whether its being and validity may not be dependent and contingent. Some, like Quine, have embraced the full implications of such a view and have argued that not even the most austere laws of logic are in principle "unrevisable," while others, like Alvin Plantinga, have resisted this view.[38] In any case, the seemingly inexorable recrudescence of the subject-object schema and (from within that perspective) the question of the origin of the a priori, seems a foregone conclusion. The problem is as old as the Aristotelian question concerning the primacy of truth or being, of the epistemological or the metaphysical. Some have asked whether there is not some other irreducible "third factor," some sort of aboriginal "structural a priori," as Husserl suggests, that generates the interface between the subjective and the objective "sides" of the correlation. Others, like Merleau-Ponty, have suggested the possibility of retrieving a pre-theoretical "third dimension" beneath the level of the distinction between constituting subjectivity and constituted objectivity.[39] Mikel Dufrenne has asked whether we cannot speak of some sort of an "*a priori* of the *a priori*."[40] Such questions often seem destined to lead either to an impasse in phenomenological reflection or into the turbid waters of speculation. Dufrenne's own discussion flirts with the Leibnizian notion of a "pre-established harmony." But even if the impasse and turbid waters are avoided, it is not immediately clear what more can be said about this quest for the anterior origin and unity of the two "sides" of the a priori, or what more light, if any, such an undertaking may yield. If current discussions among analytic philosophers on the nature of "necessity" and its relation to the "a priori" and "analyticity" are any indication, prospects may seem pretty grim.[41]

Admittedly, these are questions about the a priori that Scheler's account hardly answers, and which probably no account answers conclusively. And they are by no means the only unanswered questions. Paul Ricoeur, for example, has also asked (like Schlick) whether any *limits* can be set on experiences yielding the a priori once the dam of formalism has burst, or whether we find ourselves on a "slippery slope" (Preface, xi; cf. xvi). Ronald Perrin raises a different question about how Scheler can preserve any distinction between form and matter after his "materialist reduction" of the a priori; and, again, in another connection, he asks whether Scheler, despite his sharp attack on the Kantian dichotomy between thought and sensibility, does not reopen a similar kind of dichotomy in his distinction between "logical" and "emotive" acts. ("A Commentary," 357, 359).

None of these questions may pose insurmountable problems. The problem of whether a limit can be imposed upon the a priori is no more of a problem for the phenomenologists, certainly, than it was for Kant, who lacked conclusive justification for fixing the number of categories (or judgments on which they are based) exactly at twelve. More importantly, once the stock distinctions of Kantian critical philosophy are abandoned—especially as interpreted in the legacy of logical empiricism (Schlick, Ayer, et al.)—such issues as the "slippery slope" may cease to present the kind of problem envisioned by Ricoeur. If the question is finally, as Parmenides asked Socrates, whether there must be essential forms even for such things as hair, mud, and dirt, the answer obviously must be: Why, of course. These are nothing but their recognitional forms.

Perrin's question about how Scheler can preserve any form/matter distinction after his "materialist reduction" of the a priori does not pose a fundamental problem. Although Scheler does not offer an explicit answer to this question, or even a well-developed account of how the form/matter distinction is preserved in phenomenology, Perrin's question overlooks the fact that Scheler employs it as a *secondary* distinction *within* both the sphere of the a priori and of the a posteriori, as we have seen.[42] Hence, there is no real problem here.

A more serious problem may be how to understand the underlying unity between "logical" and "emotive" acts in Scheler's account, as Perrin suggests. This problem, in turn, involves the problem of the ultimate relationship between various "orders of experience."[43] Borrowing from Pascal's idea of a "logic of the heart," according to which the heart has its own reasons of which the understanding knows nothing, Scheler seems to posit the existence of two utterly independent orders—one logical, the other emotional—each with its utterly unique a priori principles. This view offers, it seems to me, an insight as well as a difficulty. The insight lies in Scheler's discernment that experience presents us with a diversity of orders (the emotional, logical, moral, legal, religious, and so forth), which subsist in relative autonomy and resist reductionistic strategies. Here I think Scheler is right: one order cannot be reduced to another, any more than the emotional can be reduced to the logical. But there is a twofold difficulty with his position: First, his recognition of an "emotional a priori" alone is insufficient. There are other orders besides the emotional (e.g., the moral, legal, religious, logical, etc.) whose principles cannot be subsumed without violence under the a priori of "feeling."[44] Scheler does say that his a priori of feeling is grounded in an order of phenomenological "preferences" (F, 107/89), but this does not really seem to alleviate the difficulty at issue.[45] Second, he offers no clear way of understanding how different orders are related. Is there an underlying unity and harmony here, or not? Are the principles of logic and feeling ultimately compatible, or do they perhaps conflict? Scheler offers little help here.[46] As Perrin says, "at the very moment when he seemed on the verge of healing the rift between phenomenal and noumenal man, he reinvoked the distinction between a realm of sensibility (now characterized in terms of Pascal's order of the heart) and a realm of thought, each unique and irreducible" (359).

As suggested near the beginning of this chapter, a factor that seriously complicates matters for anyone trying to understand the meaning of the a priori in the history of philosophy generally is the mutual isolation and independent development of the analytic and phenomenological traditions. Anyone wishing to undertake an evenhanded and broad-based assessment of a critique of Kantian views such as Scheler's should probably face, at some point, the legacies of both traditions. One ought to confront the legacy of logical empiricism, because this legacy, despite trenchant criticism, continues to exercise widespread residual influence in the form of basic epistemological assumptions that, though widely admitted to be problematic, continue to influence Kant-interpretation. One must confront the legacy of phenomenology, not only in order to come to an understanding of its proper representatives, but in order to try to understand why it has been so badly misrepresented in the analytic tradition.[47] If one seeks to be accountable to the philosophical community as a whole, and not merely to court the approval of one portion of it, then one cannot simply ignore such interpretations as seem disagreeable. One must try to understand them. That sufficient consideration cannot be given to these matters within the scope of the present study means, of necessity, that it must be provisional and incomplete. For the present, let it suffice to draw a number of tentative conclusions from a preliminary analysis I have offered elsewhere.[48]

In conclusion, then, it may be said that, in phenomenology, the term "a priori" refers to a cluster of things including essences (e.g., the sound of middle C on a piano), the intuition of essences (the hearing or envisioning of the sound), and the co-presentation of qualities of essences (the intensity of the sound), as well as the logical relations of substantives within propositions or judgments ("Every sound has an intensity"). The a priori in phenomenology *may* refer, in an altogether conventional sense, to formal logical analyticity of the ordinary sort recognized by any logical empiricist. In a more uniquely phenomenological sense, it may refer also, among other things, to the *content* of categorial or material intuition. In view of the problems of understanding and of terminology that have developed around these notions in the wider philosophical community, perhaps it is unfortunate that Scheler and others in the phenomenological movement chose to speak of a "material" a priori in this latter sense. They might have created less of a problem if they could have distinguished their references to the a priori knowledge of propositions, on the one hand, from their references to simple intuited essences, on the other.

It is in this last sense of a "material" a priori—an a priori of essential intuition—that phenomenology finds the means by which to link the identificational form of material essences with their co-presented or concomitant "properties," the means by which to ground a priori judgments conjoining the substantives within what Quine calls "non-logical" analytic statements (43). Much as Rudolf Carnap sought successive approximations of "meaning postulates" to analogues in natural language (*Meaning and Necessity*, 22, 235), so phenomenologists have employed reflective techniques of successive imaginative variations to clarify "essences." Such techniques yield, not the logical and syntactical relations between the substantives of propositions, but the invariant identificational forms and constant structural features of essences, on the basis of which a priori judgments may be formed about these essences and what we may call their "qualities." The invariant features of intuited essences, in other words, furnish the *conditions* necessary for discerning the logical and syntactical relations between the substantives of propositions. Until phenomenologists find a way to avoid conflating these propositional and intuitional meanings under the single expression of the "a priori," they are likely to continue having difficulty making themselves understood to the greater philosophical community.

NOTES

1. Aristotle, *The Works of Aristotle*, ed. W. D. Ross, 12 vols. (1928; rpt. Oxford: Oxford University Press, 1966), vol. 1: *Categoriae, De Interpretatione, Analytica Priora, Analytica Posteriora, Topica, and De Sophisticis Elenchis*, "Analytica Posteriora," trans. G. R. G. Mure, Bk. 1, ch. 2, 71 b 30–72 a 5, and "Categoriae," trans. E. M. Edghill, ch. 12, 14 a 26–14 b 23; and vol. 8: *Metaphysica*, trans. W. D. Ross, Bk. 5, ch. 11, 1018 b 9–1019 a 14.

For a historical survey, see *Historisches Wörterbuch der Philosophie*, ed. Joachim Ritter, vol. 1 (Basel and Stuttgart: Schwabe & Co. Verlag, 1971), Apriori/aposteriori," coll. 462–74; "Apriori, emotionales," coll. 474–76; and "Apriorismus," coll. 476–78.

2. For Moser's discussion, see his Introduction to his *A Priori Knowledge* (Oxford: Oxford University Press, 1987)—an excellent collection of articles on the subject from an analytic perspective.

3. See my article, "The A Priori in Phenomenology and the Legacy of Logical Empiricism," *Philosophy Today* 34, No. 3 (fall 1990), 195–205. The possibility of rapprochement between analytic and phenomenological understandings is evident when the empiricists' dogma on the analyticity of the a priori is being questioned from within their own ranks by the likes of Willard Quine and Saul Kripke, and the phenomenological dogma that phenomenological propositions are synthetic a priori is being challenged from within phenomenology's own ranks by the likes of Sokolowski, who considers them tautologies, as did the logical empiricist Schlick. See Willard V. Quine, "Two Dogmas of Empiricism," in *From a Logical Point of View*, 2d ed. (Cambridge: Harvard University Press, 1953), 20–46; Saul A. Kripke, *Naming and Necessity* (Cambridge: Harvard University Press, 1980), 34–39, 54–57, 80–90, 135–38; Robert Sokolowski, *Husserlian Meditations: How Words Present Things* (Evanston, IL: Northwestern University Press, 1974), 233–70, esp. 242f.

The literature on the concept of the a priori is immense and unwieldy. But at a minimum, in addition to the aforementioned work edited by Paul Moser (n. 2, above) in the analytic tradition, one must mention the major study from a Continental perspective by Mikel Dufrenne, *The Notion of the "A Priori,"* trans. Edward S. Casey (Evanston, IL: Northwestern University Press, 1966). See also R. S. Hartman, "The Epistemology of the A Priori," *Philosophy and Phenomenological Research* 9 (June 1949), 731–36; and Robert D. Sweeney, "The Affective 'A Priori,'" *The Phenomenological Realism of Possible Worlds*, ed. Anna-Teresa Tymienicka, Analecta Husserliana, 3 (Dordrecht: D. Reidel, 1974), 80–97. Perhaps the best discussion of Scheler's conception of the a priori available is that of Eiichi Shimomissé in his *Die Phänomenologie und das Problem der Grundlegung der Ethik*, 22ff.

4. Max Scheler, "Deutsche Philosophie der Gegenwart," 197f. On the controversy over how "categorial intuition" was understood by Scheler, Husserl, and Heidegger, see David R. Lachterman's discussion in his Translator's Introduction to Max Scheler, *Selected Philosophical Essays*, xxiii–xxvi.

5. For a detailed analysis, see Iso Kern, *Husserl und Kant* (The Hague: Nijhoff, 1964), which extensively treats historical and systematic connections between Husserl, Kant and the Neo-Kantians. Also see Edmund Husserl, "Kant and the Idea of Transcendental Philosophy," and Ted Klein, "Husserl's Kantian

Meditations," both in *Southwest Journal of Philosophy* 5, No. 3 (Nov. 1974), 9–56, 69–82; and Roman Ingarden, "A Priori Knowledge in Kant vs. A Priori Knowledge in Husserl," *Dialectics and Humanism* (Poland) (autumn 1973), 5–18.

6. My usage of the expressions "categorial forms" and "presentational forms" derives from Robert Sokolowski's *Husserlian Meditations* (see n. 3, above), and his *Moral Action: A Phenomenological Study*. In the former he writes: "The fact that Paul is awake, and the fact that John is beneath the sycamore tree, are categorial objects. It is possible to isolate from categorial objects the categorial form operative in them, such as the attributive form 'S is p' or the relational form *a R b*" (32). In *Moral Action* he says, "Categorial forms are relations and articulations in things that are correlative to our thinking about things"; they "are not merely mental. They belong to the presencing [sic] of things, to how things can be given and referred to and talked about. They belong to the being of things" (3). Again, he writes that moral actions are performed with an awareness that enters into the nature of the act being performed, so that it becomes "categorially formed," acquiring a "recognitional form." " 'Being recognized' or 'being identified' in this way is a presentational form. It is like 'being a picture,' 'being a word,' 'being a perceived thing,' 'being a predicate,' 'being a state of affairs' " (55, cf. 143, 218–19).

7. We must note, of course, the striking exception of space and time, which, according to Kant, are not only "forms of intuition" but themselves "pure intuitions."

8. Cf. Kant *KrV*, B xxvi, B 71f., A 256–B 311, *KU*, §77; and Husserl, *LU*, 2, Investigation VI, ch. 6., and *Ideen*, §§3–4, 69, 136–38. Cf. Emmanuel Levinas, *The Theory of Intuition in Husserl's Phenomenology*, trans. André Orianne (Evanston, IL: Northwestern University Press, 1973), 97–151.

9. For a clear, five-point summary of Husserl's main criticisms of the Kantian conception of the a priori, see Debabrata Sinha, "Phenomenology, vis-à-vis Kant and Neopositivism, on the Issue of the Apriori," *Archiv für Geschichte der Philosophie* 53, No. 1 (1971), 41–57, esp. 49–54; cf. Philip Blosser, "Kant and Phenomenology," *Philosophy Today* 30, No. 2 (summer 1986), 168–73.

10. See my article, "The A Priori in Phenomenology," for an analysis of the senses in which the a priori in phenomenology may refer to propositions, essences, and the relations between essences and their qualities. For a helpful discussion of the Husserl's conception of the a priori and its development, see J. N. Mohanty, *The Possibility of Transcendental Philosophy*, Phaenomenologica 98 (Dordrecht: Nijhoff, 1985), 101–19 (esp. 104f.); cf. 45–56, 191–212.

11. James G. Hart develops this point very clearly in his review of *Duty and Inclination*, by Hans Reiner, *Husserl Studies* 1 (1984), 307–14. From a Husserlian perspective, he criticizes Reiner and Dietrich von Hildebrand (who is a basic source for Reiner) for their failure to see that value perception (*Wertnehmung*) is "a passive association as well as the passive synthetic result of prior active position-takings" in the same way that perception (*Wahrnehmung*) is "a passive association building on the founding prior acts (*Auffassungen*)" (313). Elaborating on this point, he writes: "The founding stratum of value perception as 'passive' is never sheerly 'receptive' in the sense intended by Reiner and von Hildebrand for it always is a result of the passive synthetic 'agency.' The I-center's being affected by the founding hyletic stratum is clearly centripedal; but Husserl rightly insists that von Hildebrand does not see the elemental cen-

trifugal achievement in 'being affected' which is at the basis of waking life and founding our active value-responses. See F I 24, especially 64b" (314 n. 8).

Two important studies in Husserl's development of the notions of "passive synthesis" and "constitution" are his analysis of "internal time-consciousness" (in Z, see esp. sec. 3 on "The Levels of Constitution of Time and Temporal Objects," and the addenda in pt. 2) and *Ideen* 1 (esp. §§97, 117, 119, 135, 149–53). But see also his *Phenomenological Psychology*, trans. John Scanlon (The Hague: Nijhoff, 1977), 160, where he says that every *ego cogito* "is restricted to the presupposition that previously the I was affected," which means "that previously a passive intentionality in which the I does not yet hold sway has already constituted in itself an object by which the I-pole has been affected and determined to the *actus*."

The best study in English of these issues is Robert Sokolowski's *The Formation of Husserl's Concept of Constitution* (The Hague: Nijhoff, 1964) see esp. 195–223, but also the discussion of "passive genesis," on 175, 193, and 207. See also the chapters in Theodor De Boer, *The Development of Husserl's Thought*, trans. Theodore Plantinga (The Hague: Nijhoff, 1978), which treat the period of *Ideen* and *Die Krisis*.

12. First published in "Wissenshaftlicher Jahresbericht der Philosophischen Gesellschaft an der Universität zu Wien für das Vereinsjahr 1930/31"; translated by Wilfrid Sellars in *Readings in Philosophical Analysis*, ed. Herbert Feigl and Wilfrid Sellars (New York: Appleton-Century-Crofts, 1949), and reprinted in *Phenomenology and Existentialism*, ed. Robert C. Solomon (Lanham, MD: University Press of America, 1980), 282–88. Cf. M. M. Van de Pitte, "Schlick's Critique of Phenomenological Propositions," *Philosophy and Phenomenological Research* 45 (Dec. 1984), 195–226, on the Husserl-Schlick controversy.

13. Not surprisingly, Scheler quotes with approval the words of Spinoza: "The Truth is the criterion of itself *and* of the false" (PE, 284/140); and he defends Husserl against the criticism of Wilhelm Wundt, who saw in his *Logical Investigations* nothing but the most "primitive" and tautological "repetition" — that is, "Evidence is evidence." Such criticism, according to Scheler, is based on a fundamental misunderstanding of the phenomenological method—namely, that "phenomenological controversy" may be resolved by recourse to some sort of extra-phenomenal criterion of verification. In fact, however, even the threat of completely illusory perception presupposes the only possible condition for its resolution: the possibility of veridical perception. (PE, sec. 3).

14. Scheler's analysis of a priority appears in the second chapter of *Formalismus*, entitled "Formalism and Apriorism." The chapter is divided into two sections: (1) "The A Priori and the Formal in General" and (2) "The Non-Formal A Priori in Ethics." In the first section Scheler defines his own view of the a priori and clarifies it by contrasting it to the Kantian view and subjecting the latter to a detailed critique. In the second section he applies his own view to the field of ethics, specifically in the classification of a priori interrelations among values. The first section concerns us here; the second will be examined in the following chapter on the nature of values. While the following analysis is based on the relevant portions of *Formalismus*, it departs from Scheler's discussion, at points, in the interests of organization and clarity.

15. Ronald F. Perrin, "A Commentary on Max Scheler's Critique of the Kantian Ethic," *Journal of the History of Philosophy* 12 (Aug. 1974), 357,

overlooks this fact when he wonders how Scheler can preserve any distinction between form and matter once he commits himself to the "materialist reduction" of the a priori. Although Scheler is not as expressly clear about how the form/matter distinction is preserved in his phenomenology as he might have been, there is no problem of principle here.

16. Scheler develops a comparable analysis in LdT, 433ff./202ff.

17. *F*, 84/63. See Scheler's essay, "*Ordo Amoris*" in *Schriften aus dem Nachlaß*. Vol. 1, *Zur Ethik und Erkenntnislehre*, ed. by Maria Scheler, 2d ed. (Bern: Francke Verlag, 1957), which has been translated by David R. Lachterman in *Selected Philosophical Essays*, by Max Scheler. Cf. also Scheler's essay, *Liebe und Erkenntnis*, 2d ed. (Bern: Francke Verlag, 1970), and Manfred S. Frings, "Der *Ordo Amoris* bei Max Scheler in seinen Beziehung zu Materialer Wertethik und Ressentiment," *Zeitschrift für Philosophische Forschung* 20, No. 1 (1966), 57–76, and his "The *Ordo Amoris* in Max Scheler: Its Relationship to His Value Ethics and to the Concept of Resentment," trans. F. J. Smith, in *Facets of Eros*, ed. F. J. Smith and Erling Eng (The Hague: Nijhoff, 1972), 40–60.

18. Scheler is referring here (*F*, 94f./74) to Kant's formal definition of "necessity" — "the contradiction of that which is in itself impossible" — in *Der einzig mögliche Beweisgrund zu einer Demonstration des Daseins Gottes*, ed. Paul Menzer, *Kants Gesammelte Schriften* (Berlin: Königliche Preußische Akademie der Wissenschaften, 1912), 2:81.

19. Scheler's analysis of "necessity" was vigorously criticized by Karl Alphéus in his earlier work, *Kant und Scheler*, later reissued in a new, expanded edition by Barbara Wolandt (Bonn: Bouvier Verlag, 1981). Alphéus defended a basically Kantian view of necessity (according to which it is grounded in the nature of our understanding), and vehemently protested Scheler's view on the grounds that it compromises the native "necessity" of necessity (63, 411 n. 25). For instance, in trying to clarify the ground of "necessity" phenomenologically, Scheler endeavors to show *how* we comprehend the impossibility of contradicting a logically necessary proposition, and states that we experience as necessary those propositions whose opposites contradict evidentially *true* propositions. However, as Alphéus pointed out, this would mean that every *true* proposition, including such empirical propositions as "This tree has leaves," is logically *necessary*, which is clearly false. To make himself clear, Scheler could have differentiated more precisely between the concepts of "necessity" and "evidence" (or "truth"). His point, after all, was not that every true proposition is necessary, but that necessity itself is a matter of truth or evidence that cannot itself be called "necessary." Cf. also Shimomissé, *Die Phänomenologie*, 22–36: "Die Lehre vom Apriori."

20. Shimomissé, points out, for instance, the ambiguity deriving from the fact that "necessity" is set in opposition to *contingency* in the sphere of cognition, but in opposition to *freedom* in the sphere of volition — a fact of which Scheler usually takes no clear notice. Still, Shimomissé himself finds in the Kantian definition of "necessity" ("The contradiction of that which is in itself impossible") the suggestion of several kinds of necessity, insofar as what is in itself "possible" may mean something (1) *logical* (possible in thought), (2) *ontological* (possible in reality), and (3) *moral* (morally possible); he notes, moreover, that "necessity" has a distinctively (4) *transcendental* sense as one of the categories of modality (*Die Phänomenologie*, 25, n. 55).

21. Hans Reiner, *Duty and Inclination*, makes a similar point against Kant when he writes: "The objectivity that grounds the bindingness [sic] of a moral demand does not depend on whether the assumption that my insight is right can be confirmed by demonstrating the demand's general validity 'for all rational beings'" (67). The personal call to rescue a drowning man, he says, is recognized a priori as categorical, even though it is particular, not universal (76).

22. Cf. the similar view of Jean-Paul Sartre in his *The Transcendence of the Ego*, trans. Forrest Williams and Robert Kirkpatrick (New York: Farrar, Straus and Giroux, 1957), see esp. secs. 1 B, and 2 D.

23. By this I mean the concern for identifying the "conditions for the possibility of [coherent and intelligible] experience" (e.g., *KrV*, A 158–B 129), which constitutes the hallmark of Kantian transcendental a priorism.

24. On this usage of "categorial and recognitional form," as well as of "identificational structure," see n. 6, above.

25. See n. 23, above.

26. The notion of reality as "resistance" was developed by Scheler in his later period, but it is not entirely absent from *Formalismus* (e.g., *F*, 154 n. 3/135 n. 25). For the later development of this notion in his work, see his discussions in "Die Stellung des Menschen im Kosmos" and "Idealismus–Realismus" (both 1927). Especially interesting is Scheler's claim that "resistance" is not an "experience of the will" as in Dilthey's theory, but rather an experience of spontaneous, involuntary impulse (*Drang*); and, therefore, that it does not presuppose, as Heidegger charged, an ontology of mere presence-at-hand or an inadequate analysis of *Dasein's* Being-in-the-world (IR, 214–16/324–27). In fact, in his posthumously published manuscripts on the subject, Scheler reverses Heidegger's thesis and declares that *Dasein's* Being-in-the-world presupposes "resistance"! See *Späte Schriften*, 1 (*GW*, 9), in the section entitled "Das emotionale Realitätsproblem," 264.

27. Cf. n. 23 above, in the discussion of the eighth point in this paragraph, and the discussion of Scheler's "transcendentalism" earlier in this chapter.

28. See n. 26, above.

29. Martin Heidegger, *Being and Time*, trans. John Macquarrie and Edward Robinson (New York: Harper & Row, 1962), 252–54, 493. Cf. n. 26, above, for Scheler's response to Heidegger's charge, which was directed particularly at his notion of reality as "resistance."

30. Gerhard Funke, *Zur Transzendentalen Phänomenologie* (Bonn: Bouvier, 1957), *Phenomenology: Metaphysics or Method?*, 41–59 and 31, where he quotes from another relevant work in this connection, Thomas M. Seebohm's *Die Bedingungen der Möglichkeit einer Transzendentalphilosophie* (Bonn: Bouvier, 1962). Also see the collection of relevant essays in Mohanty, *The Possibility of Transcendental Philosophy*.

31. A less hopeless face is put on Scheler's "transcendental inference" of a "person of persons" by Lachterman, xxvi n. 35, in light of Heidegger's comments on a similar issue in Schelling. See M. Heidegger, *Schellings Abhandlung über das Wesen der Menschlichen Freiheit* (1829; Tübingen: Niemeyer, 1971), 196–98. Cf. Francis Dunlop, "Scheler's Idea of Man: Phenomenology vs. Metaphysics in the Late Works," *Aletheia* 2 (1981), 220–34.

32. For a unique and compelling recent defense of moral realism and intuitionism, see Tapio Puolimatka, *Moral Realism and Justification* (Helsinki:

Finnish Academy of Science and Letters, 1989). See my "Critical Study of *Moral Realism and Justification*," in *Philosophia Reformata* (Netherlands) 55, No. 2 (1990), 177–83. Cf. also Sokolowski, who presents his work as resting on the twin supports of Husserl's phenomenology and the ethics of Plato and Aristotle, both of which he regards as underscoring the *public, objective* nature of moral action in contrast to the subjectivizing tendency evident from the Stoics through Abelard, Montaigne, Descartes, and Kant. In a realist strain, evident throughout *Moral Action*, Sokolowski declares: "The description of moral thinking that we have given places the categorialities of reasoning in things, as forms of presentation and identification and differing *of* things." (211; cf. 5). Reiner, *Duty and Inclination*, falls in this class as well.

33. It is an altogether different question whether conclusive justification is possible or even necessary in ethical theory. Both Reiner and Puolimatka deny that it is. Reiner insists that ethics is "not bound to supply conclusive metaphysical proofs of the moral demands it discovers," but only (1) to clarify them as they are given, and (2) to refute attempts to invalidate their claim upon us (*DI*, 108). In *Moral Realism*, Puolimatka argues on behalf of moral realism (1) that the difficulties of conclusively proving moral realism are due to the inherent limitations of theoretical thought; (2) that a commonsense realism is practically an incorrigible and necessary part of ordinary moral experience; and (3) that it is therefore rationally justifiable to accept moral realism even without being able to prove it conclusively.

34. Paul Ricoeur raises this problem in connection with Dufrenne's phenomenological analysis of the a priori in his Preface to Mikel Dufrenne, *Notion of the "A Priori*," xi; cf. xvi.

35. See Quentin Lauer, *Edmund Husserl: 1859–1959* (The Hague: Nijhoff, 1956), "The Subjectivity of Objectivity," 167–74.

36. Cf. n. 11, above.

37. Nor is the problem avoided or solved by means of recourse to the primacy of practical over theoretical reason, as one finds in Funke or Apel. For the relation of this primacy to the correlations in question (subject/object, consciousness/world, order/transcendental ground) and to the original ordering principle have still not been elucidated adequately. See Gerhard Funke, "The Primacy of Practical Reason in Kant and Husserl," in *Kant and Phenomenology*, ed. Thomas M. Seebohm and Joseph J. Kockelmans, Current Continental Research, No. 4 (Washington, DC: Center for Advanced Research in Phenomenology and University Press of America, 1984), 1–29; and Karl-Otto Apel, *Transformation der Philosophie* (Frankfurt a.M.: Suhrkamp, 1973), 2:358ff.

38. Many contemporary analytic philosophers have largely abandoned the conventional distinctions and correlations between a priori/a posteriori, analytic/synthetic, and necessity/contingency as hopelessly ambiguous and unsalvageable. This is the view of Willard V. Quine, for example, in "Two Dogmas of Empiricism," (43; 63 in Moser's reprint in *A Priori Knowledge*). Alvin Plantinga, *The Nature of Necessity* (Oxford: Clarendon Press, 1974), 3–9, offers a nice summary of the state of the problem as well as a detailed defense of a traditional notion of logical necessity against Quine. Cf. Gregory W. Fitch, "Plantinga's Necessary A Posteriori Truths," *Canadian Journal of Philosophy* 8, No. 2 (June 1978), 323–27.

39. Merleau-Ponty points to this as an unthought element in Husserl's work that "opens out on something else," in *Signs*, trans. Richard C. McCleary (Evanston, IL: Northwestern University Press, 1964), 160. He makes a similar point regarding the fundamental chiasm underlying the relationship between consciousness and the body, in *The Visible and the Invisible*, trans. Alphonso Lingis (Evanston, IL: Northwestern University Press, 1968), 259. On Merleau-Ponty, see also John Sallis, *Phenomenology and the Return to Beginnings* (Pittsburgh: Duquesne University Press, 1973), ch. 6, "The Fundamental Chiasm."

40. Mikel Dufrenne, *Notion of the "A Priori*," 202, 219ff. Cf. H. Dooyeweerd, who distinguishes a *"structural a priori"* from a *"subjective a priori*," describing the former as "an *a priori* complex in the *cosmological* sense of the *structural horizon of human experience*" that has "the character of *law*" for both subjective and objective experience. The latter, on the other hand, he calls an *a priori* complex in the sense of a *"merely subjective a priori insight into that horizon."* Hence, "Only the subjective *a priori* can be *true* or *false* in an epistemological sense. . . . In other words, the subjective *a priori* always remains determined and delimited by the *a priori structure* of all human experience" (*A New Critique of Theoretical Thought*, 2:548).

41. See n. 38, above.

42. See n. 15 above.

43. The expression "orders of experience" as used here and in the following discussion can refer both to (subjective) structures of the person and to (objective) realms of activities in which the person is involved. This duality of reference is intentional. Even when limiting my attention to the logical/emotional distinction, I do not wish to restrict my reference to the (subjective) structure of the person, but to allow for reference to the (objective) realms of activity in which the person is involved as well. Logic and emotion are certainly constitutive features of human subjectivity; but they are also subjects (or realms of reality) in their own right in which people are actively involved.

44. Cf. previous note. Scheler's use of "emotional" and "feeling" here is ambiguous, since it can refer both to the (subjective) faculty by which the a priori is apprehended in intuition and to the (objective) realm of psychology, as opposed to, say, logic, biology, economics, or religion. This ambiguity suggests that the human subject has only one other (subjective) constitutive structure besides the logical, namely the emotional; and that these two structures together define human involvement in every conceivable (objective) realm of activity, not only in logic and psychology, but in art, religion, sociology, law, linguistics, politics, etc. This account strikes me as inadequate. It explains neither why the logical a priori cannot be apprehended by means of the faculty of emotional feeling, nor why there are not as many modes of apprehending the a priori as there are distinct realms of human involvement. See n. 46, below.

45. It does not diminish the ambiguities and shortcomings of his conception of the "emotional a priori" referred to in the previous note. Cf. below, ch. 4, n. 24.

46. I offer a more detailed analysis of this problem in my article "Moral and Nonmoral Values: A Problem in Scheler's Ethics," *Philosophy and Phenomenological Research* 48, No. 1 (Sept. 1987), 139–43, where I argue against the implicit claim in Scheler's theory that the realization of any nonmoral value always produces only a *moral* value. This is the sort of reductionism to which

Scheler himself is opposed in principle. It would require every appearance of "good" (whether "aesthetic good," "economic good," "social good," etc.) to be regarded as a species of "moral good," a view which I regard not only as simplistic, but as simply mistaken. It is ironic that Scheler, at this point, contradicts directly his own argument on behalf of the relative autonomy of principles belonging to distinct orders, such as the "logical," the "emotional," and the like.

47. Van De Pitte says, for example, that "phenomenology in general, and the nature of phenomenological propositions in particular, have long been misrepresented to English-speaking readers by Moritz Schlick's stylistically lucid, forceful, and much anthologized article entitled 'Is There a Factual A Priori?' " ("Schlick's Critique of Phenomenological Propositions," 195). An attempt to clear up some basic misunderstandings is also made in Van De Pitte's article, "Comments on a Claim that Some Phenomenological Statements May Be A Posteriori," *Metaphilosophy* 15, Nos. 3–4 (July–Oct. 1984), 248–55.

48. The following two paragraphs draw from material in my article, "The A Priori in Phenomenology and the Legacy of Logical Empiricism." Cf. Sinha, "Phenomenology, vis-à-vis Kant and Neopositivism, on the Issue of the Apriori"; and Robert C. Solomon's excellent article, "Sense and Essence: Frege and Husserl," in his *Phenomenology and Existentialism* (Lanham, MD: University Press of America, 1980), 258–82, originally printed in the *International Philosophical Quarterly* 10, No. 3 (1970).

Moral Good and the Nature of Values 3

THE KANTIAN SYSTEM OF ETHICS has been classified traditionally as "deontological," as one concerned chiefly with the definition of duty, not with a theory of ends or values—indeed, as one whose theory of obligation is not even made to depend upon a theory of value. Scheler's ethics, by contrast, is overtly axiological and has been called "*a priori* teleological intuitionism" (Shimomissé, *Phänomenologie*, 129, cf. 22 n. 47; cf Frankena, *Ethics*, 14). In this chapter we will be looking at the reasons for these differences, as well as calling some of them into question. First, we will examine briefly the Kantian rationale for opposing a teleological ethics of empirical ends. Then we shall analyze Scheler's reasons for rejecting Kant's deontological ethics as an "empty formalism" incapable of offering direction. Following this, we will enter into a critical appraisal of the presuppositional differences between the two perspectives. This will involve an examination of the "material" and "teleological" elements present also within Kantian ethics, as well as an extended assessment of the ontological questions underlying Scheler's phenomenology of values and surrounding the Heideggerian repudiation of all theories of value.

Formalism in Kant's Ethics

WHILE IT MAY BE TRUE, as Hans Reiner points out, that Kant made use—even frequent use—of the term "value," and that his ethics may even presuppose some sort of implicit notion of moral value,[1] it is nevertheless certain that Kant did not consider "value" to be among the fundamental concepts of his ethics. He offered no definition of it. He devoted no effort to analyzing it. More importantly, he remained unequivocally opposed to any theory presuming to ground ethics teleologically in the anticipated realization of ends; and Scheler's theory, whatever else it may be, falls within that class, even though Kant nowhere appears to have entertained the possibility of a teleological ethics of *values* such as we find in *Formalismus*. More particularly, Kant rejected the attempt to found ethics upon the anticipated realization of *empirical ends*. He spurned the notion that anything as arbitrary and circumstantial as empirical ends, no matter how well-intended, could secure the rigorous demands of morality. He insisted that moral demands are binding—not only necessarily and universally, but unconditionally. They are expressed in categorical, not hypothetical, imperatives. They must therefore be based on rationally necessary formal principles, not contingent material rules. They find their source, neither in natural inclinations nor in divine commands, but exclusively in the self-legislation of reason.

A central part of Kant's philosophical struggle involved carving out a legitimate sphere of jurisdiction and competence for ethics within the increasingly mechanistic worldview of his time, as we have seen.[2] The mathematical physics of his day and the deterministic view of nature it countenanced appear to leave no room for free moral agency. This helps to explain his distinction between phenomena and noumena, and why he sequestered the practical principles of morality within the *sanctum sanctorum* of the rationally free *homo noumenon*, thus endeavoring to safeguard them from the contaminating wiles of the pathologically determined *homo phaenomenon*. Furthermore, the empiricist theory of the will, which he himself appropriated uncritically, led Kant to conclude that any attempt to determine the morality of willing by reference to the empirical contents or objects of the will must inevitably result in a consequentialist ethics of contingent results and ends, as we have also seen.[3] These features, both of his contemporary cultural ethos and of his own thinking, help us to understand the motives behind Kant's ethical apriorism and formalism. Let us review his theory briefly.

Nothing captures with such lucid brevity the essence of Kant's ethics as the famous passage where he says: "Nothing in the world—indeed nothing even beyond the world—can possibly be conceived which could be called good without qualification except a *good will*" (*GMS*, 393f.). What is a good will? Simply one that is *rational*. In fact, will is by definition "rational," for Kant. This is what distinguishes it from inclination. Morality, for Kant, is practical rationality. That is why the task of the second *Critique* is to answer the question: How can pure reason be practical? (*KpV*, 3, 15). A perfectly rational being such as God, which had no sense complement to its nature, would be perfectly good without having the *constraint* of obligation experienced by human beings. Its will would be simply "holy."[4] But for creatures of sense as well as reason, such as mortal human beings, a "good" will is one that is constrained to act for the sake of *duty* independently of any desire or inclination. Not that all inclinations are bad. In fact, our inclinations may sometimes *coincide* with our duties, as when it is in our self-interest to do our duties.[5] But it is not yet enough for an action to *conform* to duty. That is "legality," but not yet "morality" (*KpV*, 71f.), for one may have ulterior motives. Therefore one must shun the "secret impulse of self-love, falsely appearing as the idea of duty," and do one's duty for its own sake, for the moral worth of an action resides in its having been done from duty alone (*GMS*, 407, 399).

But what is "duty?" What is it about an action done from duty that gives it moral worth? Such an action, according to Kant, does not get its moral worth from any *purpose*, *object*, or hoped-for *effect* to be realized through it, but from a principle of will that disregards all such ends (*GMS*, 399f.). For morality cannot find support in principles catering to desires as the basis for willing, not only because such principles are invariably empirical, but because the objects of desire they presuppose belong to the principle of self-love or seeking one's own happiness (*KpV*, Theorems I and II). This does not mean that we may not morally seek to realize our own ends of personal happiness, or even that securing our own happiness may not be (at least indirectly) a duty.[6] But while we may be free to pursue our own ends and even to satisfy our desires for pleasure, this is morally permissible only when we have made certain that the means we have chosen to these ends are consistent with our character as rational agents. This aspect of Kant's thought has sometimes been misunderstood.[7] The inclination to seek our own happiness, although it is purely natural and may even coincide with morality, does not define the nature of morality or furnish the basis of moral obligation. Indeed, such a basis cannot be found in anything in either "heaven or earth" (*GMS*, 425, 389, 415). For morality is concerned, in principle, with "actions of which perhaps the world has never had an example, with actions whose feasibility might be seriously doubted by those who base everything on experience, and yet with actions inexorably commanded by reason (*GMS*, 408). Moral duty, in other words, is the necessity of an action obliged by respect for moral law (*GMS*, 400).

But what kind of a "law" can it be that determines the will without reference to expected results? Initially, Kant's descriptions strike one as horribly stark: he refers to the *universal* conformity of one's actions to *law as such* (*GMS*, 401f.). What can this mean? It means, he says, that one can think of one's moral principles as universal *laws* only by considering them as principles that determine the will because of their *form* and not because of their *matter* (content) (*KpV*, Theorem III). In other words, Kant is saying that the law governing moral behavior must be the formal principle of *universalizability*. In order to be moral, one's principles must be universalizable. They must present an action "as of itself objectively necessary, without regard to any other *end*" (*GMS*, 414). Only in this way are principles, so far as they constrain the will, truly *commands of reason*; and the formula of such commands is nothing but the *categorical imperative*, the fundamental law of pure practical reason (*GMS*, 413f.; *KpV*, 30).

To seek the law for moral willing anywhere else than in these principles of reason's own self-legislation, to seek it, for example, in the objects of willing or their properties, can only result in "heteronomy"—the determination of the will by something foreign to reason.[8] This is the case whether the principles involved are *empirical*, as in hedonism (Epicurus) and in the ethics of moral feelings (Hutcheson); or whether they are *rational*, as in the ethics of metaphysical perfection (Wolff) or of divine command (Crucius) (*KpV*, 40; *GMS*, 441ff.). In either case, the will is not rationally self-determining but determined by an alien incentive in the foreseen result of the action. Instead of telling myself "I ought to do my duty," I tell myself: "I ought to do something because I desire something else." I presuppose, in effect, "still another law" besides the moral law—a law commensurate to my natural inclinations and their contingent ends, and so unfit to be an apodictical rule for moral action (*GMS*, 444). Hence, "the *autonomy* of the will is the sole principle of all moral laws," and *heteronomy* stands opposed to it as a principle inimical to morality (*KpV*, Theorem IV).

The only proper objects of practical reason, then, are good and evil. However, since the good is an object of desire, it cannot be defined *prior* to the moral law or serve as its foundation. For then it could only be the concept of something that promises pleasure, and it would be solely a matter of experience to discern what is good or evil (*KpV*, 58, 62f.). But this cannot be right. "The good" (*das Gute*) must be carefully distinguished from "well-being" or "weal" (*das Wohl*), which is only a relative matter of natural contentment (*KpV*, 59f.). For, as Kant says, it is "a very different thing to make a man happy from making him good" (*GMS*, 442). "The good," therefore, must be always defined by reference to the moral law or law of reason (*KpV*, 60).

Hence, a rational system of ethics, on the Kantian view, must be grounded in the unconditional, a priori self-legislation of pure practical reason. All ethics that seek a foundation in the material content of moral experience—in the material objects of the will or the relation of the will to its anticipated ends or purposes—are conditional, a posteriori, and heteronomous. They fall short of the unconditional necessity required by Kant, and for this reason he rejects them.

Scheler's Critique of Kantian Formalism

SCHELER BEGINS HIS EVALUATION of this Kantian position by conceding Kant's major thesis: all ethics based on the anticipated realization of particular "goods" (*Güter*), "ends" or "purposes" (*Zwecke*),[9] must be rejected as insufficient (*F*, 32/9). Kant is simply correct on this point. When he rejects "goods" as incapable of furnishing a legitimate basis for moral obligation, he is merely pointing out the absurdity of trying to make moral good and evil dependent on a relationship to a realm of contingent, empirical *things*. "Goods," after all, are nothing but such contingent, empirical entities—"things of value" (*Wertdinge*).[10] A morality defined by reference to such "things" not only would be captive to our particular whims, desires, and empirical capacities for discernment; it also would have no more than an empirical, inductive validity. The same holds for "ends" or "purposes." To seek to define moral obligation in terms of them is to relativize moral value and to subordinate it to the contingent, empirical instances of the particular "ends" or "purposes" in question. And Scheler, along with Kant, rejects this as morally inadequate.

Where Scheler parts company with Kant is in the conclusion he draws from this insight. Whereas Kant opted for ethical formalism as the only secure refuge from a sea of whim and chance, Scheler holds out for a material teleological ethics—an ethics based, not on arbitrary or contingent empirical ends, but on a priori values or value-essences. Only such an ethics, he believes, can offer actual material guidance. Kant supposed that he had demonstrated far *more* than he actually had, according to Scheler. He supposed he had shown that a well-founded ethics may not have *any* material objects of the will or desire as its basis. This would exclude, in effect, not only *goods* and *purposes* but also material *values* (*F*, 34/11). Of course, Kant made no effort to distinguish anything like material "values" from material "goods" or "ends." He simply excluded all "material objects of the faculty of desire [and will]" *simpliciter* (*KpV*, Theorem I), assuming indiscriminately that *no* kind of *experience* could yield material contents capable of providing a proper basis for ethics.

This, however, is precisely the point that Scheler contests. For the categorical exclusion demanded by Kant would preclude the possibility proposed by Scheler. But Kant's exclusion would be justified only if there were no such things as "values" distinct from goods and purposes. Specifically, it would be justified only if (1) "values" were merely abstractions from empirical goods or their sensible effects, instead of being autonomous intuitive phenomena;[11] and if (2) "values" existed only in relation to a will, which posited them in its empirical purposes, instead of being given to pre-purposive desires, drives, and impulses independently of conscious willing.[12] Scheler denies both conditions and argues that "values" are autonomous phenomena, independent of both goods and purposes, and capable of undergirding a rigorous objectivistic ethics.

The significance of Scheler's theory of the material a priori, discussed in chapter 2, now becomes clear. Once we grant his theory of the material a priori, and once we grant that values are material a priori essences, Scheler can argue that his ethics is based on material values that are not only independent of contingent goods and ends, but provide a rigorous a priori foundation without recourse to Kantian formalism. In the first place, he seeks to establish that value-essences are independent of empirical *goods*. Before he can go on to discuss the relation between values and purposes (or ends), however, he must clarify the relation between values and the will, which posits them. He therefore seeks to clarify, in the second place, what he considers the proper relation (confused by Kant) between *willing* and moral values, arguing (as we shall see) that moral values are brought into being by the will through the realization of nonmoral values. Finally, he argues that nonmoral values are intrinsically independent of *purposes*. To this effect, he offers a phenomenological analysis of the relations between values and (1) goods, (2) willing, and (3) purposes.

VALUES AND GOODS

Values, for Scheler, are a priori "qualities,"[13] which exist as essences independently of their instantiation in empirical bearers. He supports this view by drawing an intuitively suggestive comparison between values and colors. We talk easily about "red" as a pure color of the spectrum, he says, without experiencing the need to conceive of it as covering a surface or even as extended in space. In the same way, we may talk about such values as the "agreeable," "charming," "lovely," "friendly," "distinguished," "noble," and the like, without having to represent them as properties belonging to any person or thing. Like colors, values may be found attached to certain empirical objects which possess them and are made more or less valuable by them; but they are essentially qualities that exist independently of such carriers (F, 35/12).

In no case, says Scheler, are values the mere product of inductive generalization or abstraction from properties of empirical "bearers." Such properties are empirical and mutable. But values are original, irreducible essences. Just as it would be senseless to ask for the common properties of all blue or red things, since they have nothing in common except their blueness or redness, so it would be senseless, says Scheler, to ask for the common properties of good or evil deeds, dispositions, men, and so on (F, 37/15). Nor are values derived from whatever effects empirical goods may have on us, such as on our feelings or desires. This view depends on the Lockean hypothesis of a pure "occult quality," an indeterminate "X," the entire significance of which is given only through the "effect." However, such a hypothesis is not only inadequate from the point of view of furnishing a foundation for ethics, which, as Kant saw, requires more than a contingent inductive basis in empirical experience. It also conflicts, Scheler insists, with the phenomenological evidence that values are "clearly and directly given, not indirectly inferred" (F, 39/16).

Again, Scheler makes his point more by means of intuitive suggestion than by closely reasoned argument. We are acquainted, he suggests, with cases in which the value of a thing is presented to us clearly *apart from* the *bearer* of the value. For example, a person (or a work of art, or a room) may strike us as unpleasant and repugnant, or pleasant and agreeable, without our being able to show just *why* this is the case (*F*, 40/17). We may not know in the least what properties prompt this reaction. It is as if the "axiological nuance" of an object preceded its bearer as the first "messenger" of its particular nature. Such examples suggest, for Scheler, that values are independent of their bearers. We do not extract beauty from beautiful things. Rather, beauty is prior to them; and its realization in them as a real presence in them confers upon them the value of being beautiful. Furthermore, says Scheler, the meaning of value-qualities themselves does not fluctuate with the changes that occur in things: the value of friendship itself *as a value* is not tarnished if a friend turns against me and betrays me, any more than the color green *as a color* turns red when a tomato ripens (*F*, 41/18f.).

Although values are phenomenologically distinguishable from their bearers, they are not usually given as distinct in everyday experience, Scheler admits. They are usually given as realized in "goods." In this sense, values are values of things, or "thing-values" (*Dingwerten*), just as goods are "value-things" (*Wertdingen*). But "goods" must not, on that account, be reduced to "things" with superimposed values. On this score, Scheler's account differs from Husserl's. For Husserl, values are "founded" as "characters" or "predicates" to an already given object of perception in the logical sense of "object," or a noematic "nucleus" or "core."[14] Scheler, by contrast, regards values as *primordial phenomena* (*F*, 266f./252). "Goods" are essentially "permeated" by values and irreducible to mere "things," just as values, even when realized in goods, are irreducible to "goods."

Scheler therefore applauds Kant for rejecting all attempts to found ethics upon contingent *goods*—but he criticizes him for assuming that an adequate foundation could be secured by restricting oneself to the *formal* relations between the will and its objects. The problem here, according to Scheler, is that Kant failed to examine sufficiently, not only the whole realm of material values independent of goods, but also the relation between the values and *willing*.

VALUES AND WILLING

While Kant never occupied himself explicitly with the concept of "value" in Scheler's specific sense, he nevertheless did make frequent use of the term "value," as Reiner notes, and it even may have played a more basic role in his ethics than we are accustomed to believing, as Reiner claims (*DI*, 25f.). After all, Kant did describe the moral good as "absolutely good" and speak of its possessing an "inner unconditioned *value*" (*GMS*, 394). In some sense, then, we might say that Kant maintained a conception of *moral value*. In any case, where Kant went wrong, according to Scheler, was in the way he envisioned the relation between such "moral value" (the value of moral "good") and the *will*. First, Kant held that the moral value of willing is determined *only* by its conformity to law, not in any respect by the material contents or objects of willing. Second, he held that moral value attaches *only* to acts of willing.

In order to understand Scheler's critique at this point, it is important to recognize that his ethics rests on a critical distinction between *moral* and *nonmoral* values. Moral values (moral good and evil) are defined in terms of the nonmoral value that is brought into being, as in teleological theories generally (Frankena, *Ethics*, 14). According to Scheler, nonmoral values exhibit phenomenologically an order of rank based on their relative duration, simplicity, and other such criteria, and range from such values as sensible pleasure and pain (at the lower end of the scale) to cultural, aesthetic, and religious values (at the upper end). Such values not only are intentional objects, or essences, which are distinguishable apart from their possible empirical instantiation in mundane reality, but also belong to an objective hierarchy. As such, they furnish a clear basis, in Scheler's view, for establishing the moral values of good and evil; for good and evil can be defined then in terms of the relative rank of these other, nonmoral values, which are brought into being.

In other words, moral values are generated according to Scheler through *acts of willing and realizing nonmoral values*. To see what this means will take a bit of analysis, but for the moment, let me describe the matter simply as Scheler does. The value "moral good" is said to appear through the willing of those nonmoral values that are "higher" as opposed to "lower," and "positive" as opposed to "negative." For instance, when parents make material sacrifices for the education of their children, they place their children's education *before* their own physical comforts, thereby exhibiting a preference for the "intellectual" value of education over the "physical" value of their own material comfort. For Scheler, in this case, the moral value "good" appears in the act of willing the higher, positive "intellectual" value of education. Furthermore, such moral values are realized or brought into being, in Scheler's view, specifically through *willing*.[15]

In order to avert some possible confusion at this point, it may be helpful to note that the notion of "realizing" a value involves two crucially different possible meanings, corresponding to infamous ambiguities of the word "intention." In the first place, "realizing" a value may mean willing the existence of a bearer of a nonmoral value as the intended object of willing. In the second place, it may mean actually bringing about the existence of a bearer of some value whether moral or nonmoral. Scheler's position is that whenever the first occurs, moral value is actually brought into existence, regardless of whether it succeeds in bringing about the existence of the intended nonmoral value. Hence, the moral value of an act depends on the material value-content it seeks to realize, not (as Kant correctly denied) on its success in achieving the good it intends. This means that right actions always *do* in fact "realize" moral value as a byproduct of *attempting* to realize nonmoral value, whether or not they actually succeed in bringing a bearer of value into existence.[16]

Kant did not err, according to Scheler, in denying that moral value-content of the "good" *itself* can be a material object of the will to be realized. Scheler concurs on that point, though for a different reason. For Kant the reason is that the "good" can be determined only *formally*, whereas for Scheler it is that it can be determined only through nonmoral *material values*. The content of moral "good" appears only through the willing of a "positive" (as opposed to "negative") or "higher" (as opposed to "lower") nonmoral value. Thus Scheler says the moral value never appears directly as the *content* or *object* of the act of willing, but only, so to speak, "on the back" (*auf dem Rücken*) of this act (*F*, 49/27).

How, then, did Kant go wrong, according to Scheler? In the first place, he went wrong by writing off all material objects or contents of the will—specifically, *nonmoral values*. By denying material objects of the will *any* role in determining the morality of an act, Kant not only ruled out all empirical objects of desire (which, as he correctly saw, cannot provide a basis for morals), he also ruled out nonmoral values (which, in Scheler's view, furnish the only serviceable foundation for ethics). In other words, his error consists in having divested the moral "good" of all determinate content, in having excluded the possibility that it could be invested with content teleologically, by its relation to material nonmoral values and their possible realization (in the sense described above) through willing. By replacing this value-relatedness of moral willing with mere *conformity to law*, Kant ruled out the only factor that can possibly give *content* to such "lawfulness." Thus Scheler complains that, for Kant, it is a matter of complete moral indifference whether we seek to realize the "noble" or the "vulgar," the "useful" or the "harmful," as such; for the meaning of the words "good" and "evil" is wholly exhausted in *lawful* or *unlawful form* (*F*. 47/24f.).

In the second place, Kant went wrong by linking moral value originally and exclusively to acts of *willing*. This is far too one-sided a view, for Scheler. First, bearers of moral value include not only acts of willing but habits, characters, dispositions, and persons, as well as many kinds of acts that Scheler distinguishes from willing, such as forgiving, commanding, obeying, promising, and so on. Second, Kant's view, which assumes that willing involves a causal relation between objects and our affective responses, leads to his so-called "paradox of method"—namely, that good and evil cannot be defined *prior* to the moral law but only *after* and *by means of* it (*KpV*, 62f.). But if the bearers of moral value include not only acts of ("lawful" or "unlawful") *willing*, but, more fundamentally, *persons* and their *dispositions*, then moral value *precedes* all ideas of duty and lawful willing as conditions of its possibility. Hence, it cannot be true, as Kant at times seems to suggest, that the function of willing is what determines the moral worth or virtue of a person.[17]

On the contrary, there is a sense in which the opposite is true. In this sense, moral values do not originate in acts of willing, but derive from persons themselves and their characters, dispositions and virtues, in which they reside more fundamentally.[18]

VALUES AND PURPOSES

But if Scheler rejects Kant's exclusive attachment of moral value to willing, he also refuses to let nonmoral values be disqualified as a basis for ethics. He does this by refusing to let nonmoral values be identified with a teleological ethics of contingent *purposes*. For Scheler, "purposes" or "ends" (*Zwecke*) are *representations* of something to be realized through willing. They involve ideal or intuitional *images*; whereas, by contrast, values do not (F, 52/30f.). Purposes exist only in relation to a *will* that posits them. By contrast, nonmoral values are given in experience long before they are articulated or posited by the will in determinate purposes. Specifically, they are given in the pre-purposive phases of desire or "conation" (*Streben*)[19] and their *goals*. Conations, such as the drives for satisfying hunger and thirst, are not specified initially by *purposes* in a representational act, but by *goals* immanent in the non-representational conative tendencies themselves. A purpose is posited by the will as something to be realized; a goal is given in the tendencies of one's experience before one ever thinks of purposing or willing anything. Scheler is emphatic: "Nothing can become a purpose that was not first a goal! The purpose is grounded in the goal! Goals can be given *without* purposes, but no purposes can be given without previous goals. We are not able to create a purpose out of nothing, or to 'posit' a purpose without a prior 'conation toward something'" (F, 61/40). Accordingly, nonmoral values are neither dependent upon purposes nor abstracted from them, but are the foundation of goals of conation, and are hence the foundation of purposes, which are themselves founded in goals.[20]

Everything that falls under the category of what Scheler calls "conation" and so precedes "willing proper," Kant calls "inclination" and regards as *morally indifferent*. Just as he identifies the contents of intuition with a "chaos" of sensations into which the formative activity of law-giving *reason* first introduces order and intelligibility, so he identifies the contents of moral experience with a "chaos" of inclinations, drives, and impulses, into which the *will*, as practical reason, brings its own lawful order—an order to which, he seems to believe, the idea of "good" can be reduced (F, 63/41f.). But, while morally imputable "good" appears only through acts of willing—when, for example, "higher" nonmoral values are chosen rather than "low" ones from among those given in conations—the relative "height" of values that makes their choice "good" does not originate in their relation to *willing*. Rather, it is already evident in conative tendencies prior to explicit acts of purposive willing. Hence, while an ethics of material values must provide an a priori basis for determining the morality of purposes posited by the will, the nonmoral values that serve as that basis are given independently of such purposes.

The Question of "Empty Formalism" and the Concept of Material Ends in Kantian Ethics

AMONG THE VARIOUS RESPONSES to the charge of "empty formalism" leveled against Kant by Scheler and others, none have seemed more compelling, *prima facie*, than those pointing out the existence of "material" or "teleological" elements in Kant's ethics. Questions concerning these elements have been the subject of analysis and reflection for some time in Germany, where the "formalist" interpretation of Kant has been long disputed.[21] But they have come to the attention of most students in the English-speaking world only well after World War II, due partly to a considerable lag in the translation of such key works as *The Metaphysic of Morals*.[22] For example, H. J. Paton has pointed out that Kant's ethics is based on "a teleological view of man and the universe"; that Kant's argument is *not* based on "purely logical, as opposed to teleological, consistency," or on "the mere form of morality (or mere form of law) without any regard to its matter, that is, to the ends of moral action"; and that, for Kant, "the material maxim, which may embody both consequences aimed at and motives for arriving at them, is present *at the same time* as the formal maxim."[23]

Could Scheler have overlooked or misunderstood these elements in Kant's ethics? Lewis White Beck evidently thought so when he wrote that Scheler's criticism "misses the main point of Kant's distinction between the object of the will, which is always present, and the object of the will as its determining ground, which is present only to empirical practical reason" (*Commentary*, 118, n. 16). Likewise, Karl Alphéus evidently thought so when he insisted, against Scheler, that Kant's ethics is not a "blind ethics of duty" but a "rational ethics of insight" whose motive is "unconditional rational desire" (60ff.). It is quite possible that Scheler may have overlooked, misunderstood or misconstrued this teleological aspect of Kant's ethics. But even if so, this would not necessarily disprove, or even diminish the force of, his critique of Kant at this point. For the most important question at this point is not whether Scheler, in his accusations of "formalism," overlooked or misunderstood an aspect of Kant's ethics that deals with material ends, but whether that aspect of Kant's ethics actually preserves it from the kind of "empty formalism" of which Scheler accuses it.

What role do "material ends" play in this "teleological" aspect of Kant's ethics? Do they alter the basic significance of his formalism? What did Kant mean, after all, by insisting that a moral action must be determined as objectively necessary in itself *without regard to its end*; that a moral principle must determine the will by its form alone *without regard to its matter*; and that the will must seek its law in nothing outside the conformity of its maxims to universal law? What do such formal declarations mean in light of the material, teleological aspect of Kant's ethics? Let us look and see.

Every act, every volition, according to Kant, clearly must have some sort of object, material, or end (*MS*, 385; *KpV*, 34). Indeed, the "power to set an end," he says, is what distinguishes humanity from animality (*MS*, 391). Even actions conforming to moral laws must have an end, for if they did not, all ends would be only means to other ends, and a *categorical* imperative would be impossible (*MS*, 385). Objectively, the ground of practical legislation lies in the rule and form of universality; subjectively, it lies in the *end* (*GMS*, 432). But ends themselves may be subjective or objective. A subjective end is set by inclinations, rests on incentives, and is produced as an effect, which, in turn, serves merely as a means to some other end. An objective end is given by reason and is conceived, not as an effect to be produced, but as an independent (*selbständige*) end, and serves the will as the "objective ground of its self-determination"; Kant calls it an end of "absolute worth," an "end in itself" (*GMS*, 427f., 437). Principles that disregard all subjective ends are "formal"; those that are based on subjective ends are "material."

But as Ping-cheung Lo observes, this means that "for Kant *formal* is not equivalent to *empty*. A formal moral law is only empty of subjective ends, but not of an objective end. The idea of formal by no means excludes any content at all" (187). In other words, a "formal" principle is in another sense also "material"; its "matter" consists in its objective end. This is why Kant also says that such an end would be the *"material"* (content, or object) of every good will, and calls it a *material* determining ground of choice (*GMS*, 437; *MS*, 381). It is why Kant calls ethics a system of *ends* of practical reason (*MS*, 380).

If material ends occupy such a place of honor in Kant's ethics, then perhaps his ethics *must* be called "teleological" in some sense. But it cannot be so in the conventional sense of an ethics whose criterion of morality is "the nonmoral value that is brought into being" (Frankena, *Ethics*, 14). For the end Kant has in mind is not something to be "effected" or produced, but something already existing; not something whose possible realization incites desire, but whose actual nobility moves one to respect. As such, it is not an end that diminishes the unconditional and categorical force of the moral law. Kant's ethics is in this sense both "teleological" and "nonconsequentialist."

But what can serve as the *content* of such a material end? Kant answers: *humanity*. And why? Because only humanity exists as an end in itself; and nothing but the dignity of human nature, without any end or advantage to be gained by it (and thus, respect for a mere idea), serves as an inflexible precept of the will (*GMS*, 428, 439). And what gives human nature this dignity? Nothing but the capacity of rational self-legislation by which human beings are fitted for membership in a possible kingdom of ends: autonomy is thus the basis of the dignity of human nature (*GMS*, 436). And what is the basis of autonomy? Nothing but *practical rationality*. For it is only through the conformity of one's maxims to the universal legislation of practical reason that one is subjected purely to one's own self-legislation as a free, rational will.

Hence, no matter where one starts in Kant's ethics, one eventually arrives at this fact: the only ultimate control over the content of the moral "good" lies in the notion of practical "rationality." But, practically speaking, *what is "rational"*? From a Schelerian point of view, the Kantian answer to this question must always appear somewhat anemic. For no matter how fully developed the Kantian notion of rational agency may be (even with its teleology of material ends), it is prevented by its inveterate ethical formalism from delivering on its promise at that one point, which, for Scheler, is the one that finally matters: *content*. It is not a question of Kant's lacking a rich understanding and analysis of moral experience. It is a question of how that understanding and analysis is grounded. Neither in his analysis of willing nor in his analysis of ends does Kant provide, when all is said and done, more than what must for Scheler seem to be a very thin answer: recourse to the categorial form of rational universalizability. What is practically "rational" is what is universalizable rationally and what is found necessarily and universally in human beings considered as rational ends. And when it comes to explaining the unconditional necessity of willing whatever is practically "rational" in this empirically indeterminate sense, Kant can only concede that this is something that human reason is wholly incompetent to explain, something that constitutes "the supreme limit of all moral inquiry" and the "limit of human reason."[24]

Without question, this would seem a bit unfair to Kant. Kant's notion of practical rationality is a highly developed one. Its relationship to speculative reason, its role in the metaphysics of morals, and its dissimilarity as well as its connection to logic and science, are programmatically articulated in the relevant parts of his ethical works.[25] His notion is also an affectively highly nuanced one. In his *Doctrine of Virtue*, particularly, Kant offers a richly developed tapestry of descriptions and illustrations giving life and color to his notion of what practical reason morally demands. The impression created there is amplified by his elegant discussion of moral feeling in his discussion of the "The Incentives of Pure Practical Reason" in his second *Critique* (Pt. 1, ch. 3), which Heidegger calls "the most brilliant phenomenological analysis of the phenomenon of morality that we have from him" (*Basic Problems*, 133). And nowhere does this "phenomenological analysis" more powerfully invoke the majestic pathos of respect and awe for the dignity associated with practical rationality, than in the famous eulogy of duty: "Duty! Thou sublime and mighty name . . . What origin is there worthy of thee?" It is nothing less than "personality" itself, he says, that "elevates man above himself as part of the world of sense," giving him "freedom and independence from the mechanism of nature"; this alone allows him, as a person belonging to the world of sense, to be "subject to his own personality so far as he belongs to the intelligible world" (*KpV*, 86f.).[26]

Whether Scheler understood sufficiently Kant's notion of practical rationality or appreciated fully this rich, "material," "teleological" aspect of Kantian ethics is debatable. But even if he did not, his question about the moral content of Kant's ethics cannot be simply ignored, for it may not be so easily parried as may first appear. Kant's notion of practical rationality may be well-developed; he may have significant things to say about the objective, material *ends* of moral willing and about a rational, self-legislating "kingdom of ends"; there may even be broad agreement that his formulations of the categorical imperative provide effective rules for concrete decision-making. But from Scheler's perspective, a basic problem has still been overlooked. For Kant nowhere furnishes a *material* definition of practical rationality. He never spells out the *material values* presupposed by his notion of practical rationality in the way that would be needed, according to Scheler, to give demonstrable substance to his notion of moral ends and moral law. What can this mean?

Such a demand, of course, would have struck Kant as unintelligible. How could something like practical reason be defined *materially?* How could one speak of a "material content" here? The idea would have seemed as far fetched as trying to state beforehand what a rational person would do in every conceivable circumstance. Even access to Scheler's objective order of material values would seem to be of little help here.[27] On the other hand, Kant may indeed have tacitly *presupposed* some material notion of value, as we have already suggested,[28] or held some fairly specific personal assumptions about what kinds of material performances are actually moral. But he very likely would have regarded any effort to specify such assumptions as irrelevant to the task of grounding morality, and possibly even as dangerous. It would be dangerous if personal proclivities of this sort were ever thought to play a necessary role in determining the essence of morality. For in his view morality is something that must be determined as "objectively necessary in itself," and can be determined thus only by bracketing and setting aside, and in that sense *disregarding*, the question of any specific material ends (or objects) of the faculty of desire.[29]

Scheler, in turn, would find this an impossible proposition, since he would see such a procedure as requiring the disregarding of *all contents* of willing, *including material values*. Accordingly, he would see this as involving two hopeless ironies: (1) the irony of demanding the removal of the only available means, in his view, by which to determine the morality of an act; and (2) the irony of overlooking the moral insight presupposed by Kant's own notion of moral law.

In the first place, in Scheler's view, the morality of an action cannot be determined apart from a consideration of the relative ranks of the material values it is intended to realize. Hence, he would see Kant's procedure as leading to the ironic impasse of requiring that we try to determine what is morally right while excluding from consideration the only possible means of doing so. This is neither to say that it is yet clear how a consideration of material values will necessarily offer moral guidance, nor to say whether Scheler's own theory is ultimately any more successful in doing so than Kant's (a question addressed specificaly in chapter 5 below). The intuition of a hierarchy of material value-essences in itself is hardly a guarantee of moral insight. Still, it may be difficult to arrive at any certainty regarding the morality of specific deeds in actual situations without moving beyond Kant's formal conception of rational agency. Kant may have offered, like the Bible's Golden Rule, a perfectly decent and irreproachable formula for determining the morality of an act in general.[30] But unlike the Biblical formula, which is set forth within a "mythic" context of specific divine imperatives and Mosaic case laws, Kant's formula overtly eschews any material grounding whatsoever. At most, his "moral law" commands us to act "rationally." But that is not quite the same as specifying whether terminating an unexpected pregnancy is practically rational. And what Kant might have considered "rational" in this respect may not necessarily be the same as what his present-day interpreters may believe.

This is not to deny that Kant's ethics embodies a fairly clear notion of what morality is. Few would deny that it does. This is doubtless part of the reason why it has inspired such sublime respect among so many. But *presupposing* morality is not the same as *grounding* it, which is what Kant's ethics claims to do. "Kant's ethics has its mythic roots," writes John Silber, "but they lie rather in Christian pietism than in reason"; and by "eschewing mythic roots, Kant's theory only lost what it could never really have had"—that is, a determinate content. Hence, Silber concludes: "The limited incentive of moral feeling is perhaps best understood as a moral sea anchor that, although incapable of providing the motive power to move a ship to harbor, may yet prevent its foundering on the rocks" ("Mythic Roots," 32). And even this, we may add, depends on the uncertain fortunes of an historically fluid and all-but-dissipated eighteenth-century sentiment regarding the native powers of practical human "reason." Indeed, when contemporary moral philosophers are seriously discussing "rival justices" and "competing rationalities," one might quite easily suppose it had seen its day.[31]

In the second place, Scheler would see Kant's procedure as representing a significant oversight. For, according to Scheler, the "moral ought" of the categorical imperative, at the very heart of Kant's ethics, implicitly presupposes the very thing its formalism was intended to exclude—namely, material insight into the actual values underlying the Kantian notion of "moral law"—a claim more recently elaborated by Hans Reiner, as we have seen.³² Although Scheler himself makes no effort to follow up this claim by demonstrating what values he believes Kant presupposes (beyond those listed on p. 9, above), Reiner ventures a few pages and footnotes in this direction. Kant's ethics, he suggests, presupposes a philosophically significant conception of value. He finds Kant's writings pregnant with implications for value theory that might have led him to a more adequate description of moral experience had he chosen to develop them.³³ He claims that Kant, rather than Lotze, was responsible for the philosophical conception of value that flourished in German value theory. While "value" was never itself among the basic concepts defined by Kant, it was unavoidably and indispensably a concept *by means of which* he defined his basic concepts. Thus he used it to describe the "absolute" and "unconditional" quality attached to the act of moral willing, and, thereby, to define the moral "good."

What is remarkable about this, from Reiner's point of view, is that Kant's conception of value appears to exhibit certain features suggestive of a phenomenological theory. It is a conception of *absolute* value, totally independent of any need or desire.³⁴ It is a conception of value as an actually subsisting end-in-itself, not a potential effect to be produced; as a suprasensible idea to be respected, not as a hoped-for empirical result to be realized. For Reiner, such facets of Kant's thought represent insights pregnant with possibilities of where Kant *might* have been led had he pursued them. Might he have been led, for example, to distinguish explicitly, like Scheler, between value-essences and empirical goods? But, as Reiner realizes, Kant nowhere develops his thought overtly or substantially in this direction. Whether that eventually could have overcome the problem of "empty formalism," however, is a question that may be answered best by examining the relative merits of a decidedly phenomenological theory of values, such as Scheler's.

Scheler's question concerning the *content* of Kant's moral law has struck many ethicists as naive and ill-informed. It has often led them to discard his critique as superficial and insubstantial. There are undoubtedly elements in his writing and style that make this reaction understandable. But even if Scheler's question sometimes appears to be badly stated, it is not a silly one. His own ethical theory may not have succeeded in overcoming some of the same difficulties he criticized in Kant's, but this does not diminish the profundity of his insight with respect to the problem at issue. Scheler raises an important question by asking what determinate *content* is provided by Kant's notion of moral law. While many will demur, it will be hard for others to escape the conclusion that his skepticism in this matter is, at some level and to some degree, justified. Herman Dooyeweerd, to take just one example, puts the matter thus: "Perhaps never in the history of philosophy has the humanist ideal of personality received a more impressive formulation than in Kant's eulogy of duty," he says, "but, on the other hand, this ideal of personality has never before exhausted itself in an emptier formalism" (*New Critique* 1:375).

Scheler, Heidegger, and the Being of Values

BOTH THE LEGITIMACY AND necessity of Value Theory are widely denied today.[35] Many factors have contributed to this state of affairs and to the decline of interest in Value Theory over the past decades, as we saw in chapter 1. But apart from the general rejection of intuitionism in the English-speaking world, probably no single factor has done more to erode interest in the axiological ethics of Scheler, Hartmann, and others, than the influence of Heidegger. It is not merely that Scheler now seems passé. There is the pervasive impression that Heidegger's profound ontological preoccupations, together with his occasional negative remarks about Scheler and adverse assessment of Lotze and Rickert, have somehow discredited the entire enterprise of Value Theory. This impression, and the consequent widespread repudiation of the concept of value in connection with the question of Being in Western philosophy, has been abetted by the publication over the past decades of several studies of Heidegger's views on Value Theory that appear to corroborate his criticisms.[36] The fact that some of the arguments in these studies may be quite dubious and may have only a tenuous basis in Heidegger's own criticisms has not appreciably diminished the overall effects to which they have contributed. Among the most damaging results of all of these combined factors has been the wholesale foreclosure of almost all research in the phenomenology and ethics of values of the kind initiated by Scheler.

The gist of Heidegger's objections seems to be that the concept of "value" presupposes a phenomenologically untenable notion of metaphysical grounding, or a "metaphysics of presence," to use the current idiom. In *Being and Time*, for example, he claims that the idea of value contains an inappropriate *hypostatization* and stems from the "*ontology of the present-at-hand*" (332, cf. 132). Parvis Emad, particularly, presses this contention. He points out that already in his lectures of 1925–26, Heidegger can be found saying that "validity, as used by Lotze in determining the mode of being of true propositions, has the ontological meaning of *constant presence*."[37] The problem, evidently, is that such notions overlook the fact that the Being of anything is never disclosed fully in its being an object. In other words, the Being of an object is not fundamentally elucidated by an analysis of its ontical, entitative character, but only by ontologically tracing back its particular significance to the understanding that *Dasein* has of it in the context of its own horizon of possibilities. Emad argues from section 69c of *Being and Time*, further, that for Heidegger the intentionality of consciousness is *grounded* in the ecstatic temporality of *Dasein*; he also makes much of the 1928 lectures in which Heidegger accuses Scheler of misunderstanding the nature of transcendence by identifying it with intentionality and failing to see that it is grounded in *Dasein*'s own temporality.[38] Accordingly, Emad reasons that the temporal quality of "constant presence," which Heidegger finds associated with the notion of "value" in Lotze, Scheler, and others, unduly restricts temporality to the present and overlooks the "process" of rendering present, by which values, like all entities, become present only "out of a future which remains forever beyond the span of the present" (*Heidegger*, 144).

This general line of criticism can be supported by a number of Heidegger's writings. In *Platons Lehre von der Wahreheit* (1947), Heidegger links the nineteenth-century notion of "value" to the Platonic idea of *agathon*, or "good," and argues that, like the Platonic idea, it is merely the "presentative foreground" of truth, rather than that which grounds it. In his "Letter on Humanism" (1949), he declares that every "valuing" is a "subjectivising" that robs what is valued of its worth, and that "thinking in values is the greatest blasphemy imaginable against Being."[39] Again, in *Holzwege* (1950), he says that when something is reduced to an object of representation, there is, first, a loss of Being incurred by the thing and, second, a corresponding effort to compensate for this loss by ascribing "value" to it, and, finally, a tendency to reify the value itself. In this sense, value becomes the "objectification of needs as goals"; yet, as "the impotent and threadbare disguise of the objectivity of whatever is," it is a poor substitute for Being. "No one dies for mere values," he says. As Nietzsche showed, values are nothing but postulations of self-interest, which serve the will-to-power in securing itself by providing a necessary constant, a surrogate for Being.[40]

Writing from a perspective influenced by Dietrich von Hildebrand, Hans Reiner offers an interesting, concise resumé of Heidegger's critique of value theory in a critical excursus.[41] According to Reiner's analysis, the substance of Heidegger's criticism divides into three basic points: (1) that values spring from the *subjective activity of positing* values; (2) that such positing occurs through the *objectification of needs as goals*;[42] and (3) that such objectification results in the *reification of values*, with the result that the truth of Being is hidden from view and thereby deprived of appropriate dignity (*DI*, 150). Reiner examines each point in some detail and, in each case, offers a compelling rejoinder. Whether or not he does full justice to Heidegger may be another question. But his analysis shows that these specific criticisms, which can be supported by Heidegger's texts, either fail to affect or fail to preclude a phenomenology of values of the kind we find in Scheler. In what follows I shall briefly examine Reiner's analysis with an eye to its specific implications for Scheler.

First, according to Reiner, Heidegger assumes that values spring from the *subjective activity of positing* values. But in Scheler's own words, "Values cannot be created or destroyed. They exist independently of the organization of all beings endowed with spirit" (*F*, 275/261). Values are "perceived" or "felt," not "posited" by any activity of the subject.[43] Scheler stresses the objectivity and independence of values, the fact that the directed conations in which values come to givenness are not under our control, that they are not dependent upon a will to posit them as purposes. He asserts the objectivity of values and rejects, one by one, all subjectivist and relativist theories of value, including hedonism, emotivism, utilitarianism, nominalism, and any theory that would compromise the absolute objectivity of value-essences or their a priori order of ranks by making them dependent upon a relativizing relation to particular human subjects, their particular psychic or psycho-physical constitution, their particular historical ethos, their particular consciences, or the like (see esp. F, ch. 4, sec. 1; and ch. 5, secs. 3–7).

Furthermore, in one of his more interesting conjectures about ethical subjectivism, Scheler suggests that subjectivism involves a reaction of *resentment* (*Ressentiment*). The sheer difficulty of judging between objective values, as well as failure to find expected agreement, he suggests, produces feelings of inferiority, disillusionment, and skepticism. Compounded by a profound experience of personal impotence in realizing objective ideals, these feelings lead to a kind of "vengeful act" in which values are asserted to be, after all, "*only subjective*."[44] The view that values are subjective, in effect, becomes, through the psychology of resentment, a kind of testimonial to their objectivity.

Hence, while Heidegger's polemic *may* be appropriate to the conception of value found in someone like Rickert, it misses entirely the emphasis on the "receptivity" of the subject, in conjunction with the "objectivity" of values, found among members of the phenomenological school, including Brentano, Husserl, Scheler, Hartmann, von Hildebrand, and Reiner.[45] And the fact that the role of the subject in the "constitution" of its objects through "passive synthesis" was later recognized by Husserl and others does not fundamentally change this. The fact that my constitutive "agency" is involved in my passive synthesis of an intentional object, such as the color of blood, does not mean that it is no more than a subjective postulate, any more than an inadvertently witnessed bludgeoning of a homeless person in the streets of New York is. Rather, in many cases, it offers what Scheler might wish to call the rough inexorable resistance of reality.

Second, according to Reiner, Heidegger assumes that the positing activity underlying all reference to values involves the *objectification of needs as goals*.[46] But Scheler denies that values exist only in relation to the purposes posited by the will. While he admits that values are often *disclosed* in desires or conations, he denies that they essentially *depend* on them. For Scheler, values are fundamentally independent of the objectification or representation of needs or goals or purposes.[47] Heidegger's criticism here may be appropriate to the conception of value found in Nietzsche or Lotze as a nineteenth-century "descendant" of the Greek concept of *agathon* in its Platonic form as an *idea*. But it does not apply to the kind of conception found in Scheler, who distinguishes between the idea or concept of a value and the value itself. As Scheler points out, an infant son "feels the kindness of his mother without having even vaguely comprehended an idea of the good" (*F*, 184/166). We must have an idea or concept of a value before it can be posited as an objectification of our needs or desires; but no idea or concept is necessary in order to perceptually *feel* a value itself. Scheler denies, therefore, that values belong originally to the realm of representations or subjectively postulated ideal objects.

Scheler is not denying that values can in some cases be related to "needs" or that they can be conceptualized or represented as "ideal objects"; he is only denying that they are given in experience *originally* in this way (cf. *F*, 183f./165). Scheler would have no quarrel with the notion that values can be conceptualized or logically analyzed. He would probably have some difficulty with Husserl's claim that acts of feeling harbor explicitly or implicitly a "logical" factor; and that values, although originally intended affectively in acts of feeling, may be progressively brought to intentional presence also as objects of doxic and logical consciousness because of the latent *doxic content* in emotional acts that can be actualized.[48] But Scheler would have *no* difficulty with the notion that values, although originally accessible only through feelings, may be objectified eventually in conceptual representations. The only point on which he would remain adamant here is his contention that values are not originally apprehended as conceptual objectifications, particularly not as objectifications of needs as goals.[49]

Third, according to Reiner, Heidegger assumes that the objectification involved in positing values results in the reification of values, with the result that the truth of Being is hidden from view and thereby deprived of its appropriate dignity. But if Scheler denies that values are originally representations or postulations of any kind at all, it is hard to see how his conception could be saddled with the criticism that it involves a *reification* of values or presupposes an inappropriate ontology of "presence-at-hand." It is true, of course, that Scheler makes no real attempt to offer an ontological clarification of the peculiar mode of being which is *Dasein*'s, as does Heidegger. He therefore naturally makes no attempt to clarify his notion of "value" ontologically by tracing back its possible sense to the understanding *Dasein* has of some one or some ensemble of its own possibilities. This means that his conception has the unintended effect of separating the "ontic" properties of a bearer of value from what, in Heidegger's terms would make it worthy of care. Thus, on Heidegger's reading, no matter how true Scheler's value theory may be in a factual or "ontic" sense, it is ontologically inadequate. In this sense Heidegger may seem to have some justification for calling Scheler's theory "inadequate," or even for saying that it presupposes a "traditional" ontological account of our being as "presence-at-hand" (*Being and Time*, 72–75, 172–75).

But even this has been disputed.[50] And, more importantly, Scheler's descriptions of how values are disclosed in pre-purposive conative tendencies, as such, are completely compatible with Heidegger's descriptions of "Being-in-the-world," and cannot be said in themselves to essentially presuppose an ontology of "presence-at-hand."[51] Furthermore, as Manfred Frings points out, the ontology of "presence-at-hand" is decidedly avoided by Scheler's concept of "*self*-value," since Scheler takes the "self"—understood in the sense of the innermost acting person—to be non-objectifiable.[52]

It is true, certainly, that in describing such contents of passive intentionality, phenomenologists employ concepts and representations of such contents; and it is true that, by means of objectifying techniques of imaginative variation, and the like, they seek to bring such contents to clear givenness precisely in the mode of "presence-at-hand." But how is the truth of Being hidden from view by this? As Reiner says, it may be true that a concept or representation is never fully adequate to the Being of an object, but even when it grasps only the "presentative foreground" of an entity and its Being, it does grasp *something* about the entity and its Being; and while the Being of an entity may never be exhausted in its being an object, one hardly comes to the fullness of Being by excluding from philosophy, as he says, "everything that is accessible to us by virtue of its objectivity (and much of which is inaccessible to us *except* through objectification)" (*DI*, 160f).

From the perspective of Heideggerian initiatives, Scheler and the entire movement of Value Theory have come to seem helplessly caught in the "toils of onticity," unable to bring to view the radical ontological basis of the matters of fact they describe. This impression may or may not be entirely justified.[53] But as David Lachterman says, it needs to be balanced by a "home truth": "insofar as ontological truth remains germane to those experiences, facts, or beings for which it is, qua truth, foundational, the effort to disclose ontological truth cannot be divorced from the task of distinguishing and clarifying the phenomena at an ontic level."[54]

Moreover, this critique needs to be countered by an even more basic truth: even the most ontologically oblivious, superficial talk ("idle talk") about values, does not disprove the phenomenological existence of values or prove that they are comprehensible by means of the concept of *Being* as such. If there is any truth to Heidegger's remark, "No one dies for mere values," there is hardly any less in the notion that no one would die for mere "Being." It is certainly conceivable that the things for which people are willing to die—the lives of their children, freedom, justice, and truth—may be grouped under the heading of "Being" as well as "value," even though Scheler would not have wished to put the matter thus (see my discussion of "Values and Goods" in sec. 2, above). In this sense, value does not stand opposed to Being, but constitutes something in it. But this something in Being cannot be specified by means of the concept of Being as such, for, as Reiner notes, "value (as positive value) is opposed by *disvalue* (or negative value), which is clearly something in Being also."[55] Hence, it will not do to dismiss the concept of value, as Heidegger does, as a mere substitute for a lost comprehension of Being as such. For the concept of Being can conceal the specific meaning of values no less than the concept of values can conceal the meaning of Being.[56]

On the one hand, then, a phenomenology of values such as we find in Scheler may not be so vulnerable to the Heideggerian critique as has been generally supposed. Whatever it may lack in ontological profundity or adequacy cannot necessarily prevent it from showing us that we know *something*—and, quite possibly, something significant—about the nature of values in moral experience. As Robert Sokolowski argues, the categorial forms of moral performances are *publicly* recognizable, and the fact that we can point to cases of ulterior motives, hypocrisy, and the like, only confirms that the particular natures of moral transactions— and, I would add, the values they embody—are readily capable of being distinguished.[57] Instead of viewing the stated ontological inadequacy of value theory as a reason for dismissing it out of hand as irrelevant, we might choose to accept it with that ostensible limitation. On the other hand, one might arguably reject the ontological pretensions of the Heideggerian critique. Instead of viewing the apparent failure of value theory to provide adequate ontological grounding or conclusive justification for its claims simply as a refutation of them, we might use this failure as a critical tool for demonstrating the inherent limitations of theoretical thought.[58] It is quite possible that we shall never be able to justify conclusively most of what we know by means of theoretical demonstrations; which is only to say that we may always know a good deal more than we may be able to conclusively justify—and what we know might well include a good deal about values.

This does not mean that value theories such as Scheler's will not continue to face challenging difficulties, nor that one of their difficulties may not be precisely the ontological difficulty of articulating the mode in which values *exist*. Such theories are not always clear about what they mean by "values." They may refer, like Scheler, to "qualities," while denying that they originally have either *real* existence in the sense of empirical entities or *ideal* existence in the sense of concepts or Platonic ideas.[59] They may refer, like Husserl, to evaluative "characters" or "predicates" that are "founded" upon the "nucleus" or "core" of a primordially given, and therefore foundational, "noematic object."[60] And they may refer to these "characters" or "predicates" (as Husserl refers to "essences"), as "intentional," "intuitable" objects of "essential intuition," proposing that they have a phenomenologically constituted *intentional* existence; or even suggesting, perhaps, that they may have only a *functional* kind of existence, like that of primitive and irreducible intuitive qualities such as "good" or "yellow" in G. E. Moore's account.[61] But the difficulty such theories have in specifying the nature and being of values is not necessarily a sign of a fundamentally flawed theory; it may be due in part to the phenomenological impenetrability of the question at issue. In fact, as Reiner says, it may be impossible to offer a precise and direct *description* of value as such (any more than one could do so for colors), and it may be necessary to settle for a "circumscriptive" account of the *situation* in which values are experienced and to see what can be learned by way of comparison and contrast with similar or related phenomena (*DI*, 135).

Few philosophers today are patient with intuitionism and non-naturalism. Risieri Frondizi, for example, disputes Scheler's claim that values are essentially independent, either of their empirical bearers, or of our human psycho-physical constitution.[62] He argues that values are *Gestalt* qualities, neither entirely *separable* from empirical qualities nor entirely *reducible* to them. Indeed, to take one of Scheler's own examples, if it is true that we can talk about "red" as a pure color of the spectrum without experiencing the need to conceive it as covering the surface of an empirical bearer, it is no less true that we must have learned to do so from previous experiences of empirical instantiations of it. As D. W. Hamlyn points out, while there may be difficulties in trying to define terms like "red" purely ostensively, by reference to sensory experience alone, they certainly could not be understood fully without *some* sensory experience.[63] Scheler himself may well have been aware of such problems, and they may pose no intractable obstacles for a phenomenological approach. But they surely warrant a fuller consideration than Scheler gave them before such an approach can be expected to gain a wider hearing, as Reiner is keenly aware.[64]

Still, it is far from certain that a phenomenological approach could expect to make itself more readily intelligible by accommodating itself to the conceptual categories of an analytic approach. According to Nicholas Rescher, for example, two related questions at the forefront of the discussion in analytic metatheory of value have been: (1) whether value is a *property* of objects (like the color on a surface) or a *relationship* (like ownership), and (2) whether it is something grounded *subjectively* "in the mind of the beholder" (like the taste of beer and pizza) or *objectively* in "impersonally" specifiable criteria (like the nutritive properties of an apple) (*Introduction to Value Theory*, 55f.). The problem with the way these alternatives are formulated, as one might guess, is that they imply assumptions about the relationship of values to empirical bearers and percipients that are phenomenologically unacceptable. Even the conventional axiological distinction between "intrinsic" and "instrumental" values, which goes back to Aristotle's classic final cause argument (*Works*, Vol. 8, *Metaphysica*, Bk. 2, ch. 2, 994 b 9–16), typically arises only in view of the *relation* of values to their empirical bearers without even touching on the question of their own eidetic, nonempirical status. Whatever we may say about Scheler's insufficient attention to the "genetic constitution" of values, to the way consciousness of them originates and develops in empirical experience, this does not of itself rule out the legitimacy his insistence on the phenomenological point that, as intentional qualities, values are *essentially* independent of empirical subjects and objects.

Perhaps the major problem with Scheler's essentialist definition of value is that it fails to specify how values differ from other essences. Subsuming values under the category of "essence" does not in itself accomplish anything more in the way of specifying their nature than subsuming them under the heading of Heideggerian "Being." Scheler says that values are essences. But then, presumably bearers of value can be conceived as essences too. We may speak conceivably of the "essence" of a Rembrandt painting just as we may speak of the "essence" of aesthetic value. But what distinguishes a *value*-essence from a *thing*-essence? Scheler's term "quality" is not too illuminating on this point.

Most attempts to specify this distinction have been less than adequate because they have not distinguished clearly the *functional* nature of values, but settled instead for descriptions of various relations between the valuing subject and valued object. Take, for instance, the definition offered by Ralph Barton Perry in his highly respected classic, *Realms of Value* (1954): "A thing—anything—has value or is valuable, in the original and generic sense," he writes, "when it is the object of an interest—any interest" (9). Or take his statement in *General Theory of Value* (1967) that "any object, whatever it be, acquires value when any interest, whatever it be, is taken in it"—a view which he says may be otherwise formulated in the equation: "x is valuable=interest is taken in x" (115f.).[65] What does such a definition tell us? It tells us that an object, such as a painting, *acquires* value by becoming an object of "interest." Presumably, then, valu*ing* is some sort of "interest." This suggests that *value* itself must be some sort of a *relation* to interest, which is precisely what Perry concludes: "Value," he says, "is thus a specific relation into which things possessing any ontological status whatsoever, whether real or imaginary, may enter with interested subjects" (*General Theory of Value*, 116).

Such a theory may tell us a great deal about the nature of "interest," but it does not really offer a great deal of help in clarifying the phenomena of values themselves as they are given in our experience, or their functional relation to the objects that bear them. Still, without recommending Perry's view that interest is "constitutive" of value, we may find that his connection between interest and value itself provides what amounts to a phenomenological clue to the relation between values and their bearers.

An object may be an object of "interest" in an unexpected diversity of ways. For example, a painting may be an object of not just one kind of "interest," but of many kinds; we could then say that this is because it bears a corresponding diversity of values. One person may buy a painting as a financial investment; in this case it is an object of financial interest, and the focus of concern is on the economic value it bears. Another person may display the same painting on a different occasion as an object of culture and taste; in this case it is an object of artistic interest and the focus is on its aesthetic value. For yet another individual, the painting (let us say, Rembrandt's "Ascension of Christ") is primarily an object of religious interest; and here the focus is primarily on its spiritual value. This does not mean that values are merely subjective postulates; it simply means that different values manifest themselves in different functional aspects of an entity.

This suggests an illuminating analysis, developed by Dooyeweerd, of the relationship between *how* a thing functions in experience and *what* it is (*A New Critique*, 2:7ff., and 3:53ff.). On the one hand, *how* a thing functions—how it is experienced—is determined by the way in which it exhibits what he calls "functional modalities of meaning." Thus, the painting in the foregoing illustration exhibited different "functional modalities of meaning." The different interests which it served and different uses to which it was put, served also to bring to light the different functional meanings that it latently bore. On the other hand, *what* a thing is—the identity of a thing—is determined by what Dooyeweerd calls its "typical structure of individuality." This means that a thing, despite the multiplicity of meanings it may bear and corresponding variety of uses to which it may be put, has generally a "typical" functional meaning that serves to identify it. Thus, while a painting may serve as an object of financial investment because of its economic worth, or as an object of religious interest because of its spiritual subject matter, this is not the "typical" or "qualifying" functional meaning that identifies it as a painting. Similarly, a fourteenth-century chair may be displayed in a museum as an object of historical interest because of the historical significance it bears, but this is not what typically identifies it as a chair. Hence, the identity of a thing is related to how it typically functions in experience. A typical functional meaning gives a thing its identity. A painting is typically an object of perceptual enjoyment for its aesthetic function; a chair is typically something used for sitting because of its utilitarian function; and so on.

On this view, what Scheler calls a "bearer" of value, or a "good," is equivalent to *what* a thing is, and what Scheler calls a "value" (or, at least, a "rank" of value) is related roughly to *how* that object functions meaningfully in experience—that is, to what Dooyeweerd calls "functional modalities of meaning." This means that values disclose *how* a thing functions in experience—how it serves as an object of "interest." Thereby they also serve to identify *what* a thing is by manifesting its typical functional meaning. The nature of value-essences, on this view, may be distinguished from all other essences by their *functional* or "*modal*" character. Unlike thing-essences, which (like the essence of a

Rembrandt painting) may be relatively complex and bear multiple "functional meanings," value-essences are generally simple and capable of being classified within a single irreducible "modality" of meaning.

The comparison to Dooyeweerd is suggestive, but there are differences, of course. Scheler distinguishes four basic "ranks" of values (religious, spiritual, vital, and sensible),[66] whereas Dooyeweerd distinguishes fifteen irreducible "functional modalities" (religious, juridical, moral, aesthetic, economic, linguistic, social, historical, psychical, logical, biotic, physical, kinematic, spatial, and numerical) (*New Critique* 1:3; cf. vol. 2, *The General Theory of Modal Spheres*, passim). More importantly, Dooyeweerd's "functional meaning" is not quite identical to "value" in Scheler. It is closer to a "type" or "rank" (or "stratum") of value in Scheler. Thus, Scheler distinguishes a great variety of "values" in his writings (such as joy, suffering, comfort, usefulness, nobility, vulgarity, holiness, and the like), each of which can be classified within a certain type or "rank" of value (sensible, vital, spiritual, or religious). Accordingly, while "values" exhibit *how* an object is experienced—as do "functional meanings" in Dooyeweerd (or "ranks" of values in Scheler)—the category of "value" is a more expansive one than that of "functional meanings" or "ranks."

This leads to a difficulty in Scheler's value theory that we have not yet discussed, one which concerns the way in which Scheler distinguishes moral from nonmoral values.[67] As we have seen (in sec. 2, above), he says that moral values ("good" or "evil") appear in acts of willing aimed at "realizing" nonmoral values. For example, when parents make material sacrifices for the education of their children, they place their children's education before their own physical comforts, exhibiting thereby a preference for the "spiritual" value of education over the "physical" value of their own material well-being. For Scheler, moral value in such a case appears in the act of willing aimed at "realizing" a nonmoral, "intellectual" value.

The problem with Scheler's analysis lies in his basic criterion for moral value—the criterion of the *willing* and "*realization*" of any material values *other than moral values*. The problem here is not the ambiguity of the term "realize" (also noted in sec. 2 of this chapter), which might lead to a confusion between (1) willing the existence of a bearer of a nonmoral value and (2) actually bringing about the existence of a bearer of some value. The problem is of a different order, and may require an effort to step outside of Scheler's own terminological and conceptual conventions to gain a sufficient appreciation of it. The difficulty stems from his position that willing the existence of a bearer of a nonmoral value, as such, results in the realization of a specifically moral value. This means that the whole "logic of preference" upon which such willing is based—the whole schema of preference for a positive over a negative value, or for a higher over a lower value—is inseparably related to the generation of specifically *moral* value (*F*, 48f./26f.; cf. 102f./81f.). This position, I want to suggest, may need to be reconsidered.

Let us leave aside for a moment the whole question of the role of human agency and of acts of preference and willing in the realization of values. The first thing to be noted is that the mere realization of material values does not need to be regarded in itself as a specifically moral phenomenon. To be more precise, the coming into existence of bearers of nonmoral value, as such, does not need to be viewed necessarily as morally significant. More importantly, even if we allow that such actualizations of bearers of nonmoral value are accompanied in some way by the realization of moral value, this does not mean necessarily that they are themselves essentially matters of morality. In fact, considered apart from whatever moral value may accompany them, realizations of nonmoral values are essentially *amoral*. I do not think I am stating anything particularly novel or exceptional here.

But let us take this a step further—still leaving aside the question of human agency. Even considered together with any possible moral value that may appear in conjunction with them, realizations of nonmoral values may still remain refractory to classification as moral. In fact, numerous nonmoral values may be identified whose realization in some bearer one would find difficult to avoid classifying as basically "amoral." Take, for instance, the realization of a positive *aesthetic* or *economic* value. Would we wish to call the realization of such a value, even where it is accompanied by the appearance of a moral value as a byproduct, in every case a "moral" good? I think not. If the new wallpaper turns out beautifully or the stock market takes a turn for the better, these are not in themselves essentially matters of moral value—whatever the ethical permutations—but of aesthetic and economic value. This becomes all the more evident when one begins to consider a range of values not extensively dealt with by Scheler—including not only aesthetic and economic values, but also legal, historical, linguistic, logical, and even mathematical values.[68] When a mathematical calculation has been worked out correctly, the positive value that has been actualized is first and foremost a mathematical one, not a moral one. While moral good may certainly accompany the realization of such a value, the good brought into existence may not be chiefly a moral one.

Let us take this a step further still. In doing so, we shall have to revert to the question of human agency and rethink the role of acts of preference and willing in the realization of values. For it is only through acts of preference that we even begin to gain an appreciation of which values we ought to seek to realize; and it is only through acts of willing whereby we aim at bringing into existence bearers of nonmoral values, according to Scheler, that we actually realize moral value. Undoubtedly even such diverse nonmoral values as those considered above exhibit an essential normativity (or "ideal oughtness," *F*, 218/203) that makes them candidates for obligatory realization. Positive linguistic values, for example, "ought" to be realized in speech. There is a way in which one "ought" to use words—which is to say, people "ought" to employ reasonably intelligible syntax and grammar. Likewise, positive logical values "ought" to be realized in argumentation, and so forth. But when such values are harnessed to the will in acts of concrete realization, is it reasonable to regard such acts as generating specifically *moral* values, or to conceive of such acts as specifically *moral* duties? On Scheler's view there is no alternative. Acts of preference and subsequent willing are regarded as unavoidably generative of moral value. But this strikes me as confusing, even while it may not be entirely incorrect.

I have no quarrel with the notion that the realization of positive nonmoral values, or even the willingness to attempt such realization, is *commendable* somehow. But I wonder whether it should always be called *morally* commendable. Nor do I have a quarrel with the notion that such realization or willingness is accompanied by the actualization of some kind of independent positive value or virtue. But I question whether it is helpful always to describe these as *moral* value or *moral* virtue. A willingness to try to make use of intelligible syntax and logic might well be considered a *duty* in some sense. But I wonder whether it is appropriately described under every circumstance as a *moral* duty. Very likely we have some kind of *obligation* to seek the realization of such nonmoral values; and very likely such an obligation is based on acts of preference for *positive* over negative values, and the like, much as Scheler describes. My question is simply whether it is illuminating, or even accurate, to describe such obligation or preference as *essentially* moral.

This consideration suggests that Scheler's theory might be revised along the following lines. The value that appears in the act of realizing other values, as he says, is the value of "good" (or its opposite). But this is not only the value of *moral* good, but also of aesthetic good, economic good, logical good, and so forth. What Scheler calls "moral" value, then, is *only one kind* of "good" that appears in acts of realizing material values. This means that "moral good" does not appear through the realization of positive *nonmoral* values (such as the values of "utility," "frugality," "eloquence," "nobility," or even "holiness") but of positive *moral* values (such as "faithfulness," "remorse," "forgiveness," "respect," "honesty," "benevolence," and the like). This suggestion admittedly contradicts Scheler's insistence that moral values do not constitute a distinct sphere of material values or even a possible content of moral willing (*F*, 49/27). But if it is phenomenologically warranted to speak of the realization of the nonmoral "good" of aesthetic, economic, or social values, it would seem reasonable to assume that the realization of such values is governed by a normativity quite different from *moral* obligation. Moreover, if that is the case, there seems to be no overriding reason why one may not speak also of the realization of *moral* values governed by a specifically *moral* normativity.[69]

Reiner offers a slightly different but related criticism and correction of Scheler (*DI,* §30). He argues that the content of moral good and evil involves more than Scheler allows. While it is true that *some* kinds of moral value arise through acts of willing directed at realizing separate objective values (in the way claimed by Scheler), moral values are not limited to such "values of direction" (*Richtungswerte*). There are "values of bearing" (*Haltungswerte*), for example, which do not arise through the realization of separate objective values but are realized *for their own sakes,* such as industry, perseverance, bravery, self-control, forbearance, and patience (*DI,* 237). Scheler's definition of moral value prevents him from recognizing the moral good involved in acts supporting the reality of already *existing* values, as well as that attached to *judgments* (as opposed to decisions) by the will (*DI,* 238). It also keeps him from noticing that those who act from a sense of honor are concerned more with *avoiding* the realization of a *disvalue* than with seeking the realization of a positive one (*DI,* 171f.). Moreover, against Scheler's claim that moral values (independently of nonmoral values) cannot be made a direct content of willing to be realized in conduct, and that the self-deceiving attempt to do so results in "pharisaism" (*F,* 22/14), Reiner counters that the moral values attached to the *conduct* of others are readily discernible and capable of being evaluated without prejudicial self-deception; and even in one's own case, as Nicolai Hartmann admitted, striving after moral values in one's conduct is a perfectly natural and legitimate moral choice.[70]

Scheler's definition of moral value strictly by reference to the realization of nonmoral values is unduly limiting. For example, his criterion of the relative "height" of values offers no way of deciding when the value of the bare, physical survival of human life (a "lower" value) may be more pressing than that of high art and culture (a "higher" value). Additional criteria are necessary, such as the relative "strength" of values, as suggested by Hartmann (cited by Reiner, *DI,* 175). More importantly, such defects in Scheler's theory reveal a more basic deficiency in his conception of good and evil. Good and evil cannot be determined merely by reference to the choice of "higher" or "lower," "positive" or "negative," values. For such relative differences are matters about which one can be genuinely mistaken and pertain to the relative "correctness" of one's moral discernment and choices (or what Reiner calls moral "rightness" and "wrongness"); whereas moral "good" or "evil" pertain to the deliberate and unmistakable affirmation of objectively important values, or opposition to them.[71]

An ethics such as Scheler's, then, must do several things in order to restore its credibility as a phenomenological ethics of values. First, it must show that the Heideggerian critique of values does not compromise its integrity. Second, it must be clear about the functional, nonentitative yet eidetically irreducible, nature of values. Third, it must clarify the genetic constitution of values in empirical experience as well as the relation between value-essences and the bearers in which they are empirically instantiated. Fourth, it must overcome the kinds of problems produced by Scheler's teleology of nonmaterial values by showing how moral values themselves constitute a distinct and irreducible type of material value.[72] Fifth, it must articulate a more adequate set of criteria by which to define moral "good" and "evil." While *conclusive* theoretical demonstration may not be necessary to justify such definitions in ethics, there is no question of warrant for shoring up a theory where it can be shown to be inadequate. Scheler's account of the criteria for determining the relative superiority of values and for choosing between material alternatives is not only incomplete in certain respects. It also appears to overlook a number of more fundamental distinctions which it tacitly presupposes, such as those Reiner makes between absolute and relative, and objectively important and subjectively important, values (*DI*, 182, cf. 143). Until such unresolved issues are more adequately dealt with, it will be difficult to overlook the consequent problems that stand in the way of an ethics and critique of Kant such as Scheler's.[73]

NOTES

1. Hans Reiner, *DI*, 15f., 156–58. Reiner says that Kant describes moral good as an absolute, unconditional "value" attached exclusively to the will, and that he uses the term "value" in this sense over eighty times in his ethical writings and fragments, and no fewer than forty times in the *Foundations of the Metaphysics of Morals* alone.

2. See above, ch. 1, sec. 3 ("Scheler's view of the 'Kantian Problem' "), and ch. 2, sec. 2 ("The Kantian Legacy and Phenomenological Background").

3. See above, ch. 1, sec. 3 ("Scheler's view of the 'Kantian Problem'").

4. *GMS*, 414; *KpV*, 32. On Kant's doctrine of the "holy will," see ch. 4, n. 6, below (and "The Relation of Feeling to Moral Law," in sec. 1 of ch. 4).

5. Kant offers examples in *GMS*, 397–99.

6. See, for example, *GMS*, 399; *MS*, 387; *KpV*, 93.

7. As Reiner argues (*DI*, 25f.), Kant did not guard with sufficient clarity against the misinterpretation that, in order to act from duty, one must act *against* one's inclination, or at least *without* inclination. His infelicitous use of the expression "without any inclination" (*GMS*, 398) to describe an action obviously done from a sense of duty proved especially misleading, leaving the impression that an action done "with inclination" must be contrary to duty. This was certainly not Kant's opinion, as can be shown despite some ambiguous statements. His major concern was to state duty's rightful claim to outweigh inclination when they conflict. Not actions *accompanied by* inclinations, but those *motivated by* inclinations, were regarded by Kant as the actual contraries of duty. This is clear, certainly, when he later speaks of ends which are at the same time duties (*GMS*, 383–87, passim).

Scheler himself acknowledges that Kant may be "misread" in this way, but insists that the *pathos* of Kant's descriptions tends to *support* such a reading! (cf. ch. 5, below, nn. 33, 34).

8. This would not be the case, of course, where the pursuit of ends takes place within a moral framework whose demands take precedence over any such pursuit.

9. "Ends" and "purposes" are used interchangeably by Frings and Funk to translate *Zwecke*, depending on the context, which may render one of the English terms more suitable than the other, according to its particular nuances.

10. That values themselves do not have this kind of an entitative existence for Scheler, as we shall see, may have significant ontological implications for his theory in the face of the Heideggerian criticism of value theory, which is discussed in the last part of this chapter.

11. According to Shimomissé, Scheler regarded this view (which he attributed to Kant) as concealing a "naturalistic" conception of material value, much as G. E. Moore claimed to discover a "naturalistic fallacy" in various attempts to define the "good" (Shimomissé, *Die Phänomenologie*, 17 n. 28; cf. G. E. Moore, *Principia Ethica* [Cambridge University Press, 1982], ch. 2).

12. Scheler's argument against the first condition appears in *F*, ch. 2; his argument against the second, in *F*, ch. 3.

13. The term "quality" is frequently used by Scheler in reference to values. He refers, for example, to "value-qualities" (*"Wert-qualitäten"*), "non-formal qualities of contents" (*"materiale Qualitäten"*), and "a non-formal order . . . of value-qualities" (*"eine materiale Rangordnung . . . der Wert-qualitäten"*) (cf. *F*, 35/12, 37/15, 40/17, 41/18, 45/23).

14. Edmund Husserl, *Ideen*, §95, §§116–17; Paul Ricoeur, *Husserl: An Analysis of His Phenomenology*, trans. E. G. Ballard and L. E. Embree (Evanston, IL: Northwestern University Press), 40f.; Emmanuel Levinas, *The Theory of Intuition in Husserl's Phenomenology*, 128. Cf. Quentin Smith, "Scheler's Critique of Husserl's Theory of the World of the Natural Standpoint," *Modern Schoolman* 55, No. 4, (1977–1978), 393.

15. This is true, at least, of Scheler's view from his early, phenomenological period (in which he wrote *Formalismus*) through his middle, Roman Catholic period (in which he wrote *Von Ewigen in Menschen*); in his last period, values are no longer seen as realized through acts of *willing*—an act of "spirit" (*Geist*)—but through the fortuitous contingencies of "impulse" (*Drang*). No one has more thoroughly explored this shift than Peter Spader in "The Non-Formal Ethics of Value of Max Scheler and the Shift in His Thought," *Philosophy Today* 18, No. 3 (fall 1974), 217–23; and his "A New Look at Scheler's Third Period," *Modern Schoolman* 51, No. 2 (Jan. 1974), 139–58.

16. I am indebted for this clarification to one of the readers of my manuscript provided by the publisher, who, because of the latter's "blind review" policies, remains anonymous.

17. Given the whole development of his ethics, it is doubtful whether one could say with accuracy that the function of willing is what determines the moral worth or virtue of a person for Kant. After all, the reason why one ought to cultivate a good will, in his view, is because it is consistent with one's character as an autonomous end in oneself. One wills lawful acts for the sake of and out of respect for one's dignity as a person. Scheler's point seems to be that

Kant's constant identification of moral worth with acts of lawful willing has the effect of making acts of willing, rather than the personal being of the moral agents themselves, the aboriginal bearers of moral value (F, 49ff./28ff.).

18. For an analysis of Scheler's understanding of the relationships between the values of the person, the moral disposition, and the will, see ch. 6 of this book. For a discussion of how values become candidates for morally obligatory realization, see ch. 5, sec. 3.

19. "Conation," in its philosophical signification, is defined by the *Oxford English Dictionary* (Oxford: Oxford University Press, 1971), as "The faculty of volition and desire; also . . . the product of this faculty."

20. Here Scheler would agree with Alexius Meinong, who held that we desire something because we value it, over against Christian von Ehrenfels, who held that we value something because we desire it; except that Scheler would object to Meinong's identification of value with pleasure as such. We *desire* something, Scheler would say, not because the contemplation of its existence or possession gives us pleasure, in the first place, but because we *value* it. Cf. Nicholas Rescher, *Introduction to Value Theory*, 52f.

21. Among Scheler's contemporaries one finds, for example, G. Anderson, "Die 'Materie' in Kants Tugendlehere und der Formalismus der kritischen Ethik," *Kant-Studien* 26 (1921), 239; and A. Liebert, who says in *Kants Ethik* (Berlin, 1931) that "in a profound sense, Kant's ethics is not even formalistic" (36; quoted by Alwin Diemer, "Zum Problem des Materialen in der Ethik Kants," *Kant-Studien* 45, Nos. 1–4 [1953–54], 21 n. 1); as well as M. Laupichler's book by the wrenching title of *Die Grundzüge der materialen Ethik Kants* (Berlin, 1931).

Somewhat later, Otto Friedrich Bollnow could write, in "Konkrete Ethik: Vorbetrachtungen zu einer philosophischen Tugendlehre," *Zeitschrift für philosophische Forschung* 6, No. 3 (winter 1952), 328, that "the Kantian ethics, as is known, is not nearly so unequivocally formal as it appears to the ethics of values"; and Ingeborg Heidemann could claim, in *Untersuchungen zur Kantkritik Max Schelers,* Ph.D. diss., University of Bonn, 1948 (Bonn: privately published, 1955), 165f., that Scheler's critique, although it missed the point of Kant's ethics, possesses the merit of having drawn attention to "material" elements in Kant's philosophy.

In this connection it may be pointed out that the way was prepared for this "non-formal" reinterpretation of Kant, in part, by a reaction against the one-sidedly formalistic and epistemological focus of Neo-Kantianism. This reaction led to the rediscovery of the "ontological" foundations of the Kantian philosophy whose connections were seen more clearly before the advent of neo-Kantianism by members of the Hegelian school such as Johann Eduard Erdmann. Illuminating material on this aspect of Kant interpretation is furnished by Heinz Heimsoeth, "Metaphysische Motive in der Ausbildung des Kantischen Idealismus," *Kant-Studien* 29 (1924), 121ff. This ontological interpretation of Kant is developed most notably by Heidegger in his various writings on Kant.

22. A distorted formalistic interpretation of Kant may have been reinforced in the English-speaking world by the fact that his first ethical works to be translated and widely read were the *Foundations* and second *Critique* (in Abbott's translations of 1873). Both of these deal primarily with the form of morality, not its material applications; and the fact that these were being read for some time in isolation from Kant's other ethical works, and for nearly a century before

the translation (by Mary J. Gregor, in 1964) of *The Doctrine of Virtue*, may have fostered the mistaken belief that, for Kant, goodness is wholly subordinate to duty, the moral law is essentially an imperative, the ends of action must be ignored, no place can be allowed to moral feeling, and the like.

23. H. J. Paton, *The Categorical Imperative* (London: Hutchinson, 1947), 17, 136; and his Foreword to *The Doctrine of Virtue*, by Immanuel Kant, trans. Mary J. Gregor (Philadelphia: University of Pennsylvania Press, 1964), x f. For a good summary of this issue and, especially, for a discussion of the argument that Kant furnishes a material teleological principle in the second formulation of his categorical imperative, see Ping-cheung Lo, "A Critical Reevaluation of the Alleged 'Empty Formalism' of Kantian Ethics."

24. *GMS*, 462f. Kant is of course concerned here with the relationship between practical and speculative reason as they touch on the interface between phenomenal and noumenal worlds, and he would doubtless insist that human reason is *not* incompetent to explain this unconditional necessity if "reason" and "explanation" are taken in their nonspeculative, nonscientific, practical sense. The Schelerian objection, of course, would spotlight the phenomenological "contentlessness" of such "reason" and "explanation" as the inevitable result of precisely these Kantian dualizations.

Reiner, *DI*, 86f., objects to Kant's practice of rushing "to the 'extreme limits' of a subject *before* he has adequately examined and considered the things that lie *along the way*," since the likelihood of discerning anything with clarity is much less certain at the extreme limits, he says, than along the way. Reiner regards Kant as neglecting a proper phenomenology of moral experience. In this connection, see John D. Caputo's provocative essay, "Kant's Ethics in Phenomenological Perspective," in *Kant and Phenomenology*, ed. Thomas M. Seebohm and Joseph J. Kockelmans, Current Continental Research, No. 4 (Washington, DC: Center for Advanced Research in Phenomenology and University Press of America, 1984), 129–46.

25. Cf. notably *GMS*, Preface and Third Section; *KpV*, particularly the "Analytic of Pure Practical Reason"; and *MS*, Introduction to Part I, and Preface to Part II.

26. "Duty! Thou sublime and mighty name . . . What origin is there worthy of thee, and where is to be found the root of thy noble descent which proudly rejects all kinship with the inclinations and from which to be descended is the indispensable condition of the only worth which men can give themselves?" Kant replies: "It cannot be less than something which elevates man above himself as part of the world of sense . . . . It is nothing else than personality, i.e., the freedom and independence from the mechanism of nature regarded as a capacity of a being which is subject to special laws (pure practical laws given by its own reason), so that the person as belonging to the world of sense is subject to his own personality so far as he belongs to the intelligible world. For it is then not to be wondered at that man, as belonging to two worlds, must regard his own being in relation to his second and higher vocation with reverence and the laws of this vocation with the deepest respect" (*KpV*, 86f.).

27. Reiner does offer a phenomenological version of the categorical imperative in terms of Value Theory, but it, too, remains an abstract formula, even if it is a bit more detailed than Kant's: "So act that, when faced with a choice between a merely subjectively important value and a value with objective impor-

tance, you support the reality of the objectively important value by your conduct, and that, when faced with a choice between more than one objectively important value, your conduct supports the reality of the objectively important value that seems to you to have the highest objective value weight" (*DI*, 182).

28. See above, ch. 1, sec. 3; and the first paragraph of sec. 1 of this chapter (and n. 1), above.

29. Kant did not suppose, of course, that one's personal desires and assumptions couldn't be coincidentally virtuous (cf. n. 7, above); his concern was to show that duty does not *derive* from desire, and to state duty's rightful claim to outweigh the latter when they conflict.

30. Reiner's essay, "The Golden Rule and Natural Law" (in the appendix of *DI*, 271–93), offers a valuable historical interpretation of the Golden Rule as a norm of morality, and an attempt to justify natural law by means of a phenomenological argument concerning the Golden Rule.

31. Alasdair MacIntyre, *Whose Justice? Which Rationality?* (Notre Dame: University of Notre Dame Press, 1988), 1–11, discusses "rival justices" and "competing rationalities."

32. See ch. 1, n. 16, above.

33. Reiner, *DI*, 156–58. Although Reiner does not mention this, it is noteworthy that Kant was familiar with something at least analogous to value theory in the "moral sense" theories of British moralists such as Francis Hutcheson, whose psychological analysis of moral consciousness led them to postulate a "hierarchy of values and sentiments which ranged from the most sublime (i.e., moral benevolence) to the most sensuous" (Carl H. Hamburg, "Kant's First Steps toward an Ethical Formalism," *Tulane Studies in Philosophy* 8 [1959], 105). For Kant, however, such a hierarchy could not of itself furnish the determining ground of moral willing. In his *Foundations*, accordingly, he distinguished hierarchically between (1) mere technical "rules of skill," (2) pragmatic "counsels of prudence," and (3) unconditional "commands of morality"; and again, between (1) the mere "market price" of skill and diligence (in nature), (2) the "affective price" of wit, lively imagination and humor (in art), and (3) the "intrinsic worth" or "dignity" of fidelity in promises and benevolence (in morality) (*GMS*, 416f., 434). Morality clearly does not consist here in the realization of nonmoral values as it does for Scheler. Rather, it occupies the highest place within a hierarchy of values, the place of absolute value embodied by moral good.

34. This fact is of special interest to Reiner, for whom a distinction between *absolute* (independent) and *relative* (need-related) values is fundamental (*DI*, 141). Although Kant's use of the concept of value is not limited to its strictly moral, *absolute*, sense, and although there is reason to believe Kant was acquainted with the notion of a hierarchy of values including nonmoral values (see previous note), Reiner does not highlight this nonmoral aspect of Kant's conception.

35. The following analysis is based, in part, on a paper I presented at the Society for Phenomenology and Existential Philosophy in Memphis in October, 1991, entitled "Reconnoitering Heidegger's Critique of Value Theory." Cf. also Ernst Wolfgang Orth, "Husserl, Scheler, Heidegger: Eine Einführung in das Problem der philosophischen Komparatistik," in *Phänomenologische Forschungen*, vols. 6–7: *Husserl, Scheler, Heidegger in der Sicht neuer Quellen* (Freiburg i. Br. and München: Verlag Karl Alber, 1978); Manfred S. Frings,

"Scheler and Heidegger," *Philosophy Today* 12 (1968), 21–30; as well as the works cited in n. 53, below.

36. Noteworthy works include: Henri Mongis, *Heidegger et la Critique de la Notion de Valeur* (The Hague: Nijhoff, 1976), and Parvis Emad, *Heidegger and the Phenomenology of Values*.

37. *Gesamtausgabe*, 21: *Logik, Die Frage nach der Wahrheit*, ed. W. Biemel (Frankfurt: Klostermann, 1976), p. 78. Cited by Emad, *Heidegger*, 56 (emphasis added).

38. *Gesamtausgabe*, 26: *Metaphysiche Anfangsgründe der Logik*, ed. F-W. von Herrmann (Frankfurt: Klostermann, 1978); Emad, *Heidegger*, 23–48.

39. A translation by F. Capuzzi and J. Glenn Gray is included in Heidegger, *Basic Writings*, 193–242; see esp. 228.

40. The relevant essays are translated by William Lovitt under the titles, "The Age of the World Picture," and "The Word of Nietzsche: 'God is Dead,' " in Heidegger, *The Question Concerning Technology and Other Essays* (New York: Harper & Row, 1977), 115–54 and 53–112; see esp., 66, 71f., 103, 108, 142.

41. Reiner, *DI*, §21, 146–67. See also Reiner's remarks on Heidegger in his brief essay entitled "Good and Value, the Philosophical Relevance of the Concept of Value," (appended to *DI*, 295–98).

42. The term "goals" here is not used in a sense distinguished by Scheler from "purposes" posited by the will in *F*, 61/40, and discussed above in sec. 2, on "Values and Purposes."

43. Although Scheler did not take into consideration Husserl's notion of the subjective agency involved in the "passive constitution" of intentional objects (as we have seen above, ch. 2, secs. 2 and 4), I am not sure he would have rejected it. Nevertheless, it is admittedly difficult to reconcile Scheler's language with Husserl's statements (for example, in *Ideen*, §117) about feeling-consciousness having a "positional" nature, and acts of feeling being "objectifying" acts or "positings"—even if of a "non-doxic" kind. (Cf. the passage on Husserl in the fourth paragraph below.)

44. *F*, 311/318; cf. Max Scheler, *Ressentiment*, ed. Lewis A. Coser, trans. William W. Holdheim (New York: Free Press, 1961), esp. ch. 5, where he argues that this reaction characterizes modern subjectivism, relativism, utilitarianism, democracy, and even humanitarianism. Cf. M. Frings, "The *Ordo Amoris* in Max Scheler," 40–60.

45. While it is clear that Heidegger was familiar with the value theory of Rickert and Lotze, Reiner suggests that the later and quite different views of Husserl and the Munich phenomenologists were never studied very thoroughly by him (*DI*, 296). Reiner himself offers an unusual and very interesting defense of the objectivity of values in connection with a discussion of conscience. Taking cues from Husserl, Pfänder, and Scheler, he develops a distinction between "I-center" and "I-circumground" to show that the values of conscience, which arise within the horizon of the "I-circumground," are not directly under one's control, as are the experiences of the "I-center" (*DI*, 121–25).

46. See n. 42, above.

47. See, for example, *F*, 61/40, as well as the general discussion in *F*, chs. 2 and 3.

48. *Ideen*, §117; cf. n. 43, above.

49. Reiner offers a detailed critique of Heidegger's analysis of the termi-

nological and conceptual history of the modern usage and understanding of "value" (*DI*, 152–59, 295f.). A better Greek antecedent than *agathon* in the case of phenomenological theories of value, he suggests, is *axia*, which is found in Aristotle but receives a deeper philosophical development in the moral philosophy of the Stoics. From these and other antecedents, he traces the development of the conception of value as something independent of human needs and desires up through Kant's notion of "absolute" moral worth.

50. The charge of a "presence-at-hand" ontology in Scheler has been disputed especially in light of the kinds of parallels between Heidegger's analysis of *Dasein* and Scheler's description of *Person* cited by David R. Lachterman in his Introduction to Max Scheler, *Selected Philosophical Essays* (Evanston: Northwestern University Press, 1973), xxiii n. 25, and pointed out by Manfred Frings (cf. n. 53, below).

51. Scheler was acquainted, of course, with the Heideggerian distinction between the "present-at-hand" (*Vorhandensein*) and the "ready-to-hand" (*Zuhandensein*). In fact, he points to possible antecedents of the notion of "implement ready to hand" (*zuhandenes Zeug*) as described by Heidegger in *Being and Time* in his own earlier essay "Erkenntnis und Arbeit," which originated in his Munich lectures of 1909–10 (IR, 198 n./306 n. 20). Furthermore, as we saw in ch. 2, n. 26, he goes so far as to claim for his later conception of the pre-conscious, involuntary experience of "reality as resistance" an ontological primordiality surpassing even *Dasein*'s "Being-in-the-world"!

52. Manfred S. Frings, "Introduction to Three Essays by Max Scheler" in *Scheler, Person and Self-Value: Three Essays*, ed. M. S. Frings (Dordrecht: Nijhoff, 1987), xvi. Cf. Scheler's remarks about "bliss" and "despair" as "correlates of the moral value of our personal being" and preeminent instances of "self-feeling" (*F*, 355/343) and about the non-objectifiability of the person, who "lives in the execution of acts" (*F*, 397/387).

53. Scheler himself disputes this critique in "Idealismus–Realismus," as we have seen in ch. 2, n. 26. See also Manfred Frings, *Person und Dasein* (The Hague: Nijhoff, 1969), and his "Scheler and Heidegger," for interesting parallels between Scheler and Heidegger, as well as his "Background of Max Scheler's 1927 Reading of *Being and Time*"; and David R. Lachterman's comments in his Introduction to Max Scheler, *Selected Philosophical Essays*, xxiii n. 25; xxvi n. 35.

Risieri Frondizi raises the question of a "theological basis" in Scheler's ethics, quoting his remark that "*all* possible values are 'founded' in the *value* of an *infinitely personified spirit* and its correlative '*world of values*' " (*F*, 116/96; Frondizi, *What Is Value?*, 142f.). We leave this question unconsidered, except (1) to deny Frondizi's contention that if this was the case, it would necessarily constitute an annulment of the relative autonomy of the different spheres of value, (2) to recall our discussion (in ch. 2, sec. 4) of the possibility that Scheler tried to ground his phenomenology in the transcendental subjectivity of God, and (3) to observe that Husserl's later ethics, according to Ullrich Melle, has a "theological basis." (Melle, editor of Husserl's *Vorlesungen über Ethik und Wertlehre: 1908–1914*, Husserliana 28 [Dordrecht: Kluwer Academic Publishers, 1988], made this observation in his paper, "The Development of Husserl's Ethics," delivered on Oct. 14, 1989, at the annual meeting of the Society for Phenomenology and Existential Philosophy in Pittsburgh, PA.)

54. Lachterman, xxxvii. We leave unconsidered, with Lachterman, Heidegger's move to a "thinking of Being without (or apart from) being(s)" in his 1962 lecture "Zeit und Sein" (in *Zur Sache des Denkens*). But cf. John D. Caputo's *Demythologizing Heidegger* (Bloomington: Indiana University Press, 1993).

55. *DI*, 162. Reiner also rejects as phenomenologically untenable the attempt to justify the reduction of value to Being by means of the Augustinian and Scholastic doctrine that all disvalue (or evil) consists in privation of Being. The content of such negative values as pain, he says, cannot be reduced phenomenologically to a mere deficiency (ibid.).

56. Reiner claims, for example, that the phenomenon of absolute value remains concealed in Heidegger's analysis, so that all value appears to be "relative" (*DI*, 163–65). He also notes several German criticisms of Heidegger's philosophy to the effect that it is out of touch with the traditions of moral philosophy and ethically unsophisticated (*DI*, 296f.).

In the same vein, it is hard to imagine anything less compelling than Emad's suggestion that the ontological insights of Heidegger's initiatives might serve a role in our moral improvement. He suggests that insight into "the metaphysical nature of the temporal character of value" may prevent us from abandoning "ethical norms" as meaningless and enable us to begin fulfilling our "genuine ethical responsibilities" in the face of the "present world-historical crisis" (*Heidegger*, 170f.). He means that insight into the temporality of values will enable us to see them, not as meaningless postulates, but as rooted in our Being-in-the-world. But neither does Scheler regard values as meaningless postulates, nor does recognizing their rootedness in our Being-in-the-world do much, if anything, to clarify the nature of our moral responsibilities.

57. Sokolowski, *Moral Action*, 104f. While Sokolowski makes this important point about the publicly recognizable form of a moral transaction, it is also important to see that he rejects Value Theory and to understand why. He does so, in the first place, because he regards values as insubstantial postulates. He writes: "It was probably a skepticism about being able to recognize the natures of things and relationships that made philosophers in the late nineteenth century posit values as the stabilizing factors in human conduct" (189 n. 1). In the second place, he does so because he believes that values do not generate the difference between the desirable and the truly good, but *presuppose* this distinction (147). In Scheler's theory, by contrast, the *presupposed* distinction (in Sokolowski) would belong to the realm of values.

58. Cf. Puolimatka, *Moral Realism and Justification*, 21. A related point is made by Reiner, *DI*, 107f., and by Franz Brentano, *The Origin of Our Knowledge of Right and Wrong*, trans. R. M. Chisholm and E. H. Schneewind, ed. Oskar Kraus (London: Routledge & Kegan Paul, 1969), 38f., when the latter observes that our moral knowledge extends beyond our ability to give a theoretical justification of it. Cf. also Alvin Plantinga, *Warrant: The Current Debate* (New York: Oxford University Press, 1993), and *Warrant and Proper Function* (New York: Oxford University Press, 1993), where he elaborates upon his earlier discussions of "proper basicality."

59. One must advise caution, therefore, against any unqualified assertions about the axiological "idealism" or "realism" of a theorist such as Scheler. This is doubly the case in view of the position he takes in his essay "Idealismus–Realismus." Nevertheless, there is a sense in which either designation might be

warranted (though still potentially misleading): Scheler might be called an "idealist" in the sense that values, although they are not conceptual representations (like Platonic ideas), are intuitable *essences*; and he might be called a "realist" in the sense that values, although they are not empirically real, actually exist as *intuitable* essences. Thus, one must not mistakenly assume that Scheler is denying that value has an *intentional, phenomenological existence*, when he simply states that value, as such, has *no existence* ("Der Wert *ist* überhaupt nicht"), as he declares in his *Früheschriften* (*GW*, 1), ed. Maria Scheler and M. S. Frings (Berne and Munich: Francke Verlag, 1971), 98. Scheler is denying here only the *real, metaphysical existence* of values.

60. See n. 14, above.

61. "If I am asked 'What is good?' my answer is that good is good, and that is the end of the matter. Or if I am asked 'How is good to be defined?' my answer is that it cannot be defined, and that is all I have to say about it," writes G. E. Moore. "My point is that 'good' is a simple notion, just as 'yellow' is a simple notion" (*Principia Ethica*, 6f.).

I use the term "functional" to specify the peculiar nature of the existence of values at the suggestion of Manfred Frings, in his "Introduction to Three Essays by Max Scheler," who writes: "A value exists only when it realizes itself with a thing, with a state of affairs, or with a person, i.e., the value enters into a *functional* relationship with these or other factors in order for it to exist. *The existence of a value is functional existence*" (xxvii; emphasis added).

62. Frondizi, *What Is Value?*, 102f., 135; cf. 160. This is also a major argument in Imtiaz Moosa, "Scheler's Philosophy of Value and Ethics in Relation to Kant's Ethics," Part 2, Ph.D. diss., University of Toronto, 1986.

63. D. W. Hamlyn, "A Priori and A Posteriori," *The Encyclopedia of Philosophy*, ed. Paul Edwards (New York: Macmillan, 1967), 1:141; cf. also his comments about the empirical element in a priori propositions of the form "Nothing can be red and green all over at the same time in the same respect" (which one finds in Scheler), as well as his remarks about the "relative" and "absolute" a priori (143f.).

64. Reiner (*DI*, 265f.) regards his own intuitionist ethics as free of the typical objections to intuitionism and non-naturalism cited by Frankena. Cf. Frankena's remarks on Reiner's ethics in his Preface to Reiner, *DI*, xiii.

A potential gold mine of material illuminating the connections between empirical perception and eidetic intuition may be found in the psychological research being done on the phenomenon of "synesthesia." The best recent discussion is Lawrence E. Marks, "On Colored-Hearing Synesthesia, Cross-modal Translation of Sensory Dimensions," *Psychological Bulletin* 82–83 (1975), 303–31. But cf. also Odbert, Karwoski, and Eckerson, "Studies in Synesthetic Thinking, I: Musical and Verbal Associations of Colors and Mood," *Journal of General Psychology* 26 (1942), 153–73; Karwoski, Odbert, and Osgood, "Studies in Synesthetic Thinking, II: The Role of Form in Visual Response to Music," *Journal of General Psychology*, 26 (1942), 199ff. and J. G. Snider and C. E. Osgood, eds., *Semantic Differential Technique* (Chicago: Aldine, 1969).

65. Cf. also Perry, "The Definition of Value," *The Journal of Philosophy* 11 (1914), 141–62; and "Value as an Objective Predicate," *The Journal of Philosophy* 28 (1931), 477–84.

66. A discrepancy exists between the first two values in this list (based

on *F*, ch. 2, B, sec. 5) and the list of corresponding emotional strata (at *F*, ch. 5, sec. 8), where they are "spiritual" and "psychic," not "religious" and "spiritual."

67. My article, "Moral and Nonmoral Values: A Problem in Scheler's Ethics," is devoted to this problem. Its basic argument is summarized in the following discussion.

68. Dooyeweerd, of course, would consider these irreducible aspects of experience, which he would call "functional modalities of meaning" in a sense roughly analogous to Scheler's "ranks" of value, as we have seen above. See the discussion of Dooyeweerd above.

69. The idea of specifically moral values could, of course, be considered a species of what Scheler terms "spiritual values" in his value-ranking. The suggestion of specifically *moral* and *nonmoral* types of normativity and obligation implies a division within a genus calling for further examination in itself.

70. *DI*, 172f. Reference to Hartmann in Reiner (ibid.). Puolimatka accepts Scheler's remarks about "pharisaism" only in the sense that people should not intend to appear good to themselves in a self-satisfied sense. But he insists: "this does not mean that it is not legitimate to intend to be or to become benevolent" (*Moral Realism*, 147).

71. *DI*, 231–36. Hence, in an intriguing observation, Reiner points out that the thesis of Socrates that no one knowingly acts badly holds true in the case of choosing "rightly" as opposed to "wrongly" (that is, nobody knowingly chooses "incorrectly"); but it does not hold true in the case of choosing between moral "good" and "evil." Only where people can knowingly choose evil, he says, can they be held morally accountable for their acts (*DI*, 232).

For a closer inquiry into this connection, Reiner directs his readers (233 n. 1) to his lecture "Das Prinzip von Gut und Böse (Freiburg, 1949)," 20–30. But cf. also the selection by him entitled "Good and Evil: Origin and Essence of the Basic Moral Distinctions," a translation by J. J. Kockelmans of Reiner's *Gut und Böse* (Freiburg im Breisgau, 1965) 7–41, in Joseph J. Kockelmans, ed., *Contemporary European Ethics* (Garden City, NY: Anchor, 1972), 158–81.

72. Puolimatka, in particular, makes a strong case for this point, arguing on the basis of the detailed research of Henry Sidgwick that the concept of "benevolence" specifies the intuitive essence and irreducible content moral value, and rebutting objections based on J. L. Mackie's "multi-person prisoners' dilemmas" and "paradox of retribution" (*Moral Realism*, 143–55).

73. Among other things, Scheler's ranking of values alone is of no help in deciding between two alternatives where the choice is between realizing the same value for myself or for another, as Reiner points out (*DI*, 182). Furthermore, he failed to develop the implications of his analysis of "absolute" and "relative" values (*F*, 116ff./96ff.) in a way that could assist in showing when the realization of a value for another might be preferable to its realization for oneself (*DI*, 143).

In another vein, Frondizi offers several specific criticisms of the criteria Scheler offers for determining the order of ranks among nonmoral values. For instance, with reference to the criterion of "the depth of satisfaction," he asks: "In which persons are we going to 'measure' this supposed depth of satisfaction? Under what circumstances?" Again, with reference to the criterion of "duration," he asks what such a criterion could mean in light of the fact that superior values are no more or less temporal than inferior ones (*What Is Value?*, 138f.).

4 Moral Feeling and the Perception of Values

IN THE LAST CHAPTER we dealt with Scheler's critique of Kant's formal definition of the moral good and with his theory of material values, upon which his critique rests. In this chapter we shall consider how the moral good and material values are *apprehended* according to Kant and Scheler, respectively. We will see that Scheler faults Kant's view with an intellectualism that denies the affective faculties their proper role in the discernment of the moral good. For Kant such discernment always remains ultimately a matter of *rational* insight, a "fact of reason," a matter of grasping the formula of the categorical imperative through the universalizing self-legislation of reason; it cannot occur in any form other than as a species of judgment and so as a function of reason. For Scheler, by contrast, such discernment is indispensably a matter *emotional* insight, a matter of intuitively feeling the relative superiority of those values one seeks to realize. He attributes this insight to a distinctively non-rational faculty, which he calls, using a term translated inevitably with some awkwardness by Frings and Funk, "value-ception" (*Wertnehmung*).[1] This faculty differs not only from rational "con-ception" but from sensible (or phenomenological) "per-ception" (*Wahrnehmung*) in that it has a particular "pathic" quality of *feeling*. Keeping this in mind, we shall nevertheless, for the sake of linguistic ease, refer to it as "value-feeling" or the "perception of values."[2]

Of course, Kant, too, clearly (if guardedly) gives "feeling" a distinct role in moral experience, most notably in what he calls the feeling of "respect" (*Achtung*).[3] Accordingly, he refers in *The Metaphysic of Morals* to "the mind's aesthetic receptiveness to concepts of duty" (*MS*, 399); and, in a qualified analogy to the structure of the first *Critique*, he calls the chapter on moral incentives in his second *Critique* the "aesthetic of pure practical reason" (*KpV*, 90). Whatever may be true of Scheler's accusations of intellectualism, then, Kant clearly admits of an affective, "aesthetic" dimension to moral experience. Scheler recognizes this. He knows that Kant even grants a *privileged* role to the non-sensibly determined feeling of moral respect. But Scheler denies that *any* feeling has a *morally determinative* role in Kant's ethics. Moral feeling may arise as the effect of the workings of the moral principle on the affective constitution of the human subject, but, as such, it cannot be the decisive principle of moral discernment or determining ground of moral willing.

Accordingly, in what follows we shall consider, first, in some detail, Kant's theory of feeling and its role in his moral philosophy; second, Scheler's response to Kant's position; and third, the significance of Scheler's critique. In the course of examining Kant's position, we shall see that the question of whether moral feeling can serve as a moral incentive plays an important role in his discussion. This question, together with the question of the relation of moral virtue to happiness, forms the background of Scheler's response. Further, in assessing Scheler's own position, we shall consider, among other things, the question of whether the perception of values is in fact a matter of emotional feeling, as Scheler claims, or whether this view suffers from certain inadequacies.

Kant's Theory of Moral Feeling

IN THIS SECTION I shall be offering a fairly detailed analysis of Kant's theory of moral affectivity.[4] While I will be following closely what Kant says in the relevant texts, I am aware that I also shall be pressing his position at points beyond what some interpreters may find acceptable. Instead of simply accepting the way in which Kant ordinarily exploits the resources of his metaphysical dualisms (noumenal/phenomenal, etc.) in order to overcome difficulties, such as the problem of explaining how moral feeling can serve as a moral "incentive" without being "pathological," I try to press points of tension in such dualisms in order to show points of possible strain and weakness. My aim is to try to show more clearly what features of the Kantian view of affectivity may have struck Scheler as particularly objectionable and, thereby, to render Scheler's critique and alternative the more understandable.

In the Introduction to his *Metaphysic of Morals*, Kant classifies feeling under the heading of sensibility, as opposed to understanding. Sensibility has two aspects: sense and feeling. "Sense" corresponds to an intelligible object. "Feeling" refers merely to an effect, in the subject, of pleasure or pain. Pleasure may be either "contemplative," as in aesthetic taste, or "practical," as in tactile sensation. Practical pleasure evokes the appetitive power of "desire," in the narrow sense, while habitual desire is called "inclination."[5] The connection between this appetitive power and pleasure is called "interest," and in the case of natural desire, an "interest of inclination" (*MS*, 212). Objects that promise us pleasure, therefore, may be called "objects of interest or of inclination." No matter how different such objects may be, the feeling of pleasure by virtue of which they elicit our desire is the same (*KpV*, 23). It is always an empirically discerned effect upon our sensibility.

The Relation of Feeling to Moral Law

This has a direct bearing on morality. I am not concerned here with the morality of what Kant calls a purely rational or "holy" will, such as he attributes to God, but only the possible morality of wills belonging to imperfectly rational beings such as must overcome sensible disinclinations in order to assent to the demands of moral law.[6] It is only such wills, after all, to which the question of feelings are directly relevant. Accordingly, since only experience can show us whether a feeling of pleasure or pain will arise in the presence of a certain object, for Kant, no universally valid moral law can possibly be based on a maxim for the realization of practical pleasure (*KpV*, 58). If our act is motivated by feelings of personal satisfaction, it cannot have moral value, for Kant, even if what we do is right. It may have "legality," but not "morality" (*KpV*, 71). But acting from feeling offers no guarantee that an action will be right. At best, it guarantees that we will act from natural self-interest. But even if our desire was for the sublime pleasure that comes from acting morally, this still would not make such pleasure a moral *motive* for action (*KpV*, 115). The only thing that can guarantee the moral worth of our actions is that *the moral law itself directly determine the will* (*KpV*, 71).

This does not mean that our faculties of appetite and feeling enjoy no amicable relation to the moral law. Indeed, one of Kant's abiding concerns was precisely to establish the nature of such a relation. In 1773, well before his major ethical works, he made this significant statement in a letter to Marcus Herz: "The concept of morality must please in the highest degree, must have moving power; and though it is indeed intellectual, it must have direct relation to the basic incentives of the will."[7] Again, in the celebrated Duisberg Fragment 6, probably written just after the first *Critique*, he offered an analysis of the desire to be worthy of happiness, calling the enjoyment of this condition an "intellectual pleasure."[8] Josef Bohatec accordingly refers to the doctrine of this fragment as "intellectual eudaemonism" (cited by Beck, *Commentary*, 216 n. 16). How does one reconcile such notions with Kant's insistence that moral law must *directly* determine the will? The best argument may turn out to be that the law determines the will "*directly*," but not *immediately*, that is causality is mediated through practical incentives. Kant's language remains puzzling. Indeed, he himself calls the very notion of intellectual feeling "self-contradictory" (*KpV*, 117).

The answer to these questions must begin with Kant's statements in his chapter on moral incentives in his second *Critique*. There he notes that the determination of the will by moral law has a two-fold effect on feeling—one negative, one positive. The negative effect, which comes through the striking down of self-conceit and the thwarting of inclinations, is the "pathological" feeling of *pain*. The positive effect, which comes through the suprasensible nature of the moral law that is made *visible* by the feeling of pain, is the "moral" feeling of *respect (KpV, 73)*. As Heidegger observes: "From the negative phenomenon of repulsion the force that performs and grounds the repelling must become visible a priori and positively."[9] The feeling of pain is effected by means of a negation (a striking down) of a negation (the rejection of law in self-conceit), which reveals practical reason in its being-other than nature.[10] The moral law elicits a positive feeling of respect by revealing itself as the source of free, intellectual causality, completely independent of natural inclination. Kant seems reluctant to call this moral feeling "pleasure," because of its suprasensible origin. There can be no feeling, he says, for the moral law *itself (KpV, 75)*. The feeling of respect arises only mediately by means of the removal of the resistance offered by the appetitive powers to suprasensible determination. For this reason Kant is willing to call the feeling of respect "negative pleasure" *(KU, §23)*; and even though it has "sensuous feeling" as its underlying condition, he contrasts it with "pathological" feeling by calling it "moral" feeling *(KpV, 75)*.

CONSCIOUSNESS OF THE LAW AND MORAL INCENTIVE

Granting that the moral law produces such effects on the faculty of feeling, it is still not clear how the human will is furnished with moral incentives. Can a feeling, such as respect, furnish a moral incentive? It would seem not. For Kant declares clearly that "respect for the law is not the incentive to morality" and that the moral incentive of the human will "can never be anything other than the moral law" *(KpV, 76, 72)*. But then the question becomes: How does the moral law, which is suprasensible, become an incentive for the human will? To answer this question, it is necessary to understand that, for Kant, a feeling may be either a *cause* or an *effect* of an appetitive act. Typically, practical pleasure precedes an appetitive act as its *cause*, and the object producing the sensible pleasure is an object of an "interest of inclination." But when the practical pleasure follows from a preceding appetitive act as its *effect*, then it is an "intellectual pleasure" and the interest in the object is an "interest of reason" *(MS, 212)*.

Hence, it would appear that Kant allows for something like "intellectual feeling," despite what he says about the "self-contradictory" character of such an expression *(KpV, 117)*. Correlatively, he does allow for a kind of rational inclination *(propensio intellectualis)*, which is not the cause of this pure rational interest, but rather its effect *(MS, 213)*. Thus, not all desire is sensuously determined; one must distinguish a "higher" and "lower" faculty of desire *(KpV, 22)*, following the scholastic distinction between *passion* and *will*. Practical intellectual pleasure, then, is pleasure determined by an act of the *will*, or what is the same in this case, *practical reason*.[11]

In the case of such intellectual feeling or pleasure, the connection between the appetitive power and the pleasure, as we have seen, may be called "an interest of reason" (*MS*, 212). "Interest" is that by which reason becomes practical, for Kant, a cause determining the will, or an "incentive" of the will (*GMS*, 460 n.; *KpV*, 79). But how can an interest *of reason* become an "incentive" of the will? On the one hand, Kant denies that the will can be morally determined by any antecedent feeling, even the feeling of respect. On the other hand, he insists that only the moral law itself can directly determine the will as its incentive. But as Lewis White Beck observes: "In spite of what Kant says, the law *itself* is not the incentive. A law is just not the sort of thing that can be an incentive. At most, consciousness of a law can be an incentive. If the law itself were a determinant of conduct, without the intervention of consciousness (which means, for us men, also feeling), it would not be a practical law, and men would not be free agents" (*Commentary*, p. 221f.). For Kant, after all, *consciousness* of the moral law is "a fact of reason" (*KpV*, 31). Hence, the question becomes: What is the nature of this consciousness of the law, such that it can be an incentive? If the second *Critique* leaves any room for doubt on this, it is removed by *The Metaphysic of Morals*, where Kant writes: "Reverence (*Achtung*) for the law, which on the side of the subject can be designated as moral feeling, is one with man's consciousness of duty" (*MS*, 464). This means that man's consciousness of moral law is identical with moral feeling. But then, the feeling of respect, in some sense, must be a moral incentive.

This would seem to directly contradict Kant's statements denying that any feeling, even moral feeling, can be an incentive to morality. However, this would be a true contradiction only if the feeling of respect were a feeling *preceding* the consciousness of the law—if it had to be *presupposed* in order for the law to become a determining ground of the will (*KpV*, 71). But moral feeling cannot *precede* consciousness of the law if, as Kant suggests in *The Metaphysic of Morals*, it *is* consciousness of the law. Only by means of this identification can we make sense of Kant's statements that respect is "the sole and undoubted moral incentive," and that "the incentive to be employed must be only the respect for duty, the sole genuine moral feeling" (*KpV*, 78, 85).

If the feeling of respect is a moral incentive, then, like all incentives, it must in some sense be "a subjective determining ground of a will" (*KpV*, 71f.). But this does not mean that it determines the will in the sense of an "antecedent feeling tending to morality."[12] Such an incentive would be the *cause*, not the *effect*, of the appetitive power or will, and therefore neither intellectual nor moral; and a will so determined would be sensibly determined and therefore neither free nor rational. Rather, moral feeling is itself objectively determined *by the will* insofar as it is effected by the legislation of practical reason. But then how can it be an *incentive*? The answer is not immediately clear. According to Heidegger, respect is the means by which the law first becomes accessible to me as law: "This means at the same time that this feeling of respect for the law also does not serve, as Kant puts it, for substantiating the law; the law is not what it is *because* I have respect for it, but just the reverse: my having a feeling of respect for the law and with it this specific mode of revelation of the law is the only way in which the moral law is able to approach me" (*Basic Problems*, 135). Again, Beck says that the subjectivity of the incentive "refers to the workings of the moral principle, which is itself objective, upon the constitution of the human subject, and this working is the incentive which is obviously subject-conditioned as well as objectively determined."[13] But how the moral feeling of respect for the law can be both (1) an affective response objectively determined *by the will* (as practical reason) and (2) a practical incentive serving as a subjective determining ground *of the will*, is not immediately apparent.

MORAL FEELING AS RATIONAL SELF-DISCLOSURE

Perhaps the clearest sense that can be made of Kant's notion of moral incentive is by thinking of it as some sort of rational self-disclosure. Heidegger points out that, for Kant, respect for the *law* is conjointly a specific revelation of one's *self* to oneself as a rational-moral agent (*Basic Problems*, 132). Respect for the law involves respect for oneself as the self that is not bound by self-conceit and self-love, but transcends its natural conditions by virtue of its suprasensible freedom and rationality. Nowhere is this dimension of moral feeling more powerfully invoked by Kant than in his famous eulogy of duty, where he points to the suprasensible personality as the seat of human dignity.[14] Through submission to the law, I experience not only self-humiliation but the self-elevation of myself to myself as autonomous *homo noumenon*. I experience the humiliation of my heteronomous natural self by my autonomous suprasensible self as consciousness of my higher vocation.[15]

If such an experience can serve as a moral incentive, it would not be, first of all, an antecedent feeling tending to morality, but one that proceeds from and, eventually, reinforces the determination of the will by reason. This seems evident from Kant's chapter on the *summum bonum* in his second *Critique*, where he speaks of the determination of the will by reason as the "ground of the feeling of pleasure" (*KpV*, 116). While denying any necessary empirical connection between moral virtue and happiness, Kant nevertheless insists on an *analogue* of happiness that necessarily accompanies the consciousness of virtue but does not involve a gratification, as happiness does; and he calls this a *"self-contentment"* or *"intellectual contentment"* that arises from consciousness of our independence from inclinations as motives determining our desiring (*KpV*, 117f.). He goes even further in *Religion within the Limits of*

Reason Alone, describing the aesthetic character or temperament of virtue as "*joyous.*" Moral resolve, he says, begets a "joyous frame of mind," assuring us of having attained a "love for the good," of having incorporated it into our maxim (*R*, 23f., n./19, n.; also *KU*, §29, "General Remark").

There are passages in Kant's works, as Beck notes, where he appears to cross over the line and speak about the necessity of rewards and punishments as spurs to morality in a way that suggests a perverse kind of "religious eudaemonism" (*Commentary*, 214). In his first *Critique*, for example, Kant says that "without a God and without a world invisible to us now but hoped for, the glorious ideas of morality are indeed objects of approval and admiration, but not springs (*Triebfeder*) of purpose and of action" (*KrV*, A 812f.–B 840f.). It is true that Kant does insist, at least in his second *Critique*, that future rewards and happiness can never serve as the *determining ground* of morality (cf. *KpV*, 146ff.) But such passages underline the difficulty of conceptualizing incentives for morality within Kant's dualistic framework of reason and sensibility.

For Kant, feeling—whether sensibly or suprasensibly determined—is fundamentally *sensually* conditioned. Whether it is the cause of appetitive desire (and therefore pathological), or the effect of rational willing (and therefore moral), it belongs essentially to the genus of sensibility. For this reason it cannot serve as the objective determining ground of moral value. Still, it is significantly related to morality. Consciousness of the moral law itself is identified with moral feeling. In this sense, feeling can serve, at least, as the subjective determining ground of morality and, he claims, as an incentive. In this capacity, moral feeling—or, what is the same, consciousness of the moral law, moral insight, or the perception of moral value—reveals its negative side in the pain of subjection to law, and its positive side in the intellectual pleasure of moral self-contentment and the joyous temperament of virtue.

Scheler's Critique and Alternative

SCHELER RECOGNIZES THE ROLE played by the moral feeling of respect in Kant's ethics.[16] He recognizes that, unlike sensibly determined feelings, respect is a non-sensibly determined feeling—an intellectual feeling "effected by the moral law" (*F*, 255/241). But he denies that any feeling can have a morally determinative role for Kant. After all, Kant does say that respect is merely an *effect* of the moral law, and that the moral law *alone* serves as the moral determining ground of the will. Hence, despite the place Kant allots to the feeling of respect in his ethics, he still holds, according to Scheler, that "only a formal ethics, which, as a rational ethics, eschews all references to the emotive life, can avoid those errors to which all imaginable forms of eudaemonism lead" (*F*, 254/239).

No kind of feeling, for Kant, can furnish the unconditional basis needed for ethics.

The basic problem with Kant's theory of feeling, according to Scheler, is that it presupposes an understanding of human affectivity that is altogether *eudaemonistic*, or, more basically, *hedonistic*.[17] It assumes that human beings naturally desire and strive for nothing but pleasure; that they are determined thus by nature, unalterably and invariably; that nothing within affective human nature—the nature of human beings qua natural animal—is capable of altering this natural inclination. The only thing capable of superseding it is a determination of the will by something beyond affective human nature—namely, the moral law. Apart from such determination, even the value of striving for someone else's pleasure is genetically reducible to that of vicariously striving for one's own. All happiness and pleasure, furthermore, are regarded as qualitatively identical insofar as they are *sensible*. And all feelings, even the non-sensibly determined feeling of respect, are, by definition, *sensible* feelings.[18] This view, of course, is based on Kant's mechanistic view of the phenomenal world and on an empiricist theory of will, which he took over uncritically from his contemporaries, as we have seen (see above, ch. 1, sec. 3; and ch. 3, sec. 1).

Thus, when Kant rejects practical principles presupposing a material object of *desire* as a suitable determining ground of the will, he does so, Scheler suggests, because of a thoroughly hedonistic conception of desire. Desire, for Kant, is an effect of the sensible feeling of pleasure produced by an object of desire. But since the relation between desire and its objects is empirical, a posteriori, and inevitably contingent, it is unable to furnish the unconditioned ground necessary for true morality. Kant therefore excludes as untenable all ethics based on material objects of desire (including objects of inclination or willing).

As Scheler points out, however, this means that, on Kant's view, an ethics based on material *values* would have to be excluded as well, since values must be regarded, in effect, as resting on the contingent relation between empirical objects and their effects on sensible feelings.[19] Likewise, this means that Kant's ethics effectually excludes any kind of feeling, including Scheler's *value-feeling*, from having a legitimate role in discerning or determining the moral lawfulness of willing and acting. There cannot be, for Kant, anything like Scheler's immediately *felt* values that can serve as the a priori ground of moral discernment or action. The reason for this is that Kant assumes, in his account of the emotions, an anthropological hedonism such as he condemns in his ethics. As Scheler notes, although Kant never undertook a special study of pleasure and value, "it follows from his work that, for him, the fact that a thing has a value means that man attributes a value to it in the form of a judgment," and that this "occurs when a thing's effects on the psychophysical organism cause a state of *pleasure*" (F, 254/239). But since this would make values dependent upon the pathological relation between objects of desire and their effects on sensible feelings, any ethics based on value-feeling could only be a form of hedonism.

But as Scheler aims to show, Kant's view is based on the mistaken assumption that there can be no other kind of ordering principle in moral experience than reason and no other kind of discernment of orderedness (or of an ordering principle) than a rationally determined one. Kant therefore mistakenly assumes that awareness of moral lawfulness must be (as in the case of the feeling of respect) some mode of *rationally* determined awareness. He lacks any clear conception of an *ordo amoris*—a nonrational order (and ordering principle) proper to our affective life. He has an impoverished view of emotive life and offers no clear way of differentiating the diverse strata of feelings, and of the corresponding strata of values and their interrelations, which those feelings are able to apprehend. He indiscriminately reduces all feeling—including moral feeling—to *sensible* feeling, thereby entrapping his account of affective life in a rigid dualistic scheme of "reason" and "sensibility."

With rare exceptions such as St. Augustine and Blaise Pascal, says Scheler, philosophers since antiquity have been bound by the ancient prejudice that everything in the mind belongs either to "reason" or to "sensibility," and that the whole of emotional life is therefore, in principle, reducible to "sensibility." As a consequence, ethical theories have been construed either as rational, and therefore absolute and a priori, or as nonrational (and noncognitive), and therefore relative, empirical, and emotional. But entirely overlooked in this dualism is the irreducible originality of non-logical yet non-sensible forms of intuitive givenness. This is what Pascal had in mind, according to Scheler, when he wrote: "The heart has its reasons, which reason does not know."[20] Thus Scheler writes that "there is a type of experiencing whose 'objects' are completely inaccessible to reason; reason is as blind to them as ears and hearing are blind to colors. It is a kind of experience that leads us to *genuinely* objective objects and the eternal order among them, i.e., to *values* and the order of ranks among them. And the order and laws contained in this experience are as exact and evident as those of logic and mathematics."[21]

Values, then, are a type of object entirely inaccessible to reason, according to Scheler. This does not mean that reason cannot speak for emotional feelings for values and their order of rank, or make pronouncements concerning the morality of realizing particular values or appropriateness of certain emotions in certain situations. It only means that reason itself lacks any direct, original access to values and, therefore, cannot speak knowingly of values in the "first-person," so to speak, at all.[22] Neither ancient nor modern rationalism, neither Plato nor Kant, grasped this fact, according to Scheler. Restrained by their bifurcations of reason and sense, they either relegated values to an inferior plane of irrational affectivity or endeavored to merge them with entities of the intellect. But values are apprehended neither sensibly nor rationally. They belong to an order of their own with an ordering principle of its own that has nothing to do with the logic of the intellect. Values belong to an affective order—an *ordo amoris*—and are revealed to us through emotive experiences of value-feeling, preference, love, and hate.

In support of his view, Scheler undertakes a detailed phenomenological analysis of emotive life, which enables him to reveal various levels of affectivity not often clearly distinguished.[23] By means of this analysis, he intends to show the distinct, and irreducibly non-sensible, nature of value-feeling. Only by clearly distinguishing the objective, essential nature of value-feeling from the subjective, empirical nature of sensible feelings can Scheler rebut the hedonistic psychology of Kant and show that values are not reducible to relations between objects and feelings of pleasure or pain.

A fundamental distinction that runs through Scheler's analysis is that between "intentional feeling" (*intentionales Fühlen*) and "feeling-state" (*Gefühlszustand*). The former refers to the apprehension of an experience, whereas the latter refers to an experience as directly lived-through. The former has an intentional element, whereas the latter does not. For example, a sensible feeling-state such as pain, can occur together with various intentional feelings *of* this feeling-state. I may "suffer," "endure," "tolerate" or even "enjoy" pain; but the feeling-state of pain itself does not vary. There is no intrinsic object-relatedness in the feeling-state. Any reference to what may have caused the sensation of pain, for instance, is only established by means of an intellectual reflection subsequent to the moment in which the pain itself is felt. Intentional feeling, on the other hand, is directly and immediately object-related. It bears an inherent intentional reference to objects. This reference is not intellectual. It is not established externally by thought or by means of a mental representation or image. Rather, it is immediately evident in the intentionality of the feeling itself. According to Scheler, it is through such intentional feeling that values are revealed to us.

If values are given to us in emotive experiences of intentional value-feeling, their relative superiority is given to us in acts of "preferring."[24] As "acts," these differ from "functions" of value-feeling. They are "executed"; they do not simply "happen" like functions.[25] Yet "preference" must not be confused with "choice." One must not assume that the height of a value is "*felt*" in the same manner as the value itself, and that the higher value is *subsequently* "preferred." Rather, the height of a value is given immediately *in* the act of preferring. As a cognitive act, "preferring" differs from (and occurs in the absence of) conative acts of "choosing," which strictly can occur only between alternative actions. We may prefer roses to carnations regardless of any choice we may make regarding a purchase of one or the other. We choose between alternative actions, but we prefer one object of value to another, or one value to another (regardless of the bearers of value) (*F*, 274/260, cf. 107/87).

Love and hatred, for Scheler, form the highest level of intentional emotive life, the level farthest removed from feeling-states and most straightforwardly intentional. Even language reveals this: we speak not of loving or hating "about something" or "in something," but of loving or hating *something*. Loving and hating therefore are not to be confused with reactions such as rage, anger, fury, or even less with emotions that "well up" within us and "take their course" in us without any intentional connection with what they are "about." Like preferring, loving and hating are "acts," not "functions," and they contain no element of conation or striving.[26] But they must not be confused with acts of preference: preference involves a *plurality* of values, while love and hate involve only a *single* value. Furthermore, love and hate are spontaneous acts, unlike thought-out reactions, such as vengeance. Unlike preferring and value-feeling, love and hate are not *cognitive* acts. They are not even modes of value-apprehension at all; rather, they lie at the base of all value-apprehension and value-cognition.[27] More specifically, they are acts in which the realm of values, perceived through value-feeling, is *extended* or *narrowed*. This does not mean that values are created or destroyed by love and hate, since values exist independently of us. Nor does this mean that love or hate are directed in a "responding" manner to a value *after* that value is first perceived or preferred. Rather, love and hate *precede* value-perception and preference, *disclosing* or *concealing* values (F, 275/261).

History offers few examples of philosophers who have shared Scheler's appreciation of the rich diversity of affective life and its capacity for disclosing a world of values. This is true especially of the history of modern philosophy. Scheler distinguishes two periods in modern philosophy in which, he says, erroneous theories of affectivity have been set forth: the first, from Descartes through the eighteenth century; the second, from Kant onward. Until the nineteenth century, he says, it was widely recognized that there are intentional feelings that cannot be reduced to sensible feeling-states. The error of major rationalists, such as Descartes, Spinoza, and Leibniz, was their assumption that intentional feeling, love, hate, and the like, are "obscure" and "confused" *forms of thought*. As a result, good and evil and other values apprehended by such "confused" thoughts were reduced to degrees of perfection of being. By the beginning of the nineteenth century (after Tetens and Kant), it was increasingly recognized that feelings cannot be reduced to confused forms of thought. However, under the influence of the earlier rationalism, everything emotional was degraded to sensible feeling-states. The error of Tetens, Kant, and their successors was their assumption that feelings lack the intentional character of thought (F, 275f./262f.).

This background underlines the uniqueness of Scheler's position. Intentional feeling is reducible neither to a mode of rational thought nor to a type of sensible feeling-state. It is an autonomous form of intuition belonging to an order (*ordo amoris*) whose laws are non-rational and yet as exact as those of logic and mathematics. This does not mean that perceptions and estimations of values do not vary from one historical and cultural ethos to another and from one individual to another. That is a fact of historical development and of individual capacities for value-feeling. But the most radical relativity of moral value-estimations gives us no reason for assuming a relativism of moral values themselves (F, 317/303). For Scheler, as for Auguste Comte, it is no less preposterous to speak of "freedom of conscience" in morals than it is in mathematics, physics, or chemistry.[28] The fact that values are not derived from the rational analysis of ideas does not mean they are not absolute. Nor does the fact that they are apprehended by means of feeling mean that they consist in the relation between objects of desire and sensible feeling-states, as suggested by the hedonistic psychological assumptions of Kant.

In light of this, Scheler is prepared to show clearly why he rejects Kant's view of the role of affectivity in moral experience. Specifically, he is prepared to show two things: first, why he rejects Kant's hedonistic assumptions regarding human affective life, and second, why he rejects Kant's view of the relation between moral virtue and happiness.

Why Scheler Rejects Kant's Psychological Hedonism

For Kant, as we have seen, all feeling is subsumed in the final analysis under the faculty of *sensibility*. This means that feeling has nothing of the intentionality or spontaneity possessed by the faculty of reason. All feelings are reduced to sensible feeling-states. For Kant, as we have also seen, every natural desire is desire for sensible *pleasure*. There is nothing of the lawful ordering principle of reason in it that would empower it to supersede its inherently hedonistic inclinations. All natural desires, therefore, aim at fulfilling themselves in feeling-states of sensible pleasure.

But as Scheler shows, Kant's view is mistaken on at least four counts. First, it not only overlooks the fact that not all feelings are *feeling-states*, but that not all feelings are *sensible* feelings. Not only does Kant fail to discern the *intentional* character of many feelings and emotions such as love and hate, he also fails to distinguish the specific types and levels of feeling corresponding to respective ranks of value. For example, in addition to the "sensible" feelings recognized by Kant, Scheler distinguishes "vital," "psychic," and "spiritual" feelings.[29] Only by distinguishing such strata of feelings can we account for the fact that more than one feeling can coexist in a single experience, such as the experience of enjoying the pleasant bouquet of a glass of wine while feeling depressed and unhappy (F, 343/330f.).

Second, Kant overlooks the fact that there are goals or ends of conation and desire other than the realization of *pleasure*. He fails to note that conations and desires can be directed toward values as their goals and that these values may include others besides sensible pleasure. He does not recognize the existence of *pre-purposive* desires or conations, in which purposes have not yet been consciously posited by the will, but in which there is nevertheless a directedness toward values as their goals. And he overlooks the fact that such conations may be directed not only toward values of sensible pleasure but also toward other higher values, such as the values of vital well-being, aesthetic beauty, or spiritual joy.

Third, Kant fails to recognize that the motive or incentive of desire and conation lies not only in the final causality of "attraction" exercised by their goals, but also in the efficient causality of "propulsion" (*vis a tergo*) exercised by the feeling-state from which the striving or willing issues forth as its source or mainspring.[30] The ultimate origin of all desire and willing, finally, is a person's felt self-worth, or, in Scheler's words, the "inner value" of the person and the innermost feeling-state or "central emotional fulfillment" that accompanies it.

Fourth, Kant does not recognize that the direction of striving or willing is ultimately determined by one's deepest personal feeling-states.[31] Furthermore, he failed to see that not all of our natural striving and willing is hedonistic. In fact, says Scheler, hedonistic inclinations often may be only a sign of deeper vital and spiritual feelings of misery and despair. In other words, an inclination toward pleasure and self-gratification at the level of more superficial, peripheral, and manipulable *sensible* feelings is determined by emotional discontentment and distress at the level of deeper, more central, *spiritual* feelings. It seeks surrogates, at the more superficial level of sensible pleasure, for feelings of vital well-being, spiritual joy, and happiness at a deeper level. On the other hand, the deeper the feeling of well-being and joy, the less dependent such feeling is on the vicissitudes of external life. This is why spiritually contented people can suffer misfortune with joy and without the need to deaden their sense of pain at more peripheral levels, as seen in the ethos of early Christians martyred and persecuted for their faith (F, 358/346). This means that one's innermost feeling of self-worth determines the *moral value* of one's striving and willing. The desire and inclination to realize higher values has its source in "a *surplus* of positive feelings at the deepest stratum" (F, 360/349).

Why Scheler Rejects Kant's View of Virtue and Happiness

In light of this, Scheler rejects Kant's view of the relation between moral virtue and happiness. For Kant, happiness can never be a *source* of moral virtue. It can be only a *result* or *effect* of virtue. Even then, it is related necessarily to human virtue only through the ideal of justice in a world to come. Scheler has no quarrel with Kant's denial either that striving for happiness produces moral virtue or that moral virtue necessarily produces happiness. What he rejects is Kant's view that happiness is of no significance in the *determination* of moral virtue, as its source. He writes:

> For all *feelings* of happiness and unhappiness have their foundation in *feelings of values*. Deepest happiness and complete bliss are dependent in their being on a consciousness of one's own moral goodness. *Only the good person is blissful.* This does *not* preclude the possibility that this very blissfulness is the *root* and *source* of all willing and acting. But happiness can *never* be a goal or even a "purpose" of willing and acting. *Only the happy person acts in a morally good way.* Happiness is therefore in no way a "reward for virtue," nor is virtue the *means* to reach blissfulness. Nevertheless, happiness is the *root* and *source* of virtue, a fountainhead, although it is only a *consequence* of the inner *goodness* of the person. (F, 370/359)

This is not necessarily a piece of circular reasoning. Scheler is not simply saying that moral people are happy and happy people are moral. Rather, he is saying that the value of (1) *striving and willing* is grounded in the value of (2) the *central feeling-state*, which is grounded in the value of (3) the *person*. What he appears to mean is something like this: morally virtuous desires and actions are grounded in emotional well-being; and emotional well-being, in turn, is grounded in the felt self-worth of a morally virtuous disposition and character. Of course, as Aristotle saw, a virtuous disposition or character is formed only by virtuous actions; but the two are not identical, and the former eventually comes to condition the latter, even as it is initially conditioned by them. For Scheler, Kant's way of linking happiness to virtue as a promissory reward falls within the sphere of *justice* rather than *morality*.[32] It offers no clear sense—or differentiation of qualities—of the moral values implicit in actions, desires, feelings, dispositions, or persons themselves (F, 371/360).

Comparative Assessment

KANT'S THEORY OF FEELING, as Scheler saw, is bound to the classic dualist tradition for which feelings belong to the faculty of "sensibility" as opposed to "rationality." This produces a tension underlying almost everything Kant says about the feeling of respect; for respect is a feeling that must be *rationally* informed. On the one hand, feeling in general is something that belongs to the function of receptivity and to the naturally determined faculty of sensibility. But the only source of lawfulness within this system belongs to the function of spontaneity and to the autonomy of self-legislating practical reason. Hence, feeling cannot serve as the objective determining ground of moral value. In other words, if the human agent is divided into "reason" and "sensibility," then morality consists in being rational—in subduing one's sensible, pathological nature and purifying the will of all affectivity. Affectivity cannot enter into the principle of moral willing. Moral willing must be free from passion.

On the other hand, in Kant's discussion of moral feeling, this disembodied metaphysics of purism seems to give way before a richly phenomenological description of moral affectivity, which Heidegger calls "the most brilliant phenomenological analysis of the phenomenon of morality that we have from him" (*Basic Problems*, 133). In fact, his entire discussion of the feeling of respect as a moral incentive presupposes that willing is indissolubly merged with feeling in the acting person—a presupposition that the explicit dualism of his system makes rather difficult if not impossible. Whether or not there is a tacit phenomenological ethics implicit in Kant's ethical writings that can be "retrieved" from Kant's system, as John Caputo suggests ("Kant's Ethics," 141), others may judge. But Caputo is certainly right in sensing points of incompatibility between Kant's analysis of moral feeling and his "metaphysics of purism," according to which feeling belongs wholly to the phenomenal world of our pathologically determined nature, which must be purged from the pure, moral will.

Is moral feeling phenomenal or noumenal? Is it pure or is it part of our pathological system? It cannot be both. Yet Kant's account is ambivalent. On the one hand, it is described as an affective response to the determination of the will by moral law, as an effect of rational willing on our emotions, as a practical incentive, as a subjective determining ground of the will. This suggests that it is something phenomenal, belonging to our affective nature. On the other hand, it is described as an "intellectual" feeling and identified with awareness of the moral law (a "fact of reason"), although the law itself is said to be suprasensible and not susceptible of affective feeling (*KpV*, 75). This suggests that moral feeling is something noumenal, devoid of pathological affectivity. But which is it? Within Kant's system it must either be one or the other, phenomenal or noumenal, affective or purely rational. It cannot be both.

Kant's metaphysics subverts his phenomenology. His metaphysics compels him to deny that respect can be a moral incentive, since it is a feeling and therefore sensibly conditioned (*KpV*, 76). His phenomenology compels him to recognize that human emotions furnish powerful subjective motives for actions conforming to duty, and that respect for moral law is an obvious moral incentive (*KpV*, 78, 85). But even his description of respect as an incentive betrays the subversive influence of his metaphysics. Respect is distinguished from other feelings as an *effect* rather than *cause* of willing. But then, how does it work as an incentive? How does it move the will to moral action?

One possibility is that the will may be moved by consciousness of the law. As we have seen earlier in this chapter, moral feeling is identified with this consciousness. This is evident, for instance, in Kant's discussion of a person's consciousness of being a suprasensible moral agent. But this presents a problem: since this consciousness is what *moves* the will, it cannot also be the *effect* of the will. In this instance, it may qualify as an incentive, but not as moral feeling, on Kant's grounds.

Another possibility is that the will may be moved by the affective incentives of "self-contentment" and a "joyous temperament" produced as *effects* of previous instances of moral willing. But this, too, presents a problem: since these feelings are the affective results of contingent instances of moral willing, they cannot be relied upon to *move* the will in the absence of practical rational insight into the moral law itself. In this instance, such feelings may qualify as moral respect, but they are no substitute for practical reason.

A basic ambivalence in Kant's discussion turns on two possible senses of "will"—the "executive will" (*Willkür*) and the "legislative will" (*Wille*), to borrow Abbott's terminology (*Kant's "Critique,"* 268). Only the former can be moved by moral feeling. The latter, which is equivalent to practical reason, cannot be moved at all, and, as Beck says, there is little or no justification for even calling it a "will" (*Commentary*, 179). This allows for considerable ambiguity. For one thing, it means that the will can be both mover (as "legislative") and moved (as "executive"). Furthermore, if moral feeling is identified with consciousness of the law, this means that it can be conceived both as the determining ground of the "executive will" and as an affective response determined by the "legislative will." It is possible to view Kant here, as Caputo does, as victimized by his own predilection for metaphysical dualism and purism.

Scheler offers not only a cogent critique of Kant at this point, as we have seen, but a compelling alternative. He argues that there are other kinds of lawfulness and orderedness besides the rational kind that is imposed by a reasoning subject, pointing out phenomenological evidence for a nonrational *ordo amoris*. In light of this, he rejects the "ancient prejudice" implicit in Kant's assumption that everything in the mind must belong either to "reason" or "sensibility," as well as the sensualistic presupposition that the whole of emotional life may therefore be reduced to "sensibility." Nor does he find any evidence for Kant's assumption that all conation that is not rationally determined ("willing") is an irrational, chaotic manifold of pathologically determined "desires" and "inclinations." Not only does such a view reveal an impoverished understanding of emotive life; more importantly, when coupled with a hedonistic theory of conation, as it is in Kant, it effectively excludes phenomenological value-feeling from having its proper role in discerning and determining the morality of willing and action.

For Scheler, morality can have no content whatsoever apart from the material contents of nonmoral values that can be realized through willing and action. The capacity for apprehending such values is therefore necessary for discerning the content of *moral* value. As we have seen, he calls this "value-ception" (*Wertnehmung*), or—less awkwardly—"value-feeling." According to Scheler, conative impulses, desires, and inclinations are clearly "motivated" by value-feeling and have their "source" in feeling-states such as pleasure, sorrow, happiness, or despair. At the deepest level of innermost emotional fulfillment, such feelings are feelings of personal self-worth grounded self-reflectively in the felt moral value of oneself as a person. No one saw this point better, according to Scheler, than Martin Luther, who "always emphasized not only that 'the person must be good and pious' before good acts can emanate from him, but also that the person must first be *blissful* in order to will and effect the good. How much more deeply he understood this," writes Scheler, "than Kant" (*F*, 360 n. 3/349 n. 135). In effect, then, Kant's view of the matter must be reversed. Happiness is not in any sense the *result* of moral willing and action, but rather the proximate, if not ultimate, *source*.

Scheler's criticism of Kant at this point is well-founded to the extent that Kant links the *consequence* of happiness to virtue by means of the "postulate" of God's existence as the "ground of exact coincidence of happiness with morality" (*KpV*, 125). However, it fails to take adequate account of Kant's notion of "self-contentment," which accompanies consciousness of freedom from natural determination, and his notions of "intellectual pleasure" and "joyous temperament" that accompany consciousness of being determined by moral law. Despite his metaphysics, Kant seems very close in these instances to describing just the sort of thing Scheler has in mind. This is particularly true when we recall that, for Kant, moral feeling is called a "practical incentive" and that, as Heidegger points out, it is identified with the "*self*-feeling" of the person as a suprasensible moral agent (cf. the last part of sec. 1, above). The parallels one finds in Kant, at this point, to Scheler's notion of felt *self-worth* as the primordial motive of all desiring, willing, and acting, are remarkable.

There is, in fact, considerable warrant for Scheler's view that there are forms of lawfulness and orderedness independent of those imposed by the rational subject. One finds such warrant not only in the principles and laws discovered by the natural sciences, such as physics and biology, but in those of the human sciences, such as psychology, linguistics, and aesthetics. So, too, it may be found in the phenomenology of moral experience.[33] Scheler insists that the whole hierarchy of values constituting the basis of moral experience is given emotionally and constitutes an "*ordo amoris.*" But this raises questions. What about those other values that Scheler doesn't focus upon? What about linguistic, mathematical, and logical values, for example? Do they belong to this hierarchy of values too? If so, are they given emotionally also, and may their principles be subsumed appropriately under the heading of an "ordo amoris"? One could argue that Scheler would insist that every order of material universals has its own particular manner of givenness and mode of being apprehended. But then, what are these? How are mathematical values given and apprehended, for example? In the same way that moral values are? It might be argued that there are various manners of givenness and of grasping what is given besides the emotional, which are not capable of being subsumed easily under the heading of "feeling" in the ordinary sense.³⁴ There are certainly other orders or regions of experience besides the moral; and one may be forgiven for wondering at times whether Scheler does not improperly conflate the orders of morality and psychology, as well as different possible manners of givenness and modes of apprehending what is given.³⁵

Likewise, one may agree with Scheler that the principles of morality and feeling are irreducible and still question whether they are as completely separable from logical and rational factors—even in their original apprehension—as Scheler suggests. There is no question in Scheler about the possibility of rationally analyzing values apprehended by feeling. The question is whether reason is not also involved, in some sense, in value-feeling. Puolimatka, for example, accepts Scheler's claim that axiological principles are not mere "applications" of logical principles to values, but rejects Scheler's thesis that axiological principles are wholly independent of logical ones as too extreme (*Moral Realism*, 163. cf. Dooyeweerd, "Epistemological-Logical Gegenstand Relation"). Reiner insists that the act of value-feeling "does not consist in a feeling that is isolated or separate from the whole of personality," but is an integral act of the *self*, in which "the sensuous and intellectual elements of the self stand in the closest possible relation to each other and form a unity" (*DI*, 135). Furthermore, if Dooyeweerd's analysis is accurate, then no functional aspect of our experience—whether moral, psychological, or logical—is ever entirely separate from any other in experience, even if analytically distinguishable in thought.³⁶ I am not sure Scheler would have a quarrel with everything just said, but the thrust and pathos of his writing would not rest comfortably with it apart from some careful qualification.

Furthermore, one may even question whether the intuition of values is properly the function of *feeling* at all—at least, not unless the notion of "feeling" is expanded considerably beyond its ordinary sense.³⁷ It was Franz Brentano and the "Second Austrian School of Values" who first installed the entire problematic of value theory within the framework of human *emotions*. Scheler followed Brentano in this respect, as did Husserl, Meinong, and others, and was probably also influenced by Dilthey, who attributed to feeling (empathy) a basic epistemological function in the human sciences.³⁸ The identification of values as objects of *emotional feeling* and of value-intentions as *feelings* has been sharply contested by Quentin Smith, who argues that values are not objects of feeling but of *presentation*, that value-intentions belong not to "feeling consciousness" but to "presenting consciousness."³⁹ Smith says that no *argument* has ever been offered for the identification, though Nietzsche's account of the "priestly" arguments of the resentful "slave morality" in "The Genealogy of Morals" certainly could be taken as such (esp. 469–71). Smith suggests that the identification is very likely based on the fact that value-intentions *elicit* affective responses, which are undeniably "feelings" in the ordinary sense.

Puolimatka also rejects the identification of moral intuition with affective feeling, pointing out that intuition can provide us with real theoretical insight only when it distinguishes and identifies phenomena logically (156f.; cf. Dooyeweerd, *New Critique*, 2:483). Thus, as Reiner also acknowleddges, it may be argued that value-intuition includes an element of rationality. This does not mean that value-intuition is *reducible* to logical analysis, any more than affective feeling is. But it does mean, as Dooyeweerd suggests, that intuition is not purely a matter of affective feeling and is inseparably united to the function of logical analysis in concrete experience.[40]

None of these differences detracts from Scheler's basic insight regarding the irreducibly nonrational nature of moral intuition and of the moral order, much less from the genius of his rich phenomenological analysis of moral psychology. For even if moral intuition contains an element of logical distinguishing, this does not mean that it is reducible to logical analysis. After all, the difference between an immoral and a moral person is *not* the difference between being irrational and pathologically determined, on the one hand, and being rational and passionless, on the other, but rather the difference between having destructive passions and thoughts, and having good and wholesome ones. Scheler recognized this in a way that Kant did not.

Kant's metaphysics did not permit him, like Aristotle, to easily allow that natural inclinations themselves could ever *become—essentially* become —morally virtuous. Natural inclinations might occasionally *coincide* with the demands of virtue, or even be *trained to conform* to these demands; but it is only the aboriginal, inner goodness of the *will*, not the derivative, external goodness of the *inclinations*, which is the source and seat of moral virtue. Inclinations belong to sensibly determined animal nature, not to free moral personality; and, as Cassirer notes, Kant's "natural man" is *fallen*, like St. Paul's.[41] The morally virtuous type, in Aristotle's sense, has no comfortable place in his moral philosophy, notwithstanding his treatment of the subject in his *Doctrine of Virtue*. Instead, as Sokolowski observes, Kant works basically within the moral types of Aristotle's morally "strong" or "self-controlled" man and the morally "weak" man (*enkratês* and *akratês*).[42] Thus, to press the point a bit—perhaps even a bit too far, in order to stress the point—the place of the virtuous will as understood by Aristotle seems in danger of being taken over by the "holy will" in Kant, which is not desire shaped by reason (as in Aristotle), but reason cut off from desire and unaffected by it. "Virtue," for Kant, does not finally seem to mean so much the accomplished domestication of desire by reason, as in Aristotle, or even the faculty of "holy will"; rather, it seems to mean the experience of reason fighting the good fight—that is, *struggling*, and prevailing in its continuing struggle, against alien desire.

Kant knew that not all inclinations are immoral or irrational; and he knew that those that were could be brought under the ordering discipline of reason. Therefore he knew, in principle, that the conflict between duty and inclination is not an inevitable one—that the rational person might achieve a state of personal harmony. Yet the voice of "virtue" does not always seem to speak with such equanimity in Kant. The "virtuous" will seems to manifest itself only amidst—and often against—the pathological pull of conflicting inclinations. Rather, it is the "holy will" that bears the marks of self-possessed equanimity and serenity in Kant's account; but the "holy will" is noumenal, pure, and free from all sensuous influences. In short, Kant's "virtuous man" seems no better off than Aristotle's "morally strong man," who is never quite at ease with himself and always somewhat wary about keeping his desires under rational control.

Hence, Kant puts no moral stock in affective nature as the source of moral action. Even the notion of disposition (*Gesinnung*) as a formal "maxim of maxims" is construed primarily as an effect of inscrutable choice rather than a discernible motive of willing. Ultimately there is only the interplay of reason and sensibility—and choice. The sedimentation of passions themselves into a settled, identifiably moral way of desiring has no place in Kant's ethics as a normative motive for moral action.[43]

As Reiner argues at length, this was the chief complaint that Kant's contemporary critic, Schiller, raised against the Kantian ethic.[44] When Schiller complained that Kant's opposition of duty to inclination could easily inspire "a gloomy and monkish asceticism," he was not objecting to Kant's practice of clarifying the nature of duty by contrasting it to inclination. Rather, he was objecting to a view of human nature in which no moral virtue attaches to an inclination to do one's duty. It was a matter of complete moral indifference to Kant, he felt, whether an action done from a sense of duty is accompanied by an inclination to do it. At most, it was a happy coincidence. For Schiller, by contrast, the harmonization of desire and reason, sensibility and rationality, is the very aim and goal of moral perfection and virtue, a *telos* in which the ultimate essence of human existence—the "beautiful soul" (*schöne Seele*)—might be realized. "Man not only may, but ought to, combine pleasure with duty," he insisted.[45] The virtuous man does his duty with joy. He no longer needs to consult reason before every action and decision, as Kant insisted, because moral law ceases to have the "imperative form" of an alien necessitation. The inclinations themselves become moral and rational.

What Scheler seems to have wanted is an ethics that, like Aristotle's, permits a proper accounting of the kind of person who is disposed by inclination to do what is morally good, the kind of person for whom the good does not intrude as a somewhat distal or alien obligation but is exactly what is affectively desired. While Scheler seems to have the mechanics of moral psychology worked out fairly accurately, what his theory lacks is a compelling criterion for prescriptivity. After all, what determines whether our passions are good or bad, constructive or destructive? For Aristotle it was reason. Natural desires and inclinations themselves could be rendered virtuous by being rationalized, for Aristotle, in a way that is inconceivable either for Kant or for Scheler—inconceivable for Kant, because natural desires and inclinations are innately *ir*-rational; for Scheler because they are primordially *non*rational.

Yet, in response to Nicolai Hartmann, who denied that it is the task of ethics to offer concrete prescriptions, Scheler wrote: *"Ultimately ethics is a 'damned bloody affair,' and if it can give me no directives concerning how 'I' 'should' live now in this social and historical context, then what is it?"* (F, 23 n./xxxi n. 14) Scheler may be begging the question here somewhat. Nevertheless, he has put his finger on a real problem. The question that remains to be faced is how phenomenological descriptions of moral value-complexes can provide grounds for moral obligation. This issue, which is also one of Kant's chief concerns as it relates to the notion of "duty," is the subject of our next chapter.

NOTES

1. F, 212/197. See the remarks by Manfred S. Frings and Roger L. Funk in the Foreword to their translation of *Formalismus* regarding Scheler's "awkward and infelicitous neologisms" (xiv f.).

2. So long as we keep in mind the "pathic" nuances of Scheler's particular notion, the term "perception" is perfectly appropriate to this use. The ordinary signification of "perception" is by no means restricted to the five senses, but includes mental awareness (or intuition) that is independent of these, and is certainly broad enough to include the sense of Scheler's expression. While other terms, such as "valuation," might seem appropriate, they usually present other problems. For example, "valuation" suggests the value-positing activity of a valuing subject, whereas Scheler's emphasis is entirely on the "receptivity" of the subject, as stressed by Hans Reiner (*DI*, 150). Hence, the *perception* of value (*Wertnehmung*) is not primarily a matter of such activities as moral judgment, deliberation or assessment, which are concerned with determining moral obligation, but of the *consciousness* to which values are most originally given.

3. See, e.g., *KpV*, 73; *GMS*, 400; and *MS*, 402, where Kant equates *Achtung* with *reverentia*, in light of which one may not improperly translate the former as "reverence" as well as respect."

4. The following examination of Kant's theory of moral feeling is based on a paper delivered at the annual conference of the North Carolina Philosophical Society at Queen's College, Charlotte, NC, on Feb. 23, 1991, which was subsequently published as "A Problem in Kant's Theory of Moral Feeling," *Lyceum* 3, No. 2 (Dec. 1991), 27–39. Used with permission of the publisher.

5. Kant develops this more technically in his second *Critique*, where he calls *desire* the faculty that a living being has "of causing, through its ideas, the reality of the objects of these ideas," and *pleasure* "the idea of the agreement of an object or an action . . . with the faculty through which an idea

causes the reality of its object" (*KpV*, 9 n.). Or, as Lewis White Beck notes, the idea itself is "one of the efficient causes of the object by virtue of being one of the factors which determine the person's action which, in turn, will produce the object" (*A Commentary on Kant's "Critique of Practical Reason"* [Chicago: University of Chicago Press, 1960], p. 91).

6. On the "holy" will, cf. sec. 3, below; ch. 3, sec. 1, above; and ch. 5, secs. 1 and 4, below (esp. the discussion of Karl Alphéus in the latter section). The "holy" will, according to Kant, is a will to which the concept of "duty" is irrelevant. "Duty" applies only to imperfectly rational beings, such as are faced with a potential conflict between their rational wills and sensible inclinations. The perfectly rational will *necessarily* affirms or assents to the moral law's requirements, while imperfectly rational beings do not assent necessarily but must overcome disinclinations in order to assent (*GMS*, 414; *KpV*, 32).

7. *KGS*, 10, 145, quoted by Beck, *Commentary*, 214; cf. John R. Silber, "The Ethical Significance of Kant's *Religion*" in Part 2 of the Introduction to *Religion within the Limits of Reason Alone*, by Immanuel Kant, trans. Theodore M. Greene and Hoyt H. Hudson (1934; rpt. New York: Harper & Brothers, 1960), xcv n. 35.

8. *KGS*, 19, 276–82; cited by Beck, *Commentary*, 215.

9. Martin Heidegger, *The Basic Problems of Phenomenology*, trans. Albert Hofstadter (Bloomington: Indiana University Press, 1982), 134, in his analysis of Kant's chapter on moral incentives.

10. This point is made with particular clarity by Alwin Diemer, "Zum Problem des Materialen in der Ethik Kants," 26.

11. This account is corroborated by Kant in a number of other passages. In one he cites a place (the *Berlinische Monatschrift*) in which he "reduced the distinction between *pathological* and *moral pleasure* to its simplest terms: the pleasure that must precede our obedience to the law in order for us to act in conformity with the law is pathological . . . but the pleasure that we can feel only after having determined to obey the law is in the *moral order*" (*MS*, 378). In a second place, he writes: "*Pathological* feeling precedes the thought of the law: *moral* feeling can only follow from the thought of the law" (*MS*, 399). In a third place, Kant writes: "The dissimilarity of rational and empirical grounds of determination is made recognizable through the resistance of a practically legislating reason to all interfering inclinations, which is shown in a peculiar kind of feeling which does not precede the legislation of practical reason but which is, on the contrary, first effected by it, as a compulsion. That is, it is revealed through the feeling of respect of a kind that no man has for any inclinations whatever, but which he may feel for the law alone (*KpV*, 92).

12. *KpV*, 75. Kant does not mean this even when he speaks of moral feeling as a "*susceptibility*" (*Empfänglichkeit*) "on the part of free choice to be moved by pure practical reason" (*MS*, 400). For by "susceptibility" he cannot mean feeling as a state of consciousness, but only a potentiality that must logically or temporally precede the actual feeling of respect.

13. *Commentary*, 217. Silber observes that, to conceive obedience to moral law as determined *by desire* to obey the law is "one of the world's oldest, most popular and enduring varieties of circular reasoning," and that to ask what incentive can prompt the will to recognize the authority of law is to fail to recognize its unconditioned nature—i.e., to fail to "comprehend its incomprehensibility." ("The Ethical Significance of Kant's *Religion*," cviii, cx–cxi; cf. *GMS*, 463).

14. *KpV*, 87f. (and see discussion in ch. 3, sec. 3, above).

15. For a seminal early study of the metaphysical interpretation of the self as *homo noumenon* in Kant, see Heinz Heimsoeth, *Studien zur Philosophie Immanuel Kants: Metaphysische Ursprünge und ontologische Grundlagen* (Köln: Balduin Pick, 1956).

16. Scheler's views on these matters are contained in his large and sprawling fifth chapter of *Formalismus*, entitled "Non-Formal Value-Ethics and Eudaemonism." His critique of the Kantian position is, at best, extremely oblique and mediated by a more immediate concern to establish and defend his own views against possible objections represented by a variety of historical and contemporary theories. Our examination of Scheler's discussion, therefore, will be selective and synoptical, keeping in view his overall "response" to Kant.

17. Over against this view, and later variations of it—such as Christian von Ehrenfels's position that we value something because we desire it—Scheler would maintain that we desire something because we value it, as did Alexius Meinong. Scheler would have objected only to Meinong's identification of value with pleasure as such. We *desire* something, Scheler would say, not because the contemplation of its existence or possession gives us pleasure, in the first place, but because we *value* it. Cf. Nicholas Rescher, *Introduction to Value Theory*, 52f.

18. When Scheler seems to deny that respect is a "sensible" feeling (*F*, 255/241), he most likely means, merely, that it is *not sensibly determined*. He is not necessarily denying Kant's claim that "sensuous feeling, which is the basis of all our inclinations, is the condition of the particular feeling we call respect" (*KpV*, 75). He simply neglects Kant's distinction between sensible *conditioning* and sensible *determination*.

19. This view would fall under what Scheler calls the "most elementary form" of the theory that values consist in the *relation* between an object and experiences of pleasure or displeasure (*F*, 256/241). A second, more complex form—that developed by F. Krüger and H. Cornelius—is discussed in *F*, ch. 5, in the last half of sec. 1 ("Value and Pleasure").

20. Blaise Pascal, "Pensées", IV, No. 277, tr. W. F. Trotter in *Blaise Pascal: The Provincial Letters, Pensées, Scientific Treatises*, Vol. 30 of *Great Books of the Western World*, 2d ed. (Chicago: Encyclopedia Brittanica, 1990), 222. Cf. also *F*, 84/63.

21. *F*, 269/255; cf. *OA*, 347–76/98–135, for the *locus classicus* of Scheler's discussions on this subject. For a brief but very accessible introduction to many of the central issues involved in this view, from the perspective of Stephan Strasser's theories, see Andrew Tallon, "The Concept of the Heart in Strasser's *Phenomenology of Feeling*," *American Catholic Philosophical Quarterly* 66, No. 3 (summer 1992), 341–60. Cf. Stephan Strasser, *Phenomenology of Feeling: An Essay on the Phenomena of the Heart*, Foreword by Paul Ricoeur, trans. with Introduction by Robert E. Wood, Philosophical Series 34 (Pittsburgh: Duquesne University Press, 1977); as well as his "Phenomenological Trends in European Psychology (Husserl, Scheler, Pfänder, and others)," *Philosophy and Phenomenological Research* 9 (1957–1958), 18–34.

22. Cf. sec. 3, below; and ch. 3, above, sec. 4, n. 43 and the passage on Husserl that follows.

23. Scheler offers two different classifications of feelings in *Formalismus*, ch. 5—the first in sec. 2 (beginning at *F*, 269/255), the second in sec. 8 (begin-

ning at *F*, 344/332). These are based on different implicit criteria, the first on distance of object-relatedness, the second on depth of ego-relatedness, according to Quentin Smith, "Max Scheler and the Classification of Feelings," *Journal of Phenomenological Psychology* 9, Nos. 1–2 (1978), 114–38; and his "Scheler's Stratification of Emotional Life and Strawson's *Person*," *Philosophical Studies* 25 (1977), 103–27.

24. This view has its roots in the so-called logic of preference or logic of valuation developed by the Austro-German school of value theorists as well as certain economic theorists. It is closely related to the theory that value-feelings are either "correct" or "incorrect" as a consequence of their relatedness to objectively founded values—a view developed by Brentano and others, which, like the theory of preference, has antecedents also in Aristotle, as noted by Nicholas Rescher, *Introduction to Value Theory*, 74–75, 129–30. Cf. also the closely related issues addressed by Roderick M. Chisholm, "Brentano's Theory of Correct and Incorrect Emotion," *Révue Internationale de Philosophie* 78 (1966), 395–415; by Chisholm together with E. Sosa, "On the Logic of Intrinsically Better," *American Philosophical Quarterly* 3 (1966), 244–49; and "Intrinsic Preferability and the Problem of Supererogation," *Synthese* 16 (1966), 321–31.

25. As Scheler says later, " '*functions*' have nothing to do with '*acts*.' . . . Acts are executed; functions happen by themselves. . . . *Functions* can have a twofold relation to *acts*. They can be objects of acts, e.g., when I try to bring my seeing to intuitive givenness; and they can also be that 'through' which an act is directed toward something objectified" (*F*, 398f./388).

26. "Love may give rise to all kinds of effort," writes Scheler elsewhere, "but these are no part of it. It follows an *opposite law to that of effort*" (*S*, 164/141).

27. Cf. *S*, 169f./148; and *F* 85 n. 1/64 n. 20, where Scheler says that the "apriorism" of love and hate is the irreducible foundation of all a priori cognition and willing and the phenomenological basis for the ultimate unity of the theoretical and practical. Also cf. Max Scheler, "Liebe und Erkenntnis," 5–28.

28. *F*, 333/320. Scheler devotes a major portion of ch. 5 (*F*, secs. 3–8) to an extensive analysis and critique of various types of relativism and subjectivism, including (but not limited to) the historical relativity of value-estimations and the subjectivity of "conscience."

Reiner offers a fascinating analysis in which he shows that "conscience" is not subject to the will but belongs to the periphery of the ego, or what he calls the "I-circumground," which is *other* to the agency of the "I-center." This leads to an effective argument for the objectivity of values, since values are shown to appear apart from the subject's wanting them (*DI*, 121–25, 200–10).

29. Two discrepancies may be noted between Scheler's discussion in *F*, ch. 5, sec. 8 (*F*, 345–56/333–43), on which our present analysis is based, and that in *F*, ch. 2, B, sec. 5 (*F*, 125–30/104–09). First, what are called "psychical" values and feelings in the former are called "spiritual" in the latter, and those that are called "spiritual" in the former are usually identified with the "religious" or "holy" in the latter. Second, whereas Scheler emphatically denies that "spiritual" feelings such as blissfulness or despair can be feeling-*states* in the former, he describes precisely these feelings as feeling-states in the latter. A possible reason for this discrepancy lies in Scheler's incongruous claims (1) that spiritual feelings are the most acutely intentional of feelings and are feelings

of the person (*F*, 355/343), and (2) that persons cannot be intentional objects (*F*, 397/386f.). Smith, who claims that the criterion of Scheler's classification of feelings beginning at *F*, 344/332 is depth of ego-relatedness (cf. n. 23 above), tries to preserve the symmetry of the classification by arguing that Scheler was simply mistaken in asserting that spiritual feelings can be directed to persons ("Scheler's Stratification of Emotional Life," 120f.).

30. *F*, 356/344. Cf. Robert Nozick's notions of "ethical pull" and "ethical push" in *Philosophical Explanations*, 401–09, 451–504, 517–22.

31. *F*, 360/348. Not all feeling-states are sensible, according to Scheler. The discrepancies in his terminology noted previously (n. 29 above) must be kept in mind.

32. In *F*, ch. 5, sec. 10 (beginning at *F*, 370/359), Scheler offers a detailed analysis of the relation of "sanction" and "reprisal" to the connection between happiness and morality. He discusses "reward" and "punishment," the relation of reprisal to "revenge," "recompense," "retaliation," and to "atonement," "satisfaction," "purification," and "forgiveness." Cf. Francis Dunlop, "Scheler's Theory of Punishment," *Journal of the British Society for Phenomenology* 9, No. 3 (Oct. 1978), 167–74.

33. Taking cues from Husserl, Pfänder and Scheler, Reiner develops a theory of "the conscious I" with a distinction between "I-center" (coterminous with the subject's will and agency) and "I-circumground" (beyond the subject's will and agency), which permits him to offer an effective argument for the objectivity of values: as objects of the I-circumground's feelings, they appear *apart* from the subject's *wanting* them (*DI*, 121–25). In the same context, he offers an especially compelling account of the phenomenon of conscience (cf. n. 28 above).

34. One could, I suppose, employ the term "feeling" to refer to the manner in which the ordering principles of any field of experience are subjectively accessed. One could then speak broadly of "religious feeling," "jural feeling," "moral feeling," "aesthetic feeling," "biotic feeling," a "feeling" for history, language, and even logic. But the last example shows the difficulty of this remedy for Scheler, who wishes to link the affective faculty of feeling narrowly to the apprehension of material values and to sharply distinguish this faculty from the logical. Cf. ch. 2, sec. 4, esp. n. 44; and ch. 3, "Values and Willing" under sec. 2 and sec. 4 following the discussion of Heidegger.

35. See the detailed discussion and caveats concerning this problem above in ch. 2, sec. 4, particularly nn. 43–45. An early German study devoted to the problem of the relation between the psychological and the moral in Scheler's ethics is J. Hermann, *Die Principien der formalen Gesetzesethik Kants und der materialen Wertethik Schelers: Beitrag zum Problem des Verhältnisses zwischen Psychologie und Ethik* (Breslau: Schelsny, 1928).

36. While Dooyeweerd insists on the irreducibility of the "nuclear meaning" of such functional modalities of experience, he points out the existence of modal interlacements in concrete experience, which he calls modal "analogies" (or "anticipations" and "retrocipations") of meaning. For example, while *feeling* is typically qualified by its *psychic* "nuclear meaning," it has "analogies" in other modalities of experience, such as the aesthetic, religious, moral, and the like. Accordingly, one can speak of "aesthetic feeling," "religious feeling," "moral feeling," and so forth (*A New Critique of Theoretical Thought*, 2:74–78).

37. See n. 34, above.

38. According to Franz Brentano, "principles of ethics are cognitions of feelings," and we attain our "knowledge of good and bad on the basis of the part played by the emotions" (*The Foundation and Construction of Ethics*, Compiled by Franziska Mayer-Hillebran, trans. Elizabeth Hughes Schneewind [1952; New York: Humanities Press, 1973], 134f.); Husserl held that values are "affectively intended" in "acts of feeling" (*Ideen*, §117); Alexius Meinong, referred to "the feelings of value" and "value feeling" (*On Emotional Presentation*, trans. Marie-Luise Kalsi, with Foreword by J. N. Findlay [1917; Evanston, IL: Northwestern University Press, 1972], 79); Nicolai Hartmann held that values are given in an "emotional consciousness of value" (*Ethics*, 1:102); on Dilthey, see Puolimatka, 156.

39. Quentin Smith, "Max Scheler and the Classification of Feelings," 129ff. Cf. the brief discussion of Husserl's position above in ch. 3, sec. 4, esp. n. 43, and the reference to Husserl in section following it on Heidegger's second criticism of value theory.

40. Dooyeweerd, *New Critique*, 2:473f. Although Reiner recognizes that value-intuition contains "intellectual elements," he continues to regard it as an "emotional" act or "feeling" (*DI*, 135). Dooyeweerd and Puolimatka, on the other hand, regard moral intuition as something irreducible to psychic feeling.

41. Heinz W. Cassirer, *Grace and Law: St. Paul, Kant, and the Hebrew Prophets* (Edinburgh: Handsel Press, 1988), a fascinating treatise by the son of the eminent Neo-Kantian, Ernst Cassirer. See my review of the volume in *Faith and Philosophy* 8, No. 3 (July 1991), 402–05.

42. For the overall argument of this and the following paragraph, as well as this point, I am indebted to Robert Sokolowski, *Moral Action*, 217 ("Appendix D: Kant"). By contrast to Kant, as Sokolowski notes, Aristotle distinguishes four clear types: (1) virtuous, (2) strong, (3) weak, and (4) vicious.

43. For a discussion of Kant's and Scheler's conceptions of the moral "disposition" (*Gesinnung*), see Appendix I, "Is Scheler's Ethic an Ethic of Virtue?"

44. The issues underlying the famous controversy between Kant and his contemporary critic, Schiller, and their well-intentioned (but often misconceived) efforts at reconciling their views, are carefully analyzed in the fine opening chapter of the first and major part of Reiner's book, providing the rationale for its name, *Duty and Inclination*.

45. Schiller, *On Grace and Dignity*, first published in *Neue Thalia* (1793); reprinted in *Schillers Philosophische Schriften und Gedichte*, ed. Eugen Kühnemann, 3d ed. (Leipzig, 1922), 130; cited in Reiner, *DI*, 31.

Duty and Its Phenomenological Basis | 5

IN THIS CHAPTER WE SHALL EXAMINE how the issues of the foregoing chapters converge in the problem of moral obligation. The lines of convergence are nearer the surface in Scheler's ethics than in Kant's. Scheler's theory of obligation is overtly axiological and rests on the notion of an ideal "ought"-structure, which, belonging to the sphere of realizable value-essences, serves as the foundation of normative conceptions of duty and obligation. By contrast, Kant's theory of obligation does not rest on any articulated theory of value, certainly not on any theory of realizable nonmoral values. Such views belong, rather, to "axiological" and "teleological" ethics. Despite the possibility, mentioned in chapter 3, that even Kant's "deontological" ethics presupposes a conception of moral value that serves as the foundation of moral obligation, one of Scheler's chief criticisms is that Kant's formal conception of duty is axiologically "blind" and not based on substantive moral "insight." In the following pages we shall examine Kant's views on the subject, Scheler's criticisms and suggestions, and then offer an assessment of the issues in question.

Kant's Theory of Moral Obligation

IN KANT'S ETHICS, MORAL OBLIGATION is something that occurs only in persons who experience the determination of their wills by objective law as a *constraint*. The only persons who experience such constraint are *rational animals*. If persons were not rational *animals*, they would be incapable of such experience. On the one hand, a being with a purely *animal* nature would be incapable of experiencing moral constraint, because it has no rational component to check its sensuous, hedonistic inclinations. On the other hand, a purely *rational* being with no animal component to its nature, such as God, would lack the sensuous incentives and inclinations common to human nature. Such a being would have a perfectly good will (or "holy" will), but could hardly be conceived as "constrained" by moral law (*GMS*, 413f.) Its *inclinations themselves,* so to speak, would be rational and moral. Accordingly, only beings that are *both* rational *and* animal, such as human beings, actually experience the moral law as obliging and feel themselves to be constrained by the demands of "duty" (*GMS*, 439).

The conception of an objective principle that constrains a will is a *command*, says Kant, and the formula of such a command is called an *imperative*. An imperative—to be moral, and therefore categorical—must imply absolute necessity and universality. It must "present an action as of itself objectively necessary, without regard to any other end" (*GMS*, 414). It must "leave the will no freedom to choose the opposite," not in the sense of denying freedom of choice, but in the sense of presenting an unconditional demand of reason (*GMS*, 389, 420). Furthermore, as a general "canon" of the moral estimation of our action, it requires that we be able to will that "a maxim of our action become a universal law" (*GMS*, 424). A maxim's form of universality is the objective ground of the moral will, the sole moral principle of the will (*GMS*, 431, 402). The implication is clear: "*Obligation* is the necessity of a free action under a categorical imperative" (*MS*, 222).

Moral obligation, therefore, cannot be conditional or hypothetical. It cannot present the practical necessity of an action as a means to some other end, whether possible or actual. It cannot, for example, make the desire for happiness the basis for one's choice, since that is a natural inclination and cannot guarantee the morality of one's choice. This is true even of the desire to further the happiness of others, which presupposes a certain, natural satisfaction. For as Kant says, even "love as an inclination cannot be commanded" (*GMS* 399). Hence, moral obligation is most easily and surely recognized where duty is *opposed* to inclinations; for where it is not, one can never be sure that one has not been moved by a "secret impulse of self-love" falsely masquerading as duty (*GMS*, 407). This does not mean that seeking one's own happiness is not "indirectly" a duty, since the lack of it leads to temptations to transgress moral law (*GMS*, 399). Nor does it mean that one may not postulate "the exact coincidence of happiness with morality" in a relation "mediated by an intelligible Author of nature" (*KpV*, 125, 115). But it does mean that we can take no account of happiness whenever duty is in question (*KpV*, 93; cf. H. J. Paton, *The Categorical Imperative*, 50).

On the one hand, Kant insists that the link between the consequence of happiness and duty by means of the "postulate" of God's existence is a matter of practical faith, not knowledge. One cannot *know* that morality will result in happiness. Indeed, such knowledge or insight would *undermine* the moral worth of actions, for Kant. Most people would do their duty from fear, a few from hope, but none from duty; and their actions would have no moral worth at all (*KpV*, 146f.). On the other hand, Kant does not seem to be saying that duties are performed blindly. For without some kind of insight into the moral law it would be impossible to discern one's moral obligation or to form judgments applying such law to specific cases (*GMS*, 389). The categorical imperative itself, as John Silber notes, is the *procedure* for such judgment, as specified by the moral law.[1] Yet the way in which such moral insight into the demands of the moral law is to be reconciled with a metaphysical purism that insists upon the law's suprasensibility is not obvious.[2]

In any case, as Silber notes, the act of moral judgment "is an act of relating form to sensibility"; accordingly, the categorical imperative exhibits "the procedure of judgment in the act of moral schematism."[3] The demand expressed by what Paton calls the "Formula of the Law of Nature," is particularly illuminating, as Silber notes: "Act as though the maxim of your action were by your will to become a universal law of nature."[4] Essentially Kant proposes a thought experiment in which the moral agent must so order events and deeds in the spatio-temporal world that time becomes a schema for the moral law no less than for the category of causality. In his discussion of the "typic" of practical judgment in his second *Critique*, Kant puts it thus: "Ask yourself whether, if the action which you propose should take place by a law of nature of which you yourself were a part, you could regard it as possible through your will" (*KpV*, 69). Such self-questioning does not serve as the determining ground of the will, but it does provide a "type" for the estimation of maxims according to moral principles. It is the way in which one's moral obligation is determined — by beginning with one's insight into moral law and proceeding to apply this insight by way of what is described by Silber as "an act of judgment to determine that concrete state of affairs which constitutes the most adequate embodiment of the highest good for each particular act of volition."[5]

It is interesting in this regard that Kant clearly believed in the possibility of some sort of moral education. In *The Doctrine of Virtue* he states that the very concept "virtue" implies that virtue is something that must be acquired, that it is not innate, and, therefore, that "virtue can and must be learned" (*MS*, 477). This means that there must be effective measures for stimulating and guiding moral development. According to Kant, the principles of morality are already embedded in the structure of every person's reason. Hence, what is needed is a method for eliciting these embedded principles (*MS*, 376). Such a method might well make use of a "moral catechism" and call notice to the purity of will by means of vivid examples.[6] This does not mean that the moral law can be derived empirically from examples, for any conceivable example "must itself have been previously judged according to principles of morality to see whether it is worthy to serve as an original example" (*GMS*, 408f.). Rather, it means that empirical means are available for eliciting respect for the suprasensible moral law, which is ultimately a matter not of behavior but of the heart.[7]

Finally, Kant holds that if one is morally obligated to do something, it follows that it must be something of which one is *capable*. Even though morality is something determined by reason and not by experience, and may therefore be concerned "with actions of which perhaps the world has never had an example" (*GMS*, 408), it never commands, as a matter of principle, what is beyond the capacity of the moral agent. People judge that they *can* do something if they know they *ought* to do it (*KpV*, 30; cf. 36f.). This "fact of reason," says Kant, is the *ratio cognoscendi* of freedom, which, in turn, is the *ratio essendi* of the moral law (*KpV*, 4 n.).

In summary we may say that moral obligation, for Kant, (1) is moral constraint and, as such, is experienced only by a rational animal; (2) has the character of unconditional necessity and universality formulated in the categorical imperative; (3) is determined apart from all conditional ends, including such natural ends as happiness, which are invariably based on inclination; (4) cannot be calculated on the basis of the postulated coincidence of virtue and happiness in the *summum bonum*, which is a matter of practical faith, not insight; (5) is determined by applying the moral law to specific cases by means of a procedure of moral judgment (and schematism) exemplified in the categorical imperative; (6) can be learned; and (7) can be fulfilled in practice.

Scheler's Critique of Kantian Deontologism

SCHELER'S MOST GENERAL CRITICISM of Kant's theory of duty is that it is "blind"—that is, that it is not based fundamentally on axiological insight. When we ask what kind of experience furnishes the material from which we make moral judgments and determine what our duties are, says Scheler, we cannot expect to find the answer in the logical forms of moral judgments, but only in what those judgments are *about*—that is, in the experience of certain "moral facts" (*sittliche Tatsachen*). The nature of moral obligation can be understood properly only from a phenomenological analysis of the origin of such "moral facts." As Scheler knows, of course, this way of speaking blatantly contradicts prevailing conventions of modern moral discourse, which have long presupposed a positivist distinction between "facts" and "values."[8] Most people are inclined to admit that there are astronomical, botanical, and chemical "facts," but not *moral* "facts."

Kant is hardly alone, of course, in neglecting to produce an account of moral obligation based on a phenomenology of the "moral facts." Other theories neglecting this basis, as Scheler points out, range from various forms of subjectivism and idealism to various types of nominalist, emotivist, and "assessment" theories.[9] Some have thought, for example, that they could find a basis for moral judgment and obligation in inner experience. But what they overlooked was the objective reference of moral predication. When I judge something to be morally "evil," I do not find this quality in my inner experience, but in something beyond this experience *to which* my judgment is directed. Others, such as Plato, believed that the basis for moral judgment could be found in the realm of *"ideal objects"* or *"pure meanings."* This view is correct insofar as "the good" does in fact have an ideal meaning-content. But moral good cannot, like numbers or triangles, be confined to the realm of ideal meanings, as if it were an object only of "reason" and not also of "intuition." As Scheler points out, a child feels the kindness of his mother long before comprehending an idea of the good (*F*, 182/166).

Others, such as Hobbes and (according to Scheler) perhaps Nietzsche,[10] have held various nominalist and emotivist views, according to which moral judgments merely express feeling-states, interests, or desires. On this view, the judgment "This is evil" might be equivalent to saying "Ouch"; or "This is a good deed" might be equivalent to saying "Do this!" But a confusion is involved here. For the judgment "This is evil" does not express a *feeling-state* any more than the statement "This is red" means "certain muscular sensations occur in my eyes while seeing the red thing" (*F*, 188/173). The moral judgment "This is a good deed" may not express my will any more than the aesthetic statement "This is beautiful."[11]

Still others, such as J. F. Herbart (following Adam Smith) and Brentano, have held that moral values could be determined on the basis of "assessments" (*Beurteilungen*) of willing and action. According to this view, moral assessments, like logical judgments, have their own laws and norms according to which they are "correct" or "incorrect." But as Scheler points out, a moral act of willing is not good or evil because a correct or incorrect assessment can be made of it. It is good or evil because it bears an independent moral quality or value, in which any possible assessment finds its fulfillment (*F*, 198/183). Hence, the basis for discerning one's duty cannot lie in moral assessments or judgments themselves, even if they stem from some sort of inner sense of "duty." For one would still need to ask why we should comply with this sense of "duty." This, in any case, is the gist of Scheler's criticism of "assessment" theories.[12]

But it is Kant's theory, or, more precisely, the theory of "duty" exemplified by Kant's deontological ethics, that elicits Scheler's most pointed and dramatic critique. Scheler's strategy, as we shall see, pits Kant's ethics of duty against his own ethics of insight, thereby isolating the concept of duty—and particularly duty's negative, restrictive side—from Kant's notions of the worth of rational agency and autonomy to which that concept is subordinate. Kant's theory, says Scheler, is a species of the foregoing "assessment" theory.[13] It claims that moral value is discerned from assessment of willing based on the idea of "duty." But this idea of "duty," Scheler says, is a deficient basis for moral judgment and for the discernment of moral obligation in at least four respects.

First, duty is essentially a "necessitation" or "compulsion" against inclination and individual willing. It is not itself a positive insight into moral value. Rather, the content of what is demanded in terms of moral law or rationality only "first becomes 'duty' when it meets an opposing and rising inclination, and also when it is posited against or at least independent of an individual's will"; by contrast, as Scheler sees the matter, when "we have the evidential insight that a deed or a will is good, we do not talk about 'duty,'" and if the insight is adequate, it determines the will "without any factor of compulsion or necessitation that might come between insight and willing" (F, 207 /192).

Second, duty "cuts off" (*abschneidet*) moral insight, or at least develops independently, without benefit of it. It obliges by a "blind inner commandment," which lacks additional grounds for the obligations it imposes. In fact, experience shows repeatedly "that the representation of 'duty' comes into play *precisely* when our moral considerations based on insight begin to *weaken*, or when our moral considerations *fall short of* resolving a situation that is too complicated" (F, 207f./192f.).

Third, duty is a compulsion or command that comes, according to Scheler, from "inside" us, as opposed to orders coming "from outside." But this does not diminish in the least its "blindness." In fact, obedience to a command from outside may stem from insight into the values presupposed by a command and therefore qualify as morally "insightful" action. In his discussion of autonomy, Scheler speaks not only of the "autonomy of willing," as did Kant, but of "autonomy of insight." This allows him to introduce distinctions between (1) forced willing, which is not autonomous in any sense; (2) blind obedience, which may be unforced but lacks autonomy of moral insight; (3) obedience, which may not only be unforced but based on autonomous insight into the moral value of a command, though only mediate (and therefore heteronomous) insight into the moral value of the commanded action; and (4) autonomous willing based on autonomous insight into the values of material performances themselves.[14]

Fourth, duty has, according to Scheler, "an essentially *negative* and *restrictive* nature." This does not mean, simply, that duty proscribes more than it prescribes. Rather, it means that duty shares with "necessity" the character of that "whose opposite is impossible."[15] By contrast, in Scheler's view, moral insight "does not require the thought of even a possible opposite," or "an attempted counterwilling against a willing whose value is in question" (F, 208f./193f.).

Thus, says Scheler, an ethics of duty is diametrically opposed to an ethics of insight. He does seem to overstate his case a bit. In fact, he comes precariously close to misconstruing Kantian duty as a completely counter-intuitive, unnatural compulsion, thus verging on a common misunderstanding of Kant (see ch. 3, n. 7). For example, he argues that where a value has been perceived, there is no reason to assume that, in order for a moral action to follow, a "duty" having the force of an alien compulsion must necessarily first impinge upon our recalcitrant inclinations. This does not *necessarily* entail a misunderstanding of Kant, but the suggestion that duty and inclination are incompatible makes it easily susceptible of being construed as such. In any case, this characterization of "duty" seems far removed from anything Kant would have intended. Alphéus argues, for example, that Kant's ethics is not a "blind ethics of duty," as Scheler asserts, but a "rational ethics of insight" (*Kant und Scheler*, 60ff. cf. ch. 2, n. 19, and ch. 3, sec. 3). And Kant's emphasis on autonomy would appear to contradict any notion of blind, uncritical obedience, even were it understood as a duty; such uncritical obedience could only be regarded by Kant as a most abject form of heteronomy. Moreover, the concept of duty in Kant is not isolated from, but always subordinate to, his notions of the worth of autonomy and rational agency. Even duty's negative, restrictive side is thus merely the underside of a positive respect for inviolable rational agents.

Still, Scheler may have a point—even if it may seem badly stated. As we saw in chapter 3 (sec. 3), Kant's ethics does have a "material" and "teleological" aspect. There are good reasons within the Kantian orbit of assumptions for arguing that his ethics should not be called simply "contentless." In the final analysis, as we saw, the "content" upon which Kant's understanding of moral law is founded is that of rational human agency, or practical rationality itself. This is an eminently reasonable and highly principled position. But as we also saw, it has at least one serious difficulty. The critical notion of rational human agency remains viable as a foundational canon of moral theory only as long as a consensus can be sustained both as to the substantive reality and the constitutive identity of practical rationality itself. But when this is called into question along with the major ancillary assumptions of the entire Enlightenment project, as it has been in postmodern currents of thought,[16] the question concerning practical reason's "content" becomes a moot point. Recourse to reason no longer has a perfectly obvious sense during a crisis over the meaning of reason itself.[17]

Scheler, of course, does not press the argument this far. His attack is limited to the "empty formalism" of Kant's "ethics of duty," which he regards as furnishing little help in the way of substantive "moral guidance." His argument is chiefly that an "ethics of duty" goes wrong by failing to recognize that moral judgments always already presuppose the comprehension of value. Whenever we speak of "duty," he says, the comprehension of a value must have already occurred. Moral obligation is always founded upon the comprehension of value, and not vice versa (*F*, 200/ 184). But the implications of his critique, I would argue, go much farther than the all-too-common superficial reading of his work suggests. Scheler sensed a difficulty underlying the "imperativistic" and "formalistic" thrust of Kant's writings. Extrapolating a bit, it is almost as if, beneath the commanding intonations of Kant's persistent "Du sollst! Du sollst!" Scheler thought he discerned a still, small, voice replying, "Warum? Warum?"—as if to ask: "Yes, Kant, but *by what standard*? After all, what do you really *mean* by 'practical reason'? What values are you *assuming*? After all, what seems 'rational' to you may well appear 'pathological,' or at least 'culturally conditioned,' to others.'"[18] The compelling power of "duty" could not last long once it was no longer believed that it really had reinforcements from "practical reason" to draw upon. With all due respect to Kant, once the very meaning of rational agency was cast fundamentally into doubt, what could the Kantian legacy offer but a system of formulas that were for all practical purposes—precisely as Scheler insisted—"empty"?

But what is this but a slightly different way of asking a question very like that raised from the perspective of the postmodern hermeneutics of suspicion—namely, what "bias" or "interest" or "value preference" is represented by the Kantian commitment to "practical reason"? The questions are not identical. The postmodernist's point is that subjective "bias" is ubiquitous and unavoidable; Scheler's point is that some perceived value underlies any conception of "duty." But even though there is a world of difference between Scheler's a priori objectivism and postmodernism's skeptical relativism, they both point to the deeper question of ineluctable presuppositions. And insofar as we are concerned with the Kantian legacy of attempting to establish duty by recourse to reason, the result is the same: Kant is being told that he has no refuge in recourse to practical reason if it is thought to provide an inviolable a priori canon of duty unencumbered by "pathological" influences of phenomenal human existence. Postmodernism would stress the historical, cultural, and prejudicial nature of these influences, while Scheler would stress the access these furnish to an eidetically definable, stable world of objective value-phenomena. But both would claim that Kant was mistaken in what he supposed he had achieved in the way of establishing a foundation for ethics.

The Phenomenological Basis of Scheler's Critique

SCHELER'S THEORY OF MORAL OBLIGATION is based on his phenomenological persuasion that our being-in-the-world is primordially emotional and characterized by value-feeling. Value-feeling, he says, always precedes any acts of representation such as one finds in moral "assessments" or "judgments" (*F*, 212/197; 216/201). This is why any reference to moral duty must already presuppose a comprehension of value. Furthermore, this is what leads Scheler to his novel view of the nature of moral obligation—a view that is both "axiological," in that it is based on values, and "teleological," in that it is based on the possibility of realizing nonmoral values.

As we saw in chapter 3, values for Scheler do not bear a necessary relation to existing, empirical "bearers" of value, such as real things, deeds, or people. Rather, they are essences, and, therefore, grasped independently of their bearers, whether those bearers are real, or ideal—or even exist. The nature of moral *obligation*, however, is *essentially* dependent on such a relation—the relation, that is, between these independent value-phenomena and their possible reality. Whenever we say that something "ought" to happen, says Scheler, we co-intuit a relation between some positive value and a possible real bearer of this value. What we are saying is that this "ought" depends on a relationship between value and reality. The "ought" always refers beyond itself to the potential realization of a value in the empirical world (F, 200/184f.). Let us consider Scheler's view more closely.

Any "ought" can only be understood, he says, in relation to specific values. The relation is not reciprocal but *unilateral*: the "ought" is grounded in *values*, and not vice versa. The sphere of value-judgments is much larger than that of the "ought." The "ought" is immediately related only to those values resting on the *being* or *nonbeing* of other values. Whereas other values are given *indifferently* with respect to existence or nonexistence, every "ought" is *related essentially* to the existence or nonexistence of values.

Before there can be any question of imposing an "ought" on the will as a moral demand to be realized, it must be grasped as a possibility. Scheler calls this possibility the *"ideal ought,"* not yet something perceived as a matter of actual moral obligation, but merely as an ideal whose reality is possible. Only when this possibility is grasped can the "ought" be represented as a demand imposed upon the will, as a moral obligation to be realized through willing (F, 200/185). Accordingly, Scheler distinguishes from the "ideal ought" what he calls the *"real ought"*—the "normative ought" or the "ought of duty."[19] The first kind of "ought" (the "ideal ought") can be illustrated by the proposition "Injustice ought not to be"; the second, by "Thou shalt not do injustice." The second type of "ought" is dependent on the first, so that the experience of obligation is not the "ideal ought" itself, but its consequence (F, 218/203).

Specifically, the difference between these two kinds of "ought" is defined by their respective relations to values. The *"ideal* ought" is defined by reference to a relation between existing and nonexisting values; the *"real* ought" is defined exclusively by reference to nonexisting values. Thus, in both cases, the "ought" is determined by a kind of *existential* index of values.

In the first place, the relation of the *"ideal* ought" to values is governed by the rudimentary intuition that anything of positive value "ought to be," and anything of negative value "ought not to be."[20] Every ideal "ought" is an "ought-to-*be*" of something. Thus, whenever we say that something "ought to be," this something is usually understood as *not* existing (or as *existing*, in the case of something that ought-*not*-to-be) (F, 221/207). The ideal ought is therefore the ought-to-be of a nonexisting value, or, to be more exact, the ought-to-be-realized of a nonrealized value.[21] Of course, in a manner of speaking, we might also say of some *existing* positive value that "it ought to be," but what we would really mean would be that it ought not *cease* to exist. We would merely be approving the existence of an already realized positive value, and implicitly disapproving the possible realization of its nonexistence. But, ordinarily, when we say that something "ought to be," we mean that some nonexistent value ought to be realized. Hence, in principle, the nonrealization of a value is presupposed by all propositions concerning what ought to be — or the realization of a disvalue, in the case of propositions about what ought not to be. But since the nonrealization of a positive value is a disvalue no less than the realization of a negative value, even *positive* ought-declarations pertain, in a sense, to *negative* values. As Scheler says: "The entire attitude of this ethics is such that it attains positive values by referring to negative values as their opposites"; that is to say, "positive values can be meant only as the opposites of evils" (F, 224/209f.).

From this it follows, says Scheler, that the "ought" as such can *never* itself determine what *positive* values are. Any ethics that tries to derive moral value from a notion of the "ought," even an "ought of duty," falls into the untenable position of Kant and Fichte, as portrayed by Hegel: it can do justice neither to the *factual* world of moral values nor to the *realization* of moral values.[22] If a real ought — an ought of duty — belonged to the essence of the good, the good as actually *realized* would become a matter of moral indifference. One who performed a morally significant action would always act "without conscience," in the words of Goethe's paradox (F, 225/210). Only an ethics founded on nonmoral values that are themselves *indifferent* to questions of existence and morality, but are *foundational* for every ought, can escape these problems.[23]

In the second place, then, moral obligation can be based only on the "moral facts" having to do with values. That is to say, the "ought of duty" (the *real* ought) can be founded only upon the ideal ought. The ideal ought (e.g., "The good ought to be") is translated into a concrete *demand* only when its content is experienced by conation as something to be realized. The question of obligation ("Why should I do what ought to be?") is possible on this basis alone.[24] Every "ought of duty," as a demand on the will, presupposes an *act of commanding*, which reaches the will by way of some authority or tradition.[25] As every ideal ought is based on some *disvalue* (such as the nonbeing of a positive value), so every moral imperative is based on an ideal ought-not-to-be of conation. That is, in prescribing the realization of certain moral values, it reveals itself to be "founded in the intuited *possible counterconation against the realization of the values*"—that is, in the "*intuition of the bad*."[26]

A deontological approach in ethics, which tries to derive moral value from duty as the ultimate moral phenomenon, is therefore essentially "*negative, critical, and repressive*," according to Scheler, and has a "constitutive distrust not only of human nature but also of the essence of moral acts in general."[27] These are strong words. One must suppose that the concept of the "holy will" in Kant and any possible role that it could have in ameliorating this view is overlooked here. This at least would help to explain why Scheler's treatment of Kant is dominated by themes of "constraint" and "duty" and leads him to such scathing criticisms of Kant's "negative" and "repressive" views. Scheler regards the role of moral imperatives within his own theory as contrasting sharply with their role in Kant's. Moral imperatives, as such, may be good or bad, wise or foolish, but can be justified only on the basis of two conditions: First, they must be based on the observed privation of an existential good that ought-to-be. Second, they must be based on the observed existence of a conative tendency against the realization of such a good. Thus, a person issuing a moral imperative must have observed such a negative conative tendency in the one to whom the commandment or prohibition is directed. Otherwise, the imperative acquires a moral disvalue and may possibly cause offense or even elicit a counterconation that was not present to begin with. Thus: "To make the medication of commandments and prohibitions our normal moral nourishment is nonsense" (F, 228f./213f.).

Moreover, obligations and imperatives can *vary*, even where the same values are recognized and the same ideal ought is affirmed, because they are determined not only by the ideal ought, but by the "value-direction" of the *conation* to which they are directed. For example, although most people recognize the principles of mutual respect and deference in polite society, they are nonetheless naturally disposed to promote their own welfare and happiness throughout the course of their lives; but there are also some exceptional individuals who suffer from a pathological urge to sacrifice and neglect their own welfare. Accordingly, obligations in the two cases will vary: the first generates imperatives of the type: "Love your neighbor as yourself" or "It is more blessed to give than to receive"; while the second generates imperatives of the opposite type stressing recognition of self-worth and self-esteem: "Love yourself" or "Attempt first to be someone so that you can give others something from yourself" (F, 229/215). Kant was therefore mistaken, according to Scheler, in assuming that all people are always naturally inclined to seek their own happiness and that, therefore, it makes no sense to command anyone to seek his or her own happiness.[28] Contrary imperatives—even contrary norms—

can be based on the *same* values because of the variable psychological dispositions of those to whom they are addressed. The fact that norms and imperatives may *vary* does not of itself support the contention of the ethical skeptic or moral relativist, since values—not norms and imperatives—are the ultimate facts of moral life.[29]

Every imperative or duty, Scheler acknowledges, is an immediate obligation to *do* something. It is not and cannot be an obligation to perform a mere *act of will*. "As Schopenhauer has observed," he writes, "an 'ought-to-will' is nonsense."[30] To this extent Kant's observation that love "cannot be commanded" is correct.[31] But, Scheler insists, his conclusion that an act of love has no moral value because it cannot be commanded is totally erroneous and rests upon false presuppositions that are basic to his entire ethics.[32] According to Kant, the moral worth of an action resides in its being done "*from duty*." An action done merely "according to duty" by inclination may have "legality" but not moral worth. This does not mean that, for Kant, one's duty and inclination may never coincide, or that one may never have a duty to perform an action corresponding to one's inclination.[33] It means that an action in which one's inclination coincides with duty can be no more than equal in value to one done from duty alone (*F*, 243/228). In other words, for Kant, moral value can apparently be attributed only to what can be commanded or prohibited.

It is possible that these restrictions of Kantian deontological ethics may be aimed at determining what can be agreed upon universally apart from the goods valued exclusively within different cultures and traditions. If so, this would suggest that for Kant the realm of goods or values is in fact much broader than the realm encompassed by obligation. The point of difference would come, of course, in Scheler's insistence that the realm of the *morally valuable* is broader than the *morally obligatory*. For although Scheler recognizes that there are many things that cannot be commanded or prohibited, this does not necessarily mean, in his view, that they are without moral value. Moral value is not restricted to what one has an obligation to *do*. Willing itself may bear a moral value, as may all kinds of conation, inclination, acts (such as love and hate), and persons themselves. In fact, according to Scheler, the person who wills and does what ideally ought to be "by *inclination*" rather than "from duty" is not merely of equal value but of *higher value*, since the conation with the least resistance to the good has the higher moral value.[34] Thus, the morally valuable cannot be restricted, for him, to the morally obligatory.

Accordingly, Scheler's concept of *moral virtue* stems from the situation in which something is given as an ideal ought and, simultaneously, as something that one has the "power" or "ability," if not the inclination, to do. Virtue is the immediately experienced *power* to do something that ought to be done, just as *vice* is the immediately experienced *impotence* to do the same (*F*, 220/205). In either case, the experience is an "ultimate, irreducible modality of conation," which leads us to *expect* that we *shall* or *shall not* do something (F, 246f./232). The relationship between moral obligation and ability has been construed in various different ways throughout the history of philosophy. Some have tried to assimilate moral obligation to ability, others, ability to moral obligation. Scheler suggests that such difficulties begin to resolve themselves as soon as one recognizes the difference between the "ought of duty" and the "ideal ought." For one thing, he says, values of the ideal ought-to-be are as independent of the question of ability as commands and prohibitions are dependent on it. For another, the experience of the *ideal ought* and of *ability* have their foundation in equiprimordial, independent intuitions, and are therefore fundamentally irreducible to one another.[35]

Finally, Scheler therefore rejects Kant's strictly *categorical* conception of duty and his reluctance to admit distinctions in degrees of obligation, relative merit, and supererogation into his ethics. For Kant, what could not be *categorically commanded* could not be regarded as having a strictly *moral* worth, but must presuppose heteronomous incentives. On the one hand, merit or supererogation consist phenomenologically in the willing and realization of an ideal ought whose content *exceeds* in value that of generally valid "norms." On the other hand, something ideally given as ought-not-to-be may be called "permitted" if an immediate experience of inability (which does not conflict with universally valid norms) is given for the abstention. Such distinctions could be said to presuppose heteronomous incentives, according to Scheler, "only if the 'ideal' ought-to-be had its foundation in the inner necessity of the *consciousness of duty* rather than in objective value-insight" (F, 221/206). But if what "ought to be" has its foundation in the intuition of material values, such distinctions acquire an obvious place in ethics. Moral obligations may not always be categorical or absolute, but differ in degree.[36]

Critical Appraisal

BY WAY OF SUMMARY, we may note the following: (1) Scheler's disagreement with Kant is not primarily over Kant's characterization of duty or moral obligation. Scheler could agree with Kant, for example, that duty has the characteristics of "constraint" and a certain kind of "necessity," and that it must be determined independently of inclination. The person with a pathological inclination to *sacrifice*, for instance, must be constrained by the necessity of recognizing the value of self-worth and self-respect. (2) Scheler's primary disagreement with Kant concerns the *relation* between moral obligation and *moral value*. He disagrees with the view, which he attributes to Kant, that moral value may be determined by an "assessment" of a situation in terms of the idea of "duty" or by means of applying a formula of the categorical imperative; this amounts to trying to *derive* moral value from the notion of duty, which he insists is impossible. Such a view leads to a wrong-headed "imperativistic" ethics that is "blind" to the phenomenal givenness of material values and accredits moral worth only to what can be commanded or prohibited, or what is done "from duty." Such a view offers no way of recognizing or evaluating the relativity of duties resulting from the inevitable variability of personal dispositions and conations by which the ideal ought is engaged. The duty of someone with a pathological inclination to sacrifice is different from that of someone selfishly inclined. (3) According to Scheler, moral obligation must be based on moral values—that is, on the relation between positive values and possible real bearers of those values. Specifically, it must be based on the relation between the "ideal ought," governed by its axioms of the being and nonbeing of values, and the "ought of duty," governed by its criteria of the privation of a good and the existence of a conative tendency against that good's realization. In the final analysis, the problem with Kant's theory of duty, for Scheler, is that it lacks an index of material values. It is precisely such an index that Scheler claims to furnish.

One may nevertheless wish to question whether it is actually true that Kant *derives* moral value from "duty," whether the *essence* of the good consists for him in the "ought of duty," whether his ethics is in fact "imperativistic" or "blind" in the sense Scheler claims. It is true, of course, that Kant's ethics is a *deontological* moral theory, a theory centered on duties and imperatives, commands and moral obligations. But it is so only because there is some notion of a binding principle, something that obliges, something that Kant called the "moral law." As Karl Alphéus tirelessly points out, Kant's conception of the moral law is "logically independent of the concept of the categorical imperative" and has the sense of "duty" only in the case of an unholy will; for, according to Kant, "something is not good because it ought to be done, but ought to be done because it is good, i.e., practically unconditioned and rationally necessary"; hence, far from being a "blind ethics of duty," Kant's ethics is a "rational ethics of insight" (*Kant und Scheler*, 60f., 67.).

While Alphéus may be quite right from a formal point of view, the problem is that the principle of moral law upon which Kant's theory of obligation rests is not *in principle* the material sort of thing that can become an object of insight, as we have seen (ch. 3, sec. 3; and sec. 2 of this chapter). Kant may have tacitly presupposed some material notion of value *de facto*, but his grounding principle remained overtly formal *de jure*. Accordingly, his concept of "good" is defined in terms of good will or moral goodness alone. His concept of "good" must be defined, in effect, by reference to a materially *undefined* and problematic concept of practical "rationality." The same is the case, as we have seen, with his notions of humanity as an "end-in-itself" and a "kingdom of ends." As a consequence, his notion of moral value is formally "empty" and falls back, as Scheler alleges, on the moral content effectually presupposed by the agent employing the "formal" procedures prescribed by the categorical imperative and mistakenly presumed to reside normatively in the idea of "rational duty."

But, as Scheler argues, the question of *what* values exist and what values are *positive* can never be answered in terms of what is morally obligatory, or even "rationally obligatory" in Kant's sense. That is to say, the question of moral obligation—or "rational" obligation—cannot be answered in terms of itself. For what is morally or rationally obligatory can be determined only by reference to some positive value whose material essence itself has the quality of an ideal "ought-to-be." This means that the question of duty can never be answered purely formally, for some kind of material standard is required as a canon for determining what essentially ought to be.

Scheler also points out that even where this condition is fulfilled, what is morally obligatory may vary materially with the variable contents of each concrete moral situation. As we saw in his vivid illustration, what is morally obligatory for the person with a "pathological urge to sacrifice" will differ from what is obligatory for the person who is typically inclined to promote his or her own happiness. Scheler undoubtedly saw this as powerfully illustrating the necessity of an ethics of *material* values and moral *insight,* and as powerfully indicating the basic weaknesses of Kantian *formalism.* It is not clear, of course, that Kant would have been unable to rebut this criticism; he could have replied, for example, that it is precisely the underlying norm of respect for rational agency, no matter how it is manifested in oneself or in another, that his formal principle of obligation is intended to uphold. Despite this caveat, however, and for reasons I have suggested above, I do not think Kant's formal apriorism finally allows him to completely escape Scheler's critique.

Once the necessary conditions and qualifications have all been stated, Scheler's critique of Kant's notion of duty, I think, is credible enough; and his own suggestions, for the most part, are commendable as far as they go. Kant does not offer a theory of value, as such, or a clear articulation of the values underlying his notions of rationality and moral law. Scheler's theory does remedy these defects somewhat—not only by pointing out that Kant's notion of moral law presupposes some notion of value, or by stressing the importance of materially distinguishing different types and ranks of values—but by himself furnishing a reasonably detailed theory of moral and nonmoral values. But there are several important respects in which his own theory fails to present a completely convincing alternative to Kant's ethics.

One of the most persistent difficulties faced by Scheler, it seems to me, lies in the relationship between moral insight, inclination, and obligation, which he does not appear to have worked out entirely clearly. There are intimations in some of his works, to be sure, of possible directions in which these relations might be worked out more satisfactorily.[37] And it could be said fairly that such intimations in such texts point in the direction of a possible response to the following criticisms. Nonetheless, basic difficulties remain far from resolved. The emphasis on insight in itself is a good one. It is true, certainly, that moral obligation cannot ground itself and that one must look beyond the notion of "duty" to come up with the positive values that serve as the basis for what is obligatory. Likewise, it is true that one's volitional and conative orientation is determined in large part by one's insight or value-feeling, including the way one feels about oneself, one's feeling of self-worth. The problem does not lie in the notion of insight, as such, which is clearly an evident phenomenon of moral experience. The problem lies in Scheler's understanding of the relation between insight and inclination, which appears to preclude the possibility of personal moral conflict and genuine obligation.

For example, his claim that "duty" comes into play precisely when moral considerations based on insight begin to weaken (sec. 2 above) seems to suggest that moral *insight* automatically brings conformity of *will* to the ideal ought. In fact, Scheler argues that if a positive value is perfectly evident and clear, then willing follows as a veritable existential necessity, in the Socratic sense that all "good willing" follows from "cognition of the good," and that all evil willing rests on moral "deception and aberration" (F, 89/69). On this view, positive willing *inevitably* follows positive insight, just as, for Socrates, virtue inevitably follows knowledge. Any experience of moral conflict, temptation, or *knowingly* willing what ought-*not*-to-be in the absence of any kind of moral "deception" would appear to be impossible (cf. Schilpp, "Doctrine of Illusion").

This view is closely tied to Scheler's view of the autonomy of the person in ethical contexts. For Scheler, autonomy is not located merely in the spontaneity of willing, but in moral insight. Even obedience to an externally imposed command may be called autonomous, for Scheler, if it stems from autonomous insight into the value presupposed by the command. But for Scheler, one's moral disposition itself can never be commanded, nor "obey" a command, since it is the font of moral insight itself and determines the moral value of all striving and willing (Frings, "Max Scheler and Kant," 103). Hence, while he allowed for the possibility of inexplicable "conversions" or changes of moral disposition, as did Kant, Scheler denied the possibility of changing the moral disposition by means of direct moral education (F, 136/116). And while he offered brilliant analyses of cases of value-deception, his theory leaves one with the infelicitous suggestion that *any* willing that could be called immoral or evil stems from moral deception, that desires and conations never conflict with the felt value of one's own moral disposition, that the felt value of one's personal worth may never be experienced as itself divided against itself, that people are never inclined to do what they knowingly do not wish to do, that there is never any distance or tension between inclination and felt obligation.

If this were the case, there would seem to be no room for the *constraint* of moral obligation in Scheler's ethics—no place for Aristotle's *enkratês* or *akratês*, the morally "strong" or "weak" character, which must *struggle* with the tension between the demands of reason and impulses of desire. A moral person would seem to be no more than one who was naturally gifted with accurate moral insight and who simply followed his or her natural inclinations. One could ask cynically, like Heidemann, whether Scheler's theory would then not apply only to those who happen to be "moral geniuses." On this view, one could say: "As there is giftedness in the aesthetic sphere, so there is 'giftedness' in the moral sphere," and "there are men who are 'amoral' just as there are those who are a-musical" (Heidemann, 163). Any theory of ethics that fails to deal adequately with the phenomenon of personal moral conflict is critically deficient in its understanding of moral obligation.

This problem is not restricted to Scheler's theory. Kant falls victim to the same problem as a consequence of his two-world theory, which hermetically seals off pure practical reason from the contaminating wiles of phenomenal inclinations. As a result, Kant effectually precludes the possibility of the very moral conflict upon which his whole ethics turns—the conflict between duty and inclination. "Kant's theory does not explain what it is trying to explain," writes Caputo: "How can man be divided, as St. Paul says, and do not the things which he wills? Kant has invalidated this experience by identifying freedom with this noumenal and rational principle and by making the inclinations something other, something heteronomous. Kant's man is not truly divided against himself. Rather his 'proper' or 'genuine' self (*das eigentliche Selbst*) is simply being assaulted by an external invader, an outsider, and a fairly impotent one at that, one which is 'only an appearance of himself [*nur Erscheinung seiner Selbst*]' " ("Kant's Ethics," 134f. cf. Kant, *GMS*, 457f./87). Furthermore, Kant's conception of freedom as 'autonomy' (in *GMS*), in contrast to his conception of freedom as 'spontaneity' (in *KrV*), gave rise to a problematic view in which the bad or immoral will is *denied* autonomy and freedom, so that it is rendered simply *amoral* and regarded as a purely natural and heteronomous phenomenon. Kant later endeavored to correct these difficulties by means of his concept of "radical evil" as the principle on which the autonomously *evil* will acts. But his attempts to explain and integrate the key concepts of "executive will" (*Willkür*), "legislative will" (*Wille*), and "moral disposition" (*Gesinnung*) into a coherent revision of his earlier position remained bedeviled by his earlier dualisms, and his efforts were not entirely successful.[38]

But, whatever its problems, Kant's moral philosophy at least lays due emphasis on the phenomenon and necessity of moral obligation. No matter what objections one may have to his dualism of "reason" and "inclination," his descriptions of moral conflict, at least, strike us as *existentially true*. Kant did not consign cases of immorality to some sort of deficiency of moral insight or moral "deception," as Scheler sometimes seemed to. Rather, he went so far as to articulate a doctrine of "radical evil" and wrote of an "inclination to evil in human nature" (*R*, Bk. I). By contrast, it seems that in Scheler's case one may almost speak, as Heidemann says, of a supposed "radical inclination toward good" *Untersuchungen*, 159, n. 11). Whether such a supposition is phenomenologically warranted is, at least, open to serious question.

In light of these difficulties, and in view of Scheler's claim that moral obligation is based on moral *insight* (into the ideal ought and its values), one might wish to ask whether there is any way in which moral insight can be learned. Likewise, in view of his claim that virtue consists in the immediate experience of *ability* to realize what ideally ought-to-be, one may wonder whether there is any way in which such an experience can be cultivated or imparted to others by teaching. Can there be, in short, such a thing as moral education, training, or guidance? Kant's ethics, whether or not it ultimately delivers on the promise, at least clearly holds forth the possibility.[39] What about Scheler's ethics? It may strike one as unfair to ask such questions of Scheler, given his obvious attention in *Formalismus* to traditions and cultures leading one to insight. Surely Scheler would not deny the possibility of moral education and guidance. Indeed, as was noted at the end of the last chapter, he declares with great conviction that *"ethics is a 'damned bloody affair,' and if it can give me no directives concerning how 'I' 'should' live now in this social and historical context, then what is it?"* But one may then legitimately ask: Does Scheler's ethics offer moral direction and guidance, and, if so, how? At times, despite himself, he doesn't seem to offer much hope of a clear answer.[40]

Scheler's discussion of "model persons" and "pure types of the value-person" in the closing sections of *Formalismus* are instructive in this regard.[41] Quoting Kant, who writes, "Imitation has no place in moral matters" *(GMS,* 409), Scheler claims that, in contrast to Kant, he grants that the imitation of morally exemplary persons plays a determinative role in normative ethics.[42] Scheler's position, however, in contrast to Kant's, is descriptive, not prescriptive. He is not claiming that imitation should or should not have a place in moral matters, but simply that it does. Does this descriptive phenomenological approach pose problems for Scheler's ethics? There are some who seem to think so. Heidemann, for example, suggests that it entraps Scheler in an impossible quandary of trying to derive an "ought" from an "is," so that, although his ethics promises "moral direction," its "descriptive" method prevents it from delivering on this promise (162f.). Eugene Kelly claims that the "most damaging criticism to be directed at Scheler's plans for a normative ethical system concerns the possibility of applying the phenomenological *description* of values to an ethics that imagines itself capable of employment in the solution of concrete ethical problems." We may see that the "holy life" is better than the "life of sensuality," he says, "but can we know *with the same degree of evidence* in just what activities the truly holy life consists? The fact that we cannot indicates that the latter problem is *not* a phenomenological problem" (*Max Scheler*, 122).

Certainly it must be borne in mind that Scheler never conceived himself to be attempting to show how his ethics applies to all of concrete life. Indeed, as he clearly indicates in the Preface to the first edition of *Formalismus*, he conceived himself to be doing *foundational* work. He doubtless would have admitted that additional criteria or concrete specifications would be needed before his ethics could offer specific guidance to persons in actual situations. Nonetheless, while it would be unfair to ignore the philosophical level at which Scheler conceived himself to be working, surely it is not unfair to ask—or to try to imagine—how an ethics such as his would go about addressing the problem of offering concrete moral guidance.

Let us consider this problem very briefly. Granting that we can distinguish various positive material values such as pleasure, nobility, holiness, and the like, how does this help us to discover what is morally obligatory in the specific circumstances we confront in concrete life-situations? Granting, furthermore, that we can distinguish a priori a ranked hierarchy of values, and that values of a higher rank are preferable a priori to those of a lower rank, this still leaves critical questions. For one thing, it offers no direction for circumstances in which the realization of a lower value (such as famine relief in Africa, which is concerned with the "vital" or "biological" value of human life) might be *more pressing* than that of a higher value (such as building a cathedral in Washington, D.C., which is concerned with the "spiritual" or "religious" value of worship).[43] Many situations call for precisely such decisions. Furthermore, there are plenty of examples one could think of where the "higher" value would obviously not be the morally good choice. Should I rescue the drowning child in the back yard swimming pool, or continue listening to Mozart in my room? The former would realize a "lower," vital value, the latter a "higher" spiritual, aesthetic value. But my duty is obviously to save the child. The question is whether Scheler offers any clear way of showing why this is obvious. I am not sure he does.

Another difficulty is that Scheler's hierarchy of values offers no guidance as to which specific, positive values *within* a given rank are preferable to others. For example, which "vital" value should the medical profession consider more important in the care of geriatric patients, all things being equal: their physical comfort or longevity? Should doctors provide the alternative of euthanasia or "physician-assisted suicide" as a means of alleviating suffering that becomes intense and constant? Or should they do all in their power to help their patients continue to live and cope with their suffering? Which value is the "higher," the elimination of physical suffering or the preservation of life? I am not sure Scheler offers any help here either.

Even in situations presenting clear alternatives between values of *different rank*, one may ask whether what is morally obligatory can be determined adequately by means of Scheler's a priori "laws of preference." For example, what "laws of preference" would help a pregnant woman deliberating over the controversial question of abortion? What a priori "laws of preference" will offer her direction in choosing between the "vital" or "biological" value of carrying the fetus to term and bringing another human life into the world, and any number of other possible "psychological," "utilitarian" or other values that she might weigh against it? Is it sufficient or even helpful to ask *which* value is essentially "higher," "preferable," or essentially more in need of being realized? Is it enough to point out that *for some people*, the value of human life may bear not only a "biological" value but a "religious" value? Will that settle the issue? Again, I am not certain Scheler provides much help here. The choice to be made requires moral insight into the nature of the options posed by the situation itself, yet what is morally obligatory seems incapable of being adjudicated on the basis of a priori abstract, essential "laws of preference" alone.

Raising these problems is not a matter of question-begging. Each of the cases noted in the last two paragraphs presents options that are matters of deep controversy in Western society. The contemporary debates over euthanasia and abortion involve deeply held commitments on each side, stemming from traditions of long standing, such as the tradition of liberal-democratic values (which is committed to individual liberty) and the tradition of Judeo-Christian values (which is committed to the sanctity of human life). Yet there are available examples of traditional ethical theories, such as Thomistic ethics, which not only take clear positions on each of these issues but have developed traditional rationales for them. Hence, it cannot be viewed as question-begging to ask whether Scheler's ethics offers a *basis* for coming to a clear position on such questions or an adequate rationale if it does.

Part of this, of course, is simply the inescapable problem involved in the implementation of any ethical principle in a concrete, life situation. No set of ethical principles is going to do all our moral thinking for us. But this is only part of the problem, because, in the final analysis, it is not always clear in Scheler's ethics, any more than in Kant's, whether one actually has any clear material moral principles by which to plainly determine specific obligations. It is not clear whether he provides any truly adequate practical principles *to apply*. Perhaps one might protest that this is unfair to Scheler, that Scheler's work is in theoretical ethics, not applied ethics. Or one might even object that Scheler himself illustrates amply how his value theory may be applied, for example, in the whole of his work on *Ressentiment*, which utilizes his value theory to mount a brilliant critique Western bourgeois society. It is true, certainly, that Scheler's work is theoretical. It is no less true that where he does make use of his own theory it is by way of cultural critique rather than determining practical duties, more in the line of a Nietzsche than of a Richard

Brandt, for example.[44] But to say that Scheler's work is theoretical is not to deny his intention, as we have seen above, that it furnish a foundation for eventual practical applications. And to point to his own application of his theory in his criticisms of Western culture is not yet to show how exactly *such* criticisms must necessarily follow from an acceptance of his theory of values. One could argue that Scheler's critique of Western bourgeois culture could have stemmed possibly from his personal predilections as easily as from an analysis of his hierarchy of material values and a priori *ordo amoris*.

The practical problem is that Scheler's theory, even as a foundational work, offers insufficient clarity at the level of foundation to show how the structure of a normative ethics, which he aims to found, could be built directly upon it. For example, there is simply no clear mechanism in Scheler's theory by which to work out the relation between one's natural inclinations, which follow inevitably upon the heels of insight, and the constraints of moral obligation, which follow no less upon the heels of insight. What is the relation between these insights—the insight that governs inclination and the insight that governs obligation? Are they one and the same insight, or two different insights? And if they differ, can they come into conflict? And, if so—if the insight to which inclination is harnessed comes into conflict with the insight to which obligation is harnessed—what is a person to do then? Which insight *ought* to take precedence, and why? The effective result is that one has no obvious way of determining strictly what his or her moral obligation is; one apparently has no obvious, reliable moral principle to apply.

Even if this were not a problem, the disparity in Scheler's view between material value-essences themselves and the "practical morality" of the relative historical "ethos" in which they are incarnated as material conventions of moral obligation makes it doubtful whether his theory can provide the kind of reliable material foundation for morals that it claims to provide. While an attractive feature of his phenomenological approach is the promise it holds of overcoming the dichotomies of is/ought, fact/value, and inclination/rationality, upon which Kant's ethics rests,[45] Scheler's analysis of the phenomenological "facts" of moral experience—including the "fact" that moral obligations are "felt" by people—does not yet furnish adequate material evidence for *what* actually is, or *what should be*, morally obligatory.

Scheler's insight with respect to moral obligation is that every moral imperative depends for its morally obliging compulsion upon insight into the material values underlying it. What he fails to show us—and this cannot be too much to ask of any ethical theory with normative pretensions, as I have argued above—is how we are even to begin to discover *what* we are obliged to do. I am not talking about detailed rules of casuistry here, but about the most general practical principles of moral obligation. Scheler does not show us clearly how his theory of material values enables us to discern in what kinds of activities we are morally obliged to realize those values. He does not show us clearly how our natural inclinations, which flow from value-feelings, can come into conflict with our moral inhibitions, which also stem from value-feelings, or how we can resolve such conflicts.

Again, I am well aware that we must bear in mind the foundational character of Scheler's work, that it is a work of theoretical and not applied ethics, and that his own applications of his value theory were limited, by and large, to cultural critique. This is all certainly true. But Scheler's theory leaves many serious questions unanswered, honest questions which require adequate answers before his theory can be considered to provide a truly viable foundation upon which to erect a fuller normative ethical theory and an elaboration of applications to concrete situations.

In view of this, it must be admitted that some of the criticisms that Scheler levels against Kant could be leveled against his own theory. We have already suggested that Scheler's notion of moral "good" is perhaps too "formal," because it does not take into consideration nonmoral kinds of good (ch. 3, sec. 4, above). It might also be asked whether the relation between the realm of material values and the whole question of the "ought" (including both the "ideal ought" and the "ought of duty") is not conceived too "formally" by Scheler to serve as the basis for determining actual moral obligations. It is hard to see how the basic axioms governing this relation—for example, that "positive material values ought to be," and that one ought to realize the highest possible positive values—can really be effective practically in enabling us to discover what our duties are.

Probably no ethical theory can ever be expected to provide a *comprehensive* treatment of the moral cases that confront us or of the appropriate moral rules that we ought to apply in them—or even a *conclusive* justification of the principles on which such rules are founded or of the foundational presuppositions underlying them. Certainly no set of ethical formulas is going to do our moral thinking for us. We ourselves must work out the difference between what is desirable and what is good in the situation we are in, and we ourselves, not a set of formulas, will have to be the owners of the actions we take. But what would help, and what is the purpose of any normative ethical theory to provide, is a clear analysis and description of the typical way in which the good can be identified and the difference between the good and the desirable can be worked out beyond a reasonable doubt. This is what is missing in Scheler's theory. Whether a phenomenological theory can ever entirely remedy this defect or even fully address the problem, as Eugene Kelly wonders, remains to be seen.

In his phenomenological study of moral action, Robert Sokolowski suggests that the clearest way of working out the difference between the desirable and the good is by an approach that attends more directly to the *public transactional form* of moral performances (*Moral Action*, cf.

esp. 155f.). Most modern moral theories have concentrated either on the "categoriality of choice" and looked for the moral act *after* the material performance in the result (like utilitarianism or consequentialism), or on the "judgmental categoriality" and looked for it *before* the moral transaction in the intention or will (like deontologism). What both approaches neglect, he says, is the "moral categoriality," which emerges neither before nor after the moral transaction, but *within* the public material performance itself.[46] It is through this categoriality that we identify a particular performance as a moral action and discern that "an agent is taking the good or bad of another agent as such as his own good or bad in some way or other" (ibid., 156). By implication, we arrive at the following (still very abstract) formula for what is morally obligatory: what is morally obligatory is "taking the good of another as my good and the bad of another as my bad." The way we learn in what sorts of actions this consists, for Sokolowski, is related to discerning the categories of moral reasoning, which he locates in acts as their identificational and presentational forms (ibid., 5, 211). It is by means of assessing particular moral performances that one learns to discern these categories of moral reasoning, and it is by means of these categories, in turn, through a kind of interpretive dialectic, that one learns to work out the difference between the desirable and the good in assessing moral performances.

Sokolowski's analysis, despite its generality at critical points, helps to focus the public, dyadic, transactional nature of moral action. It helps us to see that a moral performance involves not merely a realization of material values through willing, as described by Scheler, but a specific relationship between "agents" and their "targets." It helps focus the commonplace moral insight that our moral obligations involve taking another's good as our good and another's bad as our bad. This observation, while unexceptional, is a helpful reminder that morality is about relationships—an idea that often seems to get lost in Scheler. But the outline of our material moral obligations that emerges in Sokolowski's account still remains sketchy and formal. Just what sorts of particular actions are involved in another's good remains unclear, and it is not enough for us to suppose, simply, that we will recognize such actions when we arrive in the situation of the moral performance itself. We need to be shown ways of recognizing them, examples of them, and rules and principles by which to interpret and understand them.

Perhaps nobody has worked out the genesis of the "ought" in moral experience from a phenomenological perspective in more intriguing detail than Reiner. Borrowing from Husserl, Pfänder, and Scheler, he develops a theory of "the conscious I" with a distinction between "I-center," which is coterminous with the subject's will and agency, and "I-circumground," which lies beyond the subject's will and agency as their surrounding environment and basis. The I-center identifies the active and responsible nucleus of spontaneous willing and acting. As I-center, it is *I* who acts.

Yet my I-center arises out of my I-circumground, the dispositional horizon of feelings and inclinations shaped by my social environment and upbringing that I carry with me, *surrounding* my I-center and *other* to it. My experience of my I-circumground may range from the conscious to the unconscious, but it furnishes the foundation and creative source upon which my I-center's agency is dependent and founded. The source—not yet the *act*—of my valuation is located in the passive intentionalities of my I-circumground, the feelings and strivings that have values as their objective correlates. The *act* of valuing is a position-taking by the will (*Willensstellungnahme*) stemming from an active desire or aversion implying approval or disapproval by the I-center. A moral *decision*, finally, is the effective self-determination involved in the active realization or bringing about of what is desired in the will's position—taking by means of an action.

The foregoing analysis permits Reiner to make several interesting theoretical claims. To begin with, it permits him to offer an effective argument for the *objectivity* of values: as objects of the I-circumground's feelings, they appear *apart* from the subject's wanting them (*DI*, 121–25). As such, they are independent of one's will or agency. They possess a "reasonable" claim in their capacity to oblige us, not only because they appeal to our rational understanding, but precisely *because* they do not present themselves originally as a matter of arbitrary choice or free will! Hence, the moral ought is neither fully autonomous nor fully heteronomous in Reiner's account: "In consequence of its *givenness*, it cannot properly be said to be subordinate to our autonomy, or to spring therefrom; but, on account of its *reasonableness*, it is by no means heteronomous in the Kantian sense. Rather, it acquires at length, despite its origin from outside, a share in the rational core of our personalities" (*DI*, 183; cf. 134). In the value-response involved in the position-taking by the will with respect to the I-circumground's passive intentionalities, the apprehension of value shifts from the inarticulate "reasons of the heart" to those of the agent's intellect and I-center. Furthermore, and most significantly for us, Reiner argues that the claims of moral obligation that present themselves to us in our experience of the phenomenon of *conscience* are not subject to the I-center's will or agency but present themselves from the ego's periphery in the I-circumground as phenomena beyond our immediate control (*DI*, 121–25, 200–10). To fully appreciate Reiner's account of how these claims of moral obligation are generated in the I-circumground, how they are apprehended, admitted, and appropriated by the I-center, and how they become effective motives of moral action, we must have a bit more background.

A significant thesis in Reiner's phenomenology of values is that values present themselves either as *relative* or *absolute*. By this, he means that they appear either as valuable "for" me or someone else, relative to our personal needs and desires, or as valuable "in themselves," apart from any relation to anybody's personal concerns. A relative value, furthermore, may present itself as merely *subjectively important* if I perceive it as being unnecessary but desirable for myself; or as *objectively important* if I perceive it as being necessary for myself or others, or even as merely desirable *for others*. A value is *objectively absolute*, then, when its importance is in itself and independent of anyone's personal life. For example, Reiner says that the "value of a man's life rests absolutely in itself whether or not a man's life is of value to him or anyone else" (*DI*, 139). Obligations, therefore, come in degrees for Reiner, and the index of the categorical ought, clearly, lies in the objectivity and/or absoluteness of the values to be realized.

Here we begin to notice how Reiner's analysis could possibly help to correct *some* of the deficiencies of Scheler's rationale for moral obligation. For we see that it allows him to retrieve the deontological thrust of Kantian ethics by restating the latter's proposed conflict between inclination and duty in terms of whether the inclination in question refers to the intentionalities of the I-center or I-circumground. This reopens the possibility of accounting for moral conflict and clarifies the issues involved in moral obligation. It does not mean that one cannot imagine someone being naturally *inclined* to do what is obligatory, so that the gap between duty and inclination disappears in the way envisioned by Scheler. But it does allow for a gap or tension, which is not always entirely clear in Scheler's account.

Furthermore, Reiner offers a fuller and more plausible account than Scheler of how the "ought" originates and engages the will to become an effective motive of moral action. While the rich detail of his theory of conscience and the origin of the moral ought cannot concern us here, it will suffice to note his description of the process of "autonomization" by which the moral ought presented in the I-circumground is authorized by the I-center through a kind of "self-entrapment." Reiner's thesis rests on a distinction between the ways in which we make moral judgments regarding ourselves and regarding others. When we judge ourselves, the voice of our conscience speaks to us as if in the voice of another. This is because our conscience is the result of those involuntary intentionalities and feelings, shaped by our personal history and socialization, that announce themselves in our I-circumground.

Such is not the case, however, when we make moral judgments regarding others. We not only praise and blame others, but often tell them, *categorically* and *unconditionally*, what they *ought* to do. In expressing ourselves thus, we are acting in complete *autonomy* and performing free, voluntary acts of judgment at our *I-center*. While our judgments of others may also have their ulterior origin in the value-feelings of the I-periphery, such judgments do not, like the voice of conscience, obtrude themselves upon us as something alien. Rather, it is precisely *we* who own and authorize them and cannot help acknowledging them as our own. But in making such judgments of others, which categorically and universally bind them to certain obligations, we implicitly "trap ourselves" and subject ourselves to the same demands. *Our* judgments of others then *obtrude* themselves upon us as a logical consequence of those judgments, by way of appeal to our rational integrity. The autonomy of our past judgments is thus transmitted to our conscience, says Reiner, thereby rendering it fully *autonomous*.

There may be still other difficulties in Scheler's account to which Reiner's discussion may also be relevant. For example, one troublesome aspect of Scheler's theory is that it offers no reason why we should ever feel obliged to prefer others over ourselves—a difficulty to which Reiner's analysis of subjectively and objectively important values provides a clear and natural solution (*DI*, 143, 182). By far the most important problem to which Reiner offers a helpful corrective, however, is the problem of moral obligation and its relation to inclination and insight. Reiner shows us clearly how the distinction between duty and inclination can be preserved within a phenomenological ethics. His distinction between I-center and I-circumground, and his discussion of the "autonomization" of conscience by means of "self-entrapping" judgments we make of others, are creative and genuinely illuminating. They show us how certain passive intentionalities and inclinations of the I-periphery could be challenged and superseded by those of the I-center when the insights implicit in our moral judgments of others obtrude themselves as moral demands upon ourselves. But while his work offers a clear indication of ways in which a theory such as Scheler's requires correction, it suffers from some of the same kinds of indefiniteness, at critical points, as Sokolowski's.

Like Sokolowski's work, Reiner's contribution to the project of a phenomenological theory of ethics is both notable and insightful. Like Sokolowski's analysis of the public, transactional form of a moral performance, Reiner's analysis of the "autonomization" of conscience and moral obligation provides a helpful corrective to certain weaknesses in Scheler's theory. But in neither case are we led to see just what sorts of particular actions and judgments are involved in another's good. It is not simply a matter of remaining ambiguities of phenomenological description. In Reiner's account, for example, one thing that remains unclear is just how moral conflict originates between the value-feelings that come to expression in our "autonomized" conscience at our I-center and those that come to expression in our involuntary inclinations at our I-periphery. If the former, like the latter, originate in the passive intentionalities of the I-periphery, where and how does the conflict begin? While such questions are of passing phenomenological interest, the question of real moment is whether Reiner's ethics, or any ethics with normative aspirations, can show us how to decide what we ought to do. It is not enough to simply describe how we "trap" ourselves in our moral obligations by the moral judgments and demands we make of others, even though this in itself is an impressive achievement of some insight, pregnant with ethical and psychological implications. In order to know what we ought to do, we need to be shown how to decide what is genuinely good.

Whether this may be too much to expect of a phenomenological theory, as Kelly suggests, is not a question to be answered here. What else is necessary, beyond what we have suggested here, to fully resolve the issues of the moral ought and the good, such as remain unsettled in Scheler's theory, is for others to conclude for themselves. If the concept of moral obligation itself is not obsolete in a world with no decided conception of moral law, as G. E. M. Anscombe has suggested, then they clearly have their work cut out for them ("Modern Moral Philosophy," esp. 6).

Notes

1. John R. Silber, "Procedural Formalism in Kant's Ethics," 198f., 203f. Silber insists, contrary to Hegel, that Kant's formalism cannot be understood either as *substantive* or *logical* formalism, but only as *procedural* formalism (233). The first to interpret Kant's moral law in a thoroughly procedural manner, according to Silber, was Paul Arthur Schilpp, in *Kant's Pre-Critical Ethics* (Evanston, IL: Northwestern University, 1938).

2. Robert Paul Wolff suggests that Kant is seeking in his ethics "substantive knowledge of the absolutely unconditioned," which was excluded in the first *Critique* as impossible. See his Introduction to the *Foundations of the Metaphysics of Morals*, by Immanuel Kant, trans. L. W. Beck (Indianapolis: Bobbs-Merrill, 1969), xiv.

Silber's interpretation of Kant's position as a *procedural* rather than a *substantive* formalism, runs counter to the suggestion of "substantive" knowledge offered by Wolff, but does not resolve the issue as to how we acquire knowledge of such procedures within a Kantian framework.

3. Silber, "Procedural Formalism," 214, 199, 208ff. Cf. also his "Der Schematismus der Praktischen Vernunft," *Kant-Studien* 56 (1966), 253–73; and Paton, *Categorical Imperative,* 143f., 158f., 146ff.

4. GMS, 421; Silber, "Procedural Formalism," 210; cf. H. J. Paton, *The Moral Law* (London: Hutchinson's University Library, 1948, 30f.; and his *Categorical Imperative,* 143f., 158f., 146ff.

5. Silber, "Procedural Formalism," 198. The general role of judgment in linking theory to practice is described, as noted by Silber, in Kant's TP, 275/61.

6. Cf. the "Methodology of Pure Practical Reason" in Part II of the second *Critique*, where, as a practical measure, Kant recommends the collection of historical examples for purposes of moral illustration. One of his own favorite examples is taken from Juvenal's *Satires*: "Be a stout soldier, a faithful guardian, and an incorruptible judge; if summoned to bear witness in some dubious and uncertain cause, though Phalaris himself should bring up his bull and dic-

tate to you a perjury, count it the greatest of all sins to prefer life to honor, and to lose, for the sake of living, all that makes life worth living" (cited in *KpV*, 158f.).

7. Thus, Kant distinguishes between an empirical "change of practice" and a suprasensible "change of heart"; the latter, clearly, requiring a change in the moral disposition itself, which cannot be directly effected by moral education (*R*, 46ff./42f.). This matter is discussed briefly in ch. 6, sec. 1.

8. *F*, 179/163. We are speaking here, of course, of the prevailing conventions of Scheler's time. The positivist paradigm has been breached in our own day. As far as its beginnings, Lotze may be the first to have actually employed the terminological distinction between "facts" and "values," but the conceptual distinction is substantively present in Kant's dualizations of phenomena/ noumena, knowledge/faith, science/religion, etc.

9. A brief explanation of "assessment" theory follows several paragraphs below.

10. Scheler makes this identification (*F*, 182/166), although it is not clear that Nietzsche would have agreed entirely with the subjectivism of Hobbes. Some might wish to argue that Nietzsche seems rather to have held that enhancement of the will-to-power is something like an *absolute* good and that some forms of the will-to-power are *objectively* superior to others.

11. Because of this confusion, neither nominalism nor emotivism can explain value diversity. If one act is contrarily called "modest" by one observer and "cowardly" by another, nominalism can account for the difference only in terms of conflicting functions of "approval" and "disapproval"; and if someone masks his deed falsely as morally praiseworthy and "good," it can be accounted for only in terms of the person's "interest." But nominalism utterly fails to provide an account of the differentiation among the values (e.g., "modest," "cowardly," and "good").

Scheler also offers a fairly detailed discussion of *utilitarianism*, arguing that it provides a theory, not of moral value, but of relative social approval and disapproval (*F*, 193ff./177ff.).

12. *F*, 206/190. It could be asked whether there is not a confusion here. In Brentano's case, for example, one could ask whether Scheler adequately distinguishes between his (1) notion of the *origin* of the concept "good" from an "impression" of inner sense, and his (2) altogether different and strictly consequentialist conception of how good and bad, better and worse, are to be *assessed*. Nevertheless, it seems to me that Scheler's main point here remains above reproach — namely, that moral "assessments" themselves are dependent upon a prior intuition of values.

13. Scheler's critical analysis of "duty," as exemplified in Kantian ethics, falls under a section of his text dealing with "assessment" theories in the first part of ch. 5 of *Formalismus*, entitled "Unsatisfactory Theories of the Origin of the Concept of Value and the Essence of Moral Facts."

14. Scheler's discussion of "The Autonomy of the Person" is found in the second part of ch. 6 of *Formalismus,* beginning at *F,* 499/494 (but see esp. 503ff./498ff.). Scheler also observes that duty, even when given as "universally valid," is subjectively conditioned and not based on "objective" insight; and that, on the other hand, the individual consciousness that something is "good" for *me alone* is not necessarily blind to objective values. In this connection, cf.

Emmanuel Levinas's view of the pre-reflective basis of moral systems in the primordial phenomenon of immediate, unrepeatable acts of "sacrifice," as contrasted with the concept of duty, which is a product of reflective and deliberative generalization, as discussed by Stephan Strasser, "Het Probleem van de Deformalisatie van de Ethiek naar Aanleiding van Kant," *Tijdschrift voor Filosofie* 43, No. 3 (Sept. 1981), 477ff.

15. Here Scheler is citing an expression used by Kant in *Der einzig mögliche Beweisgrund zu einer Demonstration des Daseins Gottes*, ed. Paul Menzer, KGS 2:81. Cf. Gordon Treash's translation, *The One Possible Basis for a Demonstration of the Existence of God* (New York: Abaris Books, 1979), 194.

16. Cf. ch. 1, n. 41. The milestone works would have to include Richard Rorty, *Philosophy and the Mirror of Nature* (Princeton: Princeton University Press, 1979); Alasdair MacIntyre, *After Virtue*, and his *Whose Justice? Which Rationality?* See also the survey by Allan Megill, *Prophets of Extremity* (Berkeley: University of California Press, 1985); and for an excellent discussion of the political dimensions of this debate, see John McGowan, *Postmodernism and Its Critics* (Ithaca: Cornell University Press, 1991). James L. Marsh, et al., eds., *Modernity and Its Discontents* (New York: Fordham University Press, 1992), contains a fascinating debate, moderated by Merold Westphal, between the Habermasian perspective of J. L. Marsh and the Derridian perspective of John D. Caputo. See also Caputo's provocative *Against Ethics: Contributions to a Poetics of Obligation with Constant Reference to Deconstruction* (Bloomington: Indians University Press, 1993). Discussions from the perspective of the Frankfort school include those of Max Horkheimer and Theodor W. Adorno, *Dialectic of Enlightenment*, trans. John Cumming (New York: Seabury Press, 1972), and Jürgen Habermas, *The Philosophical Discourse of Modernity*, trans. Frederick Lawrence (Cambridge: MIT Press, 1987).

17. John Sallis, in the opening paragraph of his often eloquent, deconstructive reading of Kant's first *Critique*, *The Gathering of Reason* (Athens: Ohio University Press, 1980), writes: "Reason—the very word now bespeaks crisis, failure of every available sense to fulfill what cannot but be intended. The crisis is radical, for in every other instance reason would serve as that to which recourse would be had in order to isolate and resolve crisis, in order to open up and appropriate a fulfilling sense. Even to thematize the conceptuality of crisis is already to lay claim in deed to a certain resolution of the crisis of reason—that is, such crisis withdraws, renders provisional, the very possibility of its being thematized as such. The crisis is so radical that even this schema itself, that of crisis, has been emptied in such fashion as to accommodate almost anything that becomes somehow problematic; the schema of crisis has itself entered upon a crisis" (1).

18. To take just one of many examples, Kant says: "*Crimina carnis* are contrary to self-regarding duty because they are against the ends of humanity. They consist in abuse of one's sexuality. Every form of sexual indulgence, except in marriage, is a misuse of sexuality, and so a *crimen carnis*" (*Lectures on Ethics*, trans. Louis Infield [1930; rpt. Indianapolis: Hackett, 1963], 169).

19. Cf. Maria Scheler's note for *F*, 200 [line 37]/185 n. 14; and also *F*, 218/203; 225/210; and 249/234.

20. *F*, 220f./206; see above, ch. 3 sec. 1. The same would apparently hold for "higher" and "lower" values, although these are *relative*, not absolute, notions.

21. Without this clarification, Scheler's language may misleadingly suggest that unrealized values do not "exist," even as intentional objects, which he would of course deny.

In view of the foregoing characterization of the ideal ought, Scheler denies that there is a special category of "ought-being" (*Soll-Seins*), as claimed by G. Simmel, *Einleitung in die Moralwissenschaft: Eine Kritik der ethischen Grundbegriffe* (Stuttgart: Cottasche, 1911).

22. See the chapter, "Morality," in Hegel's *The Phenomenology of Spirit* (§§596ff.); and Hegel's critique of Kant's categorical imperative in G. W. F. Hegel, *Gesammelte Werke*, ed. H. Büchner and O. Pöggeler (Hamburg: F. Meiner, 1968), 4:439, translated by T. M. Knox as *Natural Law* (Philadelphia: University of Pennsylvania Press, 1975), 80: "The maxim, 'Help the poor,' tested by being elevated into a principle of universal legislation, will prove to be false because it annihilates itself. If the thought is that the poor generally should be helped, then either there are no poor left or there are nothing but poor; in the latter event no one is left to help them. In both cases the help disappears. Thus the maxim, universalized, cancels itself." In defense of Kant, it could be argued against Hegel that although Kant's wording often requires the universalizability of the actions themselves (e.g., *KpV*, 69), it sometimes allows "variety in the rule" (*KpV*, 20).

Hegel's critique of Kant, which rests on *specific contents of maxims* whose universal legislation is self-annihilating, is somewhat different from (though similar to) Scheler's, which rests on Kant's *identification of moral value with duty*, which, for Scheler, entails the eclipse of the former in the apotheosis of the latter.

Cf. Karl Alphéus's detailed and critical discussion on "the supposed refutations" of the categorical imperative as a criterion of morality by Brentano, Jonas Cohn, G. Simmel, and Hegel, in *Kant und Scheler*, 320ff.

23. *F*, 224/ 210; cf. *F*, 201/185f. H. G. Stoker offers a concise discussion of Scheler's view of duty and moral obligation, with reference to the critical and supportive exchanges between Michael Wittmann, Dietrich von Hildebrand, and Erich Przywara, in *Das Gewissen: Erscheinungsformen und Theorien* (Bonn: Verlag von Friedrich Cohen, 1925), ch. 5.

24. "If the ought in general were only and originally a 'demand' or an experienced imperative, as both Rickert and Lipps have described it, this question could never be asked, and the problem of the 'binding force' of propositions of the ought would not exist" (*F*, 225/211).

25. "It makes *no* sense to speak, as Kant does, of a duty that is floating in the air, as it were, a duty vis-à-vis no one, and which is not imposed by the order of an authority. It also makes no sense to speak about 'self-obligation' " (*F*, 226/211). "One cannot 'give orders to oneself' or 'obey oneself'; one can only 'resolve to do something.' . . . One can also 'make a vow to oneself,' but only 'before' another (e.g., God)" (Ibid., n./n. 39).

26. *F*, 226/211f. Thus, Scheler claims that throughout history, *proscriptions* have always preceded *prescriptions*, and cites as an example the Decalogue (though one may note that, in the Decalogue, the proscriptions follow the prescriptions and form the *second* table of the law).

27. *F*, 226/212. But Scheler rejects completely the view propagated by Schopenhauer, which assumes a *religious* basis for an imperativistic ethics—

for example, that "Kant's imperativistic ethics is only a consequence of an enduring conception, hidden even from himself, of the divine will as the foundation of moral law" (F, 226/212). Only *some* religious ethics, according to Scheler, are imperativistic, such as Jewish ethics or the Scotistic theological ethics of late medieval Scholasticism, both of which trace the ideas of good and evil back to God's *will*. But there are other religious ethics, such as that of St. Thomas, which, according to Scheler, are not imperativistic since they hold that the good lies in God's *essence*, rather than will. Here, willing *follows* insight, and duty is *derived from* moral insight rather than consisting in "blind obedience" to God's will.

28. Cf. Henry Sidgwick, *The Methods of Ethics* (London: Macmillan, 1907; rpt. Indianapolis: Hackett, 1981). Sidgwick notes that "our conscious active impulses are so far from being always directed towards the attainment of pleasure or avoidance of pain for ourselves, that we can find everywhere in consciousness extra-regarding impulses"; in fact, we can even find examples of "the love of virtue for its own sake, or desire to do what is right as such" (52).

29. Norms themselves are relatively constant, Scheler suggests, in relation to what he calls "pedagogical advice" and "technical proposals," which they may govern (F, 231/217). Cf. Scheler's discussion (F, 218ff./203ff.) distinguishing between (1) genuine orders, or orders of authority; (2) pedagogical orders, or illusory orders; (3) advice; (4) counsel; (5) recommendations; and (6) technical proposals. Also, in this vein, see S. Strasser's discussion of Levinas's views on the pre-reflective, individual nature of "sacrifice" (n. 14 above).

30. F, 199/184; cf. 225/211. Schopenhauer's exclusion of "ought-to-will" does not pertain to the *ideal* ought. But in case of the *normative* ought, he is correct: obligation pertains, at minimum, to a *"willing-to-do"* (cf. F, 232f./218f.).

31. "Correct," not because love is a sensibly determined inclination, as Kant thought, but because love, according to Scheler, is a spiritual act of original value disclosure that, as such, always *precedes* any norm or law and whatever these may command or prohibit (F, 251/236f.; 236/233; 237f./233).

32. F, 236/211. Beginning at this point, Scheler offers a detailed critique of Kant's remarks in the second *Critique* (KpV, 83) on the Biblical commandment to "Love God above all and thy neighbor as thyself." In Scheler's view, Kant's "imperativistic" ethical presuppositions lead him "to *reinterpret* the term love *so arbitrarily* that in the end the most barren moralism is interpreted into this evangelic principle" (F, 239/225). Scheler's own view of the text in question (Matthew 22:37, 39) is that "it is meant not as a norm that commands, but as an invitation to *follow*" (F, 237/222). In this regard, he discusses at some length the Roman Catholic and Protestant (Lutheran) polemics about the propriety of calling this a "new law" or "law of love" (F 235 n./220 n. 48; 237 n. 1/222 n. 50).

33. In fact, Scheler clearly acknowledges, regarding the so-called *rigorism* of Kant, that "it has been debated whether this rigorism is really present and to what extent it can be justified" (F, 242/227). He concedes: "Insofar as Kant's descriptions lead us to conclude that a morally good action must be one *against* inclination, this would have to be attributed more to the *atmosphere* and *pathos* of his description than to the *objective sense* of his propositions" (ibid., emphasis added; but see n. 34 below).

34. F, 242/227; cf. 245/230. The opposite view would entail "a certain kind of cruelty against oneself and one's inclinations which, owing to a peculiar

value-illusion, is savored as something especially 'good' and 'noble'" (*F*, 242f./228). In this regard, Scheler notes: "I do not believe that Kant can be said to be entirely free of this inclination, or that his ethical conceptions are not influenced by it to a certain degree, at least in the *pathos* of their description" (*F*, 243/228). In particular, this can be seen in Kant's tendency to make the moral value of an action dependent on its *cost* or the *sacrifice* it requires. For example, in his discussion of moral instruction and the example of the honest witness at the trial of Anne Boleyn who refuses to be perjured despite threats and great personal hardship and loss, Kant says that "virtue is here worth so much only because it costs so much, not because it brings any advantage" (*KpV*, 156). Scheler calls this an example of "*ressentiment*-illusion" (*F*, 243/228; for a detailed discussion of this theory, see *Ressentiment*). The sacrifice and high cost involved in an action may *reveal* its high moral worth, but they do not *create* it, as Kant appears to assume (*F*, 244/229). In fact, paradoxically, Scheler points out that the morally *higher* personality is precisely the one who endeavors and sacrifices the *least* in realizing the demands of the moral law, since he who has the least resistance to the good is the best (*F*, 245/230).

35. Scheler therefore explicitly *rejects* Kant's view that knowledge of the unconditionally practical cannot come from freedom *since* we can neither know freedom immediately nor infer it from experience, that our knowledge of freedom comes from immediate consciousness of the moral law (*KpV*, 29f.). Rather, for Scheler, experience of freedom ("ability") and of the moral law (the "ideal ought") are equiprimordial (*F*, 252/237).

36. Reiner's detailed discussion of these kinds of distinctions reinforces this point (*DI*, 117, 169ff. and §25). By way of example, he writes: "Let us assume that I am out for a walk along the river with some friends who can swim as well as I, and that we all notice the drowning man at about the same time. At first I shall be bound to rescue the man from drowning by a duty that is not absolutely strict; for others who can attempt the rescue are on hand; and it would be a violation of duty to expose myself to the dangers of the rescue unnecessarily. But, if I notice that no one else can make up his mind to act, I shall be obligated immediately by a *categorical* ought to attempt the rescue myself, no matter what the others' reasons for hesitation may be" (*DI*, 198).

37. For example, in his essay on "The Nature of Philosophy and the Moral Preconditions of Philosophical Knowledge," in *On the Eternal in Man*, Scheler suggests the kinds of virtues necessary for genuine knowledge. In Section B ("Starting-Point and Elements of the Moral Upsurge"), he says, for instance, that (1) *"the whole spiritual person must love absolute value and being,"* (2) *"the natural self and ego must be humbled,"* and (3) *"self-mastery must be achieved"* (*E*, 90/95). The connotative import of such statements are compelling. Yet it is not exactly clear what they mean. What is exactly involved, for instance, in the love of "absolute value and being"? Such statements, ironically, are of little help until their "material content" can be more substantively specified and developed.

38. For example, the moral disposition (*Gesinnung*) is described as "something supersensible" whose "existence is not susceptible to division into periods of time"—in short, as something "noumenal," supratemporal, a nonexperienceable thing-in-itself (*R*, 70/64; cf. 14/13, 31/26f., 46ff./42f.). On the other hand, its existence is *inferred* and its moral value is *imputed* on the basis of phenomenal actions we can empirically observe (*R*, 20/16, 70/64). Cf. my brief discussions above in ch. 4, sec. 3 and below in ch. 6, sec. 1. John R. Silber's essay, "The

Ethical Significance of Kant's *Religion*," contains a respected introduction to the basic issues.

39. See sec. 1, above; and cf. Immanuel Kant, *Education* (Ann Arbor: The University of Michigan Press, 1960)—a translation of Kant's *Über Pädagogik*—esp. 83–94 (ch. 5: "Moral Culture"), and 95–121 (ch. 6: "Practical Education"); and Edward F. Buchner's translation of much the same material in *The Educational Theory of Immanuel Kant* (Philadelphia: J. B. Lippincott, 1904), 185–211. See also Henry E. Allison, *Lessing and the Enlightenment* (Ann Arbor: University of Michigan Press, 1966), which claims that G. E. Lessing, in "The Education of the Human Race" ("Die Erziehung des Menschengeschlechts," 1780), anticipated Kant's view that the goal of human development lies in the achievement of moral autonomy (159f.; cf. 181 n. 61).

40. Scheler denies the possibility of directly altering moral disposition through education (F, 136/116). See above, n. 38, and cf. the discussion of Scheler's notion of moral disposition, in ch. 6, sec. 1.

41. "Model persons" determine the origin of the prevailing ethos, but are themselves founded on the idea of ordered ranks among "Pure Types of the Value-Person," corresponding to the ranks of material values: "*saint*," "*genius*," "*hero*," "*leading spirit*," and "*bon vivant*" (F, 586/585; cf. 129/109).

42. Just as "there can be *no norm of duty without a person who posits it*," or "when the person 'for' whom this norm should be valid lacks the insight to see *by himself* what is good," so there "can be no 'reverence' for a norm or moral law that is not founded in reverence for the *person* who posits it—founded ultimately in love for this person as a model" (F, 575/573).

43. Reiner makes this point when, observing the insufficiency of Scheler's two criteria for value preference—the "positive" and the "higher" value—he notes that Nicolai Hartmann (in ch. 63 of his *Ethics*) points out an additional criterion, the "stronger" value, which could be rendered more clearly, says Reiner, by speaking of the "*more pressing*" value (DI, 175).

44. On Richard Brandt, see ch. 1, nn. 30 and 38, above; in addition to the work cited there, other representative writings include his *Ethical Theory* (Englewood Cliffs, NJ: Prentice-Hall, 1959), and the essays contained in Wilfrid Sellars and John Hospers, eds., *Readings in Ethical Theory*, 2d ed. (New York: Appleton-Century-Crofts, 1970), "A Quasi-Naturalist Definition" (331–34), and "Ethical Relativism" (335–45).

45. Peter Spader suggests that Scheler's modal scale of values overcomes the classical metaphysical duality between the "is" and the "ought" ("The Facts of Max Scheler," *Philosophy Today* 23, No. 3 [fall 1979], 263f.). Caputo, while not writing directly about Scheler, suggests that a "hermeneutic retrieval" of a phenomenological foundation for ethics from a reading of Kant's ethical writings would disclose a value immanent in our experience that would cut across all such dichotomies (Caputo, "Kant's Ethics," 145 n. 18).

46. In *Moral Action*, Sokolowski distinguishes three kinds of practical and moral thinking or *phronêsis*, or what he calls "categorialities": (1) the categoriality involved in "choice"; (2) the "moral" categoriality that establishes a personal transaction; and (3) the "judgmental" categoriality according to which we evaluate what is done. The first is directed toward the future; the second toward the present; the third toward the past. Again, the first is somewhat solitary; the second involves a public but dyadic transaction between agent and target; the third is communitarian, social, and traditional (155f.).

Conclusion: Some Final Thoughts on Scheler's Critique 6

Moral Action and Moral Disposition

THERE ARE OTHER IMPORTANT ISSUES in Scheler's *Formalismus* besides those we have discussed in the foregoing chapters. A few of these are of such basic importance to Scheler's critique as to warrant at least some comment. These include questions about the nature of moral action, moral disposition, and human nature. While a detailed examination of these issues lies beyond the scope of this book, a brief look at the main points of contention is in order. The first of these issues, concerning what constitutes a moral action, is related inseparably to the question of the nature of moral disposition; therefore, we shall begin by examining them together.

As we have seen, Kant argues that the morality of an action should not be determined on the basis of its success in achieving certain anticipated results. Such results are always contingent and uncertain, and have nothing to do with the morality of the action itself for which an agent may be held morally responsible. For Kant, the morality of an act lies in the character of the will, or choice, from which it issues; and, ultimately, it lies in the character of the moral disposition of the agent, which underlies all of his or her individual choices. The question, then, is how Kant's analysis of moral disposition and choice accounts for the possibility of moral conflict.

In order to allow for the obvious fact that we are free to reject the moral law, Kant concedes a sense in which our freedom of will may be identified, not with our will's "autonomy," but with its "spontaneity." This distinction is developed by Kant in his later philosophy in connection with his distinction between (1) the "legislative will" (*Wille*), which he identifies as the pure, rational, autonomous will, and (2) the "executive will" (*Willkür*), which he identifies as empirically conditioned, spontaneous willing whose task is to obey the *Wille*—which it is free to do or not to do. While this is in some ways an insightful distinction on Kant's

One other point of importance that Scheler makes in this connection is that the moral disposition is not the sole bearer of moral values, as the "pathos" of Kant's writings, at least, seems often to suggest. Rather, as Scheler argues by means of a vivid illustration about a paralytic who observes a drowning man (F, 139/119), even though the moral disposition itself bears the fundamental moral value and is the decisive source of the moral value of one's inclinations or deeds, the actual performance of a deed creates a new moral value in addition to that already evidenced in the disposition. Hence, the successful rescue of a drowning man bears a morally higher value than an unsuccessful attempt to rescue him, or merely a predisposition to rescue him. This means neither that the paralytic may be faulted morally in any way for failing to execute a successful rescue, nor that moral values are based ultimately on the successful realization of certain empirical ends. It means only that what is morally valuable in personal actions may not be restricted to the moral disposition from which they issue (F, 141f./121f.). In this regard, Scheler offers a phenomenologically accessible, insightful analysis, which ought to be exploited to full advantage in any attempt to construct a theory of moral action.

Corollaries of Scheler's theory whose implications might be explored further include his rejection of the Kantian view that the material contents of willing are inevitably conditioned by sensible states of pleasure or pain evoked by the contemplated existence or possession of some contingent empirical object or end.[2] Further, Scheler's claim that the "intended result" of an action is not part of the essential structural "unity" of the act has been called into question in interesting ways.[3] But an altogether puzzling feature of Scheler's analysis of these issues in *Formalismus* is his complete omission of the problem of evil, especially as evil relates to the issue of personal moral conflict and to the phenomenon— which both he and Kant recognized—of the "change of heart" or the "conversion" of a moral disposition. How is it that a complete transformation may occur in an otherwise constant moral disposition underlying a person's individual choices and actions? This is by no means an easy question to answer. But any attempt to do so will require confronting the issue of personal moral conflict, the phenomenon of being "in two minds," of being "at war with oneself," as described so memorably by the likes of St. Paul and St. Augustine. As we have seen, Scheler's theory simply does not account for this phenomenon adequately.

Human Nature

IF KANT'S MOST BASIC presuppositions about the value embodied in the moral law surface anywhere, they surface in his view of human nature. It is in his notion of human beings as ends-in-themselves, as beings

Conclusion: Some Final Thoughts on Scheler's Critique   6

Moral Action and Moral Disposition

THERE ARE OTHER IMPORTANT ISSUES in Scheler's *Formalismus* besides those we have discussed in the foregoing chapters. A few of these are of such basic importance to Scheler's critique as to warrant at least some comment. These include questions about the nature of moral action, moral disposition, and human nature. While a detailed examination of these issues lies beyond the scope of this book, a brief look at the main points of contention is in order. The first of these issues, concerning what constitutes a moral action, is related inseparably to the question of the nature of moral disposition; therefore, we shall begin by examining them together.

As we have seen, Kant argues that the morality of an action should not be determined on the basis of its success in achieving certain anticipated results. Such results are always contingent and uncertain, and have nothing to do with the morality of the action itself for which an agent may be held morally responsible. For Kant, the morality of an act lies in the character of the will, or choice, from which it issues; and, ultimately, it lies in the character of the moral disposition of the agent, which underlies all of his or her individual choices. The question, then, is how Kant's analysis of moral disposition and choice accounts for the possibility of moral conflict.

In order to allow for the obvious fact that we are free to reject the moral law, Kant concedes a sense in which our freedom of will may be identified, not with our will's "autonomy," but with its "spontaneity." This distinction is developed by Kant in his later philosophy in connection with his distinction between (1) the "legislative will" (*Wille*), which he identifies as the pure, rational, autonomous will, and (2) the "executive will" (*Willkür*), which he identifies as empirically conditioned, spontaneous willing whose task is to obey the *Wille*—which it is free to do or not to do. While this is in some ways an insightful distinction on Kant's part, the trouble with it, as we have seen in chapter 4, is that it cannot be consistently defended by him. For is the *Willkür* phenomenal or noumenal? It cannot be both. It must be either one or the other. As John Caputo says, "If it is phenomenal, then it is nothing but a pathological inclination and not a will at all. And if it is noumenal, then it cannot be maintained that it ever acts irrationally—not without introducing some principle of opacity, irrationality, sensuality or impurity into the noumenal sphere" ("Kant's Ethics," 135f.).

Since the disposition, in order to be imputed, must have been adopted by an act of free choice (*Willkür*), all that has been said of the *Willkür* applies to the moral disposition as well (*R, 25/20*). While Kant offers notably convincing descriptions, in places, of the phenomena of moral experience, his analysis of the moral disposition, like his analysis of *Wille* and *Willkür*, ultimately remains bound to the dualistic categorial framework of pure will and empirical interests, duty and inclination, the rational and the pathological, the formal and the material, and the autonomous and the heteronomous. Accordingly, he refers to the moral disposition as something that could only be "inferred" from phenomenal actions, as something ultimately "inscrutable."

This, of course, is the essential point of contention in Scheler's critique of Kant in this regard. For Scheler, the moral disposition, whether in ourselves or others, is a *phenomenon of experience* (*F, 132/112*); not merely a hypothesis we infer from previous actions, like the "character" we may suppose a person to have, but a phenomenon given immediately in intuition (137f./117f.). Within Kant's metaphysics, by contrast, the moral disposition remains in itself inaccessible, unknowable, inscrutable, inexperienceable. As such it serves as the noumenal determining ground of the morality of a person's actions. But it cannot possibly be useful itself in discerning the morality of such actions, since it is itself unknowable. How, then, is the morality of an act to be discerned? Kant has already excluded any appeal to the contingent *results* of actions. This leaves him with only one option: he must "infer" the probable value of a moral disposition from the contingent data of empirical actions.[1] But employing the language of "inference" requires that he implicitly abandon the strictures of his dualist metaphysics and begun speaking of the moral disposition as a phenomenon of moral experience in a way that is fundamentally impermissible within his system of a metaphysics of morals. For if there is any meaning at all to the word "inference," there must be some sort of *experienced connection* between what is inferred and that from which it is inferred. This in itself, however, only underscores the strengths of Scheler's straightforward phenomenological approach.

It might be objected here that Kant would have regarded the "strictures" referred to as imposed, not by a "dualistic metaphysics," but by the limitations of a priori reasoning. Surely from his point of view, it might be said, what is here called "moral disposition" would be more accurately thought of as a natural, cultural, and historical occurrence than as a phenomenon of moral experience; as such, it could be properly consigned to the domain of anthropology, an a posteriori discipline. Such an objection, however, would seem to overlook the difficulty underlying Kant's own discussion of the moral disposition. For Kant explicitly says of the moral disposition (*Gesinnung*), which he defines as "the ultimate subjective ground of the adoption of maxims" (R, 25/20), that it is "inscrutable" (R, 20–20 n./16–17 n., 25/20, 31/26, 43/38; cf. *KrV*, A 551 n.–B 579, n.). He refers to it as something "supersensible" whose "existence is not susceptible to division into periods of time"—in short, as something "noumenal" in the supratemporal sense of a non-experienceable thing-in-itself (R, 70/64; 14/13; 31/26f.; 46ff./42f.). To penetrate this "ground of all maxims of choice," he says, would require "the omniscience of divinity" (R, 46ff./42f.). But, if the disposition is really noumenal, then it cannot be consistently maintained that it would ever motivate an irrational act—not without introducing some principle of opacity, irrationality, sensuality or impurity into the noumenal sphere. On the other hand, Kant's definition of the disposition would seem to prevent us from consigning it, within the framework of his philosophy, to the domain of a posteriori descriptions of empirical behavioral phenomena.

There appears to be some concession of the difficulty with Kant's views at this point among some Kant interpreters. John Silber, for instance, suggests that "Kant did not err in his definition of the noumenal; he erred, rather, in placing arbitrary and uncritical limits on the phenomenal, for they forced him mistakenly and contradictorily to locate moral experience in the noumenal realm" ("Ethical Significance," cii). There also appears to be an increasing reluctance to accept Kant's typical bifurcations of reality in the analysis of human experience. This is apparent, for example, in Caputo's suggestion that, contrary to Kant,

> Reason and affectivity are not related as noumenon and phenomenon, but as the explicit to the implicit, the conceptual to the preconceptual, the articulate to the preverbal. A mistake on the passionate, affective level is a mistake on the conceptual one too. We are indeed led astray by bad instincts, but we are saved by good ones. If a man is divided against himself, it is because he is torn between conflicting tendencies and conflicting goods. . . . If there is to be a genuine conflict, it must take place on the same level and in the same order. Two orders which do not communicate with one another cannot conflict. ("Kant's Ethics," 144)

Despite the fact that Scheler's own view of the moral disposition may not have permitted an adequate understanding of the phenomenon of moral struggle, as we have seen (above, ch. 5, sec. 4), his essential insight that the moral disposition itself is a materially experienceable phenomenon remains a major contribution to the theory of moral action.

One other point of importance that Scheler makes in this connection is that the moral disposition is not the sole bearer of moral values, as the "pathos" of Kant's writings, at least, seems often to suggest. Rather, as Scheler argues by means of a vivid illustration about a paralytic who observes a drowning man (F, 139/119), even though the moral disposition itself bears the fundamental moral value and is the decisive source of the moral value of one's inclinations or deeds, the actual performance of a deed creates a new moral value in addition to that already evidenced in the disposition. Hence, the successful rescue of a drowning man bears a morally higher value than an unsuccessful attempt to rescue him, or merely a predisposition to rescue him. This means neither that the paralytic may be faulted morally in any way for failing to execute a successful rescue, nor that moral values are based ultimately on the successful realization of certain empirical ends. It means only that what is morally valuable in personal actions may not be restricted to the moral disposition from which they issue (F, 141f./121f.). In this regard, Scheler offers a phenomenologically accessible, insightful analysis, which ought to be exploited to full advantage in any attempt to construct a theory of moral action.

Corollaries of Scheler's theory whose implications might be explored further include his rejection of the Kantian view that the material contents of willing are inevitably conditioned by sensible states of pleasure or pain evoked by the contemplated existence or possession of some contingent empirical object or end.[2] Further, Scheler's claim that the "intended result" of an action is not part of the essential structural "unity" of the act has been called into question in interesting ways.[3] But an altogether puzzling feature of Scheler's analysis of these issues in *Formalismus* is his complete omission of the problem of evil, especially as evil relates to the issue of personal moral conflict and to the phenomenon—which both he and Kant recognized—of the "change of heart" or the "conversion" of a moral disposition. How is it that a complete transformation may occur in an otherwise constant moral disposition underlying a person's individual choices and actions? This is by no means an easy question to answer. But any attempt to do so will require confronting the issue of personal moral conflict, the phenomenon of being "in two minds," of being "at war with oneself," as described so memorably by the likes of St. Paul and St. Augustine. As we have seen, Scheler's theory simply does not account for this phenomenon adequately.

Human Nature

IF KANT'S MOST BASIC presuppositions about the value embodied in the moral law surface anywhere, they surface in his view of human nature. It is in his notion of human beings as ends-in-themselves, as beings distinguished from mere "things" by the rational power of their self-legislation, as beings endowed with inherent dignity and entitled to respect, that the actual content of Kant's view of the moral good becomes apparent. In this concept of the end-in-itself, and in the notions of "moral feeling" and "respect" that surround it, we find in Kant's ethics *something like a material value that is accessible in experience.* Here we see Kant articulating something resembling the "phenomenological foundation for ethics" that Caputo wishes to "retrieve" from Kant's ethical writings ("Kant's Ethics," 144). But as we have seen, it is also at this most promising point that Kant is revisited by all the devils of the old metaphysics of purism and its bifurcations of the rational and the sensible, the formal and the material, the noumenal and the phenomenal, that pervade his ethics. The question is not what Kant may have personally believed about human nature, or what we feel he may actually have believed when we read him. It is a question, rather, of warrant: what does the Kantian metaphysical framework *permit* one to say about human nature?

The human self,[4] in the preeminent sense of moral agent, as *personalitas moralis*, as the seat and substance of the personal dignity and moral worth embodied in the rational will, is effectively cut off from the world of human experience. The *personalitas moralis* is also the *homo noumenon*—inscrutable, unknowable, and inaccessible—not only to others, but even to itself. The self in the sense of *personalitas transcendentalis*, moreover, is nothing but a theoretical abstraction, a logical subject and condition for the possibility of "objectivity" as such. There is nothing of a material, phenomenal content to the self in this sense, any more than in the sense of *homo noumenon*. Not only does this concept lack sufficient concreteness to do justice to the individuality of the person, as Scheler suggests, but it involves the untenable inconsistency of postulating a logical entity (the transcendental unity of apperception) as a *condition* for the possibility of the perception of all entities. The only place in which Kant's metaphysic permits the self to emerge as a phenomenally accessible being is where the self is regarded as an object of inner intuition or empirical reflection. The self in this sense, the *personalitas psychologica*, is no less structured in accordance with forms and categories than objects of external perception; but apart from the noumenal self postulated by practical reason, this empirical self is little more for Kant than an amorphous flux of inner sense impressions such as Hume discovered in the course of his introspective search for the self. There is nothing here of personal dignity and title to respect, but only a flux of phenomena subject to pathological determination and natural causality.

There is a fundamental discrepancy between the basic dignity and importance Kant ascribes to the person, on the one hand, and the metaphysical strictures of his philosophy, which resist the realization of that ascription, on the other. Kant's metaphysics seems to militate against some of his most fundamental instincts and insights about human nature.

The concept of the person also plays a fundamental role in Scheler's philosophy. The person is the original bearer of moral values, for Scheler, and the moral value of all acts refers back to acting persons. Persons themselves bear a material value, and, as we have seen in chapter 4, it is the reflective apprehension of this value in their "central emotional fulfillment" that serves as the source of the specific moral quality of all personal striving and willing and acting. Therefore, Scheler is sharply critical of Kant's view of the human self, which either places it beyond the range of human experience, reduces it to an abstraction, or strips it of its personal identity. The self cannot be essentially a pristine, rational will, a *homo noumenon*, supersensibly separated from the phenomenal world of feelings and everyday experience; it cannot be merely a transcendental conditionality, a pure, logical subject that serves as the condition for the possibility of bare "objectivity"; and certainly it is more than a naturally determined flux of impressions observed in inner sense. In developing his own view, Scheler carefully endeavors to avoid the Scylla of "actualistic" theories, which locate the essential being of the self in its acts, and the Charybdis of "substantialist" theories, which locate it in an essence that underlies and subsists through its changing acts. His analysis is precariously subtle. His own view is that the being of the human self is located in the *execution* of its acts.

Of basic importance for Scheler's theory is the issue of how the self is *concretely given* through its acts. But another significant feature of his view is the integral *unity* of the person, which he endeavors to underline by studiously distancing himself from classical dualist theories, which invariably result in the disruption of that unity—for example, in the Cartesian dichotomy of *res cogitans* and *res extensa*. The person, in his view, has an "absolute" status, different from the "relative" status of all such phenomena as consciousness, psyche, or *res cogitans*, which always presuppose a relation to an "outer world," to a "material world," or to a "body." The self, therefore, transcends all such dichotomies. It transcends all of its psychic functions. In fact, says Scheler, it transcends phenomenal time itself: it acts *into* time without itself being *in* time.

While Scheler's emphasis on the integral unity of the person is both commendable and, I think, well founded, his own attempt to give account of how the human self is actually *given* through its acts does pose some difficulties. Scheler draws a basic distinction between personal "acts" and psychical "functions." Functions "happen by themselves"; acts are "executed." Functions are measurable in phenomenal time; acts spring from the supratemporal person into time. Functions may serve as objects of acts (as when I observe myself hearing or tasting), or they may serve as media through which acts are directed to some other object (as when I hear a melody or taste food) (*F*, 398f./388). But if the being of the self is located in its acts, and if acts, unlike psychic "functions" of the empirical ego, cannot be objectified, then the self, which lives in the execution of its acts, can never be an object (as the empirical ego can). This raises a couple of questions. First, if a person can never be an object, how, then, is a person *given* in acts? Second, if the human self is essentially "supratemporal," how is it any more accessible or knowable than Kant's *homo noumenon*?

Scheler's answer to the first question may not strike every reader as perfectly clear. The relevant passages of *Formalismus* do not explicitly address the problem and might easily leave the impression that he gets himself hopelessly entangled in contradictions. On the one hand, his remarks repeatedly imply (and his entire philosophy requires) that we do have phenomenological access to persons and to their acts. On the other hand, he clearly states (and his analysis of acts requires) that persons cannot be objects. Again, on the one hand, he repeatedly suggests (and his analysis of the person's "central emotional fulfillment" requires) that one's deepest feelings about oneself—one's spiritual feelings of happiness or despair—cannot be inert, non-referential *states*, but must be meaningfully directed *intentional* feelings about oneself as a person. But, on the other hand, he clearly states (and his view that the person cannot be an intentional object requires) that spiritual feelings, such as happiness or despair, are non-intentional feeling-*states* (see ch. 4, n. 24).

The resolution of these problems, as Peter Spader points out, rests on Scheler's tacit rejection of "the twin assumptions that the only phenomena we can be given are *objects*, and the only *way* we can reliably know anything is objectively; that is to say, as an object" ("Person, Act and Meaning," 202). This rejection, of course, stems from the distinction—first clearly articulated by Dilthey—between the methods of scientific explanation proper to the natural sciences (*Naturwissenschaften*) and the methods of human "understanding" (*Verstehen*) proper to the human sciences (*Geisteswissenschaften*).[5] The person, for Scheler, is neither an object nor given objectively. He calls the person the "most hidden of all phenomena"; but the fact that it is not an object and that it is most hidden does not prevent it from being *given* to us and *knowable* to us in our experience. The person must be known, then, in some other way than objects of natural science are known. In fact, this is just what Scheler tells us in *Wesen und Formen der Sympathie*, where he says that the person—whether oneself or another—is accessible only through the non-objectifying "participation" afforded by human "understanding" (*Verstehen*) (220/224).

But how, exactly, is the person known in this way? How is a person given? Scheler says that a person is given in the *execution* of his or her acts. But if acts cannot be objects, how can a person be given by means of acts? Scheler says: by *reflection*. Not by means of an objectifying act of intentionality, which is impossible in the case of the person, but by means of a non-objectifying act of *reflection*.[6] It is by means of reflection that one has access to one's own acts, either in the moment of execution or in immediate memory; and it is by means of reflection that one has access to the acts of others, either as experienced before, during, or after their execution. This means that, through phenomenological reflection, one grasps the essential unity of meaning underlying a given sequence of psycho-physical functions and events that occur in phenomenal time. This essential unity of meaning is what constitutes an act as an act.[7] By the same token, it is by means of reflection that one has access to the concrete *unity* of acts, which is what constitutes the person as a person.

At this point the second question raised above becomes relevant—the question concerning the "supratemporality" of the person. For, according to Scheler, the essential unity of meaning that constitutes an act as an act, although it realizes itself in the temporal manifold of mundane experience, is itself *supratemporal*. This means that the *person* always remains supratemporal for Scheler. The human self acts *into* time and lives nowhere but *in* its acts, which realize themselves *in* time, but itself remains, in some sense, supratemporal. The question, then, is: if the human self is essentially "supratemporal," how is it any more accessible or knowable than Kant's *homo noumenon*?

Scheler offers no clear or adequate answer to this second question. This poses a serious problem. While Scheler's answer to the first question may not seem perfectly transparent nor completely satisfy everyone, at least it assumes that persons and their acts are phenomenologically given and somehow knowable. But this assumption is called into serious question by his claim that the person is "supratemporal." What can he mean? One may ask whether this notion is really warranted phenomenologically. For example, one might wish to explore whether such phenomena as deliberation, indecision, hesitation, or decision-making are given in experience as temporally manifested realizations of "supratemporal" acts, or whether they are not themselves given as acts that take their points of departure *within* the temporal sequence of mundane experiences. One could reasonably ask whether Scheler's insistence on the "supratemporality" of the person does not represent, despite himself, the unresolved influence of some sort of residual Kantian distinction between the phenomenal and noumenal.

Still, to be fair to Scheler, anyone with the least bit of familiarity with philosophical anthropology and philosophical attempts to specify the ontological nature of the person must admit that the human self is a profoundly mysterious and precariously elusive subject.[8] Furthermore, Scheler's suggestions about how the human self is given in experience, whatever unresolved difficulties they may conceal, do offer significant explorations into the phenomenology of the human person and may even indicate ways in which certain recurring problems may be avoided in the development of a philosophical anthropology—such as the aforementioned Scylla of "actualistic" theories and Charybdis of "substantialist" theories. Finally, the principal focus of his philosophical anthropology must be kept in mind. Despite the substantial consideration he devotes to such matters as the problem of "other minds" in Part 3 of *Wesen und Formen der Sympathie* and to the question of self-knowledge and knowledge of persons in general in various of his works, the principal thrust of his philosophical anthropology is not in the direction of developing the epistemological problems connected with such matters, but rather the vast historical, cultural, metaphysical, religious, psychological, and even biological questions that pervade the field.[9]

Two other problems, which warrant far more discussion than we can afford here, are the problem of intersubjectivity, particularly as related to the microcosm-macrocosm theme in Scheler's later philosophical anthropology, and the problem of evil, as related to his later attempts to resolve the issue of how values are realized. A few remarks will have to suffice here.

As for the first problem, Scheler offers a variation on the ancient microcosm-macrocosm theme in his later works, in which he reasons from the act-object correlation between individual "persons" and their individual "worlds" to a structurally analogical correlation between a "person of persons" and corresponding "world of worlds."[10] One could easily wonder whether the entire microcosm-macrocosm theme, as well as the concomitant notion of a plurality of absolutely individual, correlative worlds, is not the infelicitous result of some highly metaphysical and phenomenologically groundless speculation. One might also wish to question the implications of this theme as it bears on the complete personalization and relativization, in some sense, of "truth" in Scheler's theory. Is there a ghost of solipsism here?

But Scheler's idea of individual worlds springs from his awareness of the uniqueness of each person, which parallels his awareness of distinctive cultures and traditions through which each individual comes to the "same" world.[11] He never for a moment assumes that the idea of individual "worlds" suggests even a hint of solipsism. In fact, his idea of a "person of persons" apprehending a "world of worlds" provides metaphysical support, in his view, for the notion of an "objective" world upon which individuals and cultures can come to agreement. Furthermore, Part 3 and the whole of *Wesen und Formen der Sympathie* defend the possibility of entering into another's experience as opposed to empathic theories and arguments from analogy that incline towards solipsism. One could also point to the analysis of "community of feeling" in Part 1 of *Sympathie*, in which Scheler offers the illustration of two parents standing beside the dead body of a beloved child to show how two persons may experience the same feeling of anguish without the feeling of the one being experienced in the least way as "external" to that of the other. There is no experience of an individual world here as some sort of self-enclosed Leibnizean monad; nor is there a problem of intersubjectivity. There is, rather, a *community* of feeling in an undifferentiated, pre-objectified world of anguish.

One cannot easily argue, in light of such contrary evidence, that Scheler's notion of "individual worlds" raises the specter of solipsism, even if one may question how the underlying metaphysics of his microcosm-macrocosm theme and of his theory of a "person of person" and "world of worlds" can be worked out precisely within a phenomenological framework.

In regard to the second problem—the problem of evil—Scheler increasingly became preoccupied in his later years with the problem of "reality" and "resistance." The problem was related to the question of how values, which are ideal, are *realized* in the mundane world. Are they realized through acts of *willing* by responsible moral agents, or through the fortuitous *impulses* of human nature? Specifically, the question of the origin of moral evil led Scheler to press his phenomenological concerns into the arena of traditional metaphysical problems of theodicy. As is well known, the distinction between good and evil came to be identified more and more by Scheler with the principles of "spirit" (*Geist*) and "impulse" (*Drang*) in such a way that the very *unity* of the person that Scheler wished to defend came to be increasingly threatened with disruption. As Ernest Ranly observed in the concluding remarks of his own study on Scheler, "In man, the dual principles of life and spirit tend to destroy the very unity that Scheler wished to define and to defend. Man himself becomes bifurcated in and through these two dualistic principles" (*Scheler's Phenomenology of Community*, 100). In this connection, Scheler's critical error was his identification of the ethical relation between moral good and moral evil with a metaphysical or ontological relation between structural components of human nature. In other words, he erred by collapsing the ethical antithesis between good and evil into the supposed structural antithesis between "spirit" and "impulse" in the person. But any structural division within the being of the person inevitably entails a disruption of the essential unity of human nature. In this light, it could be fruitful to explore how a non-ontological approach to the understanding of good and evil, such as one finds in Emmanuel Levinas, might preserve the structural-ontological unity and integrity of the human self.[12]

Scheler's Interpretation of Kant

HAVING REACHED THIS POINT in our study, we are now in a position to take another look at the questions we posed at the outset of this work. One of those questions, it will be recalled, concerned the accuracy of Scheler's interpretation of Kant (ch. 1, sec. 4, above). In each chapter of this study, we have tried to establish, at least briefly, Kant's own position on the subject under consideration before engaging Scheler's critique of it, in order—among other things—to answer this question. Now, we may ask, what is the verdict?

A cursory reading of *Formalismus*, as many have testified, does not leave the impression that the author is a meticulous book scholar. Scheler freely paraphrases statements by Kant, apparently from memory, and only rarely documents his references to Kantian texts. Further, he gives no more than passing attention to some fundamental features of Kant's philosophy, such as the role of transcendental freedom in the second *Critique*. These facts, in addition to Scheler's early association with such Neo-Kantians as Otto Liebmann, as well as the subsequent decline of Neo-Kantianism, have led to the view—prevalent among recent Kant scholars—that Scheler's attack on Kant's formalism misses the authentic sense of Kant's philosophy at decisive points, that it is concerned not so much with the historical Kant of the *textus receptus* as with a reconstruction of post-Kantian critical philosophy among his Neo-Kantian contemporaries (Gerd Wolandt, "Nachwort" in Alphéus, 402f.).

However, a closer reading of *Formalismus* offers a different view of the matter. For, as anyone patient enough to track down the exact sources of his citations will find, Scheler's interpretation of Kant is generally more accurate and based on a broader and more thoroughgoing acquaintance with the details of the Kantian texts than his casual approach to documentation might suggest. Indeed, not only does he appear to be reasonably conversant with the major critical works in which Kant's views of the a priori, the transcendental unity of apperception, the good will, moral feeling, duty, the moral disposition, and so forth, are the central focus of Kant's discussion (e.g., in *KrV*, *KpV*, *GMS*, *MS*, and *R*); we have found Scheler referring on occasion even to comparatively lesser-known works (e.g., his reference to *BG*, cited in ch. 2, n. 18, above). This is not to say that Scheler's interpretation is always "consistent" with every statement of Kantian doctrine. We have seen that this is not the case. Nevertheless, time after time in *Formalismus* there are indications that Scheler's apparent oversights or departures from the Kantian doctrine are due, not to ignorance of the texts, but rather to his desire to penetrate to the underlying unity and thrust of Kant's position. For example, Scheler's statement that, for Kant, "good willing occurs *against* all 'inclination' " (*F*, 91/70) clearly contradicts Kant's assertion that some inclinations, such as seeking one's own happiness, are at least indirectly one's duties (*GMS*, 399; *KpV*, 93). But in reference to this very question, Scheler just as clearly states that his interpretation is based, not on the "objective sense" of Kant's propositions, but on the "pathos" of his description (*F*, 424/227).

The importance of this distinction between the "objective sense" and the "pathos" of Kant's writing is underlined by its repeated recurrence in *Formalismus*. For example, in his discussion of the moral disposition,

Scheler concedes that Kant does state that the moral disposition is "the original, but not the sole, object of moral value" (F, 134/114). Nevertheless, he insists that the thrust of Kant's discussion suggests that everything outside the moral disposition is subject to natural causality and therefore a matter of moral indifference.[13]

More often than not, Scheler's arguments acquire an irrepressible cogency from the *implications* of Kant's views, which, if not in every detail, at least in overall *effect*, appear to confirm many of Scheler's interpretations. Thus, as we have seen (ch. 4, sec. 1, above), Scheler's suggestion that Kant's ethics is an "imperativistic ethics" that *derives* moral value from the idea of "duty" cannot be justified *textually*, except by ignoring crucial statements by Kant about the "moral law" in distinction from "duty." But at the same time, as we have also seen, Kant's concept of "moral law" suffers ultimately from the same lack of definable content as his concept of "rationality" (ch. 3, sec. 3, above). And as a consequence of this effective contentlessness, Kant must inevitably fall back, as Scheler alleges, on some formalized conception of "duty" in order to produce even the semblance of content for his notion of moral value.

The allegation of Neo-Kantian influence on Scheler is more difficult to assess, though even a cursory survey of *Formalismus* will show that Scheler himself is far from being uncritical of Neo-Kantian views. But if the final court of appeal in such matters is faithfulness to the legacy of the Kantian texts themselves, Scheler can claim, at least, fidelity to the spirit of those texts, and cannot be faulted easily with ignorance of the letter. And if Scheler felt constrained by the "pathos" he perceived in those texts to mark a discrepancy between the spirit and the letter, this only accords with the hermeneutical license that Kant himself permitted when he remarked that "it is by no means unusual, upon comparing the thoughts which an author has expressed . . . to find that we understand him better than he has understood himself" (*KrV*, A 314–B 370).

Philosophical Implications of Scheler's Critique

THIS STILL LEAVES TWO QUESTIONS. First, is Scheler's critique a convincing one? And, second, is his alternative to Kant's ethics a viable one? These questions have already been substantially addressed in the course of this study, at least with respect to each of the basic issues of the foregoing chapters. But let us summarize our conclusions. As we have seen, the questions at issue here—regarding the cogency of Scheler's critique and the viability of his alternative—are not easily separable. For neither Kant's nor Scheler's position necessarily stands or falls as a whole. Scheler's critique of Kant is legitimate at certain points but not others, and his own alternative is viable at certain points but not others. Therefore, as we have found, these questions cannot be considered entirely apart from one another—nor from the question of what other promising avenues of research in moral philosophy Scheler's critique may suggest.

Probably Scheler's most important and effective criticisms of Kant center on three points: (1) the latter's acquiescence in a metaphysical tradition that led to his proposed bifurcations of reason/sensibility, will/inclination, form/matter, and noumenon/phenomenon; (2) his presupposition that whatever order we discover in the world of desire, inclination, and moral experience can be nothing other than an order imposed practically by the law-giving rational subject; and (3) his formalistic conception of reason, moral law, and duty.

The first two points are related to a feature of Kant's philosophy that Scheler calls its "constructivism." This refers to Kant's whole new understanding of epistemology, stemming from his critical idealism and "Copernican Revolution" in philosophy, by virtue of which he invested the rational subject with the power of ordering, and in that sense "constructing," its experience. Scheler may have been aware, by his involvement in the phenomenological movement, of how the work of Husserl and others also underlined the importance of the agency of human subjectivity in the "constitution" of the world of which we are conscious. But in Scheler's view, Kant's "constructivism" led him to invest the faculty of human reason with far more powers than it justifiably may be supposed to have. It is one thing to suppose that reason plays an active role in perception or in enabling rational subjects to understand and participate in their moral experience. It is another to suggest that the principles of intelligibility governing the perceived world or the world of moral experience are themselves contributed to experience by the rational subject. It is one thing to say that the rational subject must formulate principles governing various regions of its experience by discovering what those principles are. It is quite another to suggest that there would be no ordering principles in certain regions of our experience, such as the region of moral experience, without the law-giving rational subject to provide them. Yet this is what Kant claims, or comes very close to claiming, according to Scheler, in some of his writings on ethics.

It is possible, as Scheler suggests, that Kant's "constructivist" tendencies may have prevented him from seeing that there are regions of experience whose ordering principles are not imposed, or perhaps even originally apprehended, by reason. Scheler's entire Pascalian discussion of the *ordo amoris*, the world of values and their a priori, emotional modes of givenness, highlights this point. As we have seen, however, the range of possible, objectively given, ordering principles governing various regions of experience may go beyond even the emotional (read "psychological") region embraced by Scheler's *ordo amoris* to include principles of biology, physics, linguistics, aesthetics, economics, and the like. Whatever the role may be that rational subjectivity plays in the passive synthesis, constitution, understanding, and articulation of such principles, they can hardly be imagined to reduce to innate formal qualities or a priori constructs of the mind itself. Such principles are, in some irreducible respect, objective discoveries, not merely constitutive forms of speculative or practical subjectivity, and the Kantian proclivity for ascribing all experienced lawfulness in the moral dimension of life to the auspices of law-giving reason is a reflection of a disproportionate Enlightenment confidence in the native powers of human reason.

Furthermore, these predilections lead to various problems, dilemmas, tensions, and unresolved puzzles in the Kantian philosophy itself. Some of these, like the problem of the "thing-in-itself," are notorious. More central to our own study are the problems pertaining to such matters as moral feeling, moral incentive, and moral conflict. For example, is moral feeling phenomenal or noumenal? Is it an incentive *for* moral willing or is it determined *by* the moral will? Or again, how is genuine moral conflict possible if pure practical reason is hermetically sealed off from phenomenal influences in its noumenal chamber, where the wiles of pathological inclinations and desires can never really touch it? If our true self is our rational, moral self, then how can we ever be truly divided against ourselves? While countless explanations have been offered to show how such difficulties might be resolved, it takes little effort to see that such difficulties are an unavoidable consequence of Kant's uncritical metaphysical pre-commitments.

Kant's views with respect to the third point above—his formalistic conception of reason, moral law, and duty—allow him to claim for his ethics an immediate, *prima facie* universality. However, they also prevent him, in prescribing our duties, from being specific. One's duty can be determined only according to an abstract "moral law," by means of an abstract formula of the "categorical imperative," which mandates that one's action must have the abstract virtue of being "universalizable" within an ideal community of "ends-in-themselves," by virtue of their no less abstract property of being "formally rational." Whatever may be said by way of criticism of the all-too-facile charge of "empty formalism" leveled against Kant's ethics, the fact remains, in the final analysis, that the charge is in some respect all too true: whatever overtures Kant himself may make about his ethics being a teleological system of "material ends" of practical reason, his conception of those "ends," like his conceptions of moral law, duty, and practical reason itself, were found upon closer examination to be "empty" *in effect*. These conceptions retained their apparent capacity to offer moral guidance and impose obligation only so long as they were able to draw vitality from the Enlightenment myth of instrumental reason, which, as Alasdair MacIntyre has masterfully shown, managed to retain its own viability only so long as it was not clearly understood that it was being sustained by the legacy of an earlier teleological and substantive understanding of human nature and reason for which there was no longer any clear foundation (*After Virtue*, 54 and *passim*). Another way of putting the matter is to say that Kant does not even acknowledge, let alone offer any rationale for, the actual material values presupposed by his conception of duty—a point very similar to one made by the postmodern hermeneutics of suspicion, as we have seen.[14] Hence, his notion of "duty" turns out to be as "blind," in effect, as his notion of moral "law" is formally "empty." Both presuppose a range of moral values generally accepted in Kant's time and, to a degree, in ours; but neither offers a clear way of justifying precisely those values by means of the equipment provided by Kant's ethics alone.

These difficulties result in certain troublesome consequences within the Kantian philosophy as well. For example, it leads to the curious implication that nothing can be of moral value that cannot be commanded by virtue of a categorical imperative. Since he recognizes no phenomenal or phenomenological teleology of material values in which to ground moral obligation, Kant makes moral value dependent solely on a noumenal imputation of an action's having been done "from duty." This effectively excludes a basis for the possible assessment of the relative moral value of various "pathological" dispositions, inclinations, and affective sentiments, which, of course, cannot be commanded. But is there any good reason why phenomena as basic to our moral experience as dispositions, inclinations, and sentiments should be regarded as incapable of bearing a moral value? Do we have no means at all of distinguishing morally good inclinations, for example, from morally bad ones?

Scheler's critique of Kant at these points is incisive and persuasive. Over against Kant's basic metaphysical dualism and his apotheosis of rational will as the ordering principle of experience, Scheler recognizes the existence of orders of experience that do not derive their orderedness or ordering principles from the rational subject. This recognition finds expression in his conception of an *ordo amoris*, an order of the emotions altogether autonomous and independent of the order of logic and the jurisdiction and competencies of reason. Furthermore, his theory of material values allows him to detail a fascinating analysis of how the passive intentionalities and feelings of one's most primal conative tendencies are directed at values as their targets well before the advent of value judgments in experience, or even of conscious choices. This enables him, in turn, to distinguish between the values of different conations and inclinations, and to consider what role our deepest feelings about ourselves—including our profoundest feelings of happiness and spiritual well-being or their opposites—play in our basic moral dispositions and actions.

Scheler's own theory falters, however, at a number of points. For one thing, Scheler's conception of *ordo amoris* remains ambiguous at a certain level. While his recognition of an irreducibly non-logical order of experience with its own non-rational ordering principle, or "emotional a priori," is both insightful and commendable, it remains much too indefinite. To avoid misunderstanding at this point, one must bear in mind the details of an argument made earlier in this book.[15] Briefly, however, the following may be said by way of summary.

On the one hand, if the "emotional a priori" is taken to refer specifically to the ordering principles of the (objective) realm of "psychology," as opposed to, say, "logic," "aesthetics," "economics," or "religion," it is too narrow a concept. For there are clearly other non-logical realms of activity besides the psychical—including not only the aesthetic, economic, and religious, but the linguistic, historical, and social, not to speak of the biotic, chemical, and mathematical—each with its own ordering principles. Accordingly, if the "emotional a priori" is taken in this narrow, "material-regional" sense, any attempt to ground ethics in it could be seen easily as an attempt to subsume the principles of morality under those of psychology. But such a procedure would seem to violate the integrity of ethics and fly in the face of the powerful anti-reductionist polemic running through Scheler's own work. It is highly unlikely, therefore, that he would have accepted such a reading of the matter.

On the other hand, if the "emotional a priori" is taken to refer to a (subjective) faculty of "feeling" by which the a priori is apprehended in intuition, it is too broad a concept. For then it is intended to play a multiplicity of roles as the irreducibly non-logical faculty for apprehending the ordering principles of a diversity of non-logical orders or "material regions." But if this is the case, then some careful clarifications and differentiations become necessary. For while it may be true that one can have a "moral feeling," just as one can have "religious feeling" or "aesthetic feeling"—or a "feeling" for economics, or languages, or logic, for that matter—this is not to say that the principles of any of these regions are reducible to those of psychology. Furthermore, a clearer rationale is required than Scheler offers for narrowly identifying the affective faculty of "feeling" with the apprehension of "material values" and for sharply separating this affective faculty from any notion of how logical principles are apprehended, as we have seen (cf. ch. 4, n. 34). To recast the matter in terms that would be somewhat counter intuitive for Scheler, what is needed is an explanation as to why "feeling" should be identified only with the apprehension of *certain kinds* of "material values" (such as sensible, vital, and spiritual values) *to the exclusion of others* (such as logical or mathematical "values," which are also "material" in respect of their intuitive content, despite their "formality" in respect of their universality; cf. ch. 2, sec. 3, under "Form and Content," above). In short, Scheler's insight into the irreducibility of moral experience and its norms requires further clarification and support than his own theory offers.

A related problem is Scheler's restriction of *moral* value to the positive or negative, higher or lower, values that appear through the willing and/or realization of other, *nonmoral* values. Again, while it is difficult to be brief without putting the matter in a way that could be easily misunderstood, perhaps the following may be said by way of summarizing an argument made more substantially in an earlier chapter (see ch. 3, sec. 4, and "Values and Willing" in sec. 2). The problem, briefly, is that numerous nonmoral values may be identified—such as linguistic, aesthetic, social, psychical, and even mathematical and logical (!) values—whose willing and "realization" (in many of the various possible senses of that term) one would hardly want to classify as "moral." While we might speak of an "ought" with respect to the realization of certain of these kinds of values, we would find it difficult to conceive of this "ought," in every case, as a "moral ought." The problem here stems from an inadvertent conflation of "good" in a *generic* sense with "good" in the specifically *moral* sense. There are many more kinds of "good" capable of being willed and realized than "moral good." What is necessary to resolve this difficulty, as I have argued in chapter 3, is to revise Scheler's theory to allow for some sense in which moral good can be achieved through the willing and realization of specifically *moral* values, such as "benevolence," "respect," and "faithfulness." While it might still be true, at some level, that a moral good, such as "benevolence," is brought into being through the willing or realization of other, *nonmoral* values, this would avoid the infelicitous consequence of having to call the willing or realization of every aesthetic, economic, linguistic, or logical value a *moral* good or evil.

By far the most serious shortcoming of Scheler's theory, however, as we saw in chapter 5, is his failure to present a clear basis for determining our moral obligations. This deficiency is directly the consequence of his failure either to adequately analyze or to clarify the relationship between moral insight, inclination, and duty, and it is the most troubling problem because it threatens to undermine the credibility of the normative claim underlying his ethics at a foundational level. His supposition that positive moral willing inevitably follows upon the heels of positive moral insight, for example, implies that there is no possibility of serious conflict between duty and inclination. There seems to be no room in Scheler's ethics for the possibility of moral struggle, for Aristotle's *enkratês* or *akratês*, the morally "strong" or "weak" character, which must *struggle* with the tension between the demands of reason and impulses of desire. It is possible, as Eugene Kelly has suggested (see ch. 5, sec. 4, above), that this difficulty is inherent in the phenomenological method itself, that it is an unavoidable consequence of any phenomenological approach which imagines that a phenomenological *description* of values may be employed in the service of solving actual ethical problems. Whether or not this is the case, the problem is clearly not restricted to phenomenological approaches. The inability to furnish clear grounds for moral compulsion and constraint seems almost endemic to modern moral philosophy. In any event, what is needed to remedy the problem is an ethics that can show us how to recognize our duty, and for that what is necessary is an ethics that can offer us principles by which to understand and recognize what is genuinely good and to distinguish it from the merely desirable.

In the balance, then, it may be said that although Scheler's theory is not without problems, his critique is a brilliant and necessary one. In the problem of formalism, Scheler discerned a critical flaw in the foundations underlying the imposing edifice of the Kantian philosophy. He called this formalism to task, as it manifested itself in the Kantian notions of "duty," "moral law," and, most fundamentally, "practical reason" itself. He summoned Kantian "reason" before the tribunal of "the things themselves" and demanded material evidence. In the cross-examination, old problems were brought to light, such as the entrenched legacy of metaphysical dualism, which surfaces in its particular forms within the Kantian philosophy. Some problems, like many of those incurred by Kant's uncritical acceptance of this legacy, were exposed as false problems. Other problems were reformulated altogether, such as the problem of transcendentalism in Kant's philosophy, which assumed a completely different, essentialist form in Scheler's phenomenology. Still other problems, such as the Kantian restriction of moral value to what can be commanded, were resolved in ingenious new ways in light of new insights, such as that provided by Scheler's analysis of how the moral disposition is constituted by the passive intentionalities of one's pre-rational conative tendencies, which have intuitable values as their goals. Scheler succeeded in confronting the Kantian "colossus of steel and bronze" in these ways with a cogent critique and a suggestive alternative. In some cases, this has resulted in the generation of new problems, such as the problem of how to understand the relationship between the orders of psychology and morality, which are both embraced, presumably, by Scheler's *ordo amoris*; or the problem of precisely how to understand the relationship between a "descriptive" theory of value and a "prescriptive" ethics. Significant problems still remain unresolved in Scheler's phenomenology of value and ethics. But his confrontation with Kant was a constructive one, and the engagement remains fruitful still, as, across the ages, these two brilliant thinkers add their thoughts and voices to the ongoing conversation of our minds.

Notes

1. Kant says that "we can arrive at a conclusion regarding the disposition only on the basis of *actions* (which are its *appearances*)" (*R*, 70/64; emphasis added).

2. This view is close to that held by both Meinong and Prall. See Alexius Meinong, *On Emotional Presentation*, 79; and D. W. Prall, *A Study in the Theory*

of Value, University of California Publications in Philosophy 3, No. 2 (1921), and his "The Present Status of the Theory of Value" in G. Adams and J. Lowenbert, eds., *Issues and Tendencies in Contemporary Philosophy* (Berkeley: University of California Press, 1923), 77–103; as well as Nicholas Rescher, *Introduction to Value Theory* 52f.

3. See, e.g., Alphéus, *Kant und Scheler*, 30f. This question could be profitably explored in terms of the diverse components of moral performances analyzed by Robert Sokolowski, *Moral Action*, 21, 30, 63, 150–62 (esp. 158), and 182.

4. I use the term "self" because of its stylistic ease, as a rough and ready equivalent for "person" in the following paragraphs, even though the term is employed by neither Kant nor Scheler.

5. For a discussion of this distinction, see Michael Ermarth, *Wilhelm Dilthey*, 241–67.

6. *F*, 385/374f.; 397/386f. For an elaboration of the meaning of "reflection" by Scheler, see IS, 233f./26.

7. For some illuminating phenomenological illustrations of what Scheler means by an "act," see Spader's article, "Person, Acts and Meaning," 203ff.

8. Herman Dooyeweerd, for instance, in his essay "What is Man?" in his book, *In the Twilight of Western Thought* (Nutley, NJ: Craig Press, 1960), writes: "This central I, which surpasses the temporal order, remains a veritable mystery. As soon as we try to grasp it in a concept or definition, it recedes as a phantom and resolves itself into nothingness" (181). Not far removed from this is Jean-Paul Sartre's view of consciousness as a "transparent nothingness," a view developed in his *The Transcendence of the Ego*, esp. sec. 1, B ("The *Cogito* as Reflective Consciousness"), and also in his *Being and Nothingness*, trans. Hazel E. Barnes (New York: Philosophical Library, 1956), 16–45. Cf. also Heidegger's analyses of *Dasein* in *Being and Time*, 78–90, 149–68. One could mention many other works, but for an excellent and popular introductory survey, see Leslie Stevenson, *Seven Theories of Human Nature* (New York: Oxford University Press, 1974).

9. This is evident not only in *Stellung* (1927), but his *Schriften aus dem Nachlaß*, III, *Philosophische Anthropologie*, ed. Manfred S. Frings (*GW*, 12), which begins with a review of the history and typology of classical, Judeo-Christian, and naturalistic theories of human nature; offers a thematic analysis of the notions of "soul," "body," ethical concepts such as "conscience," "duty," and cultural and linguistic phenomena; proceeds to an analysis of metaphysical notions of freedom, divinity, eros, and the like; and concludes with a detailed discussion of aging and death (based on his lectures of 1923–1924). Also worthy of note is Martin Buber, "The Philosophical Anthropology of Max Scheler," *Philosophy and Phenomenological Research* 6 (1946), 307–21; and the comparison with a prominent Japanese philosopher by Arthur R. Luther, "Scheler's Person and Nishida's Active Self as Centers of Creativity," *Philosophy Today* 21 (summer 1977), 126–42.

10. *F*, 407f./397f. Cf. ch. 2, sec. 4, above. Herman Dooyeweerd, *A New Critique*, vol. 2, claims that this microcosm-macrocosm theme reveals that Scheler's work was decisively influenced during this period by the French thinker Malebranche (589 n. 2). One also discerns here the personalistic undercurrents stemming from Rudolf Eucken's *Die Einheit des Geisteslebens in Bewußtsein*

und Tat der Menschheit (Leipzig, 1889), and Hermann Lotze's Mikrokosmus (Leipzig, 1856–1858). For concurrent developments in the English-speaking world, as well as the personalist movement as a whole, see John H. Lavely, "Personalism," *Encyclopedia of Philosophy*, ed. Paul Edwards (New York: Macmillan, 1967). On Scheler's idea of God, see S. I. M. Du Plessis, "Max Scheler's Concern with the Highest Perfection," in *Truth and Reality: Philosophical Perspectives on Reality Dedicated to Professor H. G. Stoker* (Braamfontein, South Africa: De Jong's, 1971), 86–93.

11. Scheler develops this aspect of his theory not only in *Formalismus*, but at length in his studies in the "sociology of knowledge." Cf. Max Scheler, *Die Wissensformen und die Gesellschaft*, ed. Maria Scheler, GW, 8; and in English translation, see "Problems with a Sociology of Knowledge," trans. Ernest Ranly, *Philosophy Today* 12, No. 1 (spring 1968), 42–71, and *Problems of a Sociology of Knowledge*, trans. Manfred S. Frings, ed. Kenneth W. Stikkers (London: Routledge & Kegan Paul, 1983). For an example of earlier criticisms of this aspect of Scheler's theory, see Paul A. Schilpp, "Formal Problems of Scheler's Sociology of Knowledge," *Philosophical Review* 36 (1927), 101–20.

12. When, in the preface to his *Totality and Infinity*, Levinas opposes the "eschatology of messianic peace" to the "ontology of war," he postulates an antithesis between the Jewish prophetic tradition and the whole Western metaphysical tradition, which he considers to be dominated by the concept of ontological totality. In contrast to totalitarian thinking, he suggests a kind of relational understanding of the problems of morality, expressed in terms of the relation between the "same" and the "other."

13. For other examples of this distinction between the "objective sense" and "pathos" in the Kantian text, according to Scheler, see F, 423/228 and 287/274.

14. Ch. 5, last paragraph of sec. 2. Cf. Alasdair MacIntyre, *Whose Justice?*, 1–11, where the author refers to rival conceptions of "rationality"; ch. 5, n. 17, above, where John Sallis describes a "crisis of reason"; and ch. 5, sec. 2, above, where I discuss the eroding legacy of the Age of Reason: the consensus as to what constitutes the identity of "practical rationality."

While Kant's work recognizes the formal value of the unconditioned "good" of good will, it nowhere spells out exactly what is meant by this in terms of any kind of phenomenology of the actual content of the "material values" contained in it or presupposed by it. Furthermore, it must be borne in mind that Scheler introduces the distinction of formal and material as a *secondary* distinction *within* the sphere of the "material a priori" (ch. 2, sec. 3, under "Form and Content"). Thus, while "good" may be regarded as a "material" value in one sense, in another sense it remains "formal" since its "content" (i.e "material") remains unspecified. This is the whole point of the Schelerian critique; it is why Scheler criticizes Kant's ethic as an "empty formalism"—its only mechanism for determining moral ends, the categorical imperative, remains precisely (according to Scheler) an "empty formula."

15. See the detailed discussion of these issues in ch. 2, sec. 4, above (particularly n. 44 of that chapter, as well as the note preceding and following that one). The matter also is briefly discussed in ch. 4, sec. 2, above.

APPENDIX I

Is Scheler's Ethic an Ethic of Virtue?

The Question at Issue

UNTIL RECENTLY, WHEN PHILOSOPHERS talked about ethics they spent most of their time talking about actions and consequences, about rules for decision-making in problematic situations, about laws of obligation and how to justify them.[1] With the recent resurgence of interest in the virtues, however, they have turned to reconsider another set of issues. They have begun talking again about persons as well as about actions and consequences, about moral character as well as about moral quandaries, about agents and the sorts of lives they lead as well as about rules of decision-making, about virtue as well as about obligations and the laws that enjoin these on us.[2]

This resurgence of interest in the virtues may be understood in a variety of ways. One could view it as a remedial emphasis on an unduly neglected department of ethical theory. While one might not believe that an account of the virtues in itself is sufficient for an adequate ethical theory, one might still hold, as William Frankena does, that no ethical theory can be complete without an account of the virtues (*Ethics*, 63–67). One could also view the resurgence as a reaction against an overly abstract focus of recent moral theory on such notions as "right," "good" and "ought," and as a corrective turn to a focus on richer and more concrete character traits such as "courage," "compassion," and the like. This is the view, for example, of Elizabeth Anscombe, who suggested that we should stop analyzing moral obligations and devote ourselves to the study of virtues instead! ("Modern Moral Philosophy"). Still another way of understanding the resurgence of interest in the virtues would be to see it as a retrieval of what is most fundamental in moral experience and its restoration to center stage in moral theory. On this view, aretaic concepts are seen as more fundamental than deontic or consequentialist ones; judgments about human character are seen as more basic than judgments about the rightness of actions or the value of consequences.[3]

But regardless of how this resurgence of interest in the virtues may be understood, there appears to be little disagreement about its catalyst: quite rightly, I think, this has been credited to the influence of Alasdair MacIntyre's magisterial *After Virtue* (1981).[4] MacIntyre got us thinking again about the virtues and their place in ethics. And this is especially significant, not because we have lacked traditions, such as the Thomistic, within which virtues have always had their place; but because the question of the virtues and their relevance has been raised in a new and challenging way for the philosophical community as a whole outside the cloister of such traditions. Indeed, what the concept of "virtue" might possibly mean after Heidegger's dismissal of values, the anti-foundationalism of Rorty, and the de-centering deconstructionist logic of Derrida is an interesting question.

In the following I shall consider whether Scheler's ethics may be viewed as a timely species of what is referred to in current discussions as an "ethics of virtue." First, I shall briefly follow Scheler's line of reasoning as he articulates the differences between what he calls Kant's "ethics of duty" and his own "ethics of insight." Next, focusing on a number of features implicit in Scheler's critique of Kant, I shall turn briefly to a comparative analysis of Aristotle's account of moral virtue and moral weakness in Book VII of his *Nicomachean Ethics* and ask what it is that prevents Kant's ethics from being an ethics of virtue. Finally, turning to Scheler's more thematic remarks about virtue, moral disposition, and the like, I shall argue that Scheler's ethic has some of the basic features of an ethic of virtue, but also some of the basic difficulties of "post-aretaic" ethics.

Scheler and Kant

SCHELER'S ETHICS, SET FORTH provisionally in *Formalismus* (1913–1916), is developed against the background of Kantian ethics. The Kantian ethics serves as a foil against which Scheler's ethics is articulated by way of contrast. Key elements of Kant's ethics are singled out and construed so as to set off in sharp relief the contrasting features of Scheler's ethics. Kant's "empty formalism" thus sets forth to full advantage the rich "content" of "material values" in Scheler's ethics; Kant's "subjectivism" underscores Scheler's "objectivism"; Kant's transcendental "constructivism" highlights Scheler's phenomenological "intuitionism"; and so forth. By way of critique, Scheler sets Kant's ethics of duty over against his own ethics of insight.[5]

Scheler offers a pointed critique of the concept of "duty," exemplified, in his view, by the deontological ethics of Kant. The concept of "duty" as developed in Kant, Scheler says, is a deficient basis for moral judgment in at least four respects.[6]

First, duty is essentially a "necessitation" or "compulsion" against inclination and individual willing. It is not itself a positive insight into moral value. Rather, the content of what is demanded in terms of moral law or rationality only "first becomes 'duty' when it meets an opposing and rising inclination, and also when it is posited against or at least independent of an individual's will"; by contrast, as Scheler sees the matter, when "we have the evidential insight that a deed or a will is good, we do not talk about 'duty,'" and if the insight is adequate, it determines the will "without any factor of compulsion or necessitation that might come between insight and willing" (F, 207/192).

Second, duty "cuts off" (*abschneidet*) moral insight, or at least develops independent of it. It obliges by a "blind inner commandment," which "lacks additional 'grounds'" (F, 207f./192f.). In fact, experience shows repeatedly "that the representation of 'duty' comes into play precisely when our moral considerations based on insight begin to weaken, or when our moral considerations fall short of resolving a situation that is too complicated" (F, 207/192).

Third, duty is a compulsion or command that comes, according to Scheler, from inside us, as opposed to orders coming "from outside." But this does not diminish in the least its "blindness." In fact, obedience to a command from outside may stem from insight into the values presupposed by a command and therefore qualify as morally "insightful" action. In his discussion of autonomy, Scheler speaks not only of the "autonomy of willing," as did Kant, but of "autonomy of insight." This allows him to introduce subtle distinctions between (1) forced willing, which is not autonomous in any sense; (2) blind obedience, which may be unforced but lacks autonomy of moral insight; (3) obedience, which may not only be unforced but based on autonomous insight into the moral value of a command, though only mediate (and therefore heteronomous) insight into the moral value of the commanded action; and (4) autonomous willing based on autonomous insight into the values of material performances themselves.[7]

Fourth, duty has, according to Scheler, "an essentially negative and restrictive nature" (F, 208/193). This does not mean, simply, that duty proscribes more than it prescribes. Rather, it means that duty shares with "necessity" the character of that "whose opposite is impossible."[8] By contrast, in Scheler's view, moral insight "does not require the thought of even a possible opposite," or "an attempted counterwilling against a willing whose value is in question" (F, 209/194).

Accordingly, Scheler says, "an ethics of insight should not be, as it frequently is, confused with an ethics of duty. They are in opposition to each other" (F, 209/194). Where an ethics of duty fundamentally goes wrong, according to Scheler, is in its failure to recognize that all moral judgment always already presupposes the comprehension of value. "Whenever we speak of an ought," he says, "the comprehension of a value must have [already] occurred"; and this means that "every ought has its foundation in a value (and not vice versa)" (F, 200/184). And where the comprehension of a value has occurred, there is no reason to assume that, before a moral action can follow, an "ought" having the force of an alien compulsion must first impinge upon the recalcitrant inclinations.

Kant and Aristotle

HERE ALREADY WE DISCERN certain nuances of Scheler's discussion that recall Aristotle's ethics. Aristotle, we recall, distinguished four types of moral character: (1) moral virtue, (2) moral strength, (3) moral weakness, and (4) moral vice (*Works*, Vol. 9: *Ethica Nicomachea*, trans. W. D. Ross, Bk. 7, 1–10). A morally virtuous man, in Aristotle's view, is one whose inclinations are in harmony with reason, one for whom the "good" is experienced as "desirable"; there is no moral conflict within him, for he "likes" being morally good. The morally strong man is self-controlled; he is one who has mastered his inclinations by heeding the voice of reason, but he may not entirely enjoy "having-to-do" his duty. The morally weak man lacks rational self-control; his inclinations frequently lead him to do what he later regrets doing. The morally vicious man is the exact opposite of the virtuous; he experiences no moral conflict, embracing evil without any rational resistance or regret.

Whatever his differences with Aristotle, what Scheler seems to want is an ethics that, like Aristotle's, permits a proper accounting of the kind of person who is disposed by inclination to do what is morally good, the kind of person for whom the good does not intrude as a somewhat distal or alien obligation but is exactly what is affectively desired. In Kant's ethics, however, human morality is linked inextricably to "duty"; what makes an action moral is its being done "from duty," nothing more. Inclination remains a wholly alien incentive. Not only is the morality of an action most apparent when it is perceived as a kind of "necessitation" or "compulsion" against one's natural inclinations, but if one's inclinations happen to conform to the demands of "duty," this is, at best, a happy coincidence and a matter of complete moral indifference.

One reason for this is that Kant, as Robert Sokolowski observes, works within the moral types of Aristotle's morally strong or self-controlled man and the morally weak man (*enkratês* and *akratês*) (*Moral Action*, 217). The morally virtuous or vicious type has no clear place in Kant's moral philosophy. The place of the virtuous will is taken by the "holy will," which is not desire shaped by reason, but reason cut off from desire and unaffected by it. "Virtue," for Kant, does not mean the rational domestication of desire, as in Aristotle, or the attainment of a holy will; rather, it means the experience of reason prevailing in its struggle against alien desire. In short, Kant's "virtuous man" is no better than Aristotle's "morally strong man," who takes care to keep his desires under rational control. Likewise, Kant's "vicious man" is no worse than Aristotle's "morally weak man," who rationally wishes he could be good even as he surrenders to his desire. Hence, Kant's ethics has little room for the notion of moral character as the origin of moral action. Even the notion of disposition (*Gesinnung*), as a formal "maxim of maxims," is construed primarily as an effect of inscrutable choice rather than a discernible motive of willing. Ultimately there is only the interplay of reason and sensibility—and choice. The sedimentation of passions themselves into a settled, identifiably moral way of desiring has no place in Kant's ethics as a normative motive for moral action.[9]

As Hans Reiner argued, this was the chief complaint that Kant's contemporary critic, Schiller, had against the Kantian ethic.[10] When Schiller complained that Kant's opposition of duty to inclination could easily inspire "a gloomy and monkish asceticism," he was not objecting to Kant's practice of clarifying the nature of duty by contrasting it to inclination. Rather, he was objecting to a view of human nature in which no moral virtue attaches to an inclination to do one's duty. It was a matter of complete moral indifference to Kant, he felt, whether an action done from a sense of duty is accompanied by an inclination to do it. At most, it was a happy coincidence. For Schiller, by contrast, the harmonization of desire and reason, sensibility and rationality, is the very aim and goal of moral perfection and virtue, a *telos* in which the ultimate essence of human existence—the "beautiful soul" (*schöne Seele*)—might be realized. "Man not only may, but ought to, combine pleasure with duty," he insisted (*On Grace and Dignity* in *Schillers Philosophische Schriften und Gedichte*, 130). The virtuous man does his duty with joy. He no longer needs to consult reason before every action and decision, as Kant insisted, because moral law ceases to have the "imperative form" of an alien necessitation. The inclinations themselves become moral and rational.

Aristotle and Scheler

THIS RAISES AN INTERESTING QUESTION. In *After Virtue*, Alasdair MacIntyre suggests that the Enlightenment project of justifying morality had to fail because the joint effect of its rejection of theology and Aristotelianism was to eliminate any notion of "man-as-he-could-be-if-he-realized-his-*telos*" (54). Deprived of a teleological context, he says, the relationship between the inherited conventions of morality and "untutored-human-nature-as-it-is" became unclear. Discussions about duties, actions, and consequences became separated from questions about human nature, character, and virtue. Indeed, the very notion of "moral virtue" became ambiguous. The problem was not avoided by Kant's concessive provision of a "practical" teleological framework for his ethics, because that framework effectively excluded the phenomenal component of human nature; it failed to furnish a teleological view of human nature as nature.[11] This raises the question, then, whether Scheler develops the concept of moral virtue in such a way as to provide anything like a view of "man-as-he-could-be-if-he-realized-his-*telos*."

Scheler clearly regards the theory of virtue as fundamental in moral philosophy. All moral norms are grounded ultimately in the value of persons. The question of virtue, therefore, is basic. Scheler contrasts his own view with that of Kant, who did not even furnish a theory of virtue proper, he says, because he took "virtue" to mean only the "sediment" of individual dutiful acts, which alone are originally "good." In fact, however, it is virtue (or vice) that is the foundation for the moral value of all particular acts. Accordingly, he states: "The theory of virtue precedes the theory of duty" (*F,* 50 n./28 n. 18).

How does Scheler understand "virtue" and its foundational role in ethics? First, he defines "virtue" as "the immediately experienced power to do something that ought to be done."[12] The experience is an irreducible modality of conation, which leads us to expect that we shall or shall not do something. It is an experience of "ability" that pertains to the value of actions, not to the physical or psychological strength required to perform them. "Virtue" becomes a moral "disposition" (*Gesinnung*), he says, only when its value-content is experienced as having settled into such a ready "ability" to do certain deeds (*F,* 150 n./129 n. 14).

Second, for Scheler, virtue as settled into an established moral disposition (*Gesinnung*) is an experienceable phenomenon with a discernible material content. This account differs sharply from Kant's. In Kant's view the disposition was not only the result of an inscrutable choice; it was itself, in Eugene Kelly's words, "purely the empty form in which a concrete 'intention' (*Absicht*) is posited," "a mere transcendental condition of the unity underlying our intentions" (112). In Kant's ethics the disposition does not serve as a material source of moral willing and acting; it has no phenomenal content; it cannot meaningfully be called good or bad itself. By contrast, in Scheler's ethics, the disposition serves as a phenomenally discernible source of moral action and bears a material content of moral virtue or vice.

Third, the foundational role of virtue for Scheler can be seen best in his treatment of the relationship between virtue and happiness. Almost invariably the philosophical tradition finds only one alternative in this relationship: either happiness is the consequence of moral virtue, or its goal. But this alternative misses the point, says Scheler. For there is a sense in which it is true both that only the virtuous person is happy and that only the happy person acts virtuously. Why is this? It is because moral striving and willing stem from happiness rooted in moral character or moral self-worth.[13] For Scheler, not only a virtuous character but also the affective happiness that stems from consciousness of one's moral self-worth, can serve as a motive and spring of moral action. In fact, since persons are never given as objects but only through their potential or actual performance of acts, a person's moral character (the value of the person) is only ever given through an experience of "ability" to perform certain acts and concomitant experience of happiness or unhappiness (the value of a person's central feeling-state).[14]

Scheler and the Question of Virtue

Now, IF I UNDERSTAND SCHELER correctly, "moral virtue," "moral self-worth," and the "happiness" related to these, bear an implicitly normative significance for him. "Moral virtue" and "moral self-worth" are goods to be sought. "Happiness," as an affective motive of moral action, is a morally good thing. One's moral actions "ought" to flow from such happiness. Like Schiller and Aristotle, he holds a high (though less explicitly developed) ideal of moral virtue. Within this ideal, the imperative form of duty does not even arise, for one's willing and acting is autonomous, flows from the enjoyment of one's own moral self-worth, and is grounded in the pleasure of realizing autonomously perceived moral values.[15] And insofar as this ideal of moral virtue bears, even implicitly, a normative significance for Scheler, one may find in his ethics some notion of "man-as-he-could-be-if-he-realized-his-*telos*," however ambiguous this may be.

But this raises some problems for Scheler the phenomenologist. For Aristotle and Thomas, of course, ethics was a normative discipline. Moral philosophy offered guidance. And it did so by grounding its "oughts" in an "is" about human nature. The question of human nature and its "essence" provided the keystone for a teleological framework within which the moral prescriptions governing "untutored-human-nature-as-it-is" were grounded in metaphysical descriptions about the essential nature of "man-as-he-could-be-if-he-realized-his-*telos*." But for Scheler the phenomenologist, simple recourse to this whole teleological edifice of Aristotelian metaphysics is no longer possible.

There is no question that Scheler understands ethics to be a normative discipline. He insists that it offer direction.[16] And the fact that his moral philosophy is phenomenological and essentially descriptive does not, of itself, prevent it from being normative or offering direction. But it is not clear to me that Scheler's ethic has completely succeeded in this matter. Rather, it seems to suffer some of the same problems as most modern, "post-aretaic" ethics — chiefly problems related to an unresolved philosophical anthropology underlying the failure of the Enlightenment project of justifying morality.

Scheler does not, of course, make any effort to derive his ethical principles directly from a philosophical anthropology. Why is this? One might argue that his theory of human affect may be taken to constitute a philosophical anthropology, but that this is not the source of values for Scheler. That source is rather the a priori hierarchy of values, to which his theory of affect correlates. It could be argued, then, that Scheler's philosophical anthropology does not directly furnish norms but, rather, is correlated to a non-metaphysical theory of values from which norms could be derived. In this way, one could admit that Scheler himself never developed a fully satisfactory normative ethics while claiming that he nevertheless succeeded in establishing the basis for one. Furthermore, the case could be made for viewing Scheler as drawing on the best of virtue-based and principle-based ethics.

The chief difficulty I see in this line of argument stems from the conclusions reached in the last two chapters in this study concerning unresolved problems in Scheler's theory. In the first place, as we saw in detail in chapter 5, there is his failure to show how insight into a hierarchy of nonmoral values presents a clear basis for determining actual moral obligations. It remains to be demonstrated precisely how "ethical norms" can be "derived" clearly and compellingly from an a priori hierarchy of nonmoral value-essences. Hence, how Scheler can be viewed as drawing on the best of principle-based ethics is not entirely evident. In the second place, it is fairly clear that Scheler's philosophical anthropology offers little help in this respect; which, in turn, calls into question how Scheler can be viewed as drawing on the best of virtue-based ethics. This can be seen from the most cursory review of his theory of the person.

In developing his theory of the person, upon which so much of his success depends, Scheler carefully tries to avoid either substantialist or actualist theories, the former because they presuppose a metaphysic of substance, the latter because they lose the identity of persons in their acts. But if there is anything like an "essence" or "nature" to human persons when Scheler is done with his theory, I am not sure I can find it. All he can tell us as a phenomenologist is that a person is "the concrete and essential unity of being of acts of different essences" (*F*, 393f./383). And in his later writings, even this "unity" seems jeopardized by the contrary forces of "spirit" (*Geist*) and "impulse" (*Drang*), which threaten to reopen the very kind of metaphysical rift in human nature he had denounced in Kant (see Max Scheler, *Problems with a Sociology of Knowledge*, 36; and Perrin, "Commentary," 359).

It is true that, near the end of *Formalismus*, Scheler offers an eidetic description of exemplary "model persons" and essential "types" of persons—"saint," "genius," "hero," and the like. And even though he denies that it is possible for one finite individual to represent simultaneously more than one of these types, it is conceivable that this sort of analysis might be fitted into a coherentist version of an ethic of virtue. In that case there would be no essential "human" nature as such to serve as a basis for a theory of virtue, but natures of essentially different "types," each with its own proper virtues. The trick then would be to find some means of deciding which "type" of nature and which set of virtues should be realized as one's own *telos*. But such an approach would seem to multiply, rather than reduce, the problems in Scheler's ethic, and it would appear difficult to reconcile this with his basic normative intention of offering moral direction.

To the last, human nature remains an enigma in Scheler's philosophy. And to the extent that his ethics lacks a clearly developed notion of human nature, it is incapable of developing a clear notion of the ideal person, and lacks both a means of defining the kinds of virtues that are necessary for being a person of that type, and a means of defending some view of how persons can come to possess such virtues. Is Scheler's ethic an ethic of virtue? Well, yes, of sorts. But its claim to be an ethic of virtue was never intended to be its strongest suit.

Notes

1. The material of this appendix is based on a paper I presented originally at a conference on the philosophy of Max Scheler sponsored by the Long Island Philosophical Society at SUNY-Stony Brook in 1988, which was subsequently published in revised form in *Japanese and Western Phenomenology*, ed. P. Blosser, et al. (The Hague: Kluwer Academic Publishers, 1993), 147–59. Reprinted by permission of Kluwer Academic Publishers.

2. A helpful collection of essays on this development with a good bibliography can be found in Robert Kruschwitz and Robert Roberts, eds., *The Virtues: Contemporary Essays on Moral Character* (Belmont: Wadsworth, 1986).

3. This does not mean that an ethics of virtue must necessarily assume a "foundationalist" form. There is no reason why an ethics of virtue could not assume, say, a "coherentist" form of argument.

4. Needless to say, other works of less celebrity dealing with the same sorts of issues could be mentioned that predate MacIntyre's, such as James Wallace's *Virtues and Vices* (Ithaca, NY: Cornell University Press, 1978).

5. I realize that an ethics of "insight" or "intuition" is one thing, and that an ethics of "virtue" could turn out to be another. But my expectation is that by attending closely to how Scheler contrasts Kant's ethics to his own, we may find ourselves hearing something very much like a contrast between an ethics of duty and an ethics of virtue. Furthermore, I think this will be borne out by Scheler's more thematic remarks, which I shall examine in the latter portion of this appendix.

6. Scheler's principal account of "duty" is found in ch. 4 of *Formalismus*, which is devoted to a comparison of "Value-Ethics and Ethics of Imperatives." His criticisms of an ethics of duty, as he finds exemplified in Kantian ethics,

is located in the first part of the chapter, in which he discusses at least four "Unsatisfactory Theories of the Origin of the Concept of Value and the Essence of Moral Facts."

7. Scheler's discussion of "The Autonomy of the Person" is found in the second part of ch. 6 of *Formalismus*, beginning at *F*, 499/494 (but see esp. 503ff./498ff.).

8. Here Scheler is citing an expression used by Kant in *Der einzig mögliche Beweisgrund zu einer Demonstration des Daseins Gottes*, 81. Cf. Gordon Treash's translation, *The One Possible Basis for a Demonstration of the Existence of God*, 194.

9. For Kant's discussion of the moral "disposition" (*Gesinnung*), which he distinguishes from "executive will" or "choice" (*Willkür*) and "legislative will" (*Wille*), see the opening chapters of his *Religion within the Limits of Reason Alone*.

10. The issues underlying the famous controversy between Kant and Schiller and their well-intentioned (but often misconceived) efforts at reconciling their views, are the subject of Hans Reiner's fine, thoughtful study, *Duty and Inclination: The Fundamentals of Morality Discussed and Redefined with Special Regard to Kant and Schiller*.

11. MacIntyre argues that after the teleological assumptions of Aristotelian physics were rejected, "reason" was no longer regarded—by Kant or Hume any more than by Calvin or Pascal—as capable of supplying a genuine comprehension of man's true end. He writes: "reason for [Kant], as much as for Hume, discerns no essential natures and no teleological features in the objective universe available for study by physics" (*After Virtue*, 54).

12. *F*, 220/205. The "ought" here, it should be noted, needn't be understood as bearing the imperative form of "duty," but may be regarded as an "ideal" involving the possibility of supererogation. For Scheler's distinction between the "ought of duty" and the "ideal ought," see *F*, 218/203 and 224/210.

13. In Scheler's terms, the "values of striving and willing" are founded on the "values of the central feeling-state," which, in turn, are founded on the "values of the person." For Scheler's account, see esp. *F*, 370/358f.

14. For Scheler's account of how persons are given, see *F*, 392ff./382ff., and Quentin Smith, "Scheler's Stratification of Emotional Life and Strawson's *Person*."

15. Against Scheler's claim that moral values appear only through the realization of other nonmoral values, I argue that moral values themselves represent a species of material values that may be realized. See Philip Blosser, "Moral and Nonmoral Values: A Problem in Scheler's Ethics," and ch. 3 ("Values and Willing," in sec. 2, and sec. 4) of the present study.

16. In response to N. Hartmann, who denied that it is the task of ethics to offer prescriptions, Scheler writes: "Ultimately ethics is a 'damned bloody affair,' and if it can give me no directives concerning how 'I' 'should' live . . . then what is it?" (*F*, 23 n./xxxi n. 14).

APPENDIX II

North American Dissertations on Scheler

THE FOLLOWING IS A LIST of North American dissertations in English that are devoted to Scheler or aspects of his work. It is substantially complete, though not exhaustive, and is presented in both alphabetical and chronological forms. The alphabetical listing offers the most complete bibliographical data and indicates those dissertations that have made it into print, usually in revised form.

Alphabetical Listing

Blosser, Philip Eugene. "Scheler's Alternative to Kant's Ethics." Ph.D. diss., Duquesne University, 1985. Revised and published as *Scheler's Critique of Kant's Ethics*. Series in Continental Thought, No. 22. Athens: Ohio University Press, 1995.

Commenator, George E. "The Phenomenology of Love in Max Scheler." Ph.D. diss., Boston College, 1970.

Czopek, Michael Joseph. "Max Scheler's Problem of Religion: A Critical Exposition." Ph.D. diss., De Paul University, 1981.

Deeken, Alfons Theodor. "Ethics and History in Max Scheler." Ph.D. diss., Fordham University, 1973. Revised and published as *Process and Permanence in Ethics: Max Scheler's Moral Philosophy*. New York: Paulist Press, 1974.

Funk, Roger L. "Ethics and Emotion: A Study in the Philosophy of Max Scheler." Ph.D. diss., Northwestern University, 1969.

Ibana, Rainier R. Altamarino. "The Principle of Solidarity in Max Scheler's Philosophy of Social Analysis." Ph.D. diss., Fordham University, 1989.

Kelly, Eugene. "Max Scheler and Phenomenology." Ph.D. diss., New York University, 1971. Revised and published as *Max Scheler*. Boston: Twayne, G. K. Hall & Co., 1977.

Köhle, Eckard Joseph. "Personality: A Study according to the Philosophy of Value and Spirit of Max Scheler and Nicolai Hartmann." Ph.D. diss.,

Columbia University, 1941. Published as *Personality: A Study according to the Philosophy of Value and Spirit of Max Scheler and Nicolai Hartmann*. Newton, New Jersey, 1941.

Meyer, Herbert Heinrich. "A Critical Study of Max Scheler's Philosophical Anthropology in Its Relation to his Phenomenology." Ph.D. diss., Boston University, 1972.

Miller, David George. "Nietzsche and Max Scheler on 'Ressentiment': An Inquiry into the Substructure of Hate." Ph.D. diss., De Paul University, 1988.

Moosa, Imtiaz. "Scheler's Philosophy of Value and Ethics in Relation to Kant's Ethics." Ph.D. diss., University of Toronto, 1986.

Mulligan, Thomas Michael. "Max Scheler and G. E. Moore: A Critical Comparison of Their Axiological Ethical Systems." Ph.D. diss., Northwestern University, 1976.

Munster, Ralph F. W. "The Development of Ethics in the Philosophy of Max Scheler: A Study in Personalistic Phenomenology." Ph.D. diss., Duke University, 1953.

Nabe, Clyde Milton. "Max Scheler on Phenomenology and Man's Place in the Cosmos." Ph.D. diss., Purdue University, 1975.

Perrin, Ronald Fredric. "Max Scheler's Concept of the Person: Toward a Radical Humanism." Ph.D. diss., University of California, San Diego, 1971. Revised and published as *Max Scheler's Concept of the Person: An Ethics of Humanism*. New York: St. Martin's Press, 1991.

Ranly, Ernest Willibald. "Scheler's Phenomenology of Community." Ph.D. diss., St. Louis University, 1964. Published as *Scheler's Phenomenology of Community*. The Hague: Nijhoff, 1966.

Roberts, Augustine. "Max Scheler's Phenomenology of Person." Ph.D. diss., Duquesne University, 1968.

Schneck, Frederick Stephen. "Personalism as Political Theory: A Study of the Works of Max Scheler." Ph.D. diss., University of Notre Dame, 1984. Revised and published as *Person and Polis: Max Scheler's Personalism as Political Theory*. Albany: State University of New York Press, 1987.

Schneider, Marius. "Max Scheler's Phenomenological Philosophy of Values." Ph.D. diss., Catholic University of America, 1951. Published as *Max Scheler's Phenomenological Philosophy of Values*. Washington, DC: Catholic University of America Press, 1951.

Smith, Quentin Persifor. "The Phenomenology of Feeling: A Critical Development of the Theories of Feeling in Husserl, Scheler, and Sartre." Ph.D. diss., Boston College, 1977. Revised and published as *The Felt Meanings of the World: A Metaphysics of Feeling*. West Lafayette, Indiana: Purdue University Press, 1986.

Spader, Peter. "The Realization of Value: A Study of the Philosophy of Max Scheler." Ph.D. diss., Columbia University, 1969.

Staude, John Raphael. "Max Scheler: Philosopher, Sociologist, and Critic of German Culture." Ph.D. diss., University of California, Berkeley, 1965. Revised and published as *Max Scheler, 1874–1928: An Intellectual Portrait*. New York: Free Press, 1967.

Stikkers, Kenneth W. "Toward a Sociology of Space: An Analysis of Spatial Experience in Technological Society, with Special Attention to the Philosophy of Max Scheler." Ph.D. diss., De Paul University, 1982.

Sweeney, Robert Daniel. "Max Scheler's Philosophy of Value." Ph.D. diss., Fordham University, 1962.

Vacek, Edward [Victor] Collins. "Anthropological Foundations of Scheler's Ethics of Love." Ph.D. diss., Northwestern University, 1978. Significantly influenced his later publication, *Love, Human and Divine: The Heart of Christian Ethics*. Washington, DC: Georgetown University Press, 1994.

Van De Pitte, Margaret Magdalene. "The Epistemological Function of an Affective Principle in the Phenomenology of Intersubjectivity." Ph.D. diss., University of Southern California, 1966.

Van Tuinen, Jacob. "The Phenomenological Ethics of Max Scheler." Ph.D. diss., University of Michigan, 1936.

Walraff, Charles S. "Max Scheler's Theory of Moral Obligation." Ph.D. diss., University of California, Berkeley 1939.

Weiss, Dennis Matthew. "Renewing the Anthropological Question." Ph.D. diss., University of Texas, Austin, 1991.

Welch, E. Parl. "Max Scheler's Philosophy of Religion." Ph.D. diss., University of Southern California, 1934.

Wilder, Alfred William. "The Problem of Ethical Norms in Max Scheler." Ph.D. diss., Fordham University, 1976.

Chronological Listing

THE FOLLOWING PRESENTS much less detail than the alphabetical listing, but, unlike the latter, it indicates names of dissertation advisers in parentheses following titles where this information was available. It also reveals an increased output of dissertations from the 1960s onward, marking a decided upsurge of interest coinciding with the increased availability of English translations during and since that period.

Year	Institution	Author and Title
1934	Univ. of S. California	E. Parl Welch, "Max Scheler's Philosophy of Religion."
1936	University of Michigan	Jacob Van Tuinen, "The Phenomenological Ethics of Max Scheler."
1939	UC-Berkeley	Charles S. Walraff, "Max Scheler's Theory of Moral Obligation."
1941	Columbia University	Eckhard Joseph Köhle, "Personality: A Study according to the Philosophy of Value and Spirit of Max Scheler and Nicolai Hartmann."
1951	Catholic Univ. of America	Marius Schneider, "Max Scheler's Phenomenological Philosophy of Values."

1953	Duke University	Ralph F. W. Munster, "The Development of Ethics in the Philosophy of Max Scheler."
1962	Fordham University	Robert Daniel Sweeney, "Max Scheler's Philosophy of Value" (advisor: Balduin Schwartz).
1964	St. Louis University	Ernest Willibald Ranly, "Scheler's Phenomenology of Community."
1965	UC-Berkeley	John Raphael Staude, "Max Scheler: Philosopher, Sociologist, and Critic of German Culture."
1966	Univ. of S. California	Margaret Magdalene Van De Pitte, "The Epistemological Function of an Affective Principle in the Phenomenology of Intersubjectivity" (advisor: William H. Werkmeister).
1968	Duquesne University	Augustine Roberts, "Max Scheler's Phenomenology of Person" (advisor: John Sallis).
1969	Columbia University	Peter Spader, "The Realization of Value: A Study of the Philosophy of Max Scheler."
1969	Northwestern University	Roger L. Funk, "Ethics and Emotion: A Study in the Philosophy of Max Scheler" (advisor: James M. Edie).
1970	Boston College	George E. Commenator, "The Phenomenology of Love in Max Scheler."
1971	New York University	Eugene Kelly, "Max Scheler and Phenomenology" (advisor: William Barrett).
1971	UC-San Diego	Ronald Fredric Perrin, "Max Scheler's Concept of the Person: Toward a Radical Humanism" (advisor: Herbert Marcuse).
1972	Boston University	Herbert Heinrich Meyer, "A Critical Study of Max Scheler's Philosophical Anthropology in Its Relation to his Phenomenology" (advisor: Erazim V. Kohak).
1973	Fordham University	Alfons Theodor Deeken, "Ethics and History in Max Scheler" (advisor: Quentin Lauer).
1975	Purdue University	Clyde Milton Nabe, "Max Scheler on Phenomenology and Man's Place in the Cosmos" (advisor: Richard F. Grabau).
1976	Fordham University	Alfred William Wilder, "The Problem of Ethical Norms in Max Scheler" (advisor: Quentin Lauer).
1976	Northwestern University	Thomas Michael Mulligan, "Max Scheler and G. E. Moore: A Critical Comparison of Their Axiological Ethical Systems."

1977	Boston College	Quentin Persifor Smith, "The Phenomenology of Feeling: A Critical Development of the Theories of Feeling in Husserl, Scheler, and Sartre" (advisor: Richard Stevens).
1978	Northwestern University	Edward Victor [Collins] Vacek, "Anthropological Foundations of Scheler's Ethics of Love."
1981	De Paul University	Michael Joseph Czopek, "Max Scheler's Problem of Religion: A Critical Exposition" (advisor: Parvis Emad).
1982	De Paul University	Kenneth W. Stikkers, "Toward a Sociology of Space: An Analysis of Spatial Experience in Technological Society, with Special Attention to the Philosophy of Max Scheler" (advisor: Manfred Frings).
1984	University of Notre Dame	Frederick Stephen Schneck, "Personalism as Political Theory: A Study of the Works of Max Scheler."
1985	Duquesne University	Philip Eugene Blosser, "Scheler's Alternative to Kant's Ethics" (advisor: Lester Embree).
1986	University of Toronto	Imtiaz Moosa, "Scheler's Philosophy of Value and Ethics in Relation to Kant's Ethics."
1988	De Paul University	David George Miller, "Nietzsche and Max Scheler on 'Ressentiment': An Inquiry into the Substructure of Hate."
1989	Fordham University	Rainier R. Altamarino Ibana, "The Principle of Solidarity in Max Scheler's Philosophy of Social Analysis" (advisor: Quentin Lauer).
1991	Univ. of Texas-Austin	Dennis Matthew Weiss, "Renewing the Anthropological Question" (advisor: Grayson Douglas Browning).

BIBLIOGRAPHY

Aldrich, Virgil C. "The Origin of the Apriori." *Journal of Philosophy* 60, No. 8 (April, 1954), 229–37.
Allison, Henry E. *Lessing and the Enlightenment*. Ann Arbor: University of Michigan Press, 1966.
Alphéus, Karl. *Kant und Scheler*. Ed. Barbara Wolandt. 2d ed. Bonn: Bouvier Verlag, 1981.
Anderson, G. "Die 'Materie' in Kants Tugendlehere und der Formalismus der kritischen Ethik." *Kant-Studien* 26 (1921), 288–97.
Anscombe, G. E. M. "Modern Moral Philosophy." *Philosophy* 33 (1958), 1–19; rpt. in *Collected Philosophical Papers*, by G. E. M. Anscombe. Vol. 2, *Ethics, Religion and Politics*, 26–42. Minneapolis: University of Minnesota Press, 1981.
Apel, Karl-Otto. *Transformation der Philosophie*. 2 vols. Frankfurt a.M.: Suhrkamp, 1973.
Aristotle. *The Works of Aristotle*. Ed. W. D. Ross. 12 vols. 1928; rpt. Oxford: Oxford University Press, 1966.
Ayer, A. J. *Language, Truth and Logic*. 2d ed. New York: Dover Books, 1946.
Barth, Karl. *Protestant Theology in the Nineteenth Century: Its Background and History*. Valley Forge: Judson Press, 1973.
Beck, Lewis White. *A Commentary on Kant's "Critique of Practical Reason."* Chicago: University of Chicago, 1960.
— — —. Introduction. *"Critique of Practical Reason" and Other Writings in Moral Philosophy*, by Immanuel Kant. Trans. and ed. L. W. Beck. Chicago: University of Chicago, 1949.
— — —. "Neo-Kantianism." *Encyclopedia of Philosophy*, ed. Paul Edwards. New York: Macmillan, 1967.
— — —. "Nicolai Hartmann's Criticism of Kant's Theory of Knowledge." *Philosophy and Phenomenological Research* 2 (June 1942), 472–500.
Blosser, Philip. "The A Priori in Phenomenology and the Legacy of Logical Empiricism." *Philosophy Today* 34, No. 3 (fall 1990), 195–205.
— — —. "Critical Study of *Moral Realism and Justification*." *Philosophia Reformata* (Netherlands) 55, No. 2 (1990), 177–83.
— — —. "Is Scheler's Ethic an Ethic of Virtue?" In P. Blosser et al. (eds.), *Japanese and Western Phenomenology*, 147–59. The Hague: Kluwer Academic Publishers, 1993.
— — —. "Kant and Phenomenology." *Philosophy Today* 30, No. 2 (summer 1986), 168–73.
— — —. "Moral and Nonmoral Values: A Problem in Scheler's Ethics." *Philosophy and Phenomenological Research* 48, No. 1 (Sept. 1987), 139–43.
— — —. "A Problem in Kant's Theory of Moral Feeling." *Lyceum* 3, No. 2 (Dec. 1991), 27–39.
— — —. Review of *Grace and Law: St. Paul, Kant, and the Hebrew Prophets*, by Heinz W. Cassirer. *Faith and Philosophy* 8, No. 3 (July 1991), 402–5.

Bochenski, I. M. *Contemporary European Philosophy.* Trans. D. Nicholl and K. Aschenbrenner. Berkeley: University of California, 1961.

Boelen, Bernard J. "The Question of Ethics in the Thought of Martin Heidegger." In *Heidegger and the Quest for Truth,* ed. Manfred S. Frings, 76–105. Chicago: Quadrangle Books, 1968.

Bollnow, Otto Friedrich. "Konkrete Ethik: Vorbetrachtungen zu einer philosophischen Tugendlehre." *Zeitschrift für philosophische Forschung* 6, No. 3 (winter 1952), 321–39.

Brandt, Richard B. "Epistemology and Ethics, Parallel Between." *Encyclopedia of Philosophy,* ed. Paul Edwards. New York: Macmillan, 1967.

— — —. "Ethical Relativism." In *Readings in Ethical Theory.* ed. Wilfrid Sellars and John Hospers, 335–45. 2d ed. New York: Appleton-Century-Crofts, 1970.

— — —. *Ethical Theory.* Englewood Cliffs, NJ: Prentice-Hall, 1959.

— — —. "The Future of Ethics." *Nous* 15 (1981), 31–40.

— — —. "A Quasi-Naturalist Definition." In *Readings in Ethical Theory,* ed. Wilfrid Sellars and John Hospers, 331–34. 2d ed. New York: Appleton-Century-Crofts, 1970.

— — —. *A Theory of the Good and the Right.* Oxford: Clarendon Press, 1979.

Brentano, Franz. *The Foundation and Construction of Ethics.* Compiled by Franziska Mayer-Hillebran. 1952. Trans. Elizabeth Hughes Schneewind. New York: Humanities Press, 1973.

— — —. *The Origin of Our Knowledge of Right and Wrong.* Trans. R. M. Chisholm and E. H. Schneewind. Ed. Oskar Kraus. London: Routledge & Kegan Paul, 1969.

— — —. *Psychology from an Empirical Standpoint.* Trans. A. C. Rancurello, et al. London: Routledge & Kegan Paul, 1973.

Broad, C. D. *Five Types of Ethical Theory.* Totowa, NJ: Littlefield, 1965.

Buber, Martin. "The Philosophical Anthropology of Max Scheler." *Philosophy and Phenomenological Research* 6 (1946), 307–21.

Caputo, John D. *Against Ethics: Contributions to a Poetics of Obligation with Constant Reference to Deconstruction.* Bloomington: Indiana University Press, 1993.

— — —. *Demythologizing Heidegger.* Bloomington: Indiana University Press, 1993.

— — —. "Kant's Ethics in Phenomenological Perspective." In *Kant and Phenomenology,* ed. Thomas M. Seebohm and Joseph J. Kockelmans, 129–46. Current Continental Research, No. 4. Washington, DC: Center for Advanced Studies in Phenomenology & University Press of America, 1984.

Carnap, Rudolf. *Meaning and Necessity: A Study in Semantics and Modal Logic.* 2d ed. Chicago: University of Chicago Press, 1956.

Cassirer, Ernst. *Kant's Life and Thought.* Trans. James Haden. New Haven: Yale University Press, 1981.

— — —. "Neo-Kantianism." *Encyclopaedia Britannica.* 14th ed. 1930.

Cassirer, Heinz W. *Grace and Law: St. Paul, Kant, and the Hebrew Prophets.* Edinburgh: Handsel Press, 1988.

Chisholm, Roderick M. "Brentano's Theory of Correct and Incorrect Emotion." *Révue Internationale de Philosophie* 78 (1966), 395–415.

— — —. "Evidence as Justification." *Journal of Philosophy* 68 (1961), 730–48.

Chisholm, Roderick M., and E. Sosa. "Intrinsic Preferability and the Problem of Supererogation." *Synthese* 16 (1966), 321–31.

— — —. "On the Logic of Intrinsically Better." *American Philosophical Quarterly* 3 (1966), 244–49.

De Boer, Theodor. *The Development of Husserl's Thought.* Trans. Theodore Plantinga. The Hague: Nijhoff, 1978.

Diemer, Alwin. "Zum Problem des Materialen in der Ethik Kants." *Kant-Studien* 45, Nos. 1–4 (1953–1954), 21–32.

Donagan, Alan. *The Theory of Morality.* Chicago: University of Chicago Press, 1977.

Dooyeweerd, Herman. "The Epistemological-Logical Gegenstand Relation and the Logical Subject-Object Relation." *Philosophia Reformata* (Netherlands) 41 (1976), 1–8.

— — —. *In the Twilight of Western Thought.* Nutley, NJ: Craig Press, 1960.

— — —. *A New Critique of Theoretical Thought.* Trans. David H. Freeman, et al. 4 vols. Amsterdam and Philadelphia, 1953–1958; rpt. Jordan Station, Ontario: Paideia Press, 1984.

Dufrenne, Mikel. *The Notion of the "A Priori."* Trans. Edward S. Casey. Evanston, IL: Northwestern University Press, 1966.

Duncan, A. R. C. *Practical Reason and Morality: A Study of Immanuel Kant's "Foundations for the Metaphysics of Morals."* Edinburgh: Thomas Nelson & Sons, 1957.

Dunlop, Francis. "Scheler's Idea of Man: Phenomenology vs. Metaphysics in the Late Works." *Aletheia* 2 (1981), 220–34.

— — —. "Scheler's Theory of Punishment." *Journal of the British Society for Phenomenology* 9, No. 3 (Oct. 1978), 167–74.

Du Plessis, S. I. M. "Max Scheler's Concern with the Highest Perfection." In *Truth and Reality: Philosophical Perspectives on Reality Dedicated to Professor H. G. Stoker,* 86–93. Braamfontein, South Africa: De Jong's, 1971.

Dupuy, Maurice. *La philosophie de Max Scheler, son évolution et son unité.* 2 vols. Paris: Presses Universitaires, 1959.

Eisler, Rudolf. *Kant-Lexikon.* 1930; rpt. Hildesheim: Georg Olms Verlagsbuchhandlung, 1964.

Emad, Parvis. *Heidegger and the Phenomenology of Values: His Critique of Intentionality.* Foreword by Walter Biemel. Glen Ellyn, IL: Torey Press, 1981.

— — —. "Heidegger on Transcendence and Intentionality: His Critique of Scheler." In *Heidegger: The Man and the Thinker,* ed. Thomas Sheehan, 145–58. Chicago: Precedent, 1981.

— — —. "Heidegger's Value-Criticism and Its Bearing on the Phenomenology of Values." *Research in Phenomenology* 7 (1977), 190–208.

Ermarth, Michael. *Wilhelm Dilthey: The Critique of Historical Reason.* Chicago: University of Chicago, 1978.

Findlay, J. N. *Axiological Ethics.* London: Macmillan, 1970.

———. *Meinong's Theory of Objects and Values*. 2d ed. Oxford: Clarendon, 1963.
———. *Values and Intentions: A Study in Value Theory and Philosophy of Mind*. London: George Allen & Unwin, 1961.
Fitch, Gregory W. "Plantinga's Necessary A Posteriori Truths." *Canadian Journal of Philosophy* 8, No. 2 (June 1978), 323–27.
Frankena, William K. *Ethics*. 2d ed. Englewood Cliffs, NJ: Prentice-Hall, 1973.
———. "Value and Valuation." *Encyclopedia of Philosophy*, ed. Paul Edwards. New York: Macmillan, 1967.
Frings, Manfred S. "The Background of Max Scheler's 1927 Reading of *Being and Time*: A Critique of a Critique through Ethics." *Philosophy Today*. 36, No. 2 (summer 1992), 99–114.
———. "Introduction to Three Essays by Max Scheler." In *Scheler, Person and Self-Value: Three Essays*, ed. M. S. Frings, xi–xxix. Dordrecht: Nijhoff, 1987.
———. *Max Scheler: A Concise Introduction into the World of a Great Thinker*. Pittsburgh: Duquesne University, 1965.
———. "Max Scheler and Kant: Two Paths toward the Same: The Moral Good." In *Kant and Phenomenology*, ed. Thomas M. Seebohm and Joseph J. Kockelmans, 101–14. Current Continental Research, No. 4. Washington, DC: Center for Advanced Research in Phenomenology & University Press of America, 1984.
———. "Max Scheler: Focusing on Rarely Seen Complexities of Phenomenology." In *Phenomenology in Perspective*, ed. F. J. Smith, 32–53. The Hague: Nijhoff, 1970.
———. "Der *Ordo Amoris* bei Max Scheler in seinen Beziehungen zu Materialer Wertethik und Ressentiment." *Zeitschrift für Philosophische Forschung* 19, No. 4 (1965), 57–76.
———. "The *Ordo Amoris* in Max Scheler: Its Relationship to His Value Ethics and to the Concept of Resentment," trans. F. J. Smith. In *Facets of Eros*, ed. F. J. Smith and Erling Eng, 40–60. The Hague: Nijhoff, 1972.
———. *Person und Dasein: Zur Frage der Ontologie des Wertseins*. The Hague: Nijhoff, 1969.
———. "Scheler and Heidegger." *Philosophy Today* 12 (1968), 21–30.
———. "Zur Idee des Friedens bei Kant und Max Scheler." *Kant-Studien* 66 (1975), 85–101.
———, ed. *Max Scheler (1874–1928): Centennial Essays*. The Hague: Nijhoff, 1974.
Frondizi, Risieri. *What Is Value?: An Introduction to Axiology*. 2d ed. La Salle, IL: Open Court, 1971.
Funke, Gerhard. *Phenomenology: Metaphysics or Method?* Trans. David J. Parent. Athens: Ohio University Press, 1987.
———. "The Primacy of Practical Reason in Kant and Husserl." In *Kant and Phenomenology*, ed. Thomas M. Seebohm and Joseph J. Kockelmans, 1–29. Current Continental Research, No. 4. Washington, DC: Center for Advanced Research in Phenomenology and University Press of America, 1984.

Good, Paul, ed. *Max Scheler im Gegenwartsgeschehen der Philosophie*. Bern: Francke, 1975.

Greiner, J. *Formale Gesetzethik und materiale Wertethik*. Heidelberg: Carl Winter's Universittsbuchhandlung, 1932.

Gurwitsch, Aron. "Phänomenologie der Thematik und des reinen Ich." *Psychologische Forschungen* 12 (1929), 279–381.

Habermas, Jürgen. *The Philosophical Discourse of Modernity*. Trans. Frederick Lawrence. Cambridge: MIT Press, 1987.

Hamburg, Carl H. "Kant's First Steps toward an Ethical Formalism." *Tulane Studies in Philosophy* 8 (1959), 103–10.

Hamlyn, D. W. "A Priori and A Posteriori." *The Encyclopedia of Philosophy*, ed. Paul Edwards. New York: Macmillan, 1967.

Hart, James G. Review of *Duty and Inclination*, by Hans Reiner. *Husserl Studies* 1 (1984), 307–14.

Hartman, R.S. "The Epistemology of the A Priori." *Philosophy and Phenomenological Research* 9 (June 1949), 731–36.

Hartmann, Nicolai. *Ethics*. Trans. S. Coit. 3 vols. 1932; rpt. Atlantic Highlands, NJ: Humanities, 1975.

———. "Max Scheler." *Kant-Studien* 33, Nos. 1–2 (1928), ix–xvi.

Hartmann, Wilfrid. "Max Scheler and the English Speaking World." *Philosophy Today* 12, No. 1 (spring 1968), 31–41.

Hegel, G. W. F. *Natural Law*. Trans. T. M. Knox. Philadelphia: University of Pennsylvania Press, 1975.

Heidegger, Martin. *The Basic Problems of Phenomenology*. Trans. Albert Hofstadter. Bloomington: Indiana University Press, 1982.

———. *Being and Time*. Trans. John Macquarrie and Edward Robinson. New York: Harper & Row, 1962.

———. *Holzwege*. Frankfurt am Mein: V. Klostermann, 1950.

———. "Letter on Humanism." Trans. F. Capuzzi and J. Glenn Gray. In *Basic Writings*, ed. David Farrell Krell, 193–242. New York: Harper and Row, 1977.

———. *Logik, Die Frage nach der Wahrheit*. Ed. W. Biemel. *Gesamtausgabe*, 21. Frankfurt: Klostermann, 1976.

———. "In Memory of Max Scheler." Trans. Thomas Sheehan. In *Heidegger: The Man and the Thinker*, ed. Thomas Sheehan, 159–60. Chicago: Precedent, 1981.

———. *Metaphysiche Anfangsgründe der Logik*. Ed. F-W. von Herrmann. *Gesamtausgabe*, 26. Frankfurt: Klostermann, 1978.

———. *Platons Lehre von der Wahrheit*. 1947; Bern: Francke, 1954.

———. *The Question Concerning Technology and Other Essays*. New York: Harper & Row, 1977.

———. *Schellings Abhandlung über das Wesen der Menschlichen Freiheit*. 1829; rpt. Tübingen: Niemeyer, 1971.

Heidemann, Ingeborg. *Untersuchungen zur Kantkritik Max Schelers*. Ph.D. diss., University of Bonn, 1948. Bonn: privately printed, 1955.

Heimsoeth, Heinz. "Metaphysische Motive in der Ausbildung des Kantischen Idealismus." *Kant-Studien* 29 (1924), 121–38.

———. *Studien zur Philosophie Immanuel Kants: Metaphysische Ursprünge und ontologische Grundlagen*. Köln: Balduin Pick, 1956.

Héring, Jean. "De Max Scheler à Hans Reiner: Remarques sur la Théorie des valeurs Morales dans la Mouvement Phénamenologique." *Revue d'Histoire des Sciences et de leurs Applications* (Paris) 40 (1960), 152–64.

Hermann, J. *Die Principien der formalen Gesetzesethik Kants und der materialen Wertethik Schelers: Beitrag zum Problem des Verhältnisses zwischen Psychologie und Ethik*. Breslau: Schelsny, 1928.

Horkheimer, Max, and Theodor W. Adorno. *Dialectic of Enlightenment*. Trans. John Cumming. New York: Seabury Press, 1972.

Husserl, Edmund. *Analysen zur Passiven Synthesis (1918–1926)*. Ed. Margot Fleischer. Husserliana 11. The Hague: Nijhoff, 1966.

———. *Cartesianische Meditationen und Pariser Vorträge*. 1950; rpt. The Hague: Nijhoff, 1975.

———. *Cartesian Meditations: An Introduction to Phenomenology*. Trans. Dorion Cairns. The Hague: Nijhoff, 1977.

———. *The Crisis of the European Sciences and Transcendental Philosophy*. Trans. David Carr. Evanston, IL: Northwestern University Press, 1970.

———. *Erfahrung und Urteil: Untersuchungen zur Genealogie der Logik*. Ed. Ludwig Landgrebe. Hamburg: Claassen & Goverts, 1948.

———. *Experience and Judgment: Investigations in a Genealogy of Logic*. Trans. James S. Churchill and Karl Ameriks. Evanston, IL: Northwestern University Press, 1973.

———. *Formal and Transcendental Logic*. Trans. Dorion Cairns. The Hague: Nijhoff, 1969.

———. *Formale und transzendentale Logik*. Halle: Niemeyer, 1929; rpt. The Hague: Nijhoff, 1974.

———. *Ideen zu einer reinen Phänomenologie und phäomenologischen Philosophie*. Vol. 1, *Allgemeine Einführung in die reine Phänomenologie*. Halle: Niemeyer, 1913; rpt. The Hague: Nijhoff, 1950.

———. *Ideas: General Introduction to Pure Phenomenology*. Trans. W. R. Boyce Gibson. New York: Macmillan, 1931; rpt. Collier, 1962.

———. *Ideas Pertaining to a Pure Phenomenology and to a Phenomenological Philosophy*, Book I. Trans. Fred Kersten. Norwell, MA: Kluwer Academic, 1983.

———. "Kant and the Idea of Transcendental Philosophy." Trans. Ted. E. Klein, Jr., and William E. Pohl. *Southwestern Journal of Philosophy* 5, No. 3 (Nov. 1974), 9–56.

———. *Die Krisis der europäischen Wissenschaften und die transzendentale Phänomenologie*. Ed. Walter Biemel. The Hague: Nijhoff, 1962; rpt. 1969.

———. *Logical Investigations*. Trans. John N. Findlay. New York: Humanities Press, 1970.

———. *Logische Untersuchungen*. 2 vols. Tübingen: M. Niemeyer, 1900, 1913.

———. *Phenomenological Psychology*. Trans. John Scanlon. The Hague: Nijhoff, 1977.

———. *The Phenomenology of Internal Time-Consciousness.* Trans. James Spencer Churchill. Bloomington: Indiana University Press, 1964.
———. *Vorlesungen über Ethik und Wertlehre: 1908–1914.* Ed. Ullrich Melle. Husserliana 28. Dordrecht: Kluwer Academic Publishers, 1988.
———. *Die Vorlesungen zur Phänomenologie des inneren Zeitbewußtseins.* Ed. R. Boehm. Halle: Niemeyer, 1929.
Ingarden, Roman. "A Priori Knowledge in Kant vs. A Priori Knowledge in Husserl." *Dialectics and Humanism* (autumn 1973), 5–18.
Jones, W. Tudor. *Contemporary Thought of Germany.* 2 vols. London: Williams & Northgate, 1930.
Kant, Immanuel. *Critique of Judgment.* Trans. J. H. Bernard. New York: Hafner, 1951.
———. *Critique of Practical Reason.* Trans. Lewis White Beck. Indianapolis: Bobbs-Merrill, 1956.
———. *Critique of Pure Reason.* Trans. Norman Kemp Smith. 1929; rpt. New York: St. Martin's Press, 1965.
———. *The Doctrine of Virtue.* Trans. Mary J. Gregor. Foreword by H. J. Paton. Philadelphia: University of Pennsylvania Press, 1964.
———. *Education.* Ann Arbor: The University of Michigan Press, 1960.
———. *The Educational Theory of Immanuel Kant,* trans. Edward F. Buchner. Philadelphia: J. B. Lippincott, 1904.
———. *Der einzig mögliche Beweisgrund zu einer Demonstration des Daseins Gottes.* Ed. Paul Menzer. KGS, 2:62–163.
———. *Foundations of the Metaphysics of Morals.* Trans. Lewis White Beck. Ed. Robert Paul Wolff. Indianapolis: Bobbs-Merrill, 1969.
———. *Grundlegung zur Metaphysik der Sitten.* Ed. Paul Menzer. KGS, 4:385–463.
———. *Kant's "Critique of Practical Reason" and Other Works on the Theory of Ethics.* 6th ed. Trans. Thomas Kingsmill Abbott. London: Longmans, Green and Co., 1909.
———. *Kants Gesammelte Schriften.* 28 vols. Berlin: Knigliche Preuische Akademie der Wissenschaften, 1902–.
———. *Kant's Political Writings.* Ed. Hans Reiss. Trans. H. B. Nisbet. Cambridge: Cambridge University Press, 1971.
———. *Kritik der praktischen Vernunft.* Ed. Paul Natorp. KGS, 5:1–163.
———. *Kritik der reinen Vernunft.* Ed. Raymund Schmidt. Hamburg: Felix Meiner Verlag, 1956.
———. *Kritik der Urteilskraft.* Ed. Wilhelm Windelband. KGS, 5:165–485.
———. *Lectures on Ethics.* Trans. Louis Infield. 1930; rpt. Indianapolis: Hackett, 1963.
———. *Die Metaphysik der Sitten.* Ed. Paul Natorp. KGS, 6:203–493.
———. *The One Possible Basis for a Demonstration of the Existence of God.* Trans. Gordon Treash. New York: Abaris Books, 1979.
———. *On History.* Ed. Lewis White Beck. Trans. Lewis White Beck, et al. Indianapolis: Bobbs-Merrill, 1963.

———. "On the Proverb: That May Be True in Theory, But Is of No Practical Use." In his *Perpetual Peace and Other Essays*, 61–92. Trans. Ted Humphrey. Indianapolis: Hackett, 1983.

———. *Prolegomena zu einer jeden künftigen Metaphisik*. Ed. Benno Erdmann. KGS, 4:254–383.

———. *Prolegomena to Any Future Metaphysics*. Trans. Lewis White Beck. Indianapolis: Bobbs-Merrill, 1950.

———. "Reflexion 7202." *Moralphilosophie, Rechtsphilosophie und Religionsphilosophie*. In *Kant's handschriftlicher Nachlaß*, 6. Berlin: Walter de Bruyter, 1934. KGS, 19:276–82.

———. *Die Religion innerhalb der Grenzen der bloßen Vernunft*. Ed. Georg Wobbermin. KGS, 6:1–202.

———. *Religion within the Limits of Reason Alone*. Trans. Theodore M. Greene and Hoyt H. Hudson. La Salle, IL: Open Court, 1934; rpt. New York: Harper & Brothers, 1960.

———. *Theorie und Praxis: Über den Gemeinspruch: Das mag in der Theorie richtig sein, taugt aber nicht für die Praxis*. Ed. Heinrich Maier. KGS, 8:273–313.

Kelly, Eugene. *Max Scheler*. Boston: Twayne, G. K. Hall & Co., 1977.

Kern, Iso. *Husserl und Kant: Eine Untersuchung Über Husserls Verhältnis zu Kant und zum Neukantianismus*. The Hague: Nijhoff, 1964.

Klein, Ted. "Husserl's Kantian Meditations." *Southwestern Journal of Philosophy* 5, No. 3 (Nov. 1974), 69–82.

Kockelmans, Joseph J., ed. *Contemporary European Ethics: Selected Readings*. Garden City, NY: Anchor, 1972.

Kripke, Saul A. *Naming and Necessity*. Cambridge: Harvard University Press, 1980.

Kruschwitz, Robert, and Robert Roberts, eds. *The Virtues: Contemporary Essays on Moral Character*. Belmont: Wadsworth, 1986.

Lachterman, David R. Translator's Introduction. *Selected Philosophical Essays*, by Max Scheler. Trans. David R. Lachterman. Evanston, IL: Northwestern University Press, 1973.

Lauer, Quentin. *Edmund Husserl: 1859–1959*. The Hague: Nijhoff, 1956.

———. "The Phenomenological Ethics of Max Scheler." *International Philosophical Quarterly* 1 (1961), 273–300.

Lavely, John H. "Personalism." *Encyclopedia of Philosophy*, ed. Paul Edwards. New York: Macmillan, 1967.

Levinas, Emmanuel. *The Theory of Intuition in Husserl's Phenomenology*. Trans. André Orianne. Evanston, IL: Northwestern University Press, 1973.

———. *Totality and Infinity*. Trans. Alphonso Lingis. Pittsburgh: Duquesne University Press, 1969.

Lichtigfeld, A. "A Scheler-Renaissance." *Tijdschrift voor Filosofie* 37, No. 4 (Dec. 1975), 711–15.

Luther, Arthur R. "Scheler's Person and Nishida's Active Self as Centers of Creativity." *Philosophy Today* 21 (summer 1977), 126–42.

MacIntyre, Alasdair. *After Virtue.* Notre Dame: University of Notre Dame Press, 1981.
――― . *Whose Justice? Which Rationality?* Notre Dame: University of Notre Dame Press, 1988.
Mackie, J. L. *Ethics: Inventing Right and Wrong.* Harmondsworth: Penguin Books, 1981.
Marsh, James L., et al., eds. *Modernity and Its Discontents.* New York: Fordham University Press, 1992.
Marx, Werner. *Is There a Measure on Earth? Foundations for a Nonmetaphysical Ethics.* Trans. Thomas J. Nenon and Reginald Lilly. Chicago: University of Chicago Press, 1987.
McGowan, John. *Postmodernism and Its Critics.* Ithaca: Cornell University Press, 1991.
Megill, Allan. *Prophets of Extremity.* Berkeley: University of California Press, 1985.
Meinong, Alexius. *On Emotional Presentation.* 1917. Trans. Marie-Luise Kalsi. Foreword by J. N. Findlay. Evanston, IL: Northwestern University Press, 1972.
Merleau-Ponty, Maurice. *Signs.* Trans. Richard C. McCleary. Evanston, IL: Northwestern University Press, 1964.
――― . *The Visible and the Invisible.* Trans. Alphonso Lingis. Evanston, IL: Northwestern University Press, 1968.
Mohanty, J. N. *The Possibility of Transcendental Philosophy.* Phaenomenologica 98. Dordrecht: Nijhoff, 1985.
Mongis, Henri. *Heidegger et la Critique de la Notion de Valeur.* The Hague: Nijhoff, 1976.
Moore, G. E. Review of *The Origin of the Knowledge of Right and Wrong*, by Franz Brentano. *International Journal of Ethics* 14 (1903), 115–23.
――― . *Principia Ethica.* 1903; rpt. Cambridge: Cambridge University Press, 1982.
Moosa, Imtiaz. "Scheler's Philosophy of Value and Ethics in Relation to Kant's Ethics," Ph.D. diss., University of Toronto, 1986.
Moser, Paul K., ed. *A Priori Knowledge.* Oxford: Oxford University Press, 1987.
Navickas, Joseph L. "N. Lossky's Moral Philosophy and M. Scheler's Phenomenology." *Studies in Soviet Thought* 18, No. 2 (May 1978), 121–30.
Nietzsche, Friedrich. "The Genealogy of Morals." In *The Basic Writings of Nietzsche*, trans. and ed. Walter Kaufmann, 449–599. New York: The Modern Library, 1968.
Nitta, Yoshihiro, and Hirotaka Tatematsu, eds. *Japanese Phenomenology.* Analecta Husserliana 8. Dordrecht: D. Reidel, 1979.
Nowell-Smith, Patrick Horace. *Ethics.* London: Penguin Books, 1954.
Nozick, Robert. *Philosophical Explanations.* Cambridge: Harvard University Press, 1981.
Olthuis, James H. *Facts, Values and Ethics.* Assen, The Netherlands: Van Gorcum, 1969.

Ortega y Gasset, José. "Max Scheler." *Neue Schweitzer Rundschau* 34 (Oct. 1928), 725–29.
— — —. "Max Scheler: un ubriaco di essenze." *Ethica* 7 (1968), 161–67.
— — —. *The Modern Theme*. Trans. J. Cleugh. New York: Harper, 1961.
Orth, Ernst Wolfgang. "Husserl, Scheler, Heidegger: Eine Einführung in das Problem der philosophischen Komparatistik." *Phänomenologische Forschungen*. Vols. 6–7, *Husserl, Scheler, Heidegger in der Sicht neuer Quellen*. Freiburg im Breisgau und München: Verlag Karl Alber, 1978.
Paton, H. J. *The Categorical Imperative: A Study in Kant's Moral Philosophy*. London: Hutchinson, 1947.
— — —. Foreword. *The Doctrine of Virtue*, by Immanuel Kant. Trans. Mary J. Gregor. Philadelphia: University of Pennsylvania Press, 1964.
— — —. *The Moral Law*. London: Hutchinson's University Library, 1948.
Perrin, Ronald F. "A Commentary on Max Scheler's Critique of the Kantian Ethic." *Journal of the History of Philosophy* 12 (Aug. 1974), 347–59.
Perry, Ralph Barton. "The Definition of Value." *The Journal of Philosophy* 11 (1914), 141–62.
— — —. *General Theory of Value*. New York: Longman's Green & Co, 1926; rpt. Cambridge: Harvard University Press, 1967.
— — —. *Realms of Value: A Critique of Human Civilization*. Cambridge: Harvard University Press, 1954.
— — —. "Value as an Objective Predicate." *The Journal of Philosophy* 28 (1931), 477–84.
Ping-cheung Lo. "A Critical Reevaluation of the Alleged 'Empty Formalism' of Kantian Ethics." *Ethics* 91, No. 2 (Jan. 1981), 181–201.
Plantinga, Alvin. *The Nature of Necessity*. Oxford: Clarendon Press, 1974.
— — —. *Warrant and Proper Function*. New York: Oxford University Press, 1993.
— — —. *Warrant: The Current Debate*. New York: Oxford University Press, 1993.
Prall, D. W. *A Study in the Theory of Value*. University of California Publications in Philosophy, Vol. 3, No. 2. N.p., 1921.
Puolimatka, Tapio. *Moral Realism and Justification*. Helsinki: Finnish Academy of Science and Letters, 1989.
Quine, Willard V. "Two Dogmas of Empiricism." In his *From a Logical Point of View*, 2d ed., 20–46. Cambridge: Harvard University Press, 1953.
Ranly, Ernest W. *Scheler's Phenomenology of Community*. The Hague: Nijhoff, 1966.
Regan, Tom. *Bloomsbury's Prophet: G. E. Moore and the Development of His Moral Philosophy*. Philadelphia: Temple University Press, 1986.
Reiner, Hans. *Duty and Inclination: The Fundamentals of Morality Discussed and Redefined with Especial Regard to Kant and Schiller*. Trans. Mark Santos. Phaenomenologica 93. The Hague: Nijhoff, 1983.
— — —. "Good and Evil: Origin and Essence of the Basic Moral Distinctions." Trans. Joseph J. Kockelmans. In *Contemporary European Ethics*, ed. J. J. Kockelmans, 158–81. Garden City, NY: Anchor, 1972.

Reiss, Hans, ed. *Kant's Political Writings*. Trans. H. B. Nisbet. Cambridge: Cambridge University Press, 1971.

Rescher, Nicholas. *Introduction to Value Theory*. Englewood Cliffs, NJ: Prentice-Hall, 1969; rpt. Washington, DC: University Press of America, 1982.

Ricoeur, Paul. *Husserl: An Analysis of His Phenomenology*. Trans. E. G. Ballard and L. E. Embree. Evanston, IL: Northwestern University Press.

— — —. Preface. *The Notion of the "A Priori,"* by Mikel Dufrenne. Trans. Edward S. Casey. Evanston, IL: Northwestern University Press, 1966.

Rintelen, Joachim von. *Contemporary German Philosophy and Its Background*. Bonn: Bouvier, 1970.

Ritter, Joachim, ed. *Historisches Wörterbuch der Philosophie*. Vol. 1. Basel and Stuttgart: Schwabe & Co. Verlag, 1971.

Rorty, Richard. *Philosophy and the Mirror of Nature*. Princeton: Princeton University Press, 1979.

Roth, Alois. *Edmund Husserls ethische Untersuchungen: Dargestellt anhand seiner Vorlesungsmanuskripte*. The Hague: Nijhoff, 1960.

Sallis, John. *The Gathering of Reason*. Athens: Ohio University Press, 1980.

— — —. *Phenomenology and the Return to Beginnings*. Pittsburgh: Duquesne University Press, 1973.

Sartre, Jean-Paul. *Being and Nothingness*. Trans. Hazel E. Barnes. New York: Philosophical Library, 1956.

— — —. *The Transcendence of the Ego*. Trans. Forrest Williams and Robert Kirkpatrick. New York: Farrar, Straus and Giroux, 1957.

Scheler, Max. "Deutsche Philosophie der Gegenwart." In *Deutsches Leben der Gegenwart*, ed. P. Witkop, 197–98. Berlin: Wegweiser, 1922.

— — —. *Formalism in Ethics and Non-Formal Ethics of Values*. Trans. Manfred S. Frings and Roger L. Funk. Evanston, IL: Northwestern University Press, 1973.

— — —. *Der Formalismus in der Ethik und die Materiale Wertethik*. Ed. Maria Scheler. GW, 2, 1954.

— — —. *Früheschriften*. Ed. Maria Scheler and M. S. Frings. GW, 1, 1971.

— — —. *Gesammelte Werke*. 13 vols. Bern: Francke Verlag, 1954–.

— — —. "Idealism and Realism." In his *Selected Philosophical Essays*. Trans. David R. Lachterman. Evanston, IL: Northwestern University Press, 1973.

— — —. "The Idea of Peace and Pacifism." Parts 1 and 2. *Journal of the British Society for Phenomenology* 7 (Oct. 1976), 154–66; 8 (Jan. 1977), 36–50.

— — —. "Idealismus–Realismus." *Philosophischer Anzeiger* 2 (1927); rpt. in *Späte Schriften*, ed. Manfred S. Frings. GW, 9, 1976.

— — —. "Die Idole der Selbsterkenntnis." In his *Vom Umsturz der Werte*. 4th rev. ed. Ed. Maria Scheler. GW, 3, 1955.

— — —. "The Idols of Self-Knowledge." In his *Selected Philosophical Essays*. Trans. David R. Lachterman. Evanston, IL: Northwestern University Press, 1973.

— — —. "Lehre von den drei Tatsachen." In *Schriften aus dem Nachlaß*. Vol. 1, *Zur Ethik und Erkenntnislehre*. 2d ed. Ed. Maria Scheler. GW, 10, 1957.

———. *Liebe und Erkenntnis.* 2d ed. Bern: Francke Verlag, 1970.

———. *Logik,* Vol. 1. Ed. Rudolph Berlinger and Wiebke Schrader. Elementa 3. Atlantic Highlands, NJ: Humanities Press, 1975.

———. *Man's Place in Nature.* Trans. Hans Meyerhoff. New York: Beacon, Noonday Press, 1960.

———. "Manuskripte zur Lehre vom Grunde aller Dinge." In *Schriften aus dem Nachlaß,* Vol. 2, *Erkenntnislehre und Metaphysik.* Ed. Manfred S. Frings. GW, 11, 1979.

———. *The Nature of Sympathy.* Trans. Peter Heath. New Haven: Yale University Press, 1954; rpt. Hamden, Conn.: Archon Books, 1970.

———. *On the Eternal in Man.* Trans. Bernard Noble. London: SCM Press, 1960.

———. "Ordo Amoris." In *Schriften aus dem Nachlaß.* Vol. 1, *Zur Ethik und Erkenntnislehre.* 2d ed. Ed. Maria Scheler. GW, 10, 1957.

———. "Ordo Amoris." In his *Selected Philosophical Essays.* Trans. David R. Lachterman. Evanston, IL: Northwestern University Press, 1973.

———. "Phänomenologie und Erkenntnistheorie." In *Schriften aus dem Nachlaß.* Vol. 1, *Zur Ethik und Erkenntnislehre.* 2d ed. Ed. Maria Scheler. GW, 10, 1957.

———. "Phenomenology and the Theory of Cognition." In his *Selected Philosophical Essays.* Trans. David R. Lachterman. Evanston, IL: Northwestern University Press, 1973.

———. *Philosophical Perspectives.* Trans. Oscar A. Haac. Boston: Beacon Press, 1958.

———. *Philosophische Weltanschauung.* Bonn: Verlag Friedrich Cohen, 1929; rpt. in *Dalp-Taschenbücher* CCCI, 1954; rpt. in *Späte Schriften,* ed. Manfred S. Frings. GW, 9, 1976.

———. "Probleme einer Soziologie des Wissens." In *Versuche zu einer Soziologie des Wissens,* ed. Max Scheler. Vol. 2. Schriften des Forschungsinstitutes für Sozialwissenschaften in Köln. Munich: Duncker & Humbolt, 1924; rpt. in *Die Wissensformen und die Gesellschaft.* Ed. Maria Scheler. GW, 8, 1960.

———. *Problems of a Sociology of Knowledge.* Trans. Manfred S. Frings. Ed. Kenneth W. Stikkers. London: Routledge & Kegan Paul, 1983.

———. "Problems with a Sociology of Knowledge." Trans. Ernest Ranly. *Philosophy Today* 12, No. 1 (spring 1968), 42–71.

———. "Reality and Resistance: On *Being and Time,* Section 43." Trans. Thomas J. Sheehan. *Listening* 12, No. 3 (fall 1977), 61–73; rpt. in *Heidegger: The Man and the Thinker,* ed. Thomas Sheehan, 133–44. Chicago: Precedent, 1981. This is a translation of part 5, "Das emotionale Realitätsproblem," of "Idealismus–Realismus."

———. *Ressentiment.* Ed. Lewis A. Coser. Trans. William Holdheim. New York: Free Press, 1961.

———. *Schriften aus dem Nachlaß.* Vol. 3, *Philosophische Anthropologie.* Edited by Manfred S. Frings. GW, 12, 1987.

———. "The Theory of the Three Facts." In his *Selected Philosophical Essays*. Trans. David R. Lachterman. Evanston, IL: Northwestern University Press, 1973.
———. "Die Stellung des Menschen im Kosmos." *Der Leuchter* 8 (1927); rpt. in *Späte Schriften*. Ed. Manfred S. Frings. GW, 9, 1976.
———. "Über Ressentiment und moralisches Werturteil: Ein Beitrag zur Pathologie der Kultur." *Zeitschrift für Pathopsychologie* 1, Nos. 2–3 (1912); rev. as "Das Ressentiment im Aufbau der Moralen," in *Abhandlung und Aufsätse*, vol. 1. Leipzig: Verlag der Weissen Bücher, 1915; rpt. in *Vom Umsturz der Werte*, ed. Maria Scheler. GW, 3, 1955.
———. *Vom Ewigen im Menschen*. Ed. Maria Scheler. GW, 5, 1954.
———. *Wesen und Formen der Sympathie*. Ed. Manfred S. Frings. GW, 7, 1973.
Schiller, Johann Christoph Friedrich von. *Schillers Philosophische Schriften und Gedichte*, ed. Eugen Kuhnemann, 3d ed. Leipzig: Durr, 1922.
Schilpp, Paul Arthur. "The Doctrine of Illusion and Error in Scheler's Phenomenology." *Journal of Philosophy* 24 (1927), 624–33.
———. "Ethical Formalism." *Dictionary of Philosophy*. Ed. D. D. Runes. Totowa, NJ: Littlefield, 1962.
———. "Formal Problems of Scheler's Sociology of Knowledge." *Philosophical Review* 36 (1927), 101–20.
———. *Kant's Pre-Critical Ethics*. Evanston, IL: Northwestern University, 1938.
Schlick, Moritz. "Is There a Factual A Priori?" Trans. Wilfrid Sellars. In *Readings in Philosophical Analysis*, ed. Herbert Feigl and Wilfrid Sellars. New York: Appleton-Century-Crofts, 1949; rpt. in *Phenomenology and Existentialism*, ed. Robert C. Solomon, 282–88. Lanham, MD: University Press of America, 1980.
Schroeder, H. H. "Some Common Misinterpretations of the Kantian Ethics." *Philosophical Review* 49 (July 1940), 424–46.
Schutz, Alfred. "Max Scheler's Epistemology and Ethics, I." *Review of Metaphysics* 11 (1957), 304–14; 486–501.
Seebohm, Thomas M. *Die Bedingungen der Möglichkeit einer Transzendentalphilosophie*. Bonn: Bouvier, 1962.
———. Preface. *Kant and Phenomenology*, ed. Thomas M. Seebohm and Joseph J. Kockelmans. Current Continental Research, No. 4. Washington, DC: Center for Advanced Research in Phenomenology and University Press of America, 1984.
Sheehan, J. Thomas, ed. *Heidegger: The Man and the Thinker*. Chicago: Precedent, 1981.
Shimomissé, Eiichi. *Die Phänomenologie und das Problem der Grundlegung der Ethik: An Hand des Versuches von Max Scheler*. The Hague: Nijhoff, 1971.
———. "Welches ist primär, 'sittlich gut handeln' oder 'sittlich gut sein'? (mit besonderer Rücksicht auf Max Schelers Versuch der Grundlegung der Ethik)." In *Akten des XIV Internationalen Kongresses für Philosophie, Wien: 2–9 Sept., 1968*, Part 6, 511–14. Vienna: Herder, 1968.

Shuster, George N. Introductory Statement. "Symposium on the Significance of Max Scheler for Philosophy and Social Science." *Philosophy and Phenomenological Research* 2, No. 3 (March 1942), 269–72.

Sidgwick, Henry. *The Methods of Ethics.* London: Macmillan, 1907; rpt. Indianapolis: Hackett, 1981.

Silber, John R. "The Ethical Significance of Kant's *Religion*," In Part 2 of the Introduction to *Religion within the Limits of Reason Alone*, by Immanuel Kant, lxxix–cxxxvii. Trans. Theodore M. Greene and Hoyt H. Hudson. 1934; rpt. New York: Harper & Brothers, 1960.

———. "Kant and the Mythic Roots of Morality." In *Foundations of Ethics*, ed. Leroy S. Rouner. Notre Dame: University of Notre Dame Press, 1983.

———. "Procedural Formalism in Kant's Ethics." *Review of Metaphysics* 28, No. 2 (Dec. 1974), 197–236.

———. "Der Schematismus der Praktischen Vernunft." *Kant-Studien* 56 (1966), 253–73.

Simmel, Georg. *Einleitung in die Moralwissenschaft: Eine Kritik der ethischen Grundbegriffe.* Stuttgart: Cottasche, 1911.

Singer, M. G. *Generalization in Ethics.* London: Eyre & Spottiswoode, 1963.

Sinha, Debabrata. "Phenomenology, vis-à-vis Kant and Neopositivism, on the Issue of the Apriori." *Archiv für Geschichte der Philosophie* 53, No. 1 (1971), 41–57.

Smith, Quentin. "Max Scheler and the Classification of Feelings." *Journal of Phenomenological Psychology* 9, Nos. 1–2 (1978), 114–38.

———. "Scheler's Critique of Husserl's Theory of the World of the Natural Standpoint." *Modern Schoolman* 55, No. 4 (1977–1978), 387–96.

———. "Scheler's Stratification of Emotional Life and Strawson's *Person*." *Philosophical Studies* 25 (1977), 103–27.

Sokolowski, Robert. *The Formation of Husserl's Concept of Constitution.* The Hague: Nijhoff, 1964.

———. *Husserlian Meditations: How Words Present Things.* Evanston, IL: Northwestern University Press, 1974).

———. *Moral Action: A Phenomenological Study.* Bloomington: Indiana University Press, 1985.

Solomon, Robert C. "Sense and Essence: Frege and Husserl." *International Philosophical Quarterly* 10, No. 3 (1970); rpt. in his *Phenomenology and Existentialism*, 258–82. Lanham, MD: University Press of America, 1980.

Spader, Peter H. "The Facts of Max Scheler." *Philosophy Today* 23 (fall 1979), 260–66.

———. "Language and the Phenomenologically Given." *Philosophy Today* 26 (fall 1982), 254–62.

———. "A New Look at Scheler's Third Period." *Modern Schoolman* 51, No. 2 (January 1974), 139–58.

———. "The Non-Formal Ethics of Value of Max Scheler and the Shift in His Thought." *Philosophy Today* 18, No. 3 (fall 1974), 217–33.

———. "Person, Acts and Meaning: Max Scheler's Insight." *New Scholasticism* 59, No. 2 (spring 1985), 200–12.

––––. "The Possibility of an *A Priori* Non-Formal Ethics: Max Scheler's Task." *Man and World* 9 (June 1976), 153–62.

––––. "Scheler's Phenomenological Given." *Journal of the British Society for Phenomenology* 9, No. 3 (Oct. 1978), 150–57.

Spiegelberg, Herbert. *The Phenomenological Movement*. 2 vols. 2d ed. The Hague: Nijhoff, 1976.

Staude, John R. *Max Scheler, 1874–1928: An Intellectual Portrait*. New York: Free Press, 1967.

Steiner, George. *Real Presences*. Chicago: University of Chicago Press, 1991.

Stevenson, Charles L. "The Emotive Meaning of Ethical Terms," *Mind* 46 (1937); rpt. in *Readings in Ethical Theory*, 2d ed., ed. Wilfrid Sellars and John Hospers, 254–66. New York: Appleton-Century-Crofts, 1970.

––––. *Ethics and Language*. 1944; rpt. New Haven: Yale University Press, 1976.

Stevenson, Leslie. *Seven Theories of Human Nature*. New York: Oxford University Press, 1974.

Stoker, H. G. *Das Gewissen: Erscheinungsformen und Theorien*. Bonn: Verlag von Friedrich Cohen, 1925.

Strasser, Stephan. "Phenomenological Trends in European Psychology (Husserl, Scheler, Pfänder, and others)." *Philosophy and Phenomenological Research* 9 (1957–1958), 18–34.

––––. *Phenomenology of Feeling: An Essay on the Phenomena of the Heart*. Foreword by Paul Ricoeur. Trans. with Introduction by Robert E. Wood. Philosophical Series, 34. Pittsburgh: Duquesne University Press, 1977.

––––. "Het Problem van de Deformalisatie van de Ethik naar Aanleiding van Kant." *Tijdschrift voor Filosofie* 43, No. 3 (Sept. 1981), 465–86.

Sweeney, Robert D. "The Affective 'A Priori.'" *The Phenomenological Realism of Possible Worlds, the "A Priori," Activity and Passivity of Consciousness, Phenomenology and Culture*, ed. Anna-Teresa Tymienieka, 80–97. Analecta Husserliana 3. Dordrecht: D. Reidel, 1974.

––––. "Affectivity and the Life World." *The Crisis of Culture*, ed. Anna-Teresa Tymienieka, 71–82. Analecta Husserliana 5. Dordrecht: D. Reidel, 1976.

––––. "'Cognition and Work'; *Erkenntnis und Arbeit*." *The Phenomenology of Man and of the Human Condition*, ed. Anna-Teresa Tymienieka, 97–111. Analecta Husserliana 14. Dordrecht: D. Reidel, 1983.

Swiderski, Edward M. "Phenomenology in the *Filosofskaja Enciklopedija*." *Studies in Soviet Thought* 18, No. 1 (Feb. 1978), 57–66.

Tallon, Andrew. "The Concept of the Heart in Strasser's *Phenomenology of Feeling*." *American Catholic Philosophical Quarterly* 66, No. 3 (summer 1992), 341–60.

Taylor, Richard. *Good and Evil: A New Direction*. New York: Macmillan, 1970.

Trebicki, J. "Die Kant-Rezeption in der Axiologie Max Schelers." In *Wissenschaftliche Zeitschrift der Humbolt-Universität zu Berlin. Gesellschafts- und Sprachwissenschaftliche Reihe* 24, No. 2 (1975), 179–80.

Uchiyama, Minoru. *Das Wertwidrige in der Ethik Max Schelers*. Ed. Gerhard Funke. Mainzer Philosophische Forschungen 4. Bonn: H. Bouvier Verlag, 1966.

Urmson, J. O. *The Emotive Theory of Ethics*. London: Hutchinson University Library, 1968.

Van De Pitte, M. M. "Comments on a Claim that Some Phenomenological Statements May Be A Posteriori." *Metaphilosophy* 15, Nos. 3 and 4 (July–Oct. 1984), 248–55.

— — —. "Schlick's Critique of Phenomenological Propositions." *Philosophy and Phenomenological Research* 45 (Dec. 1984), 195–226.

Wallace, James. *Virtues and Vices*. Ithaca, NY: Cornell University Press, 1978.

Williams, T. C. *The Concept of the Categorical Imperative*. Oxford: Clarendon, 1968.

Wolandt, Gerd. "Nachwort." In *Kant und Scheler*, by Karl Alphéus. Ed. B. Wolandt. Bonn: Bouvier, 1981.

Wojtyła, Karol. *The Acting Person*, trans. Andrzej Potocki. Dordrecht: D. Reidel, 1979.

— — —. "Ocena możliwośei zbudowania etyki chrześcijańskiej przy założeniach systemn Maksa Schelera" [*On the Possibility of Constructing a Christian Ethics on the Basis of Max Scheler's Philosophical System*]. Ph.D. diss., Catholic University of Lublin, 1959.

— — —. *Das Problem der Trennung von Erlebnis und Akt im Lichte der Anschauung Kants und Schelers, Primat Des Geistes*. Stuttgart: Seewald Verlag, 1979.

Wolff, Robert Paul. Introduction. *Foundations of the Metaphysics of Morals*, by Immanuel Kant, vii–xx. Trans. L. W. Beck. Indianapolis: Bobbs-Merrill, 1969.

INDEX

a posteriori, 9, 27, 29, 34f., 41, 55, 57, 106, 198, 210
a priori, xiii, 27–57, 96, 102, 106f., 144f., 160, 169, 171, 173f., 178, 186; emotional, 37, 50, 106, 173f.; Husserl and, xiii, 32, 46, 51, cf. 30; in analytic philosophy, 28, 47, 48–50, 55; in Continental philosophy, 27–30, 32, 47–51; intuition and, 6, 15f., 33, 39, 42f., 49, 51; logical empiricism, 27, 46–49, 51, 55, 57; morality and, 8, 28, 39; materialist reduction of, 47ff., 53; relative, 39, 42; subjectivity vs. objectivity of, 40–42, 43–47, 55; term, 28; values and, 16f., 52, 63, 186
Abbott, Thomas K., xvi
abbreviations, ixf., 21 n. 17, cf. xiv
Abelard, 55
ability, epistemic, 39f.; moral, 128, 136f., 142, 156, 184f.
abortion, 73, 144
absolute and relative values (see "value")
absolute good, 74, 92, 152, cf. 94
acts, 37, 40, 45, 47, 51, 61, 76, 80, 85, 88f., 108f., 116, 122, 140, 146–48, 155, 157, 162, 164–67, 169, 173, 181–83, 185f., 210; disposition and, 17, 159–62, 176; ends and, 61, 70, 162; functions and, 108f., 122, 164; logical vs. emotive, 47; moral (see "moral action"); person and, xv, 40, 186; realized in time, 166; self and, 164–67; supratemporal, 164, 166; unity of, 37, 162, 166, 186
Adorno, Theodor W., 153, 200
aesthetics, 115, 171, 175, 174
affect, 186
affectivity, xiii, 29, 99ff., 105–8, 100ff., 112, 113, 121, 161, 174, 173f.
agency, 32, 46, 51f., 61, 71, 77, 85, 93, 104, 147f., 157, 171, 179
aging, 177
Aldrich, Virgil C., 46, 195
Allison, Henry E., 157, 195
Alphéus, Karl, 22, 39, 69, 120, 138, 169; *Kant und Scheler*, 53, 131, 138, 154, 177, 195
amorality, 141
analytic philosophy, 48, 57, 74, 81, 176
analytic, and a priori, 47, 55; synthetic vs. 55
analyticity, 47

Anderson, G., 69, 195
Anscombe, G. E. M., 151, 179, 195
anthropologism, 32, 35, 40, 42, 106
anthropology (cf. "human nature," "person"), 4, 10, 31, 162–68, 177, 185–87, 191, 193
anti-foundationalism, 17, 23, 95, 180, 205
antirealism, 23, 45
Apel, Karl-Otto, 55, 195
appearance, 31, 33, 38
apperception, 40, 163, 169
approval, disapproval, 148f.
apriorism, xi, xiii, 50, 54, 60, 122, 139
Aquinas, St. Thomas, 155, 185
aretaic ethics (cf. "virtue ethics"), 179
Aristotelianism, 183, 185
Aristotle, xi, xiv, 10, 13, 27, 46, 50, 55, 81, 112, 117–19, 122, 124, 180, 182–85, 195; and value (*axia*) 94; on moral character 117, 141, 175, 182; *Metaphysica* 81; *Nicomachean Ethics* 180, 182
assessment theories, 25, 129, 152
atomism, 38
Augustine, St., 107, 162
Austin, John, 24
authority, 134, 155
autonomy, 9, 44, 48, 71, 62, 91, 94, 104, 130, 140f., 148–50, 152, 157, 173, 181, 185, 188
axiological ethics, 14f., 59, 125, 133, 190, 192, 197
axiology, 3, 5f., 14, 20, 198
Ayer, A. J., 15, 24, 47, 195

Barrett, William, 192
Barth, Karl, 1, 195
bearers, of moral value, 67f., 89f., 164, 173; of nonmoral value, 85; of value, 9, 64ff., 66–68, 78, 82f., 85, 87, 133, 138, 160–62, 164, 170, 173, 184
Beck, Lewis White, 11, 20, 22, 25, 104f., 120; *Commentary*, 69, 101, 103, 105, 114, 120, 195
being, 5, 16, 30, 35f., 40, 42, 51, 75ff., 79–82, 94f., 164, 168; Heidegger and, 16, 75ff., 82, 199; 79–81; value theory and, 76, 78f.
Being-in-the-world, 17, 54, 79, 95
benevolence, 97, 175; in Hutcheson, 92
Bergson, Henri, 4

211

biology, 56, 84, 115, 167, 171, 174
blind obedience, 130f., 155, 181
blindness, axiological, 38, 125, 127f., 130f., 138; of duty, 181
Bloomsbury Circle, 15, 204
Blosser, Philip, vii, 50f., 56f., 92f., 97, 119, 187f., 189, 193, 195
Bochenski, I. M., xi, xv, 196
body, 36, 164, 177
Boelen, Bernard J., 23, 196
Bohatec, Josef, 101
Böhm-Bawerk, Eugen, 20
Boleyn, Anne, 156
Bollnow, Otto F., 90, 195
bracketing, 46, cf. 31
Bradley, F. H., 4
Brandt, Richard B., 13, 23, 25, 144f., 157, 196
Brentano, Franz, 6f., 14, 21, 77, 95, 116, 122, 124, 129, 152, 154, 196f., 203
Broad, C. D., 11, 22, 196
Browning, Grayson D., 193
Buber, Martin, xi, 177, 196
Büchner, Ludwig, 5

Calvin, John, 188
capability (see "ability")
Caputo, John D., xv, 91, 95, 141, 153, 157, 160f., 163
Carnap, Rudolf, 49, 196
Cartesianism, 29, 164, 200
Cassirer, Ernst, xi, 19f., 124, 196
Cassirer, Heinz W., 117, 124, 195f.
casuistry, 145f., cf. 143f.
categorical imperative, xiv, 7f., 11, 22, 28, 53, 60, 62, 70, 72f., 91f., 99, 126–28, 137–39, 149, 154, 172f., 178; phenomenological version of, 91f.
categories, 31, 39, 47
Catholicism, 1, 19, 89, 155
causal explanations, 31, 37
causality, 8, 36, 72, 102, 104, 106, 163, 170, 172
central emotional fulfillment, 111f., 164f., cf. 115, 173, 184f.
character (cf. "disposition"), 117f., 141, 175, 179, 182f., 185, 189, 207
chemistry, 110, 174
Chisholm, Roderick M., 6, 16f., 25, 95, 122, 197
choice, 92, 108, 114, 141, 147f., 157, 159f., 162, 173, 183f.
Christianity, xv, 73, 191
Church, 1, 19
cognition, 5, 30, 36, 42, 109
Cohen, Hermann, 5, 20
Cohn, Johas, 154
coincidence of duty, inclination, 61, 92, 136, 149, 182f.
colors, 34, 36, 39f., 42, 64, 77, 81, 96

commands, 60–62, 73, 92, 134–38, 140, 149, 154f., 173, 176, 181
Commenator, George E., 189, 192
community (cf. "intersubjectivity"), xi, 116, 167f., 190, 192
compulsion (see "constraint")
Comte, Auguste, 4, 110
conation, 8, 63, 68, 79, 90, 108–11, 114, 134–36, 138, 140, 173, 176, 184
conditionality, 30f., 34, 41f., 44f., 49, 54, 163f., 184
conditions of experience, 31f., 41, 51
conscience, 93, 110, 122, 134, 148–50, 154, 177, 209; and self-entrapment, 149f.
consciousness, 31, 34, 36, 55f., 75, 78, 82, 87, 92, 102–4, 119, 148, 173, 177, 184f.; doxic, 78; of law, 102–5
consequences, 61, 159, 162, 179, 183
consequentialism (cf. "utilitarianism"), 6–8, 18, 29, 59–61, 147
constant presence, 75f.
constitution, 32, 44, 46f., 52, 55, 77, 87, 171f.; genetic, 82; passive, 44, 46, 93
constraint, 60, 181, 184f.
constructivism, 5, 38, 43, 171, 180
content, xiii, 2, 5, 7, 11f., 34–37, 40, 49, 61, 69, 71–73, 78, 86f., 90f., 106, 120, 144, 156, 163, 174, 178, 180, 195, 197; of "humanity," 70; of disposition, 184
contentment, 62, 104f.
contingency, 28f., 34, 46, 60, 62f., 106
conversion, moral, 140, 152 n. 7, 162
Copernican Revolution, 29f., 42f., 171
Cornelius, H., 121
correspondence, and truth, 5, 20
counsels of prudence, 92
crimen carnis (masturbation), 153 n. 18
criteria, of essence, 34; of good, evil, 88; of moral value, 87, 97; of value ranks, 66, 97, 143; preference, 87, 150, 157; value realization, 87
critical theory, xi
critique, xvi, 2, 45, 76–80
Crucius, C. A., 62
culture, 4, 66, 110, 142, 144–46, 167, 177, 190
Czopek, Michael J., 189, 193

Dasein, 17, 54, 75, 78, 94, 177
De Boer, Theodor, 52, 197
death, 177
Decalogue, 154 n. 26
deception, 35, 52, 87, 140
decision, 148; decisionism, 18
deconstruction, 17f., 45, 180, 196, 205, 209
Deeken, Alfons T., 189, 192
definition, essentialist, 82; ostensive, 81
deontological ethics, 10, 18, 59, 125, 128–32, 135f., 138, 147, 149, 179f.

Derrida, Jacques, 45, 180
Descartes, 55, 109
desirable, 149; good as, 182; moral good and, 95, 146f., 176, cf. 150
desire (cf. "inclination"), 7f., 30, 60–63, 69, 72, 90, 92, 102, 117, 118f., 120, 121, 129, 141, 148, 171f., 175, 183; and pleasure, 100, 106, 119–21; in "holy will," 182
despair, 111, 165
determination (cf. "causality"), vs. conditioning, 121 n. 18
determining ground of morality (cf. "moral justification"), xiii, 7f., 17f., 28f., 39, 60–65, 67, 70, 72, 99f., 105f., 120, 129, 131f., 138f., 143, 157, 172f., 175, 180f., 184, 186; disposition, 159, 162, 184; insight, 145, 175; moral law, 66f., 70, 101, 105; nonmoral values, 67, 186; religion, 154 n. 27; unconditional, 28, 60, 62, 106
determinism, 8, 60, 72, 106
Dewey, John, 14, 20
Diemer, Alwin, 90, 120, 197
dignity, 9, 71f., 74, 91, 104
dilemmas, 6f., 29, 45, 143–45, 150, 172
Dilthey, Wilhelm, 4f., 54, 116, 124, 165, 177, 197
disclosure, of Being, 80; of values, 76f.
disposition (cf. "character"), xvi, 9, 18, 112, 117, 118, 124, 136, 138–41, 148, 152, 156–62, 169f., 173, 175f., 179, 182–85, 188; *Gesinnung*, 21 n. 18; and conflict, 117–18, 140f., 145f., 150, 159, 161f., 172, 175; change of, 140, 152 n. 7, 162; classifications, 117, 124 n. 42, 141; experienceable, 160f., 184; inscrutable, 160f., 183f.; noumenal, phenomenal?, 161; *Wille & Willkür* and, 160, 188
disvalue, 80, 87
divinity (see "God")
Donagan, Alan, 11, 18, 22, 25, 197
Dooyeweerd, Herman, 18, 97, 116f., 123f.; *New Critique*, 56, 74, 83f., 117, 123f., 177, 197
Drang (impulse), 54, 89, 168, 186; and *Geist* (spirit), 89, 168, 186
Du Plessis, S. I. M., 178, 197
dualism, xiii, 6, 18f., 28, 30f., 32, 35–43, 91, 100, 105, 107, 112–14, 141, 145, 152, 157, 160f., 163f., 171, 173, 176, 183; in Scheler?, 47f., 166, 168, 186
Dufrenne, Mikel, 31, 41, 46f., 50, 55f., 197
Duncan, A. R. C., 11, 22, 196
Dunlop, Francis, 54, 123, 197
Dupuy, Maurice, 19, 197
duty, xiiif., 8, 18f., 59–61, 69, 72f., 99, 118f., 120 n. 6, 126, 127, 129–33, 135–41, 146, 149, 157, 169f., 170–78, 180–85, 187f.; blind, xiv, 69, 173, 181;

eulogy to, 71f., 74, 91, 104; inclination and, 60f., 88f., 136, 149, 156, 182f.; indirect, 136, 149, 169; nonmoral, 86

economics, 6, 20, 56, 84, 174
Edie, James M., 192
ego, 25, 40, 45, 54, 177
Ehrenfels, Christan von, 6, 90, 121
eidetic vs. empirical, 81, 87
Eisler, Rudolf, xvi, 197
Emad, Parvid, 18, 75f., 95, 193; *Heidegger*, 17, 25, 76, 93, 197
Embree, Lester, xiv, 89, 193
emotion (cf. "feeling"), Kant's view, 106f.; phenomenology of, 108
emotional a priori, 37, 48, 56, 173f.; modes of givenness, 171, 203; order of, 48, 56f., 173
emotivism, 13, 15f., 23f., 129
empathy, 116, 167f.
empiricism, 8f., 13, 15, 23, 29, 32, 37, 41, 47–49, 50, 60, 62f., 64, 96, 196
ends, 9, 11, 59, 61–63, 68–74, 87–89, 126, 131, 138, 172f., 178, 183
English-speaking world, and "formalism," 10f., 69, 90f.; and intuitionism, 13, 15, 75; and Scheler, 13f., 57, 189–94; and translations, xiv, 10, 13, 20, 23, 69, 90f.
Enlightenment, 10, 44, 73, 131, 172f., 178, 183, 185, 188
entities, 76, 79
Epicurus, 62
epistemology, xiii, 4–6, 13, 16f., 19, 22f., 25, 27–49, 90, 94, 167f., 171, 191, 195f., 197; intuitionism and, xi, 6, 13, 15f., 31f., 38f., 41f., 45, 75, 80f., 96, 180
Erdmann, Johann E., 90
Ermarth, Michael, 20, 177, 197
essence, 8, 10, 27–49, 57, 80–83, 186f.; intuited, 31f., 42, cf. 18, 33, 49, 80f.; in Scheler, 28, 34, 43; of values, 82ff.; values and, 63, 82
essential intuition, 7, 18, 30–33, 44, 49–51, 80f., 87; passive synthesis and, 32, 44, 51; *Wesensschau*, 7, 31, 33
essentialism, 10, 17, 82, 176, 183, 185–87
ethics, aretaic, 179; basis of (cf. "determining ground"); contentless, 71, 74, 131, 138f., 170, 172f.; consequentialist, 7–9, 18, 29, 59–61, 147; deontological, 10, 18, 59, 125, 128–32, 135f., 138, 147, 149, 180; imperativistic, 138, 154, 170, 187; normative, xiv, 12, 22, 142–46, 150, 175, 185–88; of duty vs. of insight, xiv, 69, 129–31, 138–40, 155, 180f.; of values, 9, 28f., 60, 63, 87f., 106, 121, 187; of virtue, xiv, 18, 90, 124, 179–88; phenomenological, 12, 17f., 87f., 142–51, 157, 175f.; phenomenological,

in Kant?, 157, 160, 163; post-aretaic, xiv, 180, 185; prescriptive, descriptive, 142, 176; teleological, 59, 66, 70; theological, 44, 94, 154f.; utilitarian, 6, 77, 147, 152 n. 11
Eucken, Rudolf, 4f., 177
eudaemonism, xiii, 101, 105f., 121
euthanasia, 143f.
evaluation (see "judgment," "valuation")
evidence, 25, 38f., 43f., 50, 52f., 77, 93, 148
evil, 45, 95, 134, 140–42, 162, 167f., 178, 182
existence, 5, 16–18, 31, 66f., 80, 82, 64, 66f., 80, 84, 80f., 87, 96, 133f., 138
existentialism, 16, 22, 44, 54, 75
experience, xiii, 5, 8, 16–18, 25, 28–30, 33–36, 41–44, 52, 55, 61–64, 71f., 81, 87, 99, 104, 107f., 112f., 147, 149, 160–68, 170–74, 191; of self, 163–67

fact of reason, 99, 103, 113, 128
facts, 4, 6, 20, 33–34, 37, 39, 52, 128, 134, 145, 152
factual a priori, 33, 37, 52, 207
faculties, 30, 38, 56, 72, 90, 99, 102
faculty theory, 28, 31, 42
faithfulness, 175
feeling, 7f., 12, 30, 36f., 48, 56, 73, 77f., 82, 93, 99–124, 140, 148, 165, 167f., 173f., 183; of values (see "value-feeling")
feeling-state (*Gefühlszustand*), 36f., 108–10, 114, 122f., 129, 165, 184
Feyerabend, 45
Fichte, 134
Findlay, J. N., 14, 17, 20, 124, 197
First Austrian School of Values, 6, 20
Fitch, Gregory W., 55, 198
form, 2, 5, 11f., 21, 27, 29–35, 39, 41, 43f., 47, 49, 51–55, 61, 69–72, 90f., 146f., 162, 174, 177f., 184
formalism, xiii, 2f., 5–9, 10–12, 18, 21, 28, 35, 38, 42, 47, 52, 59–63, 65, 69–74, 90–92, 105, 131f., 138f., 146, 151, 170–72, 176, 178, 180, 208
foundation, 16–18, 31, 44f., 94
foundationalism, 17f., 23, 95, 180, 187 n. 3
Frankena, William, 15, 20, 59, 66, 70, 179, 198
freedom, 8, 53f., 60, 71f., 102, 104, 128, 136f., 141f., 156, 159, 169, 177, 184
Frege, G., 57, 208
Frings, Manfred S., xi, xiv–xvi, 9, 13, 23–25, 53, 79, 89, 92–94, 96, 99, 119, 140, 177f., 193, 198
Frondizi, Risieri, 14, 20, 81, 94, 96, 198
functional modalities, 82–84, 87, 97
functions (cf. "acts"), 82–84, 108, 164, 166
Funk, Roger L., xiv, xvi, 9, 13, 89, 99, 119, 189, 192
Funke, Gerhard, 16f., 23, 25, 44, 54f., 198

Gadamer, Hans-Georg, xi
Germany, 3–7, 11–14, 16, 20, 22, 50, 69, 74, 144–46, 190
Gesinnung (cf. "disposition," "character"), xiv, xvi, 9, 21 n. 18
givenness, 31–33, 36–39, 51, 64f., 68
goals, 68, 76–78, 93
God, 8, 31, 44, 60, 93f., 94, 101, 105, 126, 134, 154f., cf. 60, 161, 167, 177f.
Goethe, 4, 134
Golden Rule, 73, 92
good, xiv, 39, 57, 60–68, 74, 76–78, 80f., 89, 93f., 96, 105, 138, 147, 150–52, 173, 178f., 182, 184; nonmoral, 56f., 85f., 146, 162, 175
good and evil, 9, 62, 64, 67, 84, 87f., 97, 168, 173, 178, 184
good will, 60, 140, 155, 169, 178, 181f.
Good, Paul, xvi, 199
goods, 7, 9, 37, 62f., 65
Grabau, Richard F., 192
Gregor, Mary J., 91
Greiner, J., 198
guidance, moral, 12, 22, 73, 119, 131, 142–46, 150, 172, 175, 185, 188; in Heidegger, 95; in Scheler, 73, 185, 187
Gurwitsch, Aron, 25, 45, 198
Gusdorf, Georges, 15

Habermas, Jürgen, 153, 199
Hall, E. W., 14
Hamburg, Carl H., 92, 198
Hamlyn, D. W., 81, 96, 199
happiness, xiii, 18, 61, 100f., 104, 111f., 123, 135, 165, 169, 173, 184f.
Hart, James G., 51, 198
Hartman, R. S., 50, 199
Hartmann, Nicolai, xi, 1, 4, 11, 14, 19, 21f., 75, 77, 87, 97, 119, 124, 157, 188–91, 195; *Ethics*, 12, 22, 199; Kant, Scheler, and, 12, 21f.; normative ethics and, 22; on Scheler, 19, 199
Hartmann, Wilfrid, 23, 199
hate, logic and, 37
heart, 37, 48, 107, 121, 128, 152, 162
Hebart, J. F., 129
hedonism, 9, 62, 77; psychological, xiii, 9, 37, 105f., 108, 110f., 114, 121
Hegel, G. W. F., 3, 19, 134, 151, 154, 199
Hegelianism, 4, 10, 18, 90
Heidegger, Martin, xif., 14, 17f., 22–25, 50, 59, 75–80, 82, 87, 90, 92–95, 102, 115, 120, 123f., 177, 180, 196–99, 203; and Scheler, xi, xv, 11f., 14, 16, 24f., 44, 54, 75ff., 80, 87, 94; *Basic Problems*, 22, 71, 104, 113, 199f.; *Being and Time*, 16, 24f., 54, 75, 78, 94; criticisms of, 17f., 76ff., 80, 87, 95; critique of values by, xi–xiii, 17f., 23, 59, 75ff., 89, 93; on Kant, 11f, 71, 102,

120; "Letter on Humanism," 23, 25, 76; visit with Scheler, 24f.
Heidemann, Ingeborg, xv, 90, 141f., 199
Heimsoeth, Heinz, 90, 121, 199f.
Herbart, J. F., 129
Héring, Jean, 199
Hermann, J., 123, 200
Hertz, Marcus, 101
heteronomy, of incentives, 62, 137, 182; of material ethics, 9, 62
hierarchy of values, 6, 8, 66, 73, 77, 84, 97, 143, 145, 186; in Kant, 74, 92
Hildebrand, Dietrich von, 22, 51, 76f., 154
history, 1f., 5, 84, 110, 122, 145, 167, 174, 177
Hobbes, Thomas, 38, 129, 152
homo noumenon, 60, 104, 121, 163–66
Horkheimer, Max, 153, 200
Hospers, John, 23, 157
human nature (cf. "anthropology," "person"), xiv, 2, 8, 10, 18, 38, 69f., 101, 162–68, 172f., 177, 183–88
humanity, in Kant, 70
Hume, David, 31, 38, 188, cf. 8, 29f.
Husserl, Edmund, xi–xiv, 6f., 14, 17, 20–22, 28, 30–33, 35, 42, 46, 50f., 55–57, 65, 77f., 80, 92f., 116, 121, 123f., 147, 171, (cf. 190, 197, 205, 207); constitution in, 52; and ethics, 12, 22, 205; and Gurwitsch, 45; and Kant, xi, 30ff., 50f.; and Neo-Kantianism, 50; and phenomenology, 6, 30ff., 52; and Scheler, 6f., 12, 21, 30, 50; and Schlick, 52; *Ideen*, 7, 30, 51f., 89, 93, 124, 200; *Logische (LU)*, 30–32, 51f., 200
Hutcheson, Francis, 62, 92
hylemorphism (cf. "form"), 5
hypocrisy, 80, cf. 87, 97

I, pure, 25; central, 177
I-center, I-circumground, 93, 147f., 149f., cf. 51 n. 11, 122 n. 28, 123 n. 33, 93 n. 45
Ibana, Rainier R. A., 189, 193
idealism, 4, 6, 10, 13, 24f., 28, 90, 95f., 129, 171
ideas, 31, 80, 96
ideation, 32
identity, 83
illustrations, abortion, 73, 144; "All Soviet flags are red," 39, 42; apple, 81; beer and pizza, 81; cathedral, 143; color, 34, 36, 39, 42, 64, 77, 81, 96; cube, 36; dead child, 167f.; drowning man, 54, 156 n. 36, 162; education of children, 66; euthanasia, 143f.; famine relief, 143; friendship, 65; homeless, 77; Japanese maple, 34; logic, 35, 51; math, 35; mother and infant son, 78; Mozart vs. drowning child, 143; "No one dies for mere values," 76, 79; "Nothing can be red and green all over . . . ," 96; paralytic and drowning man, 162; pleasant or repugnant room, 65; plums and pears, 35; Rembrandt painting, 82f.; ripening tomato, 65; sound, 36, 49; sugar, 37; survival vs. culture, 87; sycamore tree, 51; "This tree has leaves," 53; trial of Anne Boleyn, 156; wall paper, stock market, math, 85
imaginative variation, 49, 79
imitation, 142
imperative, 136f., 60, 62, 126, 135, 139, 145, 154 (see "categorical imperative")
impulse (see "*Drang*," "inclination")
imputation, 156, 160, 173
incentive, 62, 73, 99–105, 111, 113–15, 120f., 137, 148f., 172, 182, 185
inclination, xiii, 7f., 30, 38, 60, 62, 100–2, 111, 114, 117–19, 125f., 128, 130f., 135–42, 145f., 149f., 155f., 160, 162, 169, 171–73, 175, 181–83; misunderstood in Kant, 61, 88f.
individuality (see "universality")
Ingarden, Roman, xi, 51, 201
innatism, 39f., 172
inner sense, 163
insight, 35, 38–40, 42f., 72f., 99, 105, 125, 127, 130, 137, 139–42, 144f., 156, 175, 181; duty and, 69, 145, 175, 181f.
intellectualism, 99
intelligibility, 30f., 42
intention, 61, 80, 147, 162, 173
intentionality, 6, 34, 45, 75f., 108, 109, 148f., 165; passive, xiii, 32, 44, 51f., 79, 148, 150, 173, 176
interest, 82f., 100, 102f.
intersubjectivity (cf. "community"), 42, 116, 167f., 191
intuition, 6f., 15, 28, 30–35, 38f., 41–44, 49–51, 54f., 81, 87, 89, 96, 116 (see "essential intuition")
intuitionism, xi, 13, 15f., 39, 45, 75, 81, 96, 180
irrationality, 4, 31, 107, 160
irreducibility, 4f., 48, 64f., 79–81, 84, 95, 117f.

Japanese phenomenology, 13, 23, 177, 187, 202f., 207, 209
Jewish prophetic tradition, 178 n. 12, cf. 124 n. 41
Jones, W. Tudor, 20, 201
joy, 105, 183
judgment, 5, 28, 31f., 49, 99, 106, 149f., 173, 179 (see "moral judgment")
justice, 73, 92, 178
Juvenal, 151

Kant, xi–xvi, 1–5, 8, 10–13, 18–25, 27–33, 35f., 37f., 39–41, 42, 43, 47, 51, 53,

55, 57, 59–74, 88–92, 94, 99–115, 117–21, 124–32, 134–42, 146, 151–57, 159–64, 166, 168–73, 176f., 179–84; and Aristotle, 10, 182ff.; and Hartmann, 12, 21f.; and Husserl, xi, 30ff., 50f.; and Neo-Kantianism, 12, 30; and phenomenology, xi, xiii, 12, 184; *Doctrine of Virtue*, 10, 71, 91, 117, 127; *Grundlegung (GMS)*, 60–62, 65, 70f., 88, 90–92, 101, 103, 119, 126–28, 141f., 151, 169; *Kritik (KpV)*, 11, 13, 29, 60–63, 67, 70–72, 88, 90f., 99, 101–5, 113, 115, 119f., 126–28, 151f., 156, 169; *Kritik (KrV)*, 2, 29, 51, 54, 101, 105, 141, 161, 169f.; *Kritik (KU)*, 10, 29, 51, 102, 105; misreadings of, 61, 88f., 91; *Metaphysik (MS)*, 69f., 91, 99f., 102f., 119f., 126f., 169; "objective sense" vs. "pathos" of, 169f., 178; presuppositions of, xi, 8f., 73; *Religion (R)*, 104f., 142, 152, 156f., 160f., 169, 176, 188; religion and, 1, 19, 120, 208
Kelly, Eugene, 142, 146, 151, 175, 184, 189, 192, 202
Kern, Iso, 50, 202
Klein, Ted, 50f., 202
knowledge, 6, 15f., 17f., 25, 29, 33f., 52, 55, 71, 80, 87, 91, 95, 97, 140, 156, 165, 167; a priori, 17, 28f., 31f., 39, 51; of self, 163–67; sociology of, 178, 186
Kockelmans, Joseph J., 14, 25, 97, 202
Köhle, Eckard J., 189, 191
Kripke, Saul A., 50, 202
Krüger, F., 121
Kruschwitz, Robert, 187, 202

Lachterman, David R., 13, 23, 50, 53f., 79, 94f.
Lange, Friedrich, 5
language, 15, 23, 56, 84, 155, 171, 174f., 177
Latin America, 12, 23
Lauer, Quentin, 55, 192f., 202
Laupichler, M., 90
Lavely, John H., 178, 202
law, 6f., 18f., 30, 37, 40, 42–44, 48, 56, 61, 70, 73, 84, 107–10, 114–16, 126–28, 151, 154, 171f.; natural, 72, 92, 154 (see "moral law")
law-giver, 7, 18, 30, 37, 43f., 171
lawfulness, 7, 25, 30, 37, 43f., 67, 107, 112, 171f.
Le Senne, René, 14
Lebensphilosophie, 3–5
legality vs. morality, 9, 61, 101, 136
Leibniz, 109, cf. 47, 167
Lessing, G. E., 157, 195
Levinas, Emmanuel, 17, 51, 89, 153, 155, 168, 178

Lichtigfeld, A., 23, 202
Liebert, A., 90
Liebmann, Otto, 4f., 169
Lipps, T., 154
logic, 4–6, 20, 25, 28, 32–35, 37–39, 46–50, 56f., 84, 93, 107, 115, 173f.; *du coeur*, 37, 48
Lossky, N., 23, 203
Lotze, R. Hermann, 6, 20, 74f., 77, 93, 152, 178
love, 21, 37, 61, 104f., 108f., 122, 126, 135f., 155, 157
Luther, Arthur R., 177, 202
Luther, Martin, 19, 115

MacIntyre, Alasdair, 18, 92, 153, 172f., 178, 180, 187f.; *After Virtue*, xiv, 25, 173, 183, 188, 203; *Whose Justice?*, 21, 25, 92, 178, 203
Mackie, J. L., 13, 23, 97, 203
Malebranche, N., 177
manners of givenness, 34ff., 50f., 65, 76, 78, 80, 89, 115, 123, 146f., 157, 163–66, 171, 185f., 188
Mannheim, Karl, 4
Marcel, Gabriel, xi
Marcuse, Herbert, 192
Maritain, Jacques, xi
Marks, Lawrence E., 96
Marsh, James L., 153, 203
Marx, Werner, 17, 23, 203
masturbation (*crimen carnis*), 153 n. 18
material ends (cf. "ends," "object"), 61, 69f., 72
material region (cf. "orders," "region"), 171, 174f.
material values, 6, 29, 63f., 72, 86, 88, 92, 99, 106, 173–75, 180
mathematics, 84, 107, 109, 115f., 174f.
maxim, 8, 104, 183
McGowan, John, 153, 203
McTaggart, J., 4
meaning, 31–33, 42, 49, 83, 166
Megill, Allan, 153, 203
Meinong, Alexius, 6, 90, 116, 121, 124, 176, 198, 203
Melle, Ullrich, 22, 94
memory, 166
Menger, Karl, 6
merit, 137
Merleau-Ponty, Maurice, xi, 46, 56, 203
metaphysical dualism, 18, 28, 32, 43, 173, 176, 186
metaphysics, xiif., 2, 25, 27–31, 35, 40, 43, 71, 90, 121, 163–68, 172, 185f.; of presence, 17f., 54, 75f., 78, 94; of purism, 28, 60, 113f., 127, 141, 160, 163f., 172
Meyer, Herbert H., 190, 192
microcosm-macrocosm, 44, 167f., 177f.

Mill, J. S., 3f., 20
Miller, David G., 190, 193
modalities, 82–84, 87, 97
model persons, 142, 157, 186
Mohanty, J. N., 16f., 25, 51, 54, 203
Mongis, Henri, 93, 203
Montaigne, 55
Moore, G. E., 14f., 24, 81, 89, 96, 190, 192, 203
Moosa, Imtiaz, 96, 190, 193, 203
moral action (cf. "acts"), xiv, 9, 37, 17f., 51, 61, 70, 146f., 149, 157, 159–62, 173, 176f., 181–83, 185; disposition and, 17, 159–62, 176; inclination and, 88f., 140, 155, 169, 181f.; public, 80, 146f., 157
moral conflict, 117, 140f., 145f., 149f., 159, 161f., 172, 175, 182
moral education, 127, 140, 142, 155, 157
moral feeling, xiii, 12, 62, 71–73, 99–105, 107, 112–24, 120, 163, 169, 172
moral genius, 141
moral good, 59–97, 94, 99, 146f., 150, 162, 175f., 182, 185; and nonmoral good, 56f., 85f., 162, 175
moral irrelevance, 170, 182f.
moral judgment, 15–18, 23, 28, 87, 129, 131f., 147, 149f., 157, 173, 180f.
moral justification (cf. "determining ground"), 9, 17, 54f., 80, 87f., 95, 142–51, 157, 173, 175f., 183, 185
moral law, xiiif., 8f., 18f., 61f., 73f., 101–4, 106, 120 n. 13, 126–28, 138, 150, 159, 162, 170–73, 176, 181, 183
moral value (cf. "value"), 1, 2, 18, 65ff., 70, 84–89, 164, 173–75, 188; species of material value, 86, 88, 92, 175
morality (cf. "ethics"), 8f., 23, 73, 101, 136, 143–47, 157, 174, 176, 183, 185
Moser, Paul K., 27, 50, 55, 203
motive (see "incentive," "intention")
Mozart, 143
Mulligan, Thomas M., 190, 192
mundane experience, 41, 44
Munster, Ralph F. W., 190f.

Nabe, Clyde M., 190, 192
naturalism, 6, 9, 81, 89, 106, 163, 177
nature, as chaos, 38; as mechanistic, 8, 60, 106
Navickas, Joseph, L. 23, 203
Nazis, 13
necessity, 27, 30, 38f., 42, 47, 50, 55, 60; varieties of, 53 n. 20
needs, 76–79
Neo-Kantianism, 3–5, 12, 20, 30, 43, 90, 169f.
Neumann, von, 20
Nietzsche, 4, 6, 76f., 93, 116, 129, 144, 152, 190, 193, 203

Nishida, Kitaro, 177, 202
Nitta, Yoshihiro, 203
noematic object, 65, 80
noetic analysis, 31
nomena, 41
nominalism, 77, 129, 152
non-naturalism, 81
noncognitivism (cf. "emotivism"), 13, 15f.
nonmoral normativity, 85f.
nonmoral values, 56f., 65–70, 84ff., 89, 133f., 139, 162, 174f., 186, 188; amoral realizations of, 85f.
normative ethics (see "ethics")
norms, 5, 25, 66, 95, 129, 133, 135, 137, 139, 155, 157, 184, 186
noumena vs. phenomena, xiii, 2, 4, 8, 18, 30, 33, 43, 48, 60, 91, 100, 160f., 163; in Scheler?, 166
noumenal, 161, 172f.; disposition, 160f.; moral feeling?, 172; moral imputation, 173; self (see "*homo noumenon*")
Nowell-Smith, Patrick H., 24, 203
Nozick, Robert, 18, 25, 123

obedience, 130, 140, 154, 181
object, 31f, 34, 43, 46, 62, 67, 69f., 75–78, 80, 93, 101, 106, 164f., 185
objectification, 23, 76–79, 93
objectivism, 42, 45f., 63, 77, 132, 180
objectivity, 45, 53, 77, 163f., 167, 172; *Gegenstandtheorie*, 34
obligation, xiii, 2, 5, 39, 54, 59f., 70, 119, 125–57, 172f., 175, 179, 181f., 184; and insight, 39, 139f., 175, 181; basis of, xiii, 16, 18, 39, 61, 129, 131f., 138f., 143, 157, 173; conflicts in, 143; noetic, 16f., 25; nonmoral, 85ff., 97
Olthuis, James H., 6f., 20, 203
ontological vs. ontical, 75, 78f.
ontology (cf. "metaphysics"), 5, 16–18, 54, 75, 78–80, 89, 94f., 166, 168, 174f., 178
ordering principle (cf. "law"), 29, 107–10, 114–16, 171–74; nonrational, xiii, 19, 37, 107f., 173f.; rational, 18f., 30f., 43f., 68, 107, 171, 173
orders (cf. "region"), 6, 43f., 47f., 55f., 57, 72, 107–10, 114–16, 171f.; emotional, 47f., 173–76; logical, 6, 47f., 56f., 84, 173f.; nonrational, 6, 37, 48, 107f., 115f., 171–76; *ordre du coeur*, 37
ordo amoris, xiii, 18, 53, 93, 107–9, 114–15, 145, 171, 173f., 176
origin, of a priori, 46f., 195; of action, 183f.; of conscience, 149; of evil 45; of lawfulness, 44; of moral action, 183; of moral law, 170; of moral value, 18, 170; of "ought," 147, 149; of respect, 102; of value-consciousness, 82, 87, 119; of values, 18, 29, 63

Ortega y Gasset, José, 13, 23
Orth, Ernst W., 92, 204
Osgood, C. E., 96
other minds, 167
ought, 8, 17, 73, 85, 133, 137, 142, 145–51, 157, 179, 181–85, 181f., 188; and supererogation, 137, 188; ideal, 8, 17, 85f., 133–40, 142, 146, 155; non-moral, 85f., 175; of duty, 133f., 137f., 145f., 148, 155, 188

pain, 101f., 105, 108, 155, 162
Parmenides, 47
Pascal, Blaise, 37, 48, 107, 121, 171, 188
passion, 102, 161, 183
passive genesis, 52
passive synthesis, 32, 44, 46, 52, 77, 93, 171
pathos, of Kant's ethics, 155f., 162, 169f., 178; of Pietism, 1; vs. "objective sense" of Kant, 162, 169f., 178, 155f., 169f., 178
Paton, H. J., 10f., 69, 91, 127, 151, 204
Paul, St., 117, 124, 141, 162, 195
perception, illusory, 52; of values (cf. "value-feeling"), 119, n. 2; phenomenological, 36; reason and, 171; vs. eidetic intuition, 81, 87, 96
perfection, 62, 118, 178, 183
Perrin, Ronald, 47f., 52f., 186, 190, 192
Perry, Ralph Barton, 14, 82, 96, 204
person (cf. "human nature," "self"), xv, 9, 12, 18, 38, 56, 60, 67f., 70, 89, 94, 112, 114, 123, 125, 128, 138, 149, 152, 157, 162–68, 171f., 177, 179, 184–88; "model persons," 142, 157, 186; nonobjectifiable, 79, 94, 123, 164f., 185; "person of persons," 44, 54, 94, 167f.; unity of, 164, 168, 186
personalism, 177f.
personality, 8, 72, 74, 91, 104, 148
Pfänder, A., 93, 121, 123, 147
pharisaism, 87, 97 n. 70
phenomena (cf. "noumena"), xiii, 2, 4, 8, 18, 28, 30f., 33f., 41, 43, 48, 60, 91, 100, 160f., 163, 166, 172
phenomenological method, 2, 12, 81, 142, 146f., 175f.; in Husserl, 31; in Kant?, 11f., 71, 74, 91, 157, 160, 163; in Scheler, 9, 12, 16f., 28, 30, 34, 37, 44, 91; misunderstood, 34f., 52; problems of, xiv, 175f., 185
phenomenology, 6, 11–13, 16f., 21f., 25, 44, 54, 71, 74, 91, 157, 160, 163, 166, 176, 186; and analytic philosophy, 48, 57, 74, 81, 176; and Husserl, 89; and Kant, xi, xiii, 74; and Scheler, 3, 6f., 25; transcendental, 16, 25, 43–45
philosophy, analytic vs. Continental, 13, 27f., 47, 55, 48f., 50, 81; critical, xiii, 12, 17, 27–30, 44, 47, 90

physics, 10, 60, 84, 110, 115, 171, 188
Pietism, 1, 73
Ping-cheung Lo, 70, 91, 204
Plantinga, Alvin, 46, 55, 95, 198, 204
Plato, 55, 76f., 93f., 107, 129; cf. 17, 77, 80, 199
Platonic ideas, 80, 96
pleasure, 8f., 30, 61f., 66, 90, 100–6, 108, 110, 113, 115, 119–21, 155, 162, 183, 185
Polin, Raymond, 14f.
Pope John Paul II (see "Wojtyła"), xi, xv
positing (Setzung), 33, 68, 76–78, 93
positivism, 4, 6, 13, 15, 47–49, 51, 57, 152
post-aretaic ethics, 180, 185
Postmodernism, 131f., 173, 180, 185
practical rationality, 60, 68, 71f., 131f., 178
practical reason, 22, 28, 38, 41, 55, 60, 68, 71, 91, 104, 131f., 141, 172, 176, 178
Prall, D. W., 14, 176, 204
preference, 37, 48, 85–87, 108, 122; criteria of, 87, 150, 157; logic of, 8, 84f., 144, 146
prescriptions, proscriptions, 154, 181
presence-at-hand, 54, 79, 94
principles, 48, 60–62, 70, 144–47, 171, 176, 186
problems, in Kant, 71–74, 102–5, 172; in Scheler, 39, 48, 57, 80f., 84–88, 96f., 175, 185, 187
prohibition, 135, 137f.
propositions, 32f., 35, 38f., 49–51, 53, 57
Protestantism, 19, 155
Przywara, Erich, 154
psychological vs. transcendental, 4f.
psychologism, 31–32, 40
psychology, 116, 121, 167, 174; and a priori, 32, 174; faculty theory of, 28; morality and, 174, 176; of Kant, 8; of Ressentiment, 77; virtue and, 184
punishment, 105, 123
Puolimatka, Tapio, 54f., 95, 97, 116f., 124

qualities, 40, 49, 51, 64, 80f., 89
Quine, Willard V., 39, 46, 49f., 55, 204

ranks (see "hierarchy," "value")
Ranly, Ernest W., 168, 178, 190f.
rational vs. empirical, 27
rationalism, 62, 107, 109
rationality, xiii, 5, 31, 60, 62, 70–72, 99, 101, 107, 115f., 138f., 160, 170, 172, 178, 181, 183; rival views of, 73, 92, 178
realism, 24f., 95f.; metaphysical, 44f.; moral, 54f.
reality (cf. "existence"), 168; and resistance, 24f., 54, 77, 168; of values, 5, 18, 80f.; reification and, 76, 78f.
realization, 56f., 64, 66f., 70, 73, 84–87, 92, 97, 133–35, 137f., 142, 144, 146–49,

162, 166–68, 174f., 188; amoral, 85; via impulse (*Drang*), 89, 168; via willing, 64, 89, 168, 174f.
reason (cf. "intellect"), 4, 10, 18–20, 28f., 30, 44, 60, 71, 73, 91, 99, 103f., 107, 118, 131f., 141, 148, 161, 171–73, 175–77, 182f., 188, and sensibility, xiii, 18, 35–37, 43, 47f., 105, 107, 183; crisis of, 95, 131f., 153, 172f., 178; lawgiver, 7, 18, 30, 37, 43f., 171; limitations of, 55, 71, 73, 80, 91, 146, 172f. (see "practical reason")
reasoning, 29, 35–37, 42, 160
reasons of the heart, 37, 107, 148
receptivity, 32, 46, 51 ,77
reduction, phenomenological, 44, 171, cf. 47f., 53
reductionism, 16f., 23, 25, 32, 48, 53, 56f., 79f., 85ff., 95, 168, 107, 174, 182f.
reflection, 36, 165f.
Regan, Tom, 15, 204
region (cf. "orders," "functional modalities"), 171; aesthetic, 6, 56, 84; biology, 56, 84; economic, 56, 84; history, 84; language, 56, 84; law, 6, 48, 84; laws of, 107–10, 114–16, 171f.; logic, 6, 48, 56f., 84; material, 171, 174f.; math, 84f., 115, 174; moral, 6, 48, 84, 175, 188; physics, 84; political, 56; psychological, 56, 84, 174; religion, 48, 56, 84, 174; sociology, 56, 84; spatial, 84
regional ontology (cf. "ontology," "orders"), 6, 174f.
Reiner, Hans, xiv, 14f., 17f., 20–22, 25, 51, 54f., 59, 65, 73f., 76f., 78, 80, 81, 87, 91–97, 116–19, 122–24, 147–51, 156f., 183, 188, 199; and Kant, 22; contra Scheler, 87; contra Heidegger, 76ff., 93; *Duty* (DI), 21, 51, 54f., 65, 88, 79, 81, 87f., 91–97, 116, 119, 122–24, 148–50, 156f., 188, 204; normative ethics, 22; and Von Hildebrand, 22, 51, 76
relativism, 4, 39, 54, 73, 77, 132, 136, 157, 167, 173; cultural, 4f., 15, 110; ethical, 157; historical, 4f., 73, 77, 110, 122, 145, 173
religion, 1, 19, 73, 120, 144, 154, 167, 174, 177, 189; basis for ethics, 44, 94, 154f. n. 27; region, 48, 56, 84, 174
representation, 8, 78f.
Rescher, Nicholas, 20, 81, 90, 121f., 177, 205
resistance (cf. "reality"), 24, 43, 54, 77, 168; and *Dasein*, 54, 94; and evil, 168
respect (see "feeling"), 61, 70, 91, 99, 102–5, 113f., 120, 121, 163, 175; *Achtung*, 99, 103; *reverentia*, 119 n. 3
Ressentiment, 53, 77, 93, 144, 156, 206
revenge, 123
reward, 123

Rickert, Heinrich, 5, 75f., 93, 154
Ricoeur, Paul, 45–47, 55, 89, 121, 205
right and wrong, 6, 23, 87, 97, 179
rigor, 6–9, 32, 63f.
rigorism, 3, 60, 155
Rintelen, Joachim von, 20
Ritter, Joachim, 50, 205
Roberts, Augustine, 190, 192
Roberts, Robert, 187, 202
Rorty, Richard, 153, 205
Ross, W. D., 50, 182, 195
Roth, Alois, 21, 205
rules, 92, 146f.
Russell, Bertrand, 13

sacrifice, 135, 137–39, 153, 156
Sallis, John, 56, 153, 178, 192, 205
Sartre, Jean-Paul, xi, 23, 54, 177, 190, 205
Scanlon, John, xv, 52
Scheler, xi–xvi, 1–14, 16–25, 27–30, 33–45, 47f., 50, 52–54, 56f., 59f., 62–69, 71–82, 85–90, 92–97, 99f., 105–12, 114–19, 121–24., 128–47, 149f., 152–57, 159–71, 173–88; and Hartmann, 12, 14, 19, 21f.; and Heidegger, xi, 11f., 16, 24f., 75ff., 94; and Husserl, 6f., 12, 20f., 28; and religion, 1, 19; as phenomenologist, 12–14; critics of, 11, 69, 74, 97; *Ewigen* (E), 89, 156; English-speaking world and, xif., xiv, 13f., 23; *Formalismus* (F), xii, xiv, 9, 12f., 16, 21, 30, 33–35, 38–41, 48, 52–54, 60, 63–65, 67f., 77f., 85–87, 89, 93, 97, 105f., 108–12, 115, 119, 121–23, 129–37, 140, 143, 152–57, 159f., 162, 169f., 181f., 184, 186–88; "Idealismus-Realismus," 24f., 54, 94f., 205; influence of, xi, xif., xvi, 12–14, 21; Jewish background, 13, 19; Neo-Kantianism and, 4f., 169f.; on *Being and Time*, 16, 24f.; *Ordo Amoris* (OA), 53, 121; *Problems*, 178, 186, 206; *Ressentiment* (Res.), 93, 144, 156, 206; *Stellung* (Stel.), 54, 177, 206; *Sympathie* (S), 122, 165, 167, 206
Scheler, Maria, 13, 53, 96, 178
Schelling, 54, 199
schematism, 127f., 151
Schiller, Johann C. F. von, 3, 20, 118, 124, 183, 185, 188, 204, 207; vs. Kant, 183, 188
Schilpp, Paul Arthur, 11, 21, 140, 151, 178, 207
Schleiermacher, 3, 19
Schlick, Moritz, 33, 47, 52, 57, 207, 210; vs. phenomenology, 52, 57
Schneck, Frederick S., 190, 193
Schneider, Marius, 190f.
Schopenhauer, A., 3f., 20, 136, 154 n. 27, 155

Schroeder, H. H., 11, 22, 207
Schutz, Alfred, 2, 19, 44, 207
Schwartz, Balduin, 192
science, 4, 6, 8, 29, 165
Scientific Revolution, 10
Second Austrian School of Values, 116
Seebohm, Thomas M., xiv, 16, 25, 43, 54, 207
self (cf. "person"), 60, 79, 104, 116, 121, 163–68, 172, 177, 186f.
self-, authentication, 35, 52; conceit, 102, 104; control, 38, 182f.; disclosure, 104f.; entrapment, 149f.; feeling (cf. "central emotional fulfillment"), 94, 173; humiliation, 104f.; interest, 76, 101, 135; knowledge, 163–67; legislation, 60, 62, 71f., 99; perception, 140; feeling, 140; respect, 104; value, 79, 94; worth, 111f., 115, 140, 185
selfishness, 138
Sellars, Wilfrid, 23, 52, 157
sensation, 31, 36, 38, 42
sensibility, xiii, 28, 30, 33, 35–37, 96, 100f., 107, 110, 112, 114, 183
sensualism, 38
sentiments, 173
sexual ethics, 73, 144, 153
Sheehan, J. Thomas, 24f., 207
Shimomissé, Eiichi, 23, 50, 53, 59, 89, 207
Shuster, Geroge N., 23, 208
Sidgwick, Henry, 97, 155, 208
Silber, John R., 11, 73, 120, 127, 151, 156f., 161, 120, 208
Simmel, G., 4f., 154, 208
Singer, M. G., 11, 22, 208
Sinha, Debabrata, 51, 57, 208
skepticism, 8, 29, 31, 74, 132, 136
Smith, Adam, 129
Smith, Quentin P., 89, 116, 122–24, 188, 190, 193, 208
Snyder, J. G., 96
sociology, 23, 56, 84; of knowledge, 178, 186
Socrates, 47, 97, 140
Sokolowski, *Moral Action*, 25, 33, 51, 55, 95, 124, 146f., 157, 177, 182
Sokolowski, Robert, 18, 25, 50–52, 55, 80, 95, 117, 124, 146f., 157, 177, 182, 208
solipsism, 167f.
Solomon, Robert C., 57, 208
Sosa, E., 122, 197
soul, 8, 177, 183
Soviet Union, 13, 23, 203, 209
space, 32, 36, 51, 84
Spader, Peter, 89, 157, 165, 177 190, 192, 208
Spanish-speaking world, 13, 23
speculation, 4, 6f., 44f., 167f.
Spiegelberg, Herbert, 21, 209
Spinoza, 52, 109

spirit (*Geist*; see "*Drang*")
spontaneity, and receptivity, xiii, 30, 32, 37f., 43; of love, 122
Spranger, Eduard, 4
Staude, John R., 19, 190, 192, 209
Steiner, George, 25, 209
Stevens, Richard, 193
Stevenson, Charles L., 13, 23f., 209
Stevenson, Leslie, 177, (209)
Stikkers, Kenneth W., 178, 191, 193
Stoics, 94
Stoker, H. G., 134, 178, 197, 209
Strasser, Stephan, 121, 153, 155, 209
Strawson, P. F., 122, 208
striving, 111–12, 164, 184
Stumpf, Karl, 7
subject (see "self," "person," "agent"), 31, 33, 40, 46, 163; constitution of, 46, 77, 81; law-giver, 7, 18f., 30f., 36f., 43f., 171
subject-object schema, 45–47, 55
subjectivism, 15, 23, 32, 40, 42, 44–46, 76f., 122, 128, 152; Kant's, 28, 30, 35, 40, 180; transcendental, xi, 16f., 25, 31, 40, 45
subjectivity, 42, 56, 171; and objectivity, 40–42, 45f., 55; and world, 171
substance, 8
suffering, 143
summum bonum, 128
supererogation, 137, 188, 197
supersensibility, 42, 74, 104
supratemporality, 72, 91, 164–66
suspension, 31, 33, 46
Sweeney, Robert D., 50, 191f.
Swiderski, Edward M., 23, 209
synthesis (see "passive synthesis")

Tallon, Andrew, 121, 209
Tatematsu, Hirotaka, 23, 203
Taylor, Richard, 10f.
teleology, 10, 67, 69–74, 88, 126, 131, 59, 138, 172f., 178, 183f.; in Aristotle, 10, 183, 185; in ethics, 60, 63, 125, 133f., 172f.; in Kant, xiii, 10f., 59, 69–74; in Scheler, 184, 187; natural, 10, 69, 183f., 187
temporality, 75f., 95, 164, 166
temptation, 140
Tetens, J. N., 30, 109
theodicy, 45, 168
theology, 19, 94, 183
thing-in-itself, 5, 31, 172
time, 36, 52, 164f.
tradition, 142, 154, 157, 167; Western metaphysical, 27, 43, 75, 78, 171, 178
transcendence, 75f., 177
transcendental ground, 2, 31, 43–45; and Scheler, 16, 25, 45
transcendental phenomenology, 7, 16, 45, 50, 54

transcendental turn, 7, 12, 16, 30, 45
transcendentalism, 5, 27–32, 34f., 40–42, 44, 54, 163, 176
Trebicki, J., 209
Troeltsch, Ernst, 4
truth, 5, 15–17, 25, 34, 36, 52f., 56, 76, 78f., 92, 167, 195f.

Uchiyama, Minoru, 23, 209
understanding, and sensibility, 31f.; *Verstand* 38, 41; *Verstehen*, 165
unity, 30, 36, 42, 47f., 163, 166; act and, 37, 48, 116, 123, 162, 164, 166; of person, 116, 164, 168, 186
universality, 7, 30, 35, 39f., 42, 53, 70f., 99, 172, 174; and obligation, 54, 60; person-relative, 39, 42
universalizability, 22, 61, 71, 154, 172
Urban, Wilbur M., 20
Urmson, J. O., 24, 210
utilitarianism, 6, 77, 147, 152 n. 11

Vacek, Edward, 191, 193
Vaihinger, Hans, 7
valuation, the term, 119, n. 2, 121
value (see "moral value"), 5f., 17, 23, 28, 59–97, 106–8, 121f., 128, 133–39, 140, 142–49, 152f., 156f., 160–64, 168, 170f., 173–76, 178, 180f., 184, 186, 188; and ethics, 18, 66f., 134, 174f.; and Husserl, 65, 80, 89; and Kant, 8, 59, 65, 74, 88, 92, 94, 106f., 170; and metaphysics of presence, 17f., 75f., 78, 94; apprehension of, 29, 51, 108, 174; as founded, 65, 80, 89; bearers of, 63–65, 74, 78, 81, 87f., 133, 138, 160–62, 164, 170, 173, 184; classification of, 96f., 122 n. 29; existence of, 5, 16–18, 76, 78f., 80f., 87, 96, 133f., 138; object of feeling?, 103, 116, 124, 174; objectivity of, 63–65, 77f., 81f., 88, 91–93, 122f., 148–50; presupposed by Kant, 8, 21, 59, 65, 72–74, 138f., 163, 173, 178; ranks of (see "hierarchy")
value theory, xiv, 3–6, 14–16, 18, 20, 59, 74–76, 91–95, 116, 144; Heidegger and, xi–xiii, 17f., 23, 75f., 80, 87, 93
value-ception (*Wertnehmung*), 78, 114, 116; term, 99, 119 n. 2
value-essences vs. thing-essences, 83f.
value-feeling, xiii, 51, 78, 93, 99f., 105–24, 132, 146, 148, cf. 119 n. 2
valuing, 76, 82, 121

Van De Pitte, M. M., 52, 57, 191f., 210
Van Tuinen, Jacob, 191
verification, 35, 52
vice, 182, 184
Vienna Circle, 28
virtue, 18, 71, 87, 92, 104, 117, 127, 136, 141f., 155–57, 175, 179, 180, 182–85, 210; and happiness, xiii, 18, 100, 104, 110–12, 115, 123, 126, 128, 169, 184
virtue ethics, 18, 124, 179–88, 195; and Postmodernism, 180, 203

Wallace, James, 187, 210
Walraff, Charles S., 191
Weber, Max, 4
Weiss, Dennis M., 191, 193
Welch, E. Parl, 191
Werkmeister, William H., 192
Wertnehmung (see "value-ception")
Westphal, Merold, 153
Wieser, Friedrich von, 20
Wilder, Alfred W., 191f.
will, 7f., 28–30, 37, 60, 62, 65, 68, 77, 90, 101–6, 117, 120, 125ff., 136, 140f., 147–49, 155, 159ff., 164, 172f., 181f., 184, 188; and inclination, xiii, 18, 140, 155, 160, 169, 181f.; as practical reason, 60, 68, 103; good (see "good will"); holy, 60, 101, 117, 118, 120 n. 6, 126, 135, 182; Kant and, 8, 29, 37, 60, 62, 65, 68, 102ff., 106, 120, 125ff., 159ff., 173, 182, 184; phenomenal, noumenal?, 160; *Wille* vs. *Willkür*, 114, 141, 159f., 188
will-to-power, 76, 152
Williams, T. C., 11, 22, 210
willing, 29, 37, 62, 66, 72, 84ff., 89, 111f., 130, 140, 147, 159–60, 162, 164, 175, 181–85; and moral value, 67, 72, 84, 89; and nonmoral value, 66, 84ff., 89; "pharisaical," 87, 97 n. 70
Windelband, Wilhelm, 5f., 16f., 25
Witkop, P., 21
Wittgenstein, Ludwig, 24
Wittmann, Michael, 154
Wojtyła, Karol (Pope John Paul II), xi, xv, 210
Wolandt, Barbara, 53
Wolandt, Gerd, 22, 169, 210
Wolff, Christian, 30, 62
Wolff, Robert Paul, 151, 210
world, 5, 8, 31, 33, 36, 38, 44, 46, 55, 89, 167
Wundt, Wilhelm, 4, 52

A NOTE ABOUT THE AUTHOR

Philip Blosser is Associate Professor of Philosophy at Lenoir-Rhyne College. Born in China and raised in Japan, he is a graduate of Sophia University in Tokyo and received his M.A. from Villanova University, and his Ph.D. from Duquesne University. His publications include an anthology entitled *Of Friendship: Philosophic Selections on a Perennial Concern* and *Japanese and Western Phenomenology*.